BARRON'S

FORENSICS
THE
EASY
WAY

Professor Harold H. Trimm, Ph.D.
Department of Chemistry
Broome Community College

BARRON'S

Dedication

This book is dedicated to my wife, Barbara, and sons, Erik and Bryan. Their love and encouragement are always inspirational.

About the Author

Harold H. Trimm is the Chairman of the Chemistry Department at Broome Community College. This book is his first for Barron's.

All inquiries should be addressed to:
Barron's Educational Series, Inc.
250 Wireless Boulevard
Hauppauge, NY 11788
www.barronseduc.com

ISBN-13: 978-0-7641-3050-2
ISBN-10: 0-7641-3050-1

Library of Congress Catalog Card No. 2005045278

Library of Congress Cataloging-in-Publication Data

Trimm, Harold H.
    Forensics the easy way / Harold H. Trimm.
       p. cm.
    Includes bibliographical references and index.
    ISBN 0-7641-3050-1 (alk. paper)
     1. Forensic sciences—Handbooks, manuals, etc. 2. Criminal investigation—Handbooks,
    manuals, etc. 3. Evidence, Criminal—Handbooks, manuals, etc. 4. Criminal
    laboratories—Handbooks, manuals, etc. I. Title.

HV8073.T73 2005
363.25—dc22

                                                                    2005045278

Printed in the United States of America
9 8 7 6 5 4 3 2

Contents

Preface

Sherlock Holmes once said, "It is a capital mistake to theorize before one has the facts. Inevitably one begins to twist the facts to fit the theory instead of making the theory fit the facts." It is the job of the forensic scientist to discover the physical evidence that will help establish guilt and help prove innocence. Physical evidence can neither lie nor be guilty of human bias. In all violent crimes physical evidence is transferred between the victim and criminal. Locard's principle, "Every contact leaves a trace," is the basis of all forensic science.

The purpose of this book is to introduce the reader to the area of forensic science that uses science to solve crimes. The reader is not expected to have any science background but will be shown how chemistry, physics, geology, medicine, and other sciences help to convict the guilty and exonerate the innocent. The book starts with an introduction to forensic science and careers in the field. Specialized careers requiring advanced degrees, such as pathology, toxicology, odontology, and entomology, are also described. Part I ends with a description of how the modern crime laboratory operates.

Part II explains how modern police forces use chemistry, physics, and geology to help catch criminals. The application of these sciences to a crime scene is then presented.

Part III deals with physical evidence. Each chapter considers a different kind of evidence and how it should be collected, packaged, and submitted to the crime laboratory. The significance of each type of evidence is also discussed. These chapters deal with rules of probability, rules of evidence, body fluids, explosives, arson, fabrics, drugs, firearms, glass, hair, fingerprints, impressions, paint, questioned documents, computer crime, and DNA profiling. Each chapter could be a whole book, but the effort here is to introduce the reader to all the capabilities of forensic science.

Part IV looks at the future of forensic science. An attempt is made to examine present trends to try to predict where the field is heading.

A glossary of forensic science terms is included at the end of the book. Appendix A lists the various names of common street drugs.

How to Use This Book

The casual reader can use this book to gain an understanding of forensic science. It can also be used as a supplement, or as a stand-alone textbook, for an introductory course in forensic science or criminalistics. It is based on 20 years of teaching experience in the field of forensic science and work as an expert witness. The course on which it is based was originally developed for state police and arson investigators. Over the years, the class has become popular with students from every discipline. The popularity of books and television shows based on forensic science has caused many non-science majors to become interested enough to sign up for the course. Some have become so interested that they have gone on to careers in the field.

This book is written to make the extremely technical field of forensic science understandable to the everyday person. To get the most out of the book, it is recommended that the reader follow a few simple suggestions.

First, if this book is being used to supplement another textbook for a course, read the other textbook first. This is what your professor expects and will be what the tests are based on. Concepts that are unclear in the assigned textbook can then be clarified using this book. The simple explanations and examples used in this book should make these ideas readily comprehensible.

Each chapter starts with Terms You Should Know. Understanding these terms is key to understanding the concepts discussed in the chapter. You should check off each term as you discover its meaning in the chapter. In addition, there is always the glossary at the end of the book to help.

Read through the chapter and try to grasp the important concepts without worrying about all the details. You can always go back and reread a section for additional information. The first thing I tell investigators to do at the scene of a crime or suspected arson is to take a step back. Try to get the "big picture" and then start looking for all the details to put it together. Some of the chapters have math calculations that would be done by forensic scientists for a court case. If math is not your forte, don't get bogged down in the equations. Just try to understand the general concept and move on. The intent of this book is not to turn you into a forensic scientist but to provide you with an appreciation and understanding of the field.

Many of the chapters have additional resources, such as Internet links. These can be followed if the reader is interested in learning further information beyond the scope of this book.

At the end of each chapter are review questions. Read the questions and write the answers down on a separate piece of paper. Seeing how something is solved is one thing, but being able to do it yourself shows that you truly understand the material. Check your answers with the answer key at the end of the chapter. If any are wrong, go back and reread the relevant section of the chapter. If you guessed at an answer and got it right, that doesn't count. Go back and reread the appropriate section and make sure you understand the material.

Many of the later chapters build on concepts learned in earlier chapters. Try to cover the chapters in order and take your time. If you read one chapter or section at a time, you will comprehend the material better than if you try to digest too much information at one time.

PART I

INTRODUCTION TO FORENSIC SCIENCE

CHAPTER 1

INTRODUCTION

TERMS YOU SHOULD KNOW

Albert Osborn	Francis Galton	NIST
Alphonse Bertillon	Hans Gross	Paul Jeserich
anthropometry	Karl Landsteiner	physical evidence
Arthur Conan Doyle	Leone Lattes	Sherlock Holmes
Edmond Locard	Locard's principle	toxicology
FBI	Mathieu Orfila	U.S. BOI
forensic science		

WHAT IS FORENSIC SCIENCE?

In the past, when towns were small and the police force knew all the local criminals, the investigation of crime was simple. When a crime was committed, the police could round up the usual suspects, and based on interrogation, the type of crime, and how it was committed, they could determine the guilty party. As populations grew and towns turned into cities, the number of suspects expanded beyond the ability of police officers to know everyone individually and be able to determine from the crime who had perpetrated the act. Nowadays, the use of forensic science helps the police solve crimes, convict the guilty, and exonerate the innocent. Forensic science is part of almost every criminal investigation from the discovery, collection, preservation, and analysis of physical evidence to the conviction of the guilty.

The word *forensic* is based on a Latin word meaning "pertaining to law." Forensic science is the application of science to law. In its broadest sense, forensic science becomes part of almost every law. If a can of soda is labeled caffeine-free and 12 fl oz, this is a legal claim, which is controlled by the Food and Drug Administration (FDA). The FDA can check if the beverage manufacturer is following the law by having its scientists measure the caffeine content and volume of the soda to see if it is within ± 10% of the manufacturer's claim. Something as simple as the time and date stipulated by many laws can be traced back to the **National Institute of Science and Technology (NIST)** and the U.S. Naval Observatory (USNO) whose atomic clocks set the standard for the United States. This is a rather broad use of the definition, and when most people use the term *forensic science*, they are restricting it to criminal investigation. The scope of this book is based on this more common definition of **forensic science:** the application of science to the investigation and prosecution of crime.

HISTORY

As populations grew, so did the crime rate. Soon it became obvious to the public that the tried and true practices of crime investigation, knowing the criminal element in your area and selecting the perpetrator from their ranks, could not keep up with the increasing number and types of crimes. In modern crime solving there are normally two avenues of investigation, one involving people and the other involving **physical evidence.**

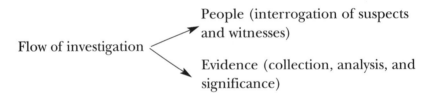

Flow of investigation — People (interrogation of suspects and witnesses) / Evidence (collection, analysis, and significance)

The police, however, were usually reluctant to change methods that had worked so well for so many years. Many people attribute the great public demand for the use of science in criminal investigation to **Arthur Conan Doyle,** author of the **Sherlock Holmes** stories. In these fictitious novels (first published in 1887) the great detective used many different scientific means to analyze the evidence left behind at the crime scene. The weight of public opinion soon forced many police departments to start hiring scientists to more thoroughly analyze this second avenue of investigation, physical evidence.

Almost all advances in science have become part of forensic science. Therefore, almost all scientists have contributed to the current state of the field. However, some of the most important early contributions were the following.

1814 **Mathieu Orfila** writes the first scientific paper on the detection of poisons. He latter published articles on the classification of poisons. The detection of poisons in body fluids, tissues, and organs is known as toxicology. For his work he is now known as the "father of toxicology."

1879 **Alphonse Bertillon** publishes his first book on **anthropometry**, a personal identification method based on 11 body measurements. This was the first system of personal identification used by the police. After a famous case showed that two different people had the same anthropometry measurements, the system was abandoned and fingerprints became the preferred tool.

1887 **Arthur Conan Doyle** publishes his first Sherlock Holmes novel, *A Study in Scarlet.* The exploits of his main character fuel the public's imagination and result in a demand for the police to use more science as part of their investigations.

1892 **Francis Galton** publishes the book *Fingerprints,* which helps police departments use fingerprints as a means of personal identification. In the book, Galton explains the many different characteristics of fingerprints and how they can combine to form a unique print for each person.

1893 **Hans Gross** publishes the book *Criminal Investigation,* which shows how the police can use science to help in criminal investigations. In it Gross shows that many different scientific fields can be of use to the police. Hans Gross is considered by many to have been the first true criminologist.

1898 **Paul Jeserich** develops forensic chemistry.

1901 **Karl Landsteiner** discovers the ABO blood groups.

1908 **The U.S. Bureau of Investigation (BOI)** is formed with 34 agents.

1910 **Albert Osborn** publishes the book *Questioned Documents,* which explains the scientific analysis of a suspected document. A questioned document is one of uncertain origin. The methods developed by Osborn are still in use today in the examination of counterfeiting, alteration, obscuring, and obliteration of written instruments.

1910 **Edmond Locard** establishes a crime laboratory in the police department in Lyon, France. For his contributions to the field, he is referred to as the "father of forensic science." His observation that "Every contact leaves a trace" is one of the guiding principles of forensic science.

1915 **Leone Lattes** discovers a method for typing dried bloodstains. Based on the pioneering work of typing whole blood done by Karl Landsteiner, Lattes developed a method to type dried bloodstains. The method is so sensitive that it has been used to determine the blood types of mummies.

1924 The first crime laboratory in the United States is set up as part of the Los Angeles Police Department.

1925 New York City establishes the Bureau of Forensic Ballistics run by C. E. Waite, Calvin Goddard, Philip Gravelle, and John Fisher.

1929 Calvin Goddard, considered the "father of firearms identification," matches the bullets recovered from the St. Valentine's Day Massacre to the weapons from which they were fired. He establishes the use of the comparison microscope for bullet identification. Goddard is credited with making the first match of a bullet from a murder victim with a suspect's gun.

1932 The U.S. BOI establishes a forensic crime laboratory, which will become the center of forensic analysis and research in the United States.

1935 The BOI changes its name to the **Federal Bureau of Investigation (FBI)**.

1953 Paul Kirk publishes the book *Crime Investigation.*

LOCARD'S PRINCIPLE

In 1910 Edmond Locard persuaded the police department of Lyon, France, to hire him as their first forensic scientist. They also provided him with two assistants and some space in the attic of police headquarters to build a makeshift laboratory. He was quickly able to help them solve many famous cases by using science to analyze the physical evidence. He solved a case involving the counterfeiting of gold coins by analyzing metal scrapings on the suspect's clothing, a case of strangulation by analyzing fingernail scrapings from the victim, and countless murders by analyzing fingerprints. **Locard's principle** can best be stated as "Every contact leaves a trace." The more violent the crime, the more likely that trace evidence has been transferred between the victim and the perpetrator. When asked to help the police with an investigation, one of the first things Locard asked for was the suspect's clothing. He hung the clothing over a clean piece of white paper and carefully brushed it to remove any trace evidence adhering to the fabric. The physical evidence was then analyzed and used to determine with what the suspect had been in contact. The following is Edmond Locard's own statement of his famous principle.

> Wherever he steps, whatever he touches, whatever he leaves, even unconsciously, will serve as a silent witness against him. Not only his fingerprints or his footprints, but his hair, the fibers from his clothes, the glass he breaks, the tool mark he leaves, the paint he scratches, the blood or semen he deposits or collects. All of these and more, bear mute witness against him. This is evidence that does not forget. It is not confused by the excitement of the moment. It is not absent because human witnesses are. It is factual evidence. Physical evidence cannot be wrong, it cannot perjure itself, it cannot be wholly absent. Only its interpretation can err. Only human failure to find it, study and understand it, can diminish its value.

As an illustration of Locard's principle consider the following hypothetical case. A motorist is driving a 2002 Suzuki XL-7 down a country road at night during a rainstorm. He picks up a hitchhiker, stabs him to death with a knife, and drives the sport utility vehicle (SUV) into the woods to dispose of the body. A few days later the body is found in the woods. How can the police investigating this crime use Locard's principle? Every contact leaves a trace. The fact that the victim was inside the vehicle means that fibers from its velour interior have been transferred onto the victim's clothing. Blood from the victim has been transferred onto the velour interior. Fiber, blood, hair, and skin cells may also have been transferred between the criminal and victim. When the XL-7 went into the woods, it left tire tracks on the ground. The police could take impressions of these tracks to determine that the tires are Cooper Lifeliner Touring SLE 235/60R16. This is not a very common size or type of tire and would lead to a very short list of suspect vehicles (mostly just Suzuki Grand Vitaras and XL-7s). The gray velour fibers from the interior of the vehicle further limit the number of vehicles. A check of Department of Motor Vehicles (DMV) records would indicate all the XL-7's in the area. If the vehicle was located, small imperfections in the tread could be used to identify it as the one that was at the crime scene. While the contact of the tires with the ground left traces of the vehicle, so would the ground leave its own traces on the wheel wells and undercarriage of the SUV. Soils samples obtained from the XL-7 could be used to confirm that the vehicle had been at the location where the body was found. The interior of the suspect's vehicle could also be checked for traces of blood, which could lead to a positive link to the victim.

The previous scenario is just one illustration of how Locard's principle can be used in crime investigation. The role of the forensic scientist is often to use Locard's principle to prove links between the victim, the criminal, and the crime scene. Physical evidence transferred by contact often provides such links. Figure 1.1 shows the association as what the author calls the physical evidence triangle. It is the job of the forensic scientist to establish these links for the police.

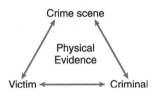

FIGURE 1.1

ROLE OF A FORENSIC SCIENTIST

As opposed to what one might see on television, the role of a forensic scientist is not to run around investigating a crime in order to catch the bad guy. The forensic scientist is one part of the criminal justice system whose function is to analyze physical evidence. To do this, he or she must be an expert in some scientific area that can be used in the investigation of crime. In the past, most forensic scientists had college degrees in chemistry, biology, or physics. They became experts in their fields by completing an apprenticeship program where they worked in a crime lab with an experienced forensic scientist until they learned their trade. Nowadays many forensic scientists graduate from college with specialized 4-year degrees in forensic science.

When evidence is brought to the crime lab, it is the role of the forensic scientist to analyze it and give the conclusions to the investigator. These conclusions could involve the identification, comparison, probability, and reliability of the results. Often, the forensic scientist must testify in court about the results of an analysis they carried out. Sometimes they are called to testify about an analysis done more than a year before. This is why it is important for the scientist to keep a good laboratory notebook and document everything that is done. These notes help refresh the forensic scientist's memory as well as document all aspects of the analysis.

A forensic scientist testifies at a trial as an expert witness. Experts are persons with special knowledge, skill, experience, training and/or education that goes beyond the experience of ordinary members of the public. Unlike an ordinary witness, an expert witness can give an opinion. The reason for this is that jurors are not expected to be experts on DNA, fingerprints, drug analysis, mass spectrometry and so on. The courts allow experts in the field to analyze the evidence and explain their results to the court. It is often the role of the forensic scientist to educate the jury about the science behind the analysis so that they have a better understanding of the significance of the results. A judge determines who can act as an expert witness. It is up to the jury to decide how much weight to give the evidence and whether or not to believe the expert. It is important that the forensic scientist explain what was done in a clear, concise manner and be able to support all the conclusions.

The forensic scientist can also be asked to train police officers about evidence types, recognition, and collection and the capabilities of the crime lab. Evidence that was once thought to be useless can now yield vital clues because of advances in science. It is the job of the forensic scientist to keep the investigators in the field current. A visitor to a state police crime lab often discovers some interesting reading material. Many drug-themed magazines can be found, which the scientist reads to keep up with the latest means of hiding contraband. For example, if a can of a certain brand of shaving cream is advertised with a secret screw-off bottom for hiding drugs, the forensic scientist will note it and the information will be passed on to those who collect the evidence from crime scenes.

Periodically the state sends proficiency samples to the crime lab. These are samples of unknown concentration that must be analyzed by crime lab personnel in the same manner as regular samples. An example of this is blood alcohol samples, which are sent to the crime lab for analysis for the determination of blood alcohol content. The results are sent back to the state and must be correct (within a narrow range of experimental uncertainty) or the lab will lose its certification for that analysis.

While the majority of a forensic scientist's time is spent analyzing physical evidence, they are also responsible for testifying about these results and training the people who collect evidence. Added to these responsibilities is the requirement to keep current with advances in their field of expertise.

CAREERS IN FORENSIC SCIENCE

Forensic science has become a popular career choice, driven not only by media attention but also by the expansion of job opportunities. The recent popularity of forensics can be traced back to the tremendous interest of the general public in the O. J. Simpson trial. People sat glued to their television sets to hear the testimony of expert witnesses and their evaluation of the physical evidence. Soon forensic science became the basis of several television series and reality programs. The publics' interest in forensics is increasing, and the prestige of the position is at an all-time high.

Two more reasons for the popularity of the field include the number of jobs available and the degree of satisfaction with the work. A

2002 report by the American Chemical Society in *Chemical and Engineering News (C&EN)* stated:

> One field on the verge of explosive growth is that of forensic chemistry, particularly DNA analysis. Experts predict that more than 10,000 new forensic scientists will be needed over the next decade to address an exponentially expanding backlog of DNA evidence. Most such work will be done in private laboratories, under contract with state and local government agencies, and on-the-job training is available. But governmental bodies are also in need of forensic scientists for crime-scene work—analyzing evidence such as bloodstains and performing firearm identification. One forensic scientist tells *C&EN*: "It's the most satisfying work you can ever do." Another says: "The knowledge that the person who has killed someone's daughter has been brought to justice—you can't put a price tag on that."

Another reason for the rapid increase in the number of crime labs is based on the U.S. Constitution. The Sixth Amendment guarantees the right of the accused to a fair and speedy trial. Specifically it says:

> Amendment VI: In all criminal prosecutions, the accused shall enjoy the right to a speedy and public trial, by an impartial jury of the state and district wherein the crime shall have been committed, which district shall have been previously ascertained by law, and to be informed of the nature and cause of the accusation; to be confronted with the witnesses against him; to have compulsory process for obtaining witnesses in his favor; and to have the assistance of counsel for his defense.

The majority of all evidence sent to a crime lab is drug-related. A forensic scientist must analyze it before the accused can be tried. The identity of the drug as well as the quantity affect what the charges against the suspect will be. It is much different, from a legal point of view, to be caught with a bag full of pancake mix as opposed to a bag full of heroin. The quantity is also important, as this can change the charges from a misdemeanor to a class A1 felony. The increasing amount of drug-related crimes has required a corresponding increase in the number of crime laboratories and forensic scientists employed to analyze evidence. In addition, advances in science, such as in forensic DNA, have greatly increased the amount of evidence that can be submitted to the crime lab for analysis.

REVIEW QUESTIONS

1. Forensic science is

   A. the application of science to government regulations
   B. the application of science to law
   C. the application of science to politics
   D. the application of law to criminal investigation

2. Whose stories about a fictional detective who used science to help solve crime are credited with increasing public awareness of forensic science?

   A. Arthur Conan Doyle   B. Jules Verne
   C. Edgar Rice Burroughs   D. Mark Twain

3. Who is known as the father of forensic science?

   A. J. Edgar Hoover   B. Paul Kirk
   C. Alphonse Bertillon   D. Edmond Locard

4. Who wrote some of the first papers on the detection of poisons and is considered the father of toxicology?

   A. Francis Galton   B. Alphonse Bertillon
   C. Mathieu Orfila   D. Calvin Goddard

5. Who wrote the book *Fingerprints*?

   A. Paul Kirk   B. Mathieu Orfila
   C. Hans Gross   D. Francis Galton

6. Who invented anthropometry?

   A. Paul Kirk   B. Alphonse Bertillon
   C. Francis Galton   D. Albert Osborn

7. Who stated the principle "Every contact leaves a trace"?

   A. Edmond Locard   B. Sherlock Holmes
   C. Leone Lattes   D. Hans Gross

8. Who wrote *Questioned Documents*?

   A. Hans Gross   B. Albert Osborn
   C. Leone Lattes   D. Francis Galton

9. What is used by forensic scientists to connect the crime scene, the victim, and the criminal?

   A. testimony   B. eyewitnesses
   C. interrogation   D. physical evidence

10. The main role of the forensic scientist is to

    A. question witnesses   B. arrest criminals
    C. analyze physical evidence   D. visit the crime scene

11. A secondary duty of the forensic scientist is to provide

    A. expert witness testimony   B. moral support
    C. training for lawyers   D. motives

12. Since the capabilities of crime labs keep changing, it is also the role of the forensic scientist to provide training to

    A. judges   B. police investigators
    C. lawyers   D. journalists

13. As opposed to a regular witness, an expert witness can give their

    A. name   B. background
    C. experience   D. opinion

14. There has been a great increase in the number of crime labs because of an increase in which type of evidence?

    A. blood   B. trace
    C. drug   D. hair

15. Another reason for the increase in the number of crime labs is the requirement for a quick analysis of physical evidence before a person is brought to trial. The right to a speedy trial is guaranteed by the

    A. First Amendment   B. Sixth Amendment
    C. Fifth Amendment   D. Twelfth Amendment

16. Most forensic scientists being hired today have 4-year degrees in

    A. police science   B. law
    C. biology   D. forensic science

17. Locard's principle states:

    A. Every contact leaves a trace   B. Never assume anything
    C. Question every suspect   D. Check all alibis

18. Experts predict that over the next decade the number of new forensic scientists hired will exceed

    A. 100   B. 1000
    C. 10,000   D. 100,000

19. One of the reasons people choose a career in forensic science is

A. salary
C. hours

B. job satisfaction
D. benefits

20. After a vehicle is driven through the woods, which are examples of contacts left by the car on the ground?

A. oil and gas
C. tire tracks and soil layers

B. paint and rubber
C. fiber and hair

21. The person who discovered how to test dried bloodstains for ABO blood type was

A. Leone Lattes
C. Calvin Goddard

B. Karl Landsteiner
D. Edmond Locard

22. The person who used the comparison microscope for bullet analysis and is considered the "father of firearms identification" was

A. Hans Gross
C. Edmond Locard

B. Paul Jeserich
D. Calvin Goddard

23. The first book on criminal investigation was written by

A. Hans Gross
C. Edmond Locard

B. Paul Jeserich
D. Calvin Goddard

24. The "father of forensic chemistry" was

A. Hans Gross
C. Edmond Locard

B. Paul Jeserich
D. Calvin Goddard

25. The FBI was started in 1908 with 34 agents in the U.S.

A. federal police force
C. Bureau of Investigation

B. Secret Service
D. federal marshals

Answers

1. B	10. C	18. C
2. A	11. A	19. B
3. D	12. B	20. C
4. C	13. D	21. A
5. D	14. C	22. D
6. B	15. B	23. A
7. A	16. D	24. B
8. B	17. A	25. C
9. D		

CHAPTER 2

SPECIALIZED FORENSIC SCIENCE CAREERS

TERMS YOU SHOULD KNOW

algor mortis	forensic	nomograph
autopsy	entomologist	odontologist
blowfly	forensic pathologist	PMI
coroner	forensic psychiatrist	puparium
forensic	larvae	rigor mortis
anthropologist	livor mortis	toxicologist
forensic engineer	medical examiner	

Some forensic scientists obtain specialized or advanced degrees in preparation for certain forensic careers. These fields include medicine, toxicology, odontology, pathology, psychiatry, engineering, entomology, and anthropology. These specialties are of great use in forensic science and are often in high demand. Sometimes a specialist in another field decides to apply their knowledge to forensic science later in their career on a part- or full-time basis.

Initially, a coroner investigated any death that was deemed suspicious. The word *coroner* comes from a Latin word meaning "from the crown." This meant that the **coroner** was an official, appointed by the king, whose job was to determine the cause of a sudden or unexpected death. These individuals could be appointed or elected to the position. Some states required coroners to be physicians, but others did not. Sometimes an undertaker took the position since they already had a hearse and knew what to do with a dead body. The coroner system has gradually been replaced by the medical examiner system. In 1915 New York City established the modern version of this system. A **medical examiner** is a physician who is authorized by state statute to investigate sudden, unexpected, violent, suspicious, or unnatural deaths of persons within the state. The purpose of this investigation is to detect the cause and manner of death. From this, the medical examiner can determine whether there was a homicide or whether a threat to public safety exists.

A **forensic pathologist** is a physician with specialized training in determining the cause of death and in forensic science. Many states now require that medical examiners also be forensic pathologists, although some states with smaller populations still use the coroner system: A pathologist aids a forensic investigation by providing information uncovered during examination of the body. One important piece of information is the time of death, which can be determined by several methods. The time since death is always an estimate because it is based on many variables that cannot be controlled exactly. For this reason a range of time is normally given. This estimate of how long a person has been dead is called the **postmortem interval (PMI)**.

Algor mortis is the process by which the body cools after death as a result of loss of heat to the surroundings. A **nomograph** is a diagram that allows a complicated mathematical relationship to be solved simply with a ruler. The time of death nomograph shown in Figure 2.1 can be used to estimate the time of death based on the deep rectal temperature of the body, surrounding air temperature, body weight, and various other correction factors such as the presence of clothing and submersion in water.

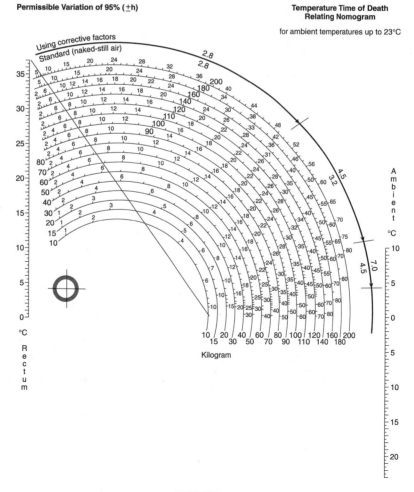

FIGURE 2.1

TABLE 2.1 Correction Factors for Body Weight in Estimating Time of Death

Wet Clothing or Wet Body Surface	Condition of Air	Condition of Water	Correction Factor
Naked	—	Flowing	0.35
Naked	—	Still	0.5
Naked	Moving	—	0.7
One or two thin layers	Moving	—	0.7

Dry Clothing or Dry Covering	Condition of Air	Correction Factor
Naked	Moving	0.75
One or two thin layers	Moving	0.9
Naked	Still	1.0
One or two thin layers	Still	1.1
Two or three thin layers	Still	1.2
One or two thin layers	Moving or still	1.2
Three or four thin layers	Moving or still	1.3
More than four thin layers	Moving or still	1.4
Thick bedspread and clothing combined	Moving or still	2.4

Table 2.1 shows correction factors used to account for nonstandard conditions such as clothing, air movement, wet clothing, and in water. The correction factor is multiplied by the body mass to give a better estimate of how long the person has been dead.

Figure 2.2 shows an example of this sort. Suppose that the body was that of a 100-kg male. The rectal temperature was 25.0°C, and the ambient temperature was 10.0°C. The body was found naked, and the air was still (so the correction factor is 1.0).

$$\text{Body mass} = 100 \text{ kg} \times 1.0 = 100 \text{ kg}$$

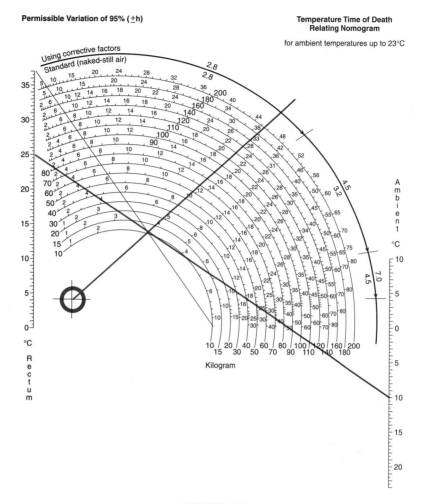

FIGURE 2.2

Draw a straight line from 25 on the rectum temperature scale to 10 on the ambient temperature scale. Mark the point where the drawn line intersects the printed diagonal line running down from the top of the rectum temperature scale. Next, draw a line from the center of the circle (on the lower left of the figure) through the intersection point you marked. The point where the line intersects the 100 kg arc indicates the hours since death can be read as about 19.0 h. Since the line intersects the outer arc in the 2.8 region, this means there is a 95% level of certainty that the estimate is correct ±2.8 h. This puts the time of death between 16.2 and 21.8 h ago.

Most pathologists use the exact formula and enter the data into a computer. This formula, where "T" stands for temperature (°C), "t" stands for time, and "e" stands for the mathematical constant, is

$$(T_{rectum} - T_{ambient}) / (37.2 - T_{ambient}) = 1.25e^{(Bt)} - 0.25e^{(5Bt)}$$

where $B = -1.2815 (kg^{-0.625}) + 0.0284$.

An example of a spreadsheet that can do this calculation can be found on the author's web site, http://hht.chem.sunybroome.edu/time.xls. Entering the correct data and pressing the Crtl-Shift-A keys simultaneously, result in the time since death being calculated automatically. With this more exact method a time of 18.6 h is obtained. A useful Java applet is *Ed's Time of Death* applet. It was written by a pathologist, Ed Friedlander, and is available at the following web site: http://www.pathguy.com/TimeDead.htm.

Livor mortis is the settling of the blood at the lowest point after death. Since the heart is no longer pumping, gravity causes the blood to pool at the lowest point of the body. At first, theses patches appear pink, however, with time the blood turns purplish blue. Places in the body where blood flow is constricted, such as where it is pressing against a hard surface, are not discolored. The process begins in as little as 30 min but does not become permanent until about 8 h after death. A forensic pathologist can use this information to determine if the body has been moved after death and also to get some idea about the time of death (PMI).

Rigor mortis is the stiffening of the muscles of the body. After death the muscles of the body relax. Then they begin to contract because of chemical changes. Rigor mortis can be observed about 2 h after death. It is usually detected in the head first and then moves into the extremities. Rigor mortis is normally complete after 6 h and begins to leave the body after 24 h. After 40 h the signs of rigor mortis are completely gone. There are many factors that affect the timing of rigor mortis, so it is not considered reliable enough to determine the time of death but can be used to help corroborate other methods.

The main tool a pathologist uses to determine the cause and manner of a suspicious death is an **autopsy**, a surgical procedure that allows a specially trained medical doctor to help determine the previous health of the deceased and the cause of death. The word *autopsy* comes from a Latin expression meaning "seeing with your own eyes."

A pathologist, with the help of an assistant called a diener, performs the autopsy. There may be investigators present, or even family members, and the whole procedure is carried out in a solemn and dignified manner. Autopsy suites often have the Latin inscription *Hic locus est ubi mors gaudet succurrere vitae*, which means "This is the place where death rejoices to teach those who live," posted on the wall.

There is always a distinct smell associated with an autopsy. It makes some people sick and some faint. Many pathologists use a small dab of oil of wintergreen below their noses and on their masks to help with the smell. The longer a person has been dead, the more the oil of wintergreen is needed. Sometimes rebreathers and filter masks are required.

First the pathologist conducts a gross examination of the exterior of the body and the sheets or bag used to cover and transport it. Records are made of the decedent's name, height, weight, and visible characteristics. Photographs are taken from every possible angle. Ultraviolet lights are also used to examine the body.

Next, samples such as blood, urine, hair, and oral swabs are taken. It is much easier to get them now then after the body has been buried. Scrapings from under the nails are also obtained. The body is also x-rayed.

The pathologist then makes a Y incision with a scalpel. Since the heart is not pumping, there is almost no bleeding. Some pathologists make two shoulder-to-midchest incisions, and others use one sweeping motion from one shoulder, under the nipples, to the other shoulder. The Y is then extended from the bottom of the Y at the midchest to the pubic bone. An incision is also made across the skull from ear to ear. The skin is pulled back and the bone cut with a vibrating saw.

The pathologist removes the brain and major organs (such as the heart, lungs, kidneys, liver, and spleen), which are carefully examined and then weighed. Small sections of the organs are routinely collected, and the samples are placed in special jars for further analysis. These samples are usually sent to a histology lab where they can be mounted as slides and any abnormalities analyzed.

The pathologist makes a detailed investigation of the internal body and examines the neck and windpipe for possible abnormalities. Once the examination is complete, the pathologist puts the organs back into the body (samples have already been removed) or has them incinerated separately. The body is then sewn back together.

A toxicologist studies toxic substances. A **forensic toxicologist** is a person, normally with an advanced degree, who detects the presence of poisons or drugs in body fluids, tissues, and organs. The forensic toxicologist is normally sent samples from a body whenever the cause of death is uncertain. The presence of poisons or drugs, as well as the quantities, is essential to the pathologist's determination of the cause of death. A forensic toxicologist normally works with specialized instruments such as high-performance liquid chromatographs, gas chromatographs, and mass spectrometers, which can detect extremely minute quantities of toxic or illegal substances in the human body.

An **odontologist** is a forensic dentist who applies the science of dentistry to police investigations. When a body has been severely burned or disfigured, an odontologist can still make a positive identification through dental records. This is especially useful in the case of a bombing or an airplane or train accident where there is a large number of victims and the damage may preclude the use of fingerprints. Even when the body is badly decomposed (such as that of a victim found in the woods after several months) or there are only skeletal remains, an odontologist can match dental records and positively identify the remains. Teeth are some of the most persistent of human remains.

In some cases an odontologist can match bite marks to the teeth of a suspect. These can include bite marks on the skin and also those left behind as an impression on some other material. In the 1970s in Endicott, NY, a string of robberies occurred in which a man broke into houses and stole various items. In one case he must have gotten hungry and started eating a roll left on a kitchen table. The roll was a bit stale, so it was left, half-eaten, at the crime scene. Using an impression from the roll and bite impressions from the police suspects, an odontologist was able to positively identify the perpetrator. This was done by measuring the distances between the points of the teeth and the spacing that make up a dental impression.

A **forensic psychiatrist** is a medical doctor who specializes in the application of psychiatry to law. In the investigation of a crime a forensic psychiatrist can be asked to develop a profile of the suspect based on all available evidence. Once a suspect is in custody, a forensic psychiatrist can testify whether the suspect is competent to stand trial and is responsible for their actions.

A **forensic engineer** applies engineering principles to law. They are often called into cases when there is a structural failure such as a bridge or building collapse. The forensic engineer can analyze the structure and determine the cause of the failure. They are also used to analyze complicated accident scenes to determine exactly what happened.

A **forensic entomologist** applies the study of insects to law. One of the most common insects used is the **blowfly**. A blowfly almost always lays its eggs in dead tissue. They are attracted by the chemicals given off by decomposition of the body, and certain varieties begin laying eggs within minutes of death. Because of the availability of moisture, blowfly eggs are normally found in open wounds and in the head orifices (nose, ears, and mouth). The eggs hatch and release blowfly **larvae** (maggots), which continue to feed on the body and grow and shed their skins. The third time they shed skin it forms a hard capsule around them called a **puparium**. Finally, the adult blowfly emerges from the puparium and after a day or two flies away. Evidence of the eggs, larvae (maggots), **puparia**, and adult flies can be collected from the body and used to determine the time of death. An accurate knowledge of the temperature and weather conditions is also needed since these greatly affect the timing of the life cycle of the blowfly. The stages of development that a blowfly undergoes are shown in Figure 2.3.

Eggs ⟶ Larvae (maggots) ⟶ Puparium ⟶ Adult fly

FIGURE 2.3

Each step takes a known amount of time at a given temperature, so by collecting samples from the corpse a forensic scientist can estimate the time since death or the **postmortem interval (PMI)**. One of the earliest recorded uses of entomology in forensics occurred in 1235 A.D. in China. A villager was murdered, and the only clue was a slash wound on the body. The murder investigator theorized that the wound was caused by a sickle and had all the local villagers bring their sickles and place them on the ground in front of them. One sickle attracted a large swarm of flies, probably because of microscopic bits of human tissue that remained on the blade. When confronted with this evidence, the owner of the sickle confessed to the murder.

A **forensic anthropologist** performs specialized examinations of human skeletal remains or badly decomposed bodies for the purpose of identification. A forensic anthropologist may be asked to help determine the cause of death, sex, age, postmortem interval, and race. They are almost always called to help identify skeletal remains found when digging. It may be a case of murder, or it may be an ancient burial site. Forensic anthropologists can also reconstruct the facial characteristics of the skull to aid in the identification process.

REVIEW QUESTIONS

1. A medical examiner must be a

   A. physician   B. pathologist
   C. funeral director   D. elected official

2. A pathologist is a physician who is trained to

   A. detect poisons
   B. reconstruct facial structures
   C. determine the cause of death
   D. make funeral arrangements

3. The cooling of the body after death resulting from the loss of heat to the surroundings is known as

   A. algor mortis   B. livor mortis
   C. rigor mortis   D. putrification

4. A figure that simplifies a more complicated calculation is called a/an

   A. *x-y* graph   B. polar graph
   C. logarithmic graph   D. nomograph

5. The time interval since death is known as the

   A. death interval   B. relaxation time
   C. PMI   D. AAS

6. Use Figures 2.1 and 2.2 to determine the time interval since death for a 100-kg man with a rectal temperature of 20.0°C found naked in still water that was 5.0°C.

   A. 6.0 h   B. 8.0 h
   C. 10.0 h   D. 12.0 h

7. What would be the uncertainty in time at 95% for problem 6.

   A. ± 2.8 h   B. ± 3.2 h
   C. ± 4.5 h   D. ± 7.0 h

8. The settling of blood by gravity and subsequent discoloration after death is known as

   A. algor mortis   B. livor mortis
   C. rigor mortis   D. decomposition

9. The stiffening of the muscles in the body that begins shortly after death is known as

   A. algor mortis   B. livor mortis
   C. rigor mortis   D. decomposition

10. In general, the settling of blood becomes permanent how many hours after death?

   A. 2   B. 4
   C. 6   D. 8

11. Rigor mortis can usually be detected in what part of the body?

   A. head   B. arms
   C. legs   D. chest

12. Rigor mortis can normally be detected how many hours after death?

   A. immediately   B. 1
   C. 2   D. 3

13. After how many hours is rigor mortis completely gone?

   A. 10   B. 20
   C. 40   D. 80

14. Toxicology is the study of

   A. death   B. poisons
   C. insects   D. cadavers

15. A toxicologist often analyzes samples of

A. insects
B. weapons
C. photographs
D. body fluids

16. An odontologist is a forensic

A. engineer
B. scientist
C. dentist
D. entomologist

17. When a badly burned body cannot be identified by finger-prints, an odontologist can often determine the victim's identity by examining the

A. teeth
B. skull
C. finger bones
D. hair

18. A forensic psychiatrist may be asked to testify about a suspect's

A. identity
B. alibi
C. competency
D. location

19. A forensic psychiatrist may help an ongoing investigation by providing the police with a suspect's

A. picture
B. behavioral profile
C. next victim
D. location

20. If a bridge has collapsed on an interstate highway, the police would probably have the scene examined by a forensic

A. psychiatrist
B. pathologist
C. entomologist
D. engineer

21. A blowfly almost always lays its eggs in

A. water
B. manure
C. rotting flesh
D. water

22. Blowfly larvae are also known as

A. maggots
B. worms
C. puparia
D. eggs

23. To estimate the postmortem interval for a corpse it is important to collect as many insects as possible and also to have a good estimate of the

A. body weight
B. temperature
C. soil conditions
D. body's clothing

24. One of the first places to look for the presence of insect eggs or larvae is in the victim's

A. pockets
B. hands
C. chest
D. nose

25. If during a construction site excavation a skeleton is uncovered, one expert normally called to the scene is a forensic

    A. entomologist   B. anthropologist
    C. toxicologist   D. psychiatrist

Answers

1. A	10. D	18. C
2. C	11. A	19. B
3. A	12. C	20. D
4. D	13. C	21. C
5. C	14. B	22. A
6. D	15. D	23. B
7. C	16. C	24. D
8. B	17. A	25. B
9. C		

CHAPTER 3

THE CRIME LABORATORY

TERMS YOU SHOULD KNOW

ATF	DOJ	PIS
biosciences unit	FBI	questioned
chemical unit	IAFIS	document
CODIS	latent	USPS
DEA	NIBIN	USSS
Department of the	physics unit	
Treasury		

ORGANIZATION

Crime laboratories in the United States are run at two levels. There are federal crimes labs run by the U.S. government and each state has its own crime labs that are normally operated under the state police. In addition, there are privately owned forensic laboratories that carry out analyses for a fee. The five main federal labs are the **Department of Justice (DOS)** laboratories at the **Federal Bureau of Investigation (FBI)** and the **United States Secret Service (USSS)**, the **Department of the Treasury** labs at the **Drug Enforcement Administration (DEA)** and the **Bureau of Alcohol, Tobacco, and Firearms (ATF)**, and the **Postal Inspection Services (PIS)** at the **U. S. Postal Service (USPS)**.

The main forensic laboratory in the United States is run by the FBI and was created on November 24, 1932. J. Edgar Hoover established the FBI as the central forensic laboratory for the United States. For example, a copy of all fingerprints taken by local police agencies in the United States is sent to the FBI. It is the central repository for many different types of forensic information. Along with fingerprints, many other types of forensic standards are kept at the FBI lab. Comparison standards for paint samples, tire patterns, DNA, bullets, explosives, and fibers are but a few of the resources available from the FBI. On April 25, 2003, the FBI opened a new state-of-the-art crime lab. This facility makes the FBI laboratory one of the most capable full-service crime labs in the world. The new laboratory incorporates clean areas into the layout, which helps prevent contamination of evidence. This is especially important as techniques become more and more sensitive.

The capabilities of the FBI crime lab can be used by any federal, state, or local police agency, but cases are handled on a priority basis. For instance, the **Integrated Fingerprinting Identification System (IAFIS)** allows local police departments to scan a suspect's fingerprints using special equipment that digitizes the pattern. The information is then sent electronically to the state government and then transmitted to the FBI. The FBI can carry out a computerized search against all known fingerprints in a matter of hours and establish the identity of the individual. DNA evidence can be searched in a similar manner using the **Combined DNA Indexing System (CODIS)** developed by the FBI. In general, the FBI accepts from state and local police departments only evidence that involves a violent crime. Since the majority of evidence that needs to be analyzed is drug-related, most evidence collected by state and local police departments is sent to state police crime labs.

When most people think of the U.S. Secret Service, they think about men in suits wearing dark sunglasses and willing to take a bullet for the president. Initially, the USSS was created to combat the increase in the counterfeiting of U.S. currency that was threatening the value of the U.S. dollar. It was established by the U.S. Congress in 1865. In 1894 the USSS began the part-time protection of President Grover Cleveland, and in 1902, after the assassination of President William McKinley, Congress officially assigned the protection of the president to the USSS. The Secret Service also maintains its own forensic lab, which specializes in the analysis of questioned documents. A **questioned document** is one whose source is uncertain. The main reason for the USSS's interest in questioned documents relates to the counterfeiting of U.S. currency. Its forensic labs can analyze the ink and paper and determine if a document is genuine or fake. They have one of the most complete collections of ink samples, spanning centuries, and can often date documents based on the ink used, the paper, and other factors.

The DEA laboratories of the Department of Justice specialize in the analysis of drugs. While most forensic labs are capable of analyzing drug samples for the major components, DEA laboratories can carry out special analyses to determine side products, solvents, impurities, and starting ingredients. This type of information often allows the authorities to determine the origin or geographical location of an illegal drug manufacturer. It can also allow the DEA to monitor patterns of drug trafficking and the development of new classes of illegal substances.

The forensic laboratories of the ATF are the best in the world at analyzing physical evidence related to arson, explosives, firearms, tobacco, and alcohol. In combination with the FBI, the ATF has developed the **National Integrated Ballistic Information Network (NIBIN)**. This network allows local police agencies to scan digitized images of bullets and cartridge casings into a computer. This information can then be used to search the NIBIN database to identify the firearm evidence or link it to other crimes.

The Postal Inspection Services at the U.S. Postal Service (USPS) are concerned with crimes that involve use of the U.S. mail. This includes crimes such as identity theft, mail fraud, letter bombs, and child pornography. In the case of a toxic substance, such as a letter containing ricin or anthrax, the PIS can analyze the envelope for the location and identity of the criminal. Sometimes something as small as a DNA sample, isolated from the saliva residue left on an envelope or stamp, can be the vital clue that solves a case.

UNITS

Because of the need for specialization, forensic labs are normally separated into functional units by scientific discipline. Most crime labs have the following sections.

Chemistry

The **chemistry unit** is often the largest unit in the modern crime lab. This unit possesses some of the most sophisticated and expensive equipment in the crime lab, such as a gas chromatograph–mass spectrometer, which is used in analyzing for drugs. Since the majority of the evidence submitted to the crime lab is drug-related, this unit is normally the largest and has the most personnel.

The Sixth Amendment guarantees the right of the accused to a speedy trial.

For this reason the evidence from an arrest involving drugs must be analyzed by the chemistry unit in a timely manner and submitted to the courts. This is one of the driving forces behind the expansion of the number of crime labs and the increase in the hiring of forensic scientists. The chemistry unit also has other instrumentation that is used for the analysis of trace evidence, explosives, metals, paints, and minerals.

Physics

The **physics unit** is often involved in the reconstruction of crime scenes. Through the use of Newton's laws of motion and the law of conservation of energy a forensic physicist can reconstruct a car accident to determine what happened and who was at fault. Lasers can be used to reconstruct a shooting to determine who fired which bullet.

Biosciences

The **biosciences unit** is staffed by specially trained biologists who analyze biological materials for DNA. The evidence can include blood, semen, saliva, skin, hair, and other samples, which can be positively linked to a person by the DNA information contained in each cell. This unit may also be asked to identify various biological samples and carry out extensive analyses of blood factors.

Toxicology

It is the function of the toxicology unit to analyze body fluids, tissues, and organs for the presence of drugs or poisons. Samples are routinely sent to this unit by a medical examiner as part of an autopsy.

Firearms

The firearms unit test-fires suspect weapons into a bullet recovery tank so that by using a comparison microscope one can link a bullet to a crime scene. A comparison microscope can also be used to match markings left on cartridge cases by the firing pin, breech-block, extractor, or ejector of the weapon.

Fingerprints

The fingerprints unit can uncover prints that are invisible to the naked eye (**latent prints**). This can be accomplished by dusting, chemical, ultraviolet, and alternate light techniques. The prints can be manually classified or scanned into an automated fingerprint identification system.

Photography

The photography unit has film and digital cameras to record the crime scene. Infrared photography is also used in the study of questioned documents and bloodstained garments. Video cameras are also used to obtain a "walkthrough" view of the crime scene.

Questioned Documents

Any document suspected of being forged, altered, or counterfeit is sent to the questioned documents unit. There, experts can analyze ink, handwriting, printing, erasures obliterations, and charred documents. Counterfeit money and forged checks can also be identified.

Evidence Collection

Many larger crime labs have a specialized evidence collection unit. Trained evidence collection technicians travel to the crime scene in specially equipped vans, sometimes mistakenly called mobile crime labs. These vans contain all the devices needed to properly collect different types of evidence from a crime scene that might otherwise be missed. For example, these vans carry special vacuum cleaners used to vacuum the crime scene for fiber evidence. The fibers are collected on a white filter that is then taken to the lab.

Evidence Submission and Holding

Evidence taken to the crime lab by crime scene investigators is logged in by the evidence submission unit. This unit maintains the legal chain of custody and is where the evidence submission form (a list of all the evidence and what analyses are to be done) is delivered. The evidence is kept in a secure, locked area and must be signed out for each analysis. It is not unusual to see all types of evidence, the front end of a Trans Am, for instance, in a vault.

REVIEW QUESTIONS

1. The main forensic laboratory in the United States is located at the

   A. FBI B. USSS
   C. ATF D. USPS

2. Ink analysis is an expertise of the laboratories at the

   A. FBI B. USSS
   C. ATF D. USPS

3. Evidence from a bomb sent through the mail is handled by the

   A. FBI B. USSS
   C. ATF D. USPS

4. Arson evidence is an expertise of the laboratories at the

A. FBI   B. DEA
C. ATF   D. USPS

5. Drug evidence is an expertise of the laboratories at the

A. FBI   B. DEA
C. ATF   D. USPS

6. Scanned images of bullets can be entered into the

A. IAFIS   B. CODIS
C. PIS   D. NIBIN

7. Scanned images of fingerprints can be entered into the

A. IAFIS   B. CODIS
C. PIS   D. NIBIN

8. Digitized DNA results can be entered into the

A. IAFIS   B. CODIS
C. PIS   D. NIBIN

9. A modern crime laboratory is separated by specialization into

A. groups   B. families
C. units   D. sections

10. The largest unit in a crime lab is the

A. chemical   B. physics
C. biosciences   D. toxicology

11. A brain requiring an alcohol level analysis would be sent to which of the following units?

A. chemical   B. physics
C. biosciences   D. toxicology

12. Skid marks from a car accident are analyzed by which unit?

A. chemical   B. physics
C. biosciences   D. toxicology

13. Cartridge case evidence is analyzed by which unit?

A. firearms   B. fingerprints
C. questioned document   D. photography

14. Counterfeit money evidence is analyzed by which unit?

A. firearms   B. fingerprints
C. questioned document   D. photography

15. A gas chromatography–mass spectrometer would most likely be found in which unit?

    A. chemical   B. physics
    C. biosciences   D. toxicology

16. Which amendment guarantees the accused the right to a speedy trial?

    A. First Amendment   B. Fourth Amendment
    C. Fifth Amendment   D. Sixth Amendment

17. A list of the evidence and tests to be done is called a/an

    A. test and evidence list
    B. evidence submission form
    C. chain of custody
    D. case form

18. A main concern of the PIS is

    A. identity thief   B. alcohol
    C. tobacco   D. drugs

19. The purpose of the special vacuum cleaners in evidence collection vans is for the collection of which type of evidence?

    A. blood   B. pills
    C. paper   D. fiber

20. Physicists use which of the following to analyze accident scenes?

    A. Newton's laws   B. conservation of energy
    C. skid marks   D. all of the above

21. A comparison microscope would be most likely be found in which unit?

    A. chemical   B. physics
    C. firearm   D. biosciences

22. Dusting is a technique used in which unit?

    A. chemical   B. firearms
    C. fingerprints   D. toxicology

23. The majority of evidence being analyzed by crime labs is related to

    A. drugs   B. forgery
    C. mail fraud   D. child pornography

24. The DEA laboratory is run under the

A. DOJ   B. DOT
C. USPS   D. FBI

25. The five federal forensic laboratories help state and local
labs based on case

A. cost   B. load
C. priority   D. complexity

Answers

1. A	10. A	18. A
2. B	11. D	19. D
3. D	12. B	20. D
4. C	13. A	21. C
5. B	14. C	22. C
6. D	15. A	23. A
7. A	16. D	24. A
8. B	17. B	25. C
9. C		

PART II
THE PHYSICAL SCIENCES

CHAPTER 4

CHEMISTRY

TERMS YOU SHOULD KNOW

AAS	GSR	MS
analytical chemistry	HPLC	NAA
atom	hypothesis	organic chemistry
atomic fingerprints	ICAP	qualitative analysis
atomic number	inorganic chemistry	quantitative analysis
Beer's law	IR	science
chemistry	LC	SEM
compounds	line spectra	spectroscopy
EDX	matter	spectrum
elements	molecule	theory
GC		

INTRODUCTION

Science is the careful observation of nature. By making careful observations scientists can develop guesses (called **hypotheses**) about why things occur the way they do. Carrying out experiments further tests these hypotheses. Other scientists also carry out these experiments independently. If any of the experiments do not support the hypothesis, it is discarded and a new one is proposed, but if all the experimentation supports the hypothesis, it is accepted by the scientific community and called a **theory**. Science is therefore testable, tentative, and explanatory. It is tested by experiment, it can be disproved at any time, and it explains why things occur in nature the way they do.

Physical sciences include those sciences that study nonliving systems. Of particular importance to the field of forensic science are chemistry, physics, and geology. The physical sciences unit is the largest unit of the crime lab, and the largest part of this unit is the chemistry division.

Chemistry is the science that studies matter and the changes it can undergo. The reason for a large proportion of the crime lab being devoted to chemistry is the need for the analysis of drug evidence. The U.S. Constitution guarantees a defendant the right to a speedy trial, and this requires a chemical analysis of drug evidence before the case can go to trial. The bulk of the physical evidence analyzed by crime labs today is drug-related.

MATTER AND ATOMS

Matter is defined as anything that has mass. Matter can be measured and classified, as illustrated in Figure 4.1.

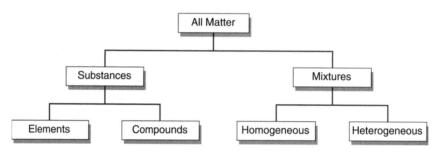

FIGURE 4.1

Matter can be divided into pure substances and mixtures. Pure substances, like water and gold, have a definite composition. Mixtures, such as saltwater and coffee, have a composition that can vary. Mixtures can further be classified as homogeneous or heterogeneous. A homogeneous mixture, such as a glass of homogenized milk, has the same composition throughout the mixture. A heterogeneous mixture, such as oil mixed with water, has a composition that varies throughout the mixture.

Pure substances can be further classified as elements or compounds. **Elements** are the basic building blocks of matter, and **compounds** are chemical combinations of two or more different elements. Gold is an example of an element, and water is an example of a compound (water is a chemical combination of the elements hydrogen and oxygen).

There are presently 115 different known elements, but all the elements after uranium (number 92) do not exist in nature. A table of all the elements is shown in Figure 4.2.

Group
1A

Key

1
Hydrogen
H
1.0079

1 — Atomic Number
Hydrogen — Element Name
H — Element Symbol
1.0079 — Atomic Mass

☐ Metals
☐ Semimetals
☐ Nonmetals

Period

Group 1A	2A	3B	4B	5B	6B	7B	8B			1B	2B	3A	4A	5A	6A	7A	8A
1 Hydrogen **H** 1.0079																	2 Helium **He** 4.0026
3 Lithium **Li** 6.941	4 Beryllium **Be** 9.0122											5 Boron **B** 10.811	6 Carbon **C** 12.0112	7 Nitrogen **N** 14.0067	8 Oxygen **O** 15.9994	9 Fluorine **F** 18.9984	10 Neon **Ne** 20.179
11 Sodium **Na** 22.989	12 Magnesium **Mg** 24.305											13 Aluminum **Al** 26.9815	14 Silicon **Si** 28.086	15 Phosphorous **P** 30.9738	16 Sulfur **S** 32.064	17 Chlorine **Cl** 35.453	18 Argon **Ar** 39.948
19 Potassium **K** 39.098	20 Calcium **Ca** 40.08	21 Scandium **Sc** 44.956	22 Titanium **Ti** 47.90	23 Vanadium **V** 50.942	24 Chromium **Cr** 51.996	25 Manganese **Mn** 54.938	26 Iron **Fe** 55.847	27 Cobalt **Co** 58.933	28 Nickel **Ni** 58.71	29 Copper **Cu** 63.546	30 Zinc **Zn** 65.38	31 Gallium **Ga** 69.723	32 Germanium **Ge** 72.59	33 Arsenic **As** 74.922	34 Selenium **Se** 78.96	35 Bromine **Br** 79.904	36 Krypton **Kr** 83.80
37 Rubidium **Rb** 85.468	38 Strontium **Sr** 87.62	39 Yttrium **Y** 88.905	40 Zirconium **Zr** 91.22	41 Niobium **Nb** 92.906	42 Molybdenum **Mo** 95.94	43 Technetium **Tc** (99)	44 Ruthenium **Ru** 101.07	45 Rhodium **Rh** 102.905	46 Palladium **Pd** 106.4	47 Silver **Ag** 107.868	48 Cadmium **Cd** 112.40	49 Indium **In** 114.82	50 Tin **Sn** 118.69	51 Antimony **Sb** 121.75	52 Tellurium **Te** 127.60	53 Iodine **I** 126.904	54 Xenon **Xe** 131.30
55 Cesium **Cs** 132.905	56 Barium **Ba** 137.34	*57 Lanthanum **La** 138.91	72 Hafnium **Hf** 178.49	73 Tantalum **Ta** 180.948	74 Tungsten **W** 183.85	75 Rhenium **Re** 186.2	76 Osmium **Os** 190.2	77 Iridium **Ir** 192.2	78 Platinum **Pt** 195.09	79 Gold **Au** 196.967	80 Mercury **Hg** 200.59	81 Thalium **Tl** 204.37	82 Lead **Pb** 207.19	83 Bismuth **Bi** 208.980	84 Polonium **Po** (209)	85 Astatine **At** (210)	86 Radon **Rn** (222)
87 Francium **Fr** (223)	88 Radium **Ra** (226)	**89 Actinium **Ac** (227)	104 Rutherfordium **Rf** (261)	105 Hahnium **Ha** (262)	106 Seaborgium **Sg** (263)	107 Nielsborium **Ns** (261)	108 Hassium **Hs** (265)	109 Meitnerium **Mt** (266)	110	111	112						

Lanthanides Series

58 Cerium **Ce** 140.12	59 Praseodymium **Pr** 140.907	60 Neodymium **Nd** 144.24	61 Promethium **Pm** 144.913	62 Samarium **Sm** 150.35	63 Europium **Eu** 151.96	64 Gadolinium **Gd** 157.25	65 Terbium **Tb** 158.925	66 Dysprosium **Dy** 162.50	67 Holmium **Ho** 164.930	68 Erbium **Er** 167.26	69 Thulium **Tm** 168.934	70 Ytterbium **Yb** 173.04	71 Lutetium **Lu** 174.97

Actinides Series

90 Thorium **Th** 232.038	91 Protactinium **Pa** (231)	92 Uranium **U** 238.03	93 Neptunium **Np** (237)	94 Plutonium **Pu** 244.064	95 Americium **Am** (243)	96 Curium **Cm** (247)	97 Berkelium **Bk** (247)	98 Californium **Cf** 242.058	99 Einsteinium **Es** (254)	100 Fermium **Fm** 257.095	101 Mendelevium **Md** 258.10	102 Nobelium **No** 259.101	103 Lawrencium **Lr** 260.105

FIGURE 4.2

Elements have one- or two-letter abbreviations called chemical symbols. Hydrogen, for example, has the symbol H, while helium has the symbol He. Two-letter symbols are needed since there are only 26 letters in the alphabet. When two letters are used to designate an element, the first is always capitalized and the second is always lowercase. Thus Co is the symbol for the element cobalt, while CO stands for the compound carbon monoxide, which is composed of the elements carbon and oxygen.

The Greek philosopher Democritus (ca. 450 B.C.) believed that if an element was cut up into smaller and smaller pieces, eventually there would come a point where the matter could no longer be divided. He called this ultimately tiny particle *atomos* from the Greek meaning "cannot be cut." From this, the present-day word *atom* originates. All matter is composed of atoms. Elements are the different types of atoms that exist. The smallest unit of an element is called an **atom**, and the smallest unit of a compound is called a **molecule**. The formula for a molecule includes not only the elements that make up the molecule but also how many of each atom are present in the molecule (Table 4.1). The molecular formula for water is H_2O. The subscript 2 after the H indicates that a molecule of water contains two atoms of hydrogen and one atom of oxygen.

TABLE 4.1

Compound	Molecular Formula	Atoms Present
Hydrogen cyanide	HCN	1 hydrogen 1 carbon 1 nitrogen
Ethyl alcohol	C_2H_6O	2 carbons 6 hydrogens 1 oxygen
Curare (curine)	$C_{18}H_{19}NO_3$	18 carbons 19 hydrogens 1 nitrogen 3 oxygens

Atoms themselves are composed of three particles, protons, neutrons, and electrons. Table 4.2 shows that protons and neutrons both have a relative mass of 1 amu and that the electron has a negligible mass (~0.0005 amu).

TABLE 4.2

Particle	Symbol	Mass (u)	Charge	Location in Atom
Proton	p+	1	1+	Nucleus
Neutron	n	1	0	Nucleus
Electron	e−	$\frac{1}{1837}$	1−	Outside nucleus

A proton has a relative charge of +1, and an electron has a relative charge of −1 (a neutron has no charge). Since all atoms have a charge of zero, the number of protons must equal the number of electrons.

Neutrons and protons are located in a region at the center of the atom called the nucleus. Electrons orbit the nucleus as shown in Figure 4.3.

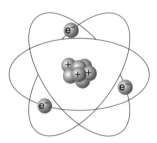

FIGURE 4.3

The number of protons in the nucleus defines what element an atom is. This quantity is so important that it is given a special name. The **atomic number** is the number of protons in the nucleus of an atom. The periodic table of the elements (Figure 4.2) arranges all the elements by atomic number (the number above the symbol for the element). For example, arsenic is a well-known poison in forensic circles. It is quickly distributed throughout the body and binds to enzymes in almost every cell. Inactivating these enzymes can lead to a swift death. Arsenic (As) has atomic number 33 (Figure 4.2). This means that each atom of arsenic has 33 protons in the nucleus and 33 electrons orbiting the nucleus.

ORGANIC CHEMISTRY

There are many branches of chemistry, but the three most important to forensic science are organic, inorganic, and analytical. **Organic chemistry** is the study of matter that contains the element carbon. **Inorganic chemistry** is the study of matter that does not contain the element carbon. Of the compounds listed in Table 4.3 the first three are inorganic and the second three are organic.

TABLE 4.3

Compound	Molecular Formula	Organic or Inorganic
Arsenic trioxide	As_2O_3	Inorganic
Silver nitrate	$AgNO_3$	Inorganic
Table salt	NaCl	Inorganic
Curare (curine)	$C_{18}H_{19}NO_3$	Organic
Strychnine	$C_{21}H_{22}N_2O_2$	Organic
Sarin	$C_4H_{10}FO_2P$	Organic

From a forensic point of view it is important to be able to distinguish between organic and inorganic compounds. Organic samples often contain a complicated mixture of compounds. Not only does this require extra steps in the laboratory analysis, but organic compounds are also more susceptible to degradation due to heat, temperature, humidity, and microorganisms. Curare can break down in body tissue in a matter of days. Therefore, the investigator has much less time to collect organic samples and submit them to the crime lab. Once at the crime lab, organic samples are normally kept in a walk-in refrigerator at 4°C to ensure preservation.

Organic chemicals offer the greatest diversity of any type of compound. Of the more than 20 million known compounds, about 95% are organic. Because of this great diversity, organic compounds are the basis of life. Many poisons, such as curare and strychnine, are isolated from living systems such as plants. Two of the most toxic compounds known are tetrodotoxin (from the puffer fish) and botulinum toxin (from the bacterium *Clostridium botulinum*). The botulinum toxin is so lethal that 1 g (about one-fifth of a teaspoon) of it could kill 1 million people.

INORGANIC CHEMISTRY

Inorganic compounds do not contain the element carbon. Metals, salts, and pure elements are normally associated with inorganic analysis. As opposed to organic compounds, inorganic samples tend to be more persistent. That is, they are more stable and normally can be analyzed long after exposure. Napoleon Bonaparte died in 1821 in exile on the remote island of Saint Helena. Locks of his hair were collected at the time of his death and handed down through generations of families as treasured heirlooms. Almost 140 years later Napoleon's hair was analyzed and found to contain traces of the element arsenic. This has led to speculation that he was poisoned during his last years. Thus inorganic compounds can be detected long after organic compounds have broken down.

Metals can be made up of pure samples of an element, or they can be mixtures known as alloys. Even in the case of pure samples other elements are present in trace amounts. These trace elements are often referred to as "invisible markers" since they can be used to associate various fragments of metal with a single source. Bullets are made of the element lead; however, trace quantities of other elements such as silver can also be found in lead bullets. Antimony is also added in small amounts to the lead to make the bullet harder. In the case of the assassination of President John F. Kennedy, the bullet fragments recovered from the president, Governor John Connally, and the presidential limousine were analyzed for the invisible markers silver and antimony. Since the amounts of silver and antimony vary from bullet to bullet, this method could be used to determine how many bullets were involved. In this case the silver and antimony concentrations were consistent with all the fragments coming from two bullets, which supported the findings of the Warren Commission.

ANALYTICAL CHEMISTRY

Analytical chemistry is the branch of chemistry involved in qualitative and quantitative analysis. **Qualitative analysis** involves the identification of a compound. **Quantitative analysis** involves the determination of the amount of a substance present. The identity of a compound is sometimes used to establish whether a law has been broken. A bag of white powder sent to the crime lab may contain cocaine, or it may contain pancake flour. It is up to the crime lab to determine the identity of the unknown chemical. The quantity also determines the crime. Table 4.4 lists the punishment for the cocaine possession in New York State.

TABLE 4.4 *Punishment for the Possession of Cocaine (Pure or Any Mixture) in New York State*

Quantity	Fine ($)	Prison Term (yr)	Class
0–⅛ oz	1,000–	Up to 1	Class A misdemeanor
500 mg	100,000	Up to 7	Class D felony
⅛–½ oz	for all offences	Up to 15	Class C felony
½–2 oz		Min 1, max 25	Class B felony
2–4 oz		Min 3, max life	Class AII felony
>4 oz		Min 15, max life	Class AI felony

The crime varies from a misdemeanor all the way to a class I felony based on the quantity present in the sample. It is important for the crime lab to determine the identity and quantity of any substance before a defendant goes to trial.

Gas Chromatography

The identification of chemicals is normally carried out by **spectroscopy**, which is the study of spectra (plural of *spectrum*). A **spectrum** is the orderly arrangement of a more complex phenomenon such as light, sound, or mass. Figure 4.4 shows a spectrum of visible light. White light is the combination of all the colors in the spectrum. It can be separated into its component colors by passing it through a prism.

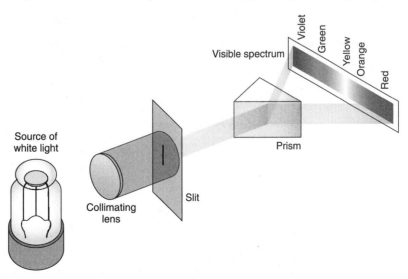

FIGURE 4.4

For forensic science, light and mass are the most important spectra because they can be used to identify chemicals. These spectra act as fingerprints and can be used in a court to prove the true identity of a material. The problem with spectroscopy is that the sample must be a pure compound or else a positive identification cannot be made. Think of ten different fingerprints superimposed on top of one another; it is very unlikely that a match could be made that would hold up in court. The same holds true for spectra from organic compounds. The superimposed spectra from a mixture of compounds is useless to a forensic investigator.

The problem of separating complicated mixtures of organic compounds was simplified by the discovery of **chromatography** in 1903 by Mikhail Tswett. Tswett used a glass column filled with calcium carbonate (chalk) to separate the pigments in a leaf. The leaf was ground up in an organic solvent, and the solution was poured into the top of the column. The solution was pulled down the column by gravity, and the different compounds that made up the pigments in the leaf were separated into brightly colored bands (Figure 4.5). Tswett called this process chromatography, which means "color writing."

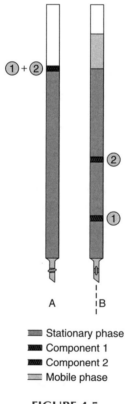

Stationary phase
Component 1
Component 2
Mobile phase

FIGURE 4.5

Chromatography involves an interaction between two phases, a stationary phase and a mobile phase. It is the function of the mobile phase to carry the compounds in the mixture through the stationary phase. Depending on the interactions, each compound travels through the column at a different speed. This causes the mixture to separate into bands of pure compounds. The type of chromatography is determined by the state of the mobile phase. In the case of Tswett's original work the mobile phase was the liquid solvent, and the process was called liquid chromatography. The most popular form of chromatography used in crime laboratories is one in which the mobile phase is a gas, what is called **gas chromatography (GC)**. A typical gas chromatograph is shown in Figure 4.6.

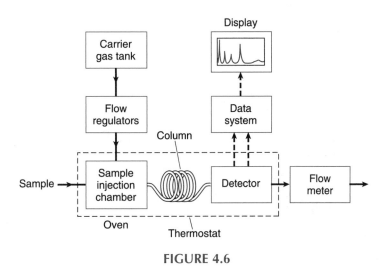

FIGURE 4.6

The gas that carries the sample through the instrument is normally helium. The sample is injected into the instrument as a liquid. If the sample is a solid, it is dissolved in a liquid such as methanol and the resulting solution is injected into the instrument. The analysis requires less than 0.5 μL (5×10^{-7} L, about one-hundredth of a drop) to be injected. The sample is injected into the sample injection chamber using a syringe and is instantly vaporized because of the high temperature (~250°C). The helium gas carries the sample through the column where the lighter compounds travel faster than the heavier compounds. The temperature of the column is carefully regulated since it is inside a thermostatically controlled oven. The temperature of the oven is set between room temperature and an upper limit of about 250°C, depending on the sample. The column itself is a long, thin tube of glass wound into a coil. Modern columns are about the thickness of a human hair and about 100 yd in length. These columns are referred to as capillary columns and can separate complicated mixtures with as many as 100 different compounds in less than 30 min. The separated chemicals then exit the column as pure compounds to be detected.

Liquid chromatography (LC) is more difficult to set up but has the advantage of operating at room temperature. Its use is normally restricted to compounds that decompose at the temperatures required for gas chromatography. Thermally unstable compounds analyzed by liquid chromatography include explosives and larger biological compounds. A liquid chromatograph is shown in Figure 4.7.

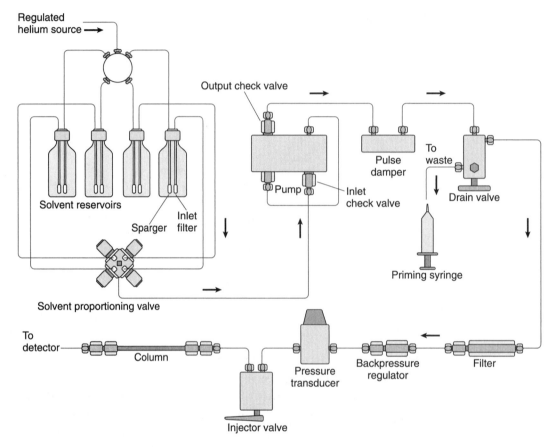

FIGURE 4.7

The sample is injected into the rotary sample inlet where a mixture of liquid solvents carries the sample through the column. The components of the mixture separate as they move through the column based on their varying affinity for the column or solvent system. Each compound moves through the column at a different rate, which causes the separated chemicals to exit the column as pure compounds. There are more choices of solvent mixtures, and it takes more time to get the combination correct.

Besides the ease and speed of use, gas chromatography has the advantage of having the separated pure compounds exit the column as gases. This allows the instrument to deliver the separated pure compounds directly into an identification tool such as a mass spectrometer.

Spectroscopy

For organic compounds the two most commonly used forms of identification are **mass spectroscopy (MS)** and **infrared (IR)** spectroscopy. Mass spectroscopy is the preferred method of analysis for organic samples because of several advantages. First, each mass spectrum produced by a compound is unique. Like a fingerprint, it can be used to prove the identity of a compound. In qualitative analysis there are tests that are presumptory (quick screening tests that sometimes give incorrect results) and there are methods that are confirmatory (tests that always give the correct results and therefore are admissible in court). Mass spectroscopy is a confirmatory technique. Second, mass spectroscopy is very sensitive. Quantities as small as 1 fg = $(1 \times 10^{-15}$ g) can be analyzed. This is very important in the analysis of many drugs that can produce physiological effects at very low concentrations. Third, mass spectra can be digitized and stored on computer hard drives. This allows large databases of several hundred thousand compounds to be searched in a few seconds, and the mass spectrometer can automatically identify the compound. Fourth, a mass spectrometer is easily combined with a gas chromatograph, which makes the analysis of complex mixtures easy.

A mass spectrometer smashes a compound into fragments and produces a mass spectrum of the compound and its fragments. Figure 4.8 shows the mass spectrum of cocaine. The number of particles counted is on the vertical axis, and the mass of each particle is on the horizontal axis. This spectrum is unique for each compound and can be used to identify a chemical in court. Figure 4.9 shows the general components of a mass spectrometer.

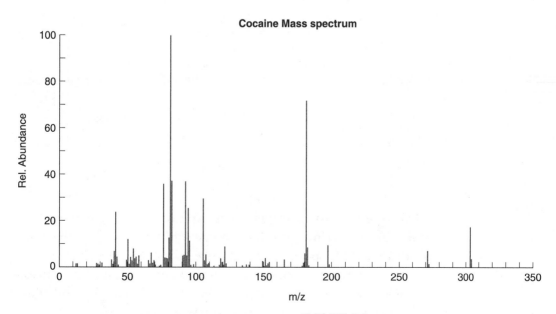

FIGURE 4.8

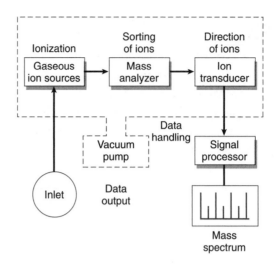

FIGURE 4.9

Two types of mass spectrometers are used in forensics. The new FBI laboratory uses a time-of-flight mass spectrometer (Figure 4.10) that measures the time it takes the particles to go from the ion source (where the compounds are smashed into charged fragments) to the electron multiplier (where the fragments are detected and counted).

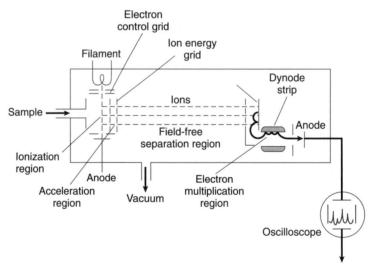

FIGURE 4.10

This type of mass spectrometer is expensive and is not commonly found in most crime labs. Most crime laboratories use a benchtop quadrupole mass spectrometer (Figure 4.11). Here the charged fragments from the ion source go through four parallel conductors called a quadrupole. The quadrupole acts as a mass filter and allows only charged particles of a certain mass to pass through. The mass allowed through is set by a radio frequency controlled by a computer. A benchtop mass spectrometer can be purchased for less than $100,000. Both instruments operate under a high vacuum to make sure that there are no other molecules inside that could cause interference.

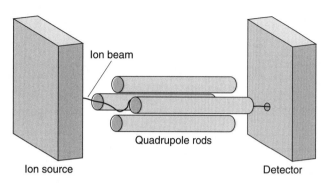

FIGURE 4.11

An infrared spectrometer (Figure 4.12) works by measuring the infrared light absorbed by a sample. Infrared light is lower in energy than visible light.

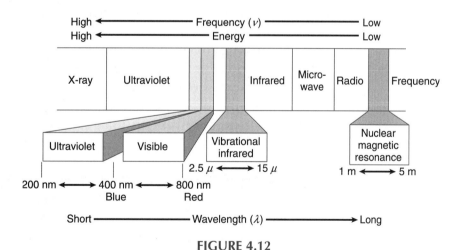

FIGURE 4.12

The human eye cannot see infrared light, but the bonds holding the atoms together in an organic compound absorb it. Each organic compound absorbs infrared light in a unique manner that allows infrared spectra to be used as fingerprints to identify chemicals. Figure 4.13 is the infrared spectrum of cocaine.

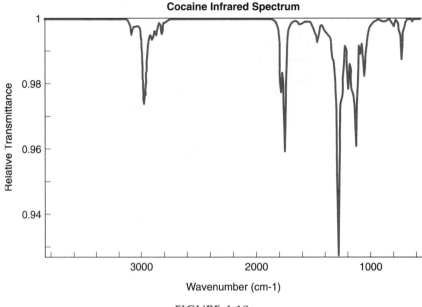

FIGURE 4.13

Sample preparation for infrared spectroscopy is normally very time-consuming. Solid samples must be ground into fine particles and mixed with potassium bromide. The mixture must then be formed into a pellet under high pressure. The pellet is mounted into the instrument, and the spectrum is obtained. Most modern infrared instruments are actually called Fourier transform infrared (FTIR) spectrometers. These instruments are much faster then the older type and can obtain a spectrum in as little as 0.1 sec. This has led to a new type of infrared spectrometer called an infrared detector (IRD), which overcomes the limitations of the old method. An IRD can be combined with a gas chromatograph. Some drug testing laboratories have gone over to using GC/MS/IRD because these dual detection devices allow independent confirmation of the identity of each substance.

The absorption of visible (VIS) and ultraviolet (UV) light can also be used to detect compounds, but the spectra are not very detailed or unique. Figure 4.14 is the UV absorption spectrum of heroin.

A lack of features makes visible and ultraviolet spectroscopy unsuitable for identification purposes. However, they are useful in determining the quantity of a material present. Instruments such as **high-performance liquid chromatographs (HPLC)** use visible and ultraviolet light spectroscopy as a detection system.

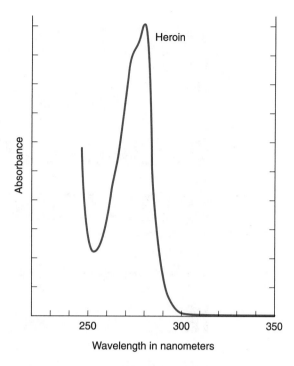

FIGURE 4.14

In the special case of the analysis of elements the spectra consists of single lines. Figure 4.15 shows the **line spectra** of several elements. Each element has a unique line spectra that can be used to identify it like a fingerprint. In fact, the spectra of the elements are often referred to as **atomic fingerprints**. Two instruments that make use of this property of atoms are the **atomic absorption spectrophotometer (AAS)** and the **inductively coupled argon plasma (ICAP** or **ICP)** spectrophotometer. These instruments can detect trace quantities of various elements down to the parts-per-billion (ppb) level or less. AAS and ICAP combine qualitative and quantitative analysis in one instrument and are the preferred method of analysis for metals. Inductively coupled argon plasma spectrophotometers can analyze more elements faster and to lower levels than atomic absorption spectrophotometers. However, ultratrace ICAPs can cost close to $500,000, while a good AAS can be purchased for about $50,000. For this reason most crime laboratories use an atomic absorption spectrophotometer for inorganic analysis.

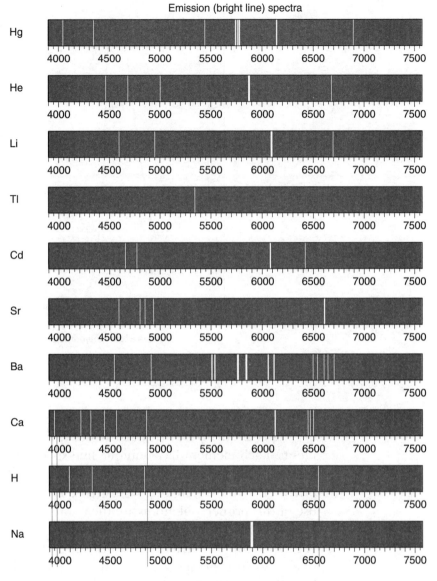

FIGURE 4.15

An atomic absorption spectrophotometer works by using the element to be analyzed to construct a light source. Figure 4.16 shows a typical AAS.

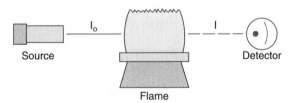

FIGURE 4.16

In detecting the presence of arsenic in hair, the first step is to place an arsenic lamp in the instrument. The lamp has a cup inside filled with arsenic, and it is excited by radio-frequency energy. This excites the arsenic atoms in the cup and causes them to give off the line spectra specific to arsenic. The only atoms that can absorb these lines are other arsenic atoms. The trick is getting the arsenic in the hair into its atomic form since only free arsenic atoms can absorb the line spectra produced by the lamp. The hair can be dissolved in concentrated nitric acid. The resulting solution is drawn through a tube, called a nebulizer, into a flame head, which burns the sample and produces the free arsenic atoms needed for the analysis. The free arsenic atoms in the flame can absorb the light from the source lamp, and the amount of absorbed light can be used to calculate the amount of arsenic in the hair using the following relationship called **Beer's law.**

Absorbance = absorptivity constant × pathlength × concentration

Often the crime lab plots the absorbance of light versus the concentration of the analyte (chemical being analyzed). This is called a Beer's law plot and is shown in Figure 4.17.

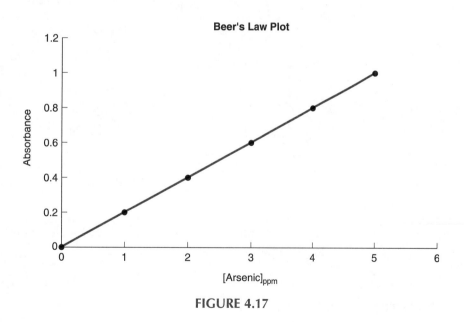

FIGURE 4.17

A common application of AAS is to determine if a suspect has recently fired a weapon. The primer blast from a center fire cartridge covers the back of a suspect's hand with elements from the primer mixture (lead styphnate, barium nitrate, and antimony sulfide). The back of a suspect's hand is swabbed with a cotton swab moistened with dilute nitric acid. The sample can be analyzed by AAS for trace amounts of the element lead to see if the suspect has fired a weapon within 24 h. After 24 h the amount of lead on the back of a shooter's hand decreases to the point where the test has difficulty determining the presence of lead.

Certain types of atomic spectroscopy make the atoms of an element in the sample produce its own light. Collectively, theses methods are referred to as atomic emission spectroscopy (AES). The AES technique most commonly used in the crime laboratory is inductively coupled argon plasma spectroscopy. Inductively coupled argon plasma spectrometers do not need to use lamps. These instruments use an argon torch to heat the sample to a temperature of about 10,000°C. At this extreme temperature the elements emit their own characteristic line spectra. The ICAP spectrophotometer measures the light given off by the excited atoms in the sample (Figure 4.18).

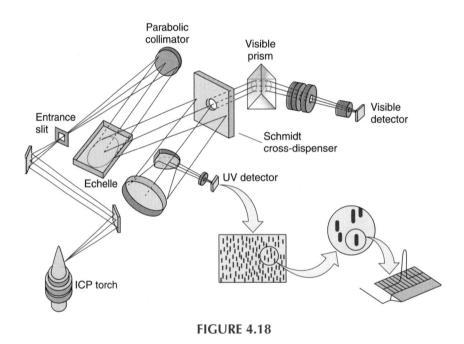

FIGURE 4.18

An ICAP instrument can measure 40 elements simultaneously down to parts-per-billion levels or less.

Neutron Activation Analysis

The most sensitive method available to forensic scientists for the analysis of trace elements is **neutron activation analysis (NAA)**. This method is rarely used in practice because it requires the use of a nuclear reactor to make a sample radioactive. Nuclear reactors produce a high concentration of neutrons. When a sample is placed inside a nuclear reactor, some of these high-speed neutrons collide with and stick to the nuclei of the atoms that make up the sample. Figure 4.19 is a flow diagram for neutron activation analysis.

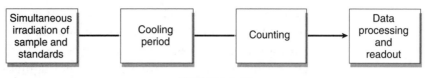

FIGURE 4.19

These nuclei become unstable (overweight) and shed some of the weight that they have gained by undergoing radioactive decay (Figure 4.20).

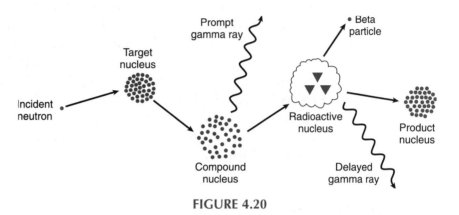

FIGURE 4.20

The sample is removed from the reactor and placed in a gamma spectrometer where the spectrum of energy emitted during the radioactive decay can be used to determine what elements are present and in what concentrations. Figure 4.21 shows the gamma spectrum of the calibration standard.

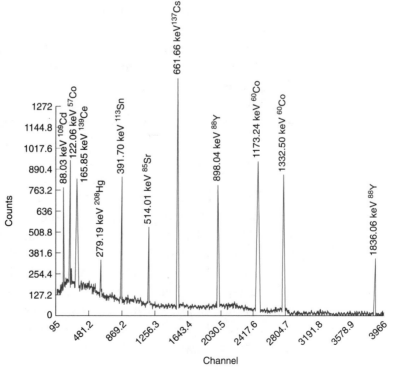

FIGURE 4.21

The bullet fragments from the assassination of President Kennedy were subjected to neutron activation analysis to determine the concentration of the trace elements silver and antimony in the lead. The results showed that one set of bullet fragments had a silver content centered around 9.3 ppm silver and an antimony content of about 815 ppm. The other fragments were consistent with a silver content of 8.1 ppm with an antimony content of about 622 ppm. This indicated that all the fragments recovered from the president, Governor Connally, and the limousine were produced by two bullets. Military ammunition has antimony added to the lead to make the bullets harder. This allows a bullet to better retain its shape in a high-velocity weapon, which results in a longer, more accurate shot. It also adds to the bullet's ability to penetrate and fragment.

Neutron activation analysis can be performed by the FBI for any local police agency, but it is done based on priority. Since reactor time is in great demand, only the highest priority cases receive this treatment. Most of the time the results from AAS or ICAP spectroscopy are sufficient and can be obtained without delay.

Scanning Electron Microscopy

Another technique for the analysis of elements is **scanning electron microscopy (SEM)**. A scanning electron microscope is used in many areas of forensics because of its ability to magnify objects to a much greater extent than an optical microscope. The maximum magnification of an optical microscope is about 600×, while an electron microscope can magnify an object up to 1,000,000×. A SEM produces a beam of electrons, which are shot out of the electron gun, focused, and strike the object (Figure 4.22).

The electrons are accelerated toward the target by 10,000 V, which gives them enough energy to knock electrons off the specimen object being viewed. This not only allows the object to be highly magnified but also causes it to emit X-rays, which can be used to determine what elements are in the sample and their concentrations. The energy-dispersive **X-ray detector (EDX)** is connected to a computer, which displays the X-ray spectrum generated by the sample. The computer identifies which elements are present in the sample and the concentrations from the spectrum. While this method is fast, easy, and an added bonus to any laboratory having an SEM, it is not very sensitive. The EDX detects only elements that are present in concentrations greater than 1%. Thus the method cannot detect trace elements and is more commonly applied in the analysis of **gunshot residue (GSR)**. When a person fires a weapon, the primer blast blows particles of the primer explosive back onto the hand holding the weapon. The primer particles contain lead, barium, and antimony that form spheres with a diameter of about 1 μm (1×10^{-6} m).

Figure 4.23 shows an SEM picture and the X-ray spectrum of a GSR particle from a shooter's hand.

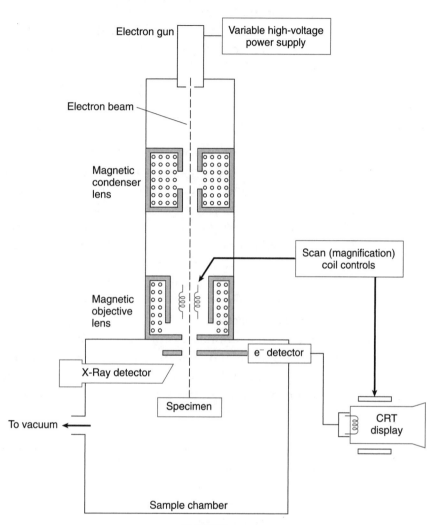

FIGURE 4.22

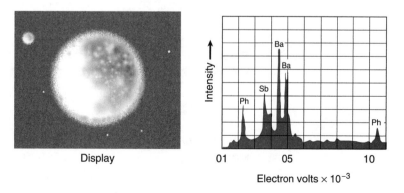

FIGURE 4.23

The sample is obtained by placing sticky adhesive on a metal stud, pressing the stud against the back of the suspect's hand in several places, and then placing the stud in the electron microscope. These gunshot residue spheres are positive proof that someone has fired a weapon up to 48 h after the incident (this does not work on 22-caliber weapons since rim fire cartridges have the primer mixture sealed inside the casing).

Summary of Techniques

The method of choice for the analysis of organic compounds is a gas chromatograph–mass spectrometer (GC/MS). This hybrid instrument separates a complicated mixture of organic compounds, identifies each compound, and also determines the amount of each chemical present in the sample. While the instrument is expensive, many samples can be loaded into its autosampler tray and it can be set to run all day and all night.

The preferred method of analyzing inorganic samples or elements is atomic spectroscopy, which includes atomic absorption and atomic emission spectroscopy. Because of its cost, the most common instrument is the atomic absorption spectrophotometer. It can determine the presence and concentration of elements in the parts-per-billion range. The ICAP can analyze more elements faster and to a lower concentration, but it is also more expensive to buy and operate.

TABLE 4.5 *Summary of Analytical Methods*

Method	Description	Advantages	Disadvantages
GC	A method of separation based on gas chromatography	Can separate a complicated mixture into pure compounds	Can decompose thermally unstable compounds such as explosives
UV	Ultraviolet light spectroscopy	Many organic compounds absorb UV light, so it can be used as a detector in HPLC	UV spectra are not unique, so it cannot be used for ID
VIS	Visible light spectroscopy	Many compounds absorb visible light	Molecular visible light spectra are not unique, so it cannot be used for identification
IR	Infrared light spectroscopy	Many organic compounds have unique IR spectra that allows positive identification	Time-consuming sample preparation and will not work on mixtures

TABLE 4.5 *(continued)*

Method	Description	Advantages	Disadvantages
AAS	Atomic absorption spectroscopy	Many inorganic elements can be determined at the sub-ppb level	Time-consuming for multiple analytes since each element requires a different lamp
ICAP (ICP)	Inductively coupled argon plasma spectroscopy	Many inorganic elements can be determined at the sub-ppb level simultaneously	High cost of buying and operating the instrument
GC/ MS	Hybrid instrument made by combining a gas chromatograph with a mass spectrometer	Method of choice for qualitative and quantitative analysis of a mixture of organic compounds	
GC/ MS/ IRD	Hybrid instrument made by combining a gas chromatograph with a mass spectrometer and an infrared spectrometer	All the advantages of a GC/MS plus independent confirmation of the identity of the compound by IR	High cost; large-sized sample required
NAA	Neutron activation analysis	Most sensitive technique for the determination of trace elements	Requires the use of a nuclear reactor
SEM/ EDX	Scanning electron microscope with an energy-dispersive X-ray detector	Quick method for determining the major elements present in a sample	Requires the lab to have an SEM (high cost); not sensitive to trace elements

REVIEW QUESTIONS

1. What is the term for a tentative proposal of a scientific principle?

   A. explanation B. assumption
   C. theory D. hypothesis

2. What is the term for a tested proposal of a scientific principle?

   A. explanation B. assumption
   C. theory D. hypothesis

3. Science is _____ , _____, and _____.

4. Chemistry is the science that studies

   A. explosions
   C. criminals

   B. matter
   D. living systems

5. What type of evidence is the bulk of the physical evidence that comes to a crime lab?

   A. arson
   C. drug

   B. murder
   D. accident

6. What is the symbol for arsenic?

   A. As
   C. Ar

   B. A
   D. AR

7. HCl is a/an

   A. organic compound
   C. element

   B. inorganic compound
   D. synthetic

8. What is the term for the smallest particle of a compound?

   A. molecule
   C. proton

   B. atom
   D. element

9. An atom is made up of _____, _____, and _____.

10. Analytical chemistry involves _____ and _____ analysis.

11. Chromatography was discovered by

    A. Edmond Locard
    C. Mikhail Tswett

    B. J. Edgar Hoover
    D. Calvin Goddard

12. Chromatography is used to

    A. identify compounds
    C. separate mixtures

    B. identify elements
    D. detect GSR

13. Liquid chromatography has an advantage for some analyses since it

    A. runs at room temperature
    B. is very fast
    C. is inexpensive
    D. can identify any compound

14. A unique spectrum of a compound can be obtained from which type of spectroscopy?

    A. ultraviolet
    C. sound

    B. visible
    D. mass

15. Sample preparation for a conventional infrared spectrom-
    eter is

    A. fast   B. time-consuming
    C. expensive   D. dangerous

16. Elements produce which type of spectra?

    A. continuous   B. line
    C. intense   D. random

17. What is the term for the plot of the light absorbance of an
    analyte versus its concentration?

    A. Tswett's law   B. Color's law
    C. Beer's law   D. Locard's law

18. What is the forensic term for the trace elements present in
    an inorganic sample?

    A. invisible markers   B. trace markers
    C. hidden elements   D. fingerprint elements

19. The two elements used to determine the number of source
    bullets, that created fragments in the Kennedy assassina-
    tion were _____ and _____.

20. The method used to analyze the bullets from the assassina-
    tion of President Kennedy was

    A. GC/MS   B. NAA
    C. ICAP   D. SEM/EDX

21. The preferred method for the analysis of a mixture of
    organic compounds in the crime laboratory is

    A. AAS   B. GC/MS
    C. IR   D. SEM

22. The line spectra of elements are often called the atomic
    _____.

23. GSR on the back of a shooter's hand contains the elements
    _____, _____, and _____.

24. In AAS analysis of GSR what is used to swab the back of a
    person's hand?

    A. dilute hydrochloric acid   B. dilute sulfuric acid
    C. dilute nitric acid   D. chloroform

25. The analysis of curare is time-dependent because curare is
    a/an _____ compound.

Answers

1. D
2. C
3. Testable, tentative, explanatory
4. B
5. C
6. A
7. B
8. A
9. Protons, neutrons, electrons
10. Qualitative, quantitative
11. C
12. C
13. A
14. D
15. B
16. B
17. C
18. A
19. Silver, antimony
20. B
21. B
22. Fingerprint
23. Lead, barium, antimony
24. C
25. Organic

CHAPTER 5

PHYSICS

TERMS YOU SHOULD KNOW

acceleration	force	polarizer
birefringence	friction	power
coefficient of	inelastic collisions	SEM
friction (μ_f)	mass	skid formula
crush depth	microscope	speed formula
crush stiffness	momentum	velocity
elastic collisions	N.A.	weight
energy	par focal	work
focal point	physics	

ACCIDENT RECONSTRUCTION

Physics is the science that deals with natural phenomena such as motion, force, work, energy, momentum, light, sound, electricity, and magnetism. A forensic physicist can use the evidence left behind at an accident scene to determine what happened and who was at fault. To do this the scientist must understand kinematics (the study of motion) and especially Newton's laws of motion and how these quantities can be used to tell what happened in a collision.

Let's start with some basic terms used in physics and what they mean.

Force: A push or a pull.

Weight: The pull of the earth on an object. A person who weighs 150 lb has the earth pulling on them with a force of 150 lb. Weight is a force. As defined in Chapter 4, weight = mass × acceleration of gravity.

Mass: A measure of the amount of an object that is present.

Friction: A special type of force that causes an object to slow down. There are two types of friction, static and kinetic. Static friction is the force that must be overcome to start an object moving. The force required to start a parked car moving while the brakes are still on is static friction. Kinetic friction is the force that slows down a moving object and the force that causes the skid marks left at an accident scene. The **coefficient of friction** (μ) is determined by dividing the force it takes to move the object by the weight of the object. μ = force/weight.

Velocity: The speed and direction an object is traveling. Velocity = distance/time. A positive or negative value is often associated with the velocity to show in what direction an object is moving.

Acceleration: The increase or decrease in the velocity of an object. Acceleration = velocity/time.

Momentum: The product of the mass of an object and its velocity. Momentum = mass × velocity.

Energy: The ability to do work. There are two types of energy, kinetic and potential. Kinetic energy is the energy of motion. A car driving down the highway at 65 mph has kinetic energy. Kinetic energy = ½ mass × velocity². Potential energy is the energy of position. A car at the top of a hill has potential energy relative to the bottom of the hill. Potential energy = mass × acceleration of gravity × height.

Work: A force acting through a distance. Work = force × distance.

Power: The rate at which work is done. Power = work/time.

Some examples of these quantities in terms of an average car would probably be useful. Consider the case of a 2000 Toyota Camry that has a weight of 3600 lb (112 lbm) and is traveling at a speed of 55 mph (81 ft/s). The calculations are normally done in the SI system in the laboratory but are presented to the jury in English units. For simplification all the calculations in this section will be done in English units. In these units mass and weight are differentiated by mass pounds (lbm) and force pounds (lbf). The units of speed in the English system are normally ft/s.

Mass: Mass = weight/g = 3600 lbf/32.2 ft/s² = 112 lbm

Kinetic energy: Kinetic energy = mass × velocity² = 112 lbm × (81 ft/s)² = 735,000 ft lbf

Momentum: Mass × speed = 112 lbm × 81 ft/s = 9100 ft lbm/s

THE SKID FORMULA

Often a forensic scientist is asked to reconstruct an automobile accident. One method frequently used is to measure skid marks left on the pavement. When a car skids to a stop, its kinetic energy is dissipated by the frictional work of the tires on the pavement. One can determine the speed at which the car was moving using the **skid formula**:

$$\text{Velocity} = 5.5 \times \text{square root } (\mu_f \times D)$$

where μ_f is the coefficient of friction for the surface of the road and D is the length of the skid mark. It is best to determine the actual value of μ_f for the accident scene. This can be done using specialized sleds or other tools to get an exact value. Some typical values of μ_f are given in Table 5.1.

TABLE 5.1

μ_f	Surface
0.25	Grass
0.4	Gravel
0.7	Paved road

A graph can also be used to simplify the calculation. In Figure 5.1 simply read up vertically from the length of the skid mark to the line corresponding to the appropriate coefficient of friction and read horizontally over to the speed that the vehicle was going.

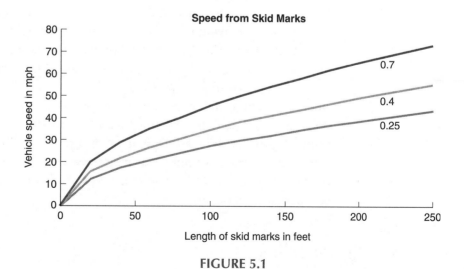

FIGURE 5.1

If the vehicle comes to a complete rest, then its initial speed can be read directly from the chart. If it was not at a stop at the end of the skid or hit another vehicle, the additional speed must be accounted for. Here are two examples using a 2000 Toyota Camry on a highway ($\mu_f = 0.7$).

CASE I
The vehicle left 150 ft of skid marks on the pavement before coming to a complete stop.

Read up from the 150 mark on the y-axis until you intersect the 0.7 curve. At the point of intersection read over horizontally to the speed in mph (~56). This means the Camry was going 56 mph when it entered the skid (bad news if the posted speed limit was 30 mph).

CASE II
The vehicle left 100 ft of skid marks before hitting a utility pole. From the crush depth of the Toyota it was determined that the vehicle was traveling 56 mph when it hit the pole. What was the initial speed of the Camry?

Read over from the 56 mph vehicle speed on the y-axis and note where it intersects the 0.7 curve. Read down to the length of the skid mark on the x-axis and note the value (~150 ft). Add this value to the length of the skid mark on the road to get a final value of 250 ft. Read up from the 250-ft mark on the x-axis to where it intersects the 0.7 curve and read over to the y-axis from that point. This means the Camry was originally going about 72 mph before it went into a skid and then hit the utility pole.

Case II required an estimate of the speed of the vehicle from the amount of damaged caused when it hit the utility pole. This is called the **crush depth**. When the crush depth is multiplied by the **crush stiffness**, it gives an estimate of how fast the car was traveling before impact. The crush stiffness is different for every vehicle and even varies somewhat with speed. It can be determined from crash test results from the National Highway Traffic Safety Administration (www.nhtsa.gov). In the case of a 2000 Toyota Camry the crush stiffness is 1.6 mph/in. In Case II the Camry was crushed 35 in when it hit the utility pole. The speed it was going before it hit the pole can be calculated by the formula: speed = crush stiffness × crush depth. In this case, speed = 1.6 mph/in × 35 in = 56 mph. There are several commercial programs available that contain all the crush stiffness values and can be used to reconstruct the most complicated scenarios.

THE SPEED FORMULA

The initial speed of the vehicle in Case II can also be calculated by determining the speeds of the individual events (the skid and the crush) and adding them together using the speed formula. The

speed formula states that the initial speed of a vehicle is equal to the square root (SQRT) of the sum of the squares of the speeds of the individual events.

$$S_{total} = SQRT(S_1^2 + S_2^2 + S_3^2 + \text{etc.})$$

In Case II the car was going 56 mph when it hit the pole, and its skid marks of 100 ft corresponded to a speed of 45 mph.

$$
\begin{aligned}
S_{total} &= SQRT(56^2 + 45^2) \\
&= SQRT(5161) \\
&= 72 \text{ mph}
\end{aligned}
$$

CONSERVATION OF ENERGY AND MOMENTUM IN ACCIDENTS

In physics, collisions can be classified as inelastic or elastic. **Inelastic collisions** occur when two objects collide and stick together and then travel together as one object in the same direction. Kinetic energy is not conserved in inelastic collisions, so the law of conservation of momentum is normally used. This law states that the total momentum before a collision must equal the total momentum after the collision. **Elastic collisions** occur when objects collide and then travel off on their own. An example of an elastic collision is when two billiard balls collide on a pool table and then go off in different directions. In the case of elastic collisions both momentum and kinetic energy are conserved. Here are two examples of collisions.

CASE III (INELASTIC COLLISION)

A 3596-lb Toyota Camry traveling at 30 mph collides with a 3527-lb Geo Tracker LSI stopped at a red light. What is the velocity of the two entangled vehicles after the collision? In this case we can use force pounds since any conversion to mass pounds would cancel out. The same holds true for using miles per hour instead of feet per second. We also assume that the vehicles are moving from left to right and make that the positive direction for the velocities.

Total momentum before collision	=	total momentum after collision
Momentum of Camry + momentum of Geo	=	(mass of Camry + mass of Geo) × velocity
3596 lb × 30 mph + 3527 lb × 0 mph	=	(3596 lb + 3527 lb) × velocity
Final velocity	=	(3596 lb × 30 mph) / (3596 lb + 3527 lb)
	=	15 mph

CASE IV (INELASTIC COLLISION, DIFFERENT DIRECTIONS)

A 3596-lb Toyota Camry traveling at 30 mph (left to right) collides head-on with a 3527-lb Geo Tracker LSI traveling 15 mph (right to left). What is the velocity of the two entangled vehicles after the collision? In this case we can use force pounds since any conversion to mass pounds would cancel out. The same holds true for using miles per hour instead of feet per second. We also assume that the positive direction for the velocities is from left to right and that the velocity for the Geo is therefore negative since it is right to left.

Total momentum before collision	=	total momentum after collision
Momentum of Camry + momentum of Geo	=	(mass of Camry + mass of Geo) × velocity
3596 lb × 30 mph + 3527 lb × (–15 mph)	=	(3596 lb + 3527 lb) × velocity
Final velocity	=	(54,975 lb mph)/(3596 lb + 3527 lb)
	=	8 mph

Since the final answer is positive, this means the entangled mass will be traveling at 8 mph from left to right.

Elastic collisions require solving equations for both the conservation of momentum and the conservation of kinetic energy. Since this can be complicated, most investigators use commercially available computer software that solves the equations automatically.

A simple example of the law of conservation of energy occurs when a car at the top of a hill rolls down to the bottom of the hill. Here the potential energy of the car at the top of the hill is turned into kinetic energy at the bottom of the hill. The following case illustrates this point.

CASE V (CONSERVATION OF ENERGY)

A 3596-lb Toyota Camry is parked at the top of a hill. The driver forgets to set the brake, and the car rolls down the hill and into a lake. What speed was the car going at the bottom of the hill if the change in elevation was 100 ft?

Potential energy at the top of the hill	=	kinetic energy at the bottom of the hill
Mass × gravity × height	=	½ Mass × velocity^2
Gravity × height	=	½ velocity^2
Velocity	=	SQRT × (2 × gravity × height)
	=	SQRT × (2 × 32.2 ft/s^2 × 100 ft)
	=	80 ft/s = 55 mph

BASIC OPTICS

Solving a crime often depends on finding trace evidence that is often referred to as the "invisible clue." While the evidence might be invisible to the naked eye, it can be easily discerned with the use of a microscope. A **microscope** is a device that can make a small object very large by the use of lenses. A lens is a curved piece of glass that magnifies objects by bending light. A single lens is the simplest type of microscope. Pictures of Sherlock Holmes often show him holding a simple magnifying glass in his hand to help enlarge the detail of some particular piece of evidence. The magnification of a lens is dependent on several factors such as the focal length of the lens and the distances between the lens and the object and the viewer. The focal length of a lens depends on the radius of curvature (how curved the glass lens is) and the refractive index (η) of the lens material (glass $\eta = 1.5$). Lenses for eyeglasses are made based on the lens maker's equation, which calculates the focal length of a lens for a given curvature (Figure 5.2):

$$\text{Focal length} = R_2R_1/((\eta-1)(R_2-R_1))$$

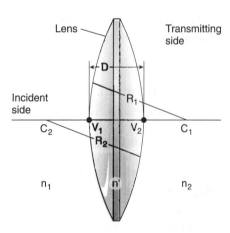

FIGURE 5.2

CASE VI

A glass lens has a radius of curvature of 10.0 cm on the front side of the lens and a radius of curvature of −15.0 cm on the back side. If it has a refractive index of 1.5, what is its focal length?

$$f = (-15.0 \text{ cm})(10.0 \text{ cm})/(1.5 - 1)(-15.0 \text{ cm} - 10.0 \text{ cm}) = 12.0 \text{ cm}$$

Once the **focal point** of a lens is known, the magnification of the lens can be calculated by a modification of the thin-lens equation:

Thin-lens equation: $\quad 1/f \quad = \quad 1/p \quad + \quad 1/q$

Magnification $\quad\quad = \quad -(q-f)/f$

where f is the focal length of the lens, p is the distance from the lens to the object being magnified, and q is the distance from the lens to the magnified image produced. A negative sign for the magnification indicates that the object is inverted, a negative sign in front of p or q indicates which side of the lens the object or image is located.

CASE VII

A glass lens has a focal length of 10.0 cm, and the distance from the lens to the image is –10.0 cm. What is the magnification?

Magnification = –(–10.0 cm – 10.0 cm)/10.0 cm = 2.0

The maximum magnification that can be obtained from a lens is limited. Many lenses have a **numerical aperture (N.A.)** value printed on the side of the lens (especially on microscopes). The maximum useful magnification that can be obtained from a lens can be calculated by multiplying the numerical aperture by 1000:

Maximum useful magnification = 1000 × numerical aperture

Any magnification beyond the maximum useful magnification causes the image to be distorted and is called empty magnification.

CASE VIII

What is the maximum useful magnification that can be obtained with a lens with a numerical aperture of 0.65 (N.A. = 0.65)?

Maximum useful magnification = 1000 × 0.65 = 650

When a combination of lenses is used, the overall magnification is the product of the magnification of each lens (Figure 5.3). This is what gives compound microscopes the ability to magnify an object to such a great extent.

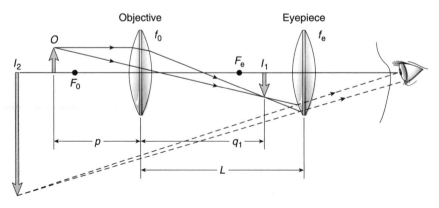

FIGURE 5.3

MICROSCOPES

Microscopes used in modern forensic laboratories are compound, which means that they contain two or more lenses. However, when the term *compound microscope* is used in forensics, it refers to the normal microscope used in the laboratory. Figure 5.4 is a diagram of a modern compound laboratory microscope.

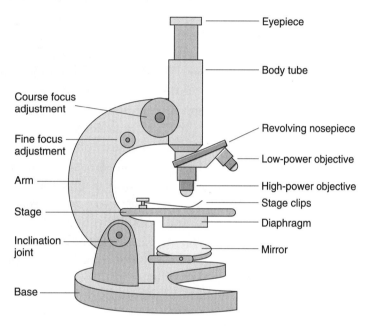

FIGURE 5.4

The eyepiece contains the ocular lens, which is the one closest to the viewer. The ocular lens normally has a magnification factor of ten (×10). The objective lens is the one closest to the object being magnified. Most compound microscopes have several objective lenses mounted in a revolving nosepiece. This allows a forensic scientist to select several different overall magnifications. Common magnifications for the objective lenses are 4×, 10×, and 40×. The overall magnification of a microscope is the product of the magnification of the ocular lens and the magnification of the objective lens (Table 5.2).

TABLE 5.2

Objective Lens	Ocular Lens	Overall Magnification
10×	4×	40×
10×	10×	100×
10×	40×	400×

The arrangement of the objective lenses on the revolving nose-piece is called **par focal**. This means that when the microscope is focused with one objective lens, another can be rotated into place and the object will still be in focus. This is a very useful feature since the working distance (the distance between the objective lens and the object) decreases with increasing magnification. At the highest magnification, the object lens almost touches the specimen and can easily scratch the objective lens or break the microscope slide on which the specimen is mounted. It is common practice to start the analysis at the lowest magnification, which gives the viewer the greatest working distance and is also the easiest to focus. Low magnification also gives the viewer the greatest field of view (amount of the specimen in view) and depth of field (how much of the specimen from top to bottom that is in focus). Once the specimen is in focus at a lower magnification, the nosepiece can be revolved to an objective lens with a higher magnification.

Five types of optical microscopes are used in forensic laboratories: compound, stereo, comparison, polarizing light, and microspectrophotometer. Each one has special uses and advantages. A sixth type of microscope, the **scanning electron microscope (SEM)** has already been discussed and normally is not included when discussing optical microscopes since it doesn't use light.

The compound microscope is the microscope most commonly used in the crime lab. These instruments can have all sorts of additional features, including light sources from above and below the specimen, ultraviolet light, filters, cameras, two eyepieces (binocular), and variable magnifications in small steps. Compound microscopes with these additional features are often referred to as universal microscopes.

A stereomicroscope is basically two microscopes focused on one object (Figure 5.5). Having two independent light paths, one for each eye, gives the viewer a three-dimensional view of the object. Also, unlike a compound microscope, moving the specimen to the left results in the image moving to the left. A stereomicroscope usually has a low magnification (~16× to 25×), which results in a large field of view and depth of field. This makes the stereomicroscope the preferred tool of forensic scientists in the screening of objects for trace evidence. When using a stereomicroscope, it is important to properly adjust the distance between the eyepieces to match the separation between the viewer's eyes so that a proper three-dimensional image is obtained.

Stereomicroscopes are often used to scan large carriers of trace evidence, such as clothing, for fibers, gunpowder particles, specks of blood, and other vital clues too small to see with the unaided eye. Once the objects are located, they can be further magnified using a compound microscope.

American Optical Cycloptic Stereomicroscope

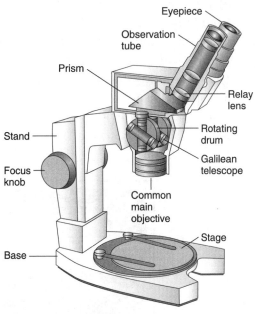

FIGURE 5.5

Comparison microscopes are basically two independent compound microscopes in which the field of view is combined (Figure 5.6). When the investigator looks through the binocular eyepieces, everything on the left side of the field of view is from the specimen in the left microscope and everything on the right side of the field of view is from the specimen in the right microscope.

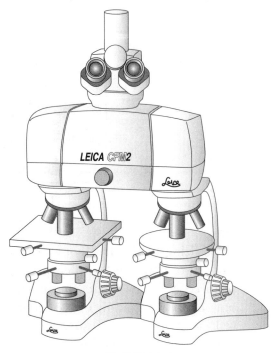

FIGURE 5.6

Comparison microscopes are extensively used in the firearms unit of the crime lab. Forensic investigators can use them to compare fired bullets and cartridge cases from the crime scene or the victim with bullets and cartridge cases test-fired from a suspect's weapon. A positive identification can be made by matching the striations (scratch marks) on each object. In Figure 5.7 a bullet test-fired from a suspect's weapon is shown on the right, and a bullet recovered from a body on the left. Both bullets must have come from the same weapon since the striation marks match.

FIGURE 5.7

They can also be used to compare fibers, hairs, and other small pieces of evidence to determine if they could have come from the same source. In Figure 5.8 a hair found on a victim's clothing is compared to a hair from a suspect. Obviously the hairs are not from the same source.

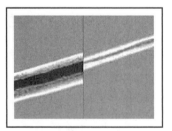

FIGURE 5.8

Polarizing light microscopes are compound microscopes that include two extra lenses called polarizers (Figure 5.9). Light can be pictured as a wave that vibrates in all directions. **Polarizers** allow only light vibrating in one direction to pass through. When light reflects off a horizontal surface, such as a road or water, it becomes horizontally polarized. Some sunglasses have polarized lenses that block horizontally polarized light from passing through. This reduces the glare caused by a flat horizontal surface. A polarizing light microscope has two polarizing lenses orientated at right angles. This blocks out all light except when examining objects that can rotate the direction in which light vibrates. This property is called **birefringence** (which means that the object has two different refractive indexes) and is quite common among fibers and minerals. Forensic scientists can identify many fibers and minerals by measuring their birefringence using a polarizing light microscope. Figure 5.10 shows a nylon fiber seen under a polarizing light microscope.

Polarized Light Microscope Configuration

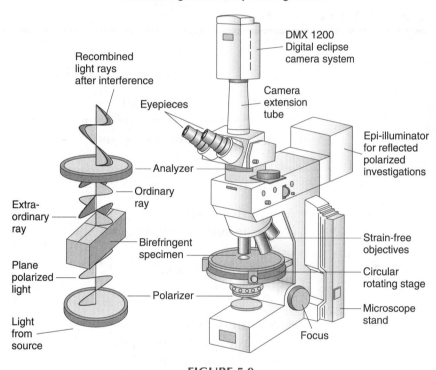

FIGURE 5.9

Nylon Fiber in Polarized Light

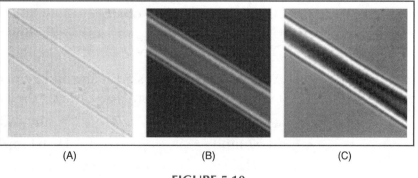

(A)   (B)   (C)

FIGURE 5.10

Microspectrophotometers are compound microscopes that are also connected to spectrophotometers that can analyze the light from a specimen. They are used in crime labs for the analysis of fibers and ink. A microspectrophotometer can focus in on a single line of ink on a questioned bill to determine if it is counterfeit. To the unaided eye, the colors of ink on a counterfeit bill might look exactly the same as those on a genuine bill, but they show a different pattern of light absorption (spectrum). This is because the inks used to produce the bills are unique combinations of dyes that are kept secret by the Bureau of Engraving and Printing, which is part of the U.S. Department of the Treasury.

REVIEW QUESTIONS

1. Physics is the science that deals with

   A. force, work, and motion
   B. energy, magnetism, and momentum
   C. light, electricity, and sound
   D. all of the above

2. Force is

   A. a push or pull
   B. the amount of an object
   C. distance per time
   D. mass times velocity

3. Velocity is

   A. a push or pull
   B. the amount of an object
   C. distance per time
   D. mass times velocity

4. Momentum is

   A. a push or pull
   B. the amount of an object
   C. distance per time
   D. mass times velocity

5. A car leaves a 100-ft skid mark on dry pavement ($\mu_f = 0.7$) before coming to rest. How fast was the car going?

   A. 20 mph   B. 46 mph
   C. 57 mph   D. 64 mph

6. A car hits a utility pole and is crushed 24 in. If it has a crush stiffness of 1.7 mph/in, what speed was it going when it hit the pole?

    A. 24 mph   B. 30 mph
    C. 41 mph   D. 45 mph

7. A cars leaves a 150-ft skid mark on dry pavement ($\mu_f = 0.7$) before hitting the side of a bridge. If the car was crushed 30 in (its crush stiffness is 1.5 mph/in), how fast was the car going before it entered into the skid?

    A. 72 mph   B. 45 mph
    C. 128 mph   D. 56 mph

8. A 3000-lb vehicle traveling 45 mph hits a stopped vehicle weighing 2300 lb. If both vehicles stick together in an inelastic collision, how fast will the two vehicles be going after the collision?

    A. 15 mph   B. 25 mph
    C. 10 mph   D. 5 mph

9. A 4000-lb SUV rolls down a hill. If the change in elevation is 200 ft, how fast is the vehicle traveling at the bottom of the hill?

    A. 57 mph   B. 68 mph
    C. 87 mph   D. 77 mph

10. A glass lens ($\eta=1.5$) has a curvature of 10.0 cm on the front side and –10.0 cm on the back side. What is the focal length of the lens?

    A. 5 cm   B. 10 cm
    C. 15 cm   D. 20 cm

11. A lens has a focal length of 5 cm and an object is located at –2.0 cm. What is the magnification?

    A. 1.0×   B. 1.2×
    C. 1.4×   D. 1.6×

12. A microscope has a 10× ocular lens and a 40× objective lens. What is the total magnification?

    A. 400×   B. 50×
    C. 100×   D. 1000×

13. A microscope lens has N.A. 0.60 written on its side. What is the maximum useful magnification that can be obtained from this lens?

    A. 60×   B. 600×
    C. 650×   D. 1000×

14. As the magnification increases, the working distance and depth of field

    A. increase   B. decrease
    C. stay the same   D. cannot be determined

15. The property of being able to rotate the objective lens while the object is still in focus is called

    A. numerical aperture   B. useful magnification
    C. field of view   D. par focal

16. Which type of microscope is used to match test-fired and questioned bullets?

    A. compound   B. stereo
    C. comparison   D. polarizing

17. Which type of microscope provides a three-dimensional image of evidence?

    A. compound   B. stereo
    C. comparison   D. polarizing

18. Which type of microscope can determine the birefringence of a fiber?

    A. compound   B. stereo
    C. comparison   D. polarizing

19. Which type of microscope uses electrons instead of light to produce an image?

    A. SEM
    B. microspectrophotometer
    C. polarizing
    D. universal

20. Which type of microscope can be used to analyze the chemical composition of the ink on a questioned bill?

    A. SEM
    B. microspectrophotometer
    C. polarizing
    D. universal

21. The part of a microscope that the objective lens is mounted into is called the

    A. base   B. diaphragm
    C. nosepiece   D. body tube

22. The part of a microscope that the ocular lens is mounted into is called the

    A. base   B. diaphragm
    C. nosepiece   D. body tube

23. A microscope with two or more lens is normally referred to as

    A. compound   B. stereo
    C. comparison   D. polarizing

24. Magnification beyond the maximum useful magnification of a lens is referred to as

    A. useless   B. empty
    C. questioned   D. fuzzy

25. Moving a specimen to the right in a compound microscope causes the image to move in which direction in the field of view?

    A. up   B. down
    C. left   D. right

Answers

1. D	10. B	18. D
2. A	11. C	19. A
3. C	12. A	20. B
4. D	13. B	21. C
5. B	14. B	22. D
6. C	15. D	23. A
7. A	16. C	24. B
8. B	17. B	25. C
9. D		

CHAPTER 6

GEOLOGY

THE EARTH'S CRUST AND MINERAL COMPOSITION

Geology is the study of the earth. The earth is divided into many layers (Figure 6.1). Starting with the center of the earth we have the core, which is split into an **inner core** and an **outer core**. The core is thought is be composed mostly of the element iron, with the inner core being solid and the outer core being liquid. It is the liquid outer core that is thought to be responsible for the earth's **magnetic poles**. Next comes the **mantle**. The mantle is composed of solid rock and is the largest of the layers in volume. The outer skin of the earth is called the **crust**. In comparison to that of the other layers, its thickness is analogous to that of the skin on an apple.

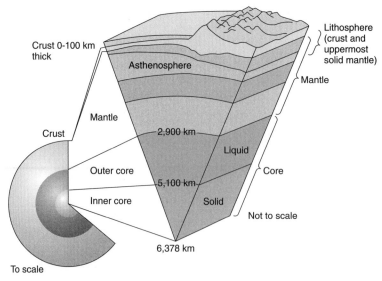

FIGURE 6.1

It is the crust of the earth that we come in contact with everyday. The soil we walk on has been created by the weathering of the underlying bedrock over a long period of time. Since crime scenes occur on the surface of the earth, it is common to find the elements present in the earth's crust also present at the crime scene. The eight most common elements in the earth's crust are

Oxygen (O), 46.6%

Silicon (Si), 27.7%

Aluminum (Al), 8.1%

Iron (Fe), 5.0%

Calcium (Ca), 3.6%

Sodium (Na), 2.8%

Potassium (K), 2.6%

Magnesium (Mg), 2.1%

The two most common elements in the earth's crust are oxygen and silicon, and together they make up 75% of the crust. A **mineral** is an inorganic chemical compound that is a naturally occurring crystalline solid with a definite chemical composition. The most common mineral in the earth's crust is **quartz**. Quartz has the chemical formula SiO_2.

SOIL ANALYSIS

While thousands of different minerals occur in the earth's crust, only about 40 common minerals are normally found in forensic investigations. These can be transferred by contact to a criminal's shoes, tires, clothing, vehicle, and so on. The famous criminologist Hans Gross once said, "Dirt on shoes can often tell us more about where the wearer of those shoes has last been than toilsome inquiries." Forensic geologists can provide valuable information in the course of an investigation. They can identify mineral compounds, suggest where they came from, see if the samples are consistent with the scene of the crime, and provide clues about the circumstances of burial. Soils can also be classified based on color. A sample of soil is thoroughly dried and then compared to a standard soil color comparison chart. There are 1100 different classifications of soil color. Samples from a suspect's shoe can be compared to soil samples collected from the crime scene to see if the minerals and the color match.

DENSITY GRADIENT TUBE

A simpler method of comparing two soil samples is to make use of the fact that each mineral has its own unique density. A tube can be constructed containing a solution of increasing density from top to bottom. This is called a **density gradient tube**. The solution is made by mixing two solutions, ethanol (density 0.789 g/mL) and bromo-form (density 2.96 g/mL), in varying proportions. The solution at the top of the tube has a density of about 0.789, and the density of the solution increases steadily to a value of about 2.96 at the bottom of the tube. If a small sample of soil is dried, finely ground, and placed in the tube, each mineral will sink to a level where its density is the same as that of the surrounding solution. At that point the mineral remains suspended in space. Since soil samples from different locations contain different combinations of the possible minerals, they each produce a unique pattern when placed in density gradient tubes. Samples from various sources are shown in density gradient tubes in Figure 6.2. Soil samples from three suspects are put into three separate density gradient tubes, and a soil sample from the crime scene is put into a fourth tube. Which sample is consistent with the soil from the crime scene?

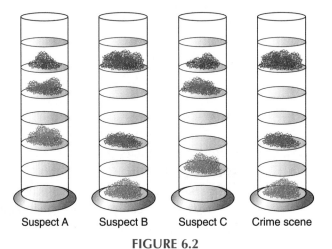

Suspect A   Suspect B   Suspect C   Crime scene

FIGURE 6.2

The answer is the sample from suspect B. The pattern of the soil from this suspect matches the pattern of the soil from the crime scene. Density gradient tubes are also useful in comparing glass samples and other types of evidence that have slightly different densities. They provide a very powerful visual piece of evidence to the jury, which can see if the patterns match even if they don't understand the science behind the demonstration.

SAMPLE COLLECTION

When collecting soil samples, it is important for the investigator to collect whole clumps of dirt if possible. Clumps of dirt often contain layers of different types of soil, which can be read as a history of where someone has been. In the case of a hit-and-run accident the violent nature of the impact often causes pieces of dirt to be dislodged from the driver's car and left at the crime scene. These clumps of dirt often contain layers of dirt indicating different geographical regions over which the car has traveled. The investigator should collect whole clumps of dirt from the vehicles of any suspects in the case. When collecting soil samples, the investigator should scrape off whole clumps of dirt right down to the surface of the car. The best place to collect dirt is from under the wheel wells and from the areas under the car directly behind the tires. Layered clumps of dirt can be almost as good as a fingerprint in connecting a suspect's vehicle with a crime scene. These whole clumps should be carefully packaged in separate containers. Careful handling, as well as the use of cotton or some other suitable packing material, helps keep the layers intact.

Soil samples obtained from a suspect's clothing and shoes can also be used to connect the individual with a crime scene. If the suspect claims the dirt was from another location, the investigator must be sure to collect soil samples from the alibi location as well. When collecting soil samples from an alibi location or crime scene, it is important to collect several samples in a 100-yd radius to allow for natural variation in the composition of the soil. The FBI recommends that the following procedure be used when collecting soil samples.

Collect soil samples as soon as possible.

Collect samples from the immediate crime scene as well as from any access or escape routes.

Collect soil samples where there is a noticeable change in color, texture, or composition.

Collect soil samples at a depth consistent with that where they may have originated.

Collect soil samples from alibi locations.

Include a map detailing where the soil samples were collected.

Do not scrape soil off clothing or shoes; instead air-dry and package whole items in separate paper bags.

Carefully remove whole clumps of soil adhering to suspect's vehicle, air-dry, and package in separate paper bags.

Pack to keep lumps intact.

Through the comparison of soil samples by color and mineral composition a link between the suspect and the crime scene can be established. Alternatively, the evidence may show that the suspect was at an alibi location and not at the crime scene. The use of density gradient tubes provides a powerful visual image for the jury to see the connection between the suspect and the crime scene.

One of the first recorded uses of geology in forensic science occurred in 1904. In this case the famous German criminologist Georg Popp was asked to investigate the murder of Eva Disch. Forensic specialists Murray and Tedrow state:

> In October 1904 a dirty handkerchief containing bits of coal, snuff, and grains of the mineral hornblende was found at the murder scene of a seamstress named Eva Disch. A suspect was found who used snuff, and worked part-time at both a coal burning gas works and a quarry that had an abundance of the mineral hornblende in the rock that it produced. The suspect also had two layers of dirt in his pant cuffs. The lower layer matched the soil at the crime scene and the upper layer, characterized by a particular type of mica particle, matched the soil found on the path to the victim's home. When confronted with the evidence the suspect confessed.

Another excellent example of the use of soil in forensic investigation involved the kidnapping and murder of a USDEA agent, Enrique Camarena, in 1985. While working in Mexico, Enrique Camarena was abducted. His body was discovered near a known drug trafficker's ranch. However, the soil found on the dead agent's body did not match that of the location where the body was found. The FBI finally determined that Special Agent Enrique Camarena's body had originally been taken to the another location, 881 Lope De Vega, where he was murdered. The house was operated by the Caro-Quintero drug gang, and they disposed of the body at a rival drug gang's ranch to throw the police off track.

REVIEW QUESTIONS

1. Geology is the science that deals with the study of

   A. rocks
   C. dirt
   B. the earth
   D. weather

2. The outermost layer of the earth is called the

   A. mantle
   C. crust
   B. core
   D. asthenosphere

3. The innermost layer of the earth is called the

   A. mantle   B. core
   C. crust   D. asthenosphere

4. The earth's magnetic poles are thought to be caused by the flow of electricity in the earth's

   A. inner core   B. outer core
   C. mantle   D. crust

5. Which of the earth's layers is thought to be composed of molten iron?

   A. inner core   B. outer core
   C. mantle   D. crust

6. Which of the earth's layers is of most interest to forensic science?

   A. inner core   B. outer core
   C. mantle   D. crust

7. Which two elements make up 75% of the earth's crust?

   A. H and O   B. C and O
   C. C and H   D. Si and O

8. What is the most common mineral in the Earth's crust?

   A. quartz   B. mica
   C. feldspar   D. calcite

9. SiO_2 is the chemical formula for which mineral?

   A. quartz   B. mica
   C. feldspar   D. calcite

10. A simple means of separating minerals in a soil sample based on density is the

    A. flotation method   B. refractometer
    C. density gradient tube   D. SEM

11. Solutions of ethanol mixed with bromoform are used in the

    A. gas chromatograph   B. refractometer
    C. density gradient tube   D. SEM

12. Visual comparisons of soil samples can be shown to a jury using the

    A. flotation method   B. refractometer
    C. density gradient tube   D. SEM

13. In collecting samples of soil the investigator should

    A. scrape off layers   B. collect whole clumps
    C. wash soil off with water   D. vacuum off soil

14. If the suspect claims the soil came from gardening in his backyard, the investigator should

    A. believe the alibi
    B. collect soil from the backyard
    C. not believe the alibi
    D. look for recent gardening activity

15. When collecting soil samples from a crime scene, the investigator should collect several samples in a 100-yd radius to allow for

    A. natural variability   B. wind drift
    C. soil erosion   D. uncertainty of location

16. Besides collecting soil samples from the immediate area of the crime, the investigator should also collect samples from

    A. drainage ditches   B. under trees
    C. under large rocks   D. access and escape paths

17. Soil samples should always be packaged

    A. wet   B. together to avoid loss
    C. separately   D. in airtight plastic bags

18. Soil evidence present as whole clumps should be packaged

    A. carefully in cotton
    B. dried and ground to a fine powder
    C. as a wet slurry
    D. broken into smaller pieces for ease

19. There are about _____ minerals that are common in the earth's crust.

    A. 10   B. 20
    C. 40   D. 80

20. There are about _____ different colors of soil that can be used for comparison.

    A. 200   B. 600
    C. 1100   D. 2000

21. In the investigation of the murder of Eva Disch one of the important minerals was

    A. quartz   B. feldspar
    C. montmorillonite   D. hornblende

22. In the Eva Disch case, soil from the suspect matched both the crime scene and the

    A. suspect's backyard
    B. path to the victim's house
    C. victim's garden
    D. victim's work

23. In the Eva Disch case, soil from the suspect was found on the victim's

    A. shoes   B. blouse
    C. handkerchief   D. floor

24. In the murder of DEA Special Agent Enrique Camarena, soil evidence was used to show that the body was

    A. moved from the crime scene
    B. badly decomposed
    C. buried at a great depth
    D. buried during the rainy season

25. Soil from a suspect's shoes should be

    A. washed off with water
    B. wiped off with a cloth
    C. left on the shoes
    D. scraped off with a scalpel

Answers

1. B	10. C	18. A
2. C	11. C	19. C
3. B	12. C	20. C
4. B	13. B	21. D
5. B	14. B	22. B
6. D	15. A	23. C
7. D	16. D	24. A
8. A	17. C	25. C
9. A		

CHAPTER 7

THE CRIME SCENE

TERMS YOU SHOULD KNOW

accelerants	evidence submission	quadrant search
annotated	form	search patterns
photographs	forceps	search warrant
chain of custody	Fourth Amendment	spiral search
controls	grid search	Tyvek
crime scene	native photographs	
reconstruction	protective clothing	

LEGAL CONSIDERATIONS

Forensic scientists can analyze only the physical evidence brought to the crime lab by investigators. Therefore it is imperative that investigators locate all the physical evidence that has a bearing on the case and correctly package and submit it to the crime lab. Once at the crime lab, the forensic scientists can use their expertise to gain as much information from the evidence as possible. One of the fastest ways for an investigator to lose friends at the crime lab is to collect the evidence improperly. There is nothing worse for a forensic scientist than to painstakingly go through mountains of trace evidence, spend hundreds of hours identifying and comparing pieces that prove the suspect guilty, and then have the whole thing thrown out of court because the evidence was collected improperly at the crime scene.

There are certain legal considerations, which the investigator must be aware of, that govern the collection of physical evidence at crime scenes. The **Fourth Amendment** of the U.S. Constitution protects us against unreasonable search of our houses and seizure of our property. It states:

86

The right of the people to be secure in their persons, houses, papers, and effects, against unreasonable searches and seizures, shall not be violated, and no Warrants shall issue, but upon probable cause, supported by Oath or affirmation, and particularly describing the place to be searched, and the persons or things to be seized.

The courts go a long way in admitting physical evidence into a case. Physical evidence cannot be bribed, it cannot suffer a loss of memory, and it cannot see things from a biased perspective. Physical evidence is available to both the prosecution and the defense. It is often said that if five people witness a crime, they will give five different versions of what happened. Physical evidence is not subject to this human frailty. Thus the courts want the jury to be able to use the results to determine the "truth" of the matter. However, all physical evidence must be collected legally, which means adhering to the Fourth Amendment.

In order to legally collect physical evidence at a crime scene the investigator must first obtain a **search warrant**. The search warrant must be obtained from a judge, and the investigator must give a good reason (probable cause) why they believe the evidence is present. The warrant must specify the location to be searched and what is to be seized.

While the best policy for an investigator is to always obtain a search warrant, there are four common exceptions that allow a warrantless search and seizure. The situations are as follows.

1. **Emergency:** In the case of an emergency the police do not require a search warrant. For example, the police are responding to a phone call by a neighbor about a domestic disturbance. They are standing outside the door of an apartment, and they hear gunshots and someone calling for help. The police have reason to believe an emergency exists and do not need a warrant to enter the apartment.

2. **Prevent destruction of evidence:** A fire department does not need a warrant to enter a burning building to put out a fire. This could also fall under the first exception—emergency. Once in the building the firefighers can battle the blaze and put out the fire, and then the fire investigators can search the fire scene and collect evidence without obtaining a search warrant. The courts recognize that the chemicals (accelerants) used to start a fire quickly evaporate and that during the time required to obtain a search warrant the evidence may disappear or be destroyed. Therefore fire investigators are allowed to remain at the fire scene, search the area, and collect evidence to see if a crime has been committed.

3. **Consent:** A savvy investigator can often get a suspect to give their consent for a search. Once consent is given, an officer can conduct a search as if a warrant had been obtained. It is important to document the consent in some way, such as a written release signed by the suspect.

4. **Pursuant to a lawful arrest:** When an arrest is made, a police officer is allowed to search the person and their immediate surroundings. The definition of immediate surroundings is somewhat vague and is the center of much legal debate. In 2004 the U.S. Supreme Court expanded the search limits to include the search of a car after a suspect has left it and the search of passengers and the passenger compartment. It is important to note that the initial arrest must be valid (lawful). If the initial arrest was in error, any subsequent search and seizure will also be ruled invalid.

If there is any question in the investigator's mind, a search warrant should always be obtained. If time permits, the courts always require that a warrant be obtained. In the case of *Mincey* v. *Arizona*, the U.S. Supreme Court looked at a murder case where an undercover police officer was killed in a suspected drug dealer's apartment. The police entered the apartment, conducted a 4-day search, and collected evidence without a search warrant. While the initial entry into the home was considered legal, the courts did not agree that the subsequent searches were legal since there was no indication that evidence would be destroyed or that a search warrant could not be obtained. The interpretation of the Fourth Amendment by the Supreme Court means that if there is sufficient time to get a search warrant, one must always be obtained.

PROCEDURES

There are five basic steps that an investigator must follow at any crime scene:

1. Obtain a search warrant.

2. Secure and protect the scene.

3. Search the scene.

4. Document and record the scene.

5. Collect and package the evidence.

6. Submit the evidence to the crime lab.

A search warrant is a must unless the case clearly falls into one of the four noted exceptions. If in doubt, get a search warrant, and be sure all the details listed on the warrant are correct.

One of the most important duties of the first responding officer is to secure and protect the crime scene. This means that barriers must be set up to exclude unauthorized personnel from entering the crime scene. This includes even high-ranking police officers and politicians who have come for a look. Often, the more high profile the crime, the more difficult it is to keep the crime scene secure. In the O. J. Simpson case, many of the investigators wandered through the crime scene without **protective clothing**. Such clothing is meant to protect the crime scene from contamination. The advent of DNA fingerprinting makes the integrity of the crime scene even more important. If a crime scene is left unsecured, all subsequently collected evidence is likely to be questioned and even thrown out of court.

SEARCH PATTERNS

The crime scene should be searched in a systematic fashion. An initial walkthrough is often recommended, with a more thorough search to follow. The four standard **search patterns** used are strip, grid, spiral, and quadrant. The actual pattern used varies, and the shape and size of the crime scene can influence the choice, as well as the number of search personnel and the preferences of the lead investigator. A spiral search is well suited to round crime scenes, while a strip or lane search is well suited to large areas when there are multiple searchers.

A **spiral search** is shown in Figure 7.1. A single investigator at an outdoor crime scene often uses the spiral search pattern. It has also been employed in underwater searches.

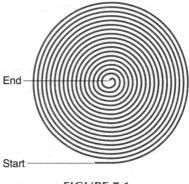

FIGURE 7.1

A **strip** or **lane search** is shown in Figure 7.2. A strip search pattern is often used to cover large areas. Each searcher travels at a fixed distance from the other searchers and all travel in the same direction. Large areas of land can be covered quickly using this method.

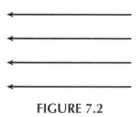

FIGURE 7.2

A **grid search** is shown in Figure 7.3. A grid search is similar to a strip search but after completing the search in one direction, say east to west, the search is then done at a 90° angle, say south to north. A grid search takes longer to conduct but has the benefit of double-checking the area.

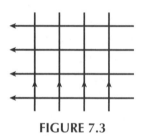

FIGURE 7.3

A **quadrant** or **sector search** is shown in Figure 7.4. A quadrant search pattern can be applied to small or large crime scenes. In the case of a small area the scene can be divided into four quadrants and each quadrant can be searched separately. In the case of a larger area the scene can also be divided into four quadrants, and so on, until the sectors are of reasonable size.

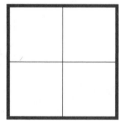

FIGURE 7.4

While there are many different patterns that can be used, the most important thing is that the search be systematic, with no areas left unsearched.

RECORDING THE SCENE

The crime scene must be documented in the investigator's field notes as well as in a sketch. There must also be a visual record of the crime scene consisting of photographs. While there has never been a case of a crime scene being overdocumented, there have been many cases where vital clues have been overlooked, lost, or misplaced. A thorough documentation of the crime scene is of importance to both the investigator and the jury. An investigator is often called to testify about an investigation several months, or sometimes years, after the crime occurred, and a careful documentation of the crime scene helps refresh the investigator's memory. In addition, good photographs and sketches of the crime scene allow the jury to see exactly what happened and how all the physical evidence is related.

The field notes should provide a description of all the evidence found at the crime scene. This description should include measurements that allow the evidence to be exactly located at the crime scene. The description and measurements in the field notes should go hand and hand with the sketch and photographs. The sketch should show the general dimensions of the crime scene along with all the evidence and its location. The sketch does not have to be artistic (round circles can indicate tables and chairs), but it does have to be complete. The rough sketch done at the crime scene can be redone by a forensic artist for presentation at the trial.

The preferred manner of recording a crime scene starts with a camera. In the past all crime scene photographs were taken with a film camera. Film has the advantage of producing enlargements with minimal distortion and of being difficult to alter. While digital pictures are fast and easy to print, they are also easy to digitally alter and these alterations can be difficult to detect.

In 2003 Victor Reyes went on trial for a 1996 murder. A smudged handprint found on duct tape recovered from the victim's body originally could not be used by the state police crime lab. Later the print was digitally enhanced and matched to Reyes by a computer software program called More Hits. The judge allowed this evidence to be introduced as part of his gatekeeping role. The defense attacked the evidence as having undergone digital manipulation and compared the software to digital image editing programs such as Adobe Photo-Shop. In the end the jury acquitted Reyes because they did not believe the evidence.

For this reason it is important to make digital pictures as reliable as possible. Approximately one-third of the police departments in the United States use digital photography to record crime scenes, and the numbers are increasing. In Oregon, the state police crime lab encrypts the images from its digital cameras and burns them onto compact discs, producing the digital equivalent of a film negative. The encryption prevents any alterations, and digital enhancements are done only on copies, never on the originals.

Photographs should be taken of everything that could be a potential piece of evidence. Initially, photographs should be taken of the evidence just as it is found (**native photographs**). Next, a measuring device (to show the size of a footprint, for instance) or an explanatory note can be added (**annotated photographs**). These shots can then be taken to help the jury. An example is a photograph, made by a local odontologist, showing the feet of a man in a prone position protruding from behind a van. No part of the man's body could be seen except the feet. A small object, which was difficult to discern, was on the ground near the feet. The next picture, which was annotated, identified this object as the man's nose. He had died of a self-inflicted gunshot wound, and because of the extensive damage to his face, the forensic odontologist was called in to positively identify him from dental records. All photographs should be recorded in the field notes along with the f-stop and shutter speed (for film cameras), distance to the object, and what was being photographed. It is important to be able to reproduce the entire crime scene from the notes, sketches, and photographs.

The crime scene can also be videotaped. While this is of limited use in presenting evidence, it does allow a walkthrough of the crime scene. This, plus the added benefit of narration, allows an exceptional overview of the crime scene, which is of great value in presenting the "big picture" to the jury.

COLLECTION AND PROPER PACKAGING OF PHYSICAL EVIDENCE

It is extremely important that evidence be collected properly or all its value may be lost. The guidelines for collecting physical evidence can vary slightly from agency to agency, but the standards set by the Federal Bureau of Investigation (FBI) are practiced almost universally. These can be found in the *FBI Handbook of Forensic Science*. The ever-increasing sensitivity of the analytical instrumentation used in modern crime labs means that a great deal more information can be obtained from physical evidence. It also means that there is a much greater chance that contamination of the evidence can render it useless. Contamination can come from the investigator or the environment or can be cross-contamination from other evidence. The general guidelines that follow are aimed at preserving the integrity of the evidence from the time it is collected at the crime scene until the time it is turned over to the court. First and most important, the investigator should never directly come in contact with the evidence themselves. This can lead to the investigator's own blood or DNA being deposited on the evidence. The investigator should wear a disposable hair net, latex gloves, and protective shoe coverings at all crime scenes. At sensitive crime scenes a full protective **Tyvek** jumpsuit and a protective mask may be required. At a minimum, evidence can be collected using **forceps** or gloves and must never be directly touched by the investigator.

For the purpose of packaging, evidence can generally be separated into four main categories, trace, nonbiological, biological, and arson, with general guidelines for each.

Trace evidence, such as fibers, hairs, and skin cells, can be very difficult if not impossible to detect with the unaided eye. Instead, the carrier of the trace evidence is carefully collected and packaged. Each carrier of evidence must be packaged separately to avoid cross-contamination. Of what use would it be to put the blouse from a victim in the same bag as the shirt from a suspect? Any fibers that might have been transferred during the crime could also be easily transferred if the clothes were packaged together, rendering the evidence useless. This is a very obvious example, but the possibilities of cross-contamination exist in more subtle situations. In the O. J. Simpson case many of the investigators walked through the original crime scene without wearing protective clothing (hair nets, latex gloves, shoe coverings, and so on) that would keep them from contaminating the scene. On June 12, 1994, the bodies of Nicole Brown Simpson and Ronald Goldman were found murdered outside Nicole Simpson's home. Photographs of the crime scene actually show the investigators walking through the area and scattering vital evidence, such as blood. Worse yet, some of the investigators then went to the next investigation site, the home of O. J. Simpson, and tracked evidence from the initial crime scene along with them. Crime lab techniques are so sensitive now that a single hair, eyelash, skin cell, clothing fiber, drop of blood, or shoeprint can be a vital clue. Care must be taken to prevent the contamination of evidence from any source. Trace evidence is routinely collected in plastic evidence bags of various sizes (Figure 7.5). These bags have a white area on the front, which allows for documentation, and a strip running across the top, which when pulled, exposes a contact adhesive that seals the bag closed. The adhesive is strong enough that opening the bag again will cause a tear in the plastic. This feature is designed to make the evidence bag tamper-proof. A plain envelope should not be used unless precautions are taken to seal the flaps at the top where evidence could be lost.

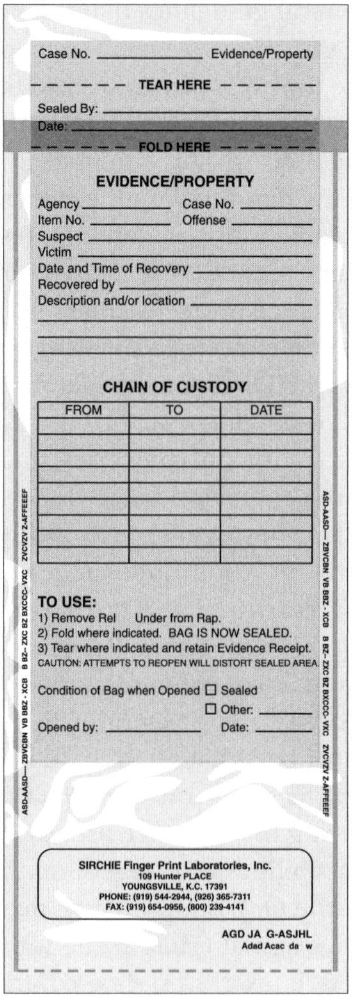

FIGURE 7.5

For most nonbiological evidence the standard plastic evidence bags work very well. In a pinch, 35-mm plastic film containers also work very well. A druggist's fold, or bindle, is also a suitable way to package evidence. A clean piece of paper is folded into thirds and then folded into thirds again. The evidence is placed in the center of the paper, and then the paper is folded. Finally, one flap is tucked inside the other. This is the way people used to obtain medicine from drugstores a long time ago. Many times the evidence is already in a suitable container, such as pills in a pill bottle.

Biological evidence is normally collected in nonairtight containers. The reason for this is that humidity can be trapped and concentrated in an airtight container, leading to the growth of mold or bacteria that feed on the evidence. This contamination can render the evidence worthless, so to prevent potential destruction by this mechanism, biological evidence is normally dried first and then packaged loosely in a paper bag (Figure 7.6).

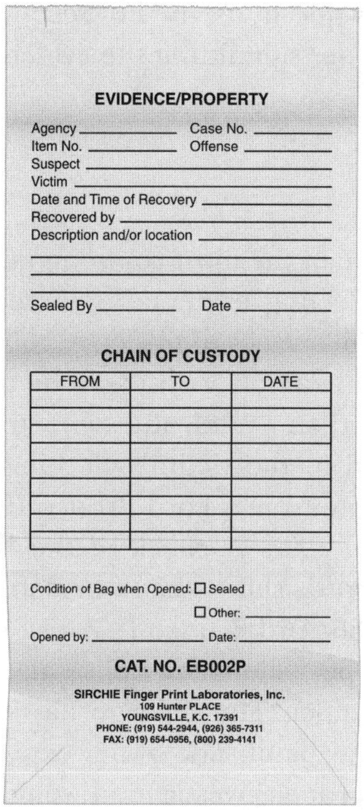

EVIDENCE/PROPERTY

Agency _____ Case No. _____
Item No. _____ Offense _____
Suspect _____
Victim _____
Date and Time of Recovery _____
Recovered by _____
Description and/or location _____
_____
_____
_____

Sealed By _____ Date _____

CHAIN OF CUSTODY

FROM	TO	DATE

Condition of Bag when Opened: ☐ Sealed

☐ Other: _____

Opened by: _____ Date: _____

CAT. NO. EB002P

SIRCHIE Finger Print Laboratories, Inc.
109 Hunter PLACE
YOUNGSVILLE, K.C. 17391
PHONE: (919) 544-2944, (926) 365-7311
FAX: (919) 654-0956, (800) 239-4141

FIGURE 7.6

Since air is allowed to circulate freely around the item, the growth of microorganisms is reduced. The evidence is stored in a walk-in refrigerator and kept at 4°C to prevent the growth of any mold or bacteria. In certain circumstances there are special packaging requirements for biological samples. Spots of dried blood can be picked up with a cotton swab that has been premoistened with distilled water. Liquid blood (from a live subject or found pooling at a crime scene) can be drawn into an evacuated vial containing preservatives that keep the blood from clotting and prevent bacterial growth.

Arson evidence normally involves a search for accelerants. **Accelerants** are chemicals that can be used to start a fire, such as gasoline and kerosene. These chemicals would react with the plastics in sealed evidence bags and would evaporate from nonairtight paper. For this reason arson evidence is collected in a metal container and sealed airtight. Paint cans that have never been used make excellent containers for arson evidence.

While these guidelines give a good general overview of the proper way to package evidence, it is important to note that specific types of evidence have specific requirements. The chapters in Part III of this book describe the various types of physical evidence and the proper way to collect and package each. Even FBI agents normally carry a small flipbook listing the various types of physical evidence and the proper way to collect and package each. If a police department has any questions, the FBI recommends that they check with the bureau before submitting the evidence.

CONTROLS

One of the most common mistakes made by new investigators when collecting evidence is forgetting to collect controls. **Controls** are similar types of evidence collected away from the area of the crime. For example, consider a hit-and-run car accident. A person is found dead on a road, and some small chips of car paint are found embedded in the victim's clothing. The paint is analyzed and found to come from a Ford Bronco II or a Ford Ranger made between 1985 and 1990. A check of the Department of Motor Vehicles (DMV) records shows that a person living in the surrounding area owns a 1988 Ford Bronco II. A visit is made to the suspect's house, and the suspect shows the police his vehicle, which has a damaged left front bumper. The damage has been hastily fixed with body filler and spray paint. The owner explains that he hit a deer a few nights ago. A proper investigation would include collecting paint samples from the damaged area, as well as control samples from areas away from the damage.

A common example of what can happen when a control sample is not collected occurred in an arson investigation. In this case a fire burned down a building, and arson by the owner was suspected. A dark area of a carpet was the suspected point of origin of the fire, and samples of the carpet from this area, and this area alone, were collected. When analyzed by the crime lab, the samples were found to contain traces of an organic solvent. Armed with this evidence the police charged the owner with the crime of arson. During the trial the defense produced documents showing that a contractor who used organic solvents as part of the cleaning process had professionally cleaned the carpet. Since the investigators had not collected control samples from other parts of the carpet, they could not prove that the chemicals detected were accelerants used to start the fire or residue from the cleaning process. The defendant was found not guilty.

SUBMISSION OF EVIDENCE AND CHAIN OF CUSTODY

Once evidence is submitted to the court, it is no longer the concern of the police department. However, from the time the first officer responds to the crime scene until the time the evidence is delivered to the court, it is the responsibility of the police to maintain the integrity of the evidence. The first concern is that all the legalities are carried out correctly. This normally means obtaining a search warrant. Next, the crime scene must be secured. This means that no unauthorized persons are allowed into or out of the crime scene. The scene should also be secured and sealed if no police personnel will be present. Next, the evidence must be protected from contamination from the investigator or the environment (in an outdoor location, for example) and from cross-contamination. The investigator must not touch the evidence and should wear a protective hair net, gloves, and shoe coverings. The evidence should be packaged separately in the proper container.

Once all the following have been taken care of, the investigator can start thinking about delivering the evidence to the crime lab. First, the investigator should prepare a chain of custody for each piece of evidence. A **chain of custody** is a document that records the date, the time, and the person who has possession of the evidence from the time it is collected at the crime scene to the time it is turned over to the court. Any break in the chain of custody or any period of time when the evidence was not secure is grounds to have it thrown out of court. Many pieces of evidence have been rendered worthless by being left on the dashboard of an unlocked, empty patrol vehicle or left overnight on someone's desk. Once at the crime lab the chain of custody is maintained, and each time a scientist removes the evidence from the secure area for analysis and then returns it, an entry is made. Most plastic and paper evidence bags have a preprinted chain of custody form on the front.

The investigator has the option to mail the evidence to the crime lab or to deliver it in person. There are exceptions to what can be mailed, and in general it is better to take the evidence to the crime lab in person. But there are exceptions. Let's say a small town has only one police officer and that it is a 3-h drive, one way, to the regional crime lab. The town would be without police protection for a minimum of 6 h if the evidence were transported by the police. The U.S. Postal Service is considered a secure means of sending evidence since it is part of the federal government and articles of mail are kept secure at all times during delivery. There are exceptions to what can be sent through the U.S. mail, however, and they include explosives, ammunition, and hazardous materials. In the case of explosives it is important to make sure the device is safe before giving it to the crime lab. The receptionist at the crime lab would not appreciate getting a brown box from a police officer with something ticking inside. They also would not appreciate receiving loaded weapons. All ammunition should be removed from weapons (and packaged separately) before submission to the crime lab, and explosives should be rendered harmless by the bomb squad (some labs also limit the maximum amount of an explosive they will accept).

Once a police officer brings the evidence to the crime lab, a receptionist normally collects it and signs the chain of custody. The evidence is then transported to a secure location, normally a large, locked room with many storage compartments and shelves for the systematic storage and retrieval of evidence. The room is like a safe, only much bigger to accommodate all the different types of evidence that can be collected in an investigation. On a trip to the local New York State police crime lab, I was escorted into the evidence lockup room and saw the front end of a Trans Am that had been involved in a hit-and-run accident.

The investigator is asked to fill out a form listing the following.

The submitting officer's name, agency, address, and telephone number

The case number

A basic summary of the case

Names and descriptions of the individuals involved

A list of the evidence being submitted

The types of examinations required.

Where the evidence should be returned and where the report should be sent.

Different crime labs have different requirements. That is why it is best for the investigator to bring the evidence to the crime lab in person. This way the investigator can ask the experts if there are any examinations that they would recommend or the scientist can recommend additional analysis to the investigator based on the physical evidence collected and the particulars of the case. A copy of an **evidence submission form** from the Georgia Bureau of Investigation, Division of Forensic Sciences, is shown in Figure 7.7.

Georgia Bureau of Investigation
Division of Forensic Sciences
EVIDENCE SUBMISSION FORM

Received by:_____

DOFS Case #_____

THIS FORM MUST BE COMPLETED IN ITS ENTIRETY
INCIDENT REPORT MUST BE SUBMITTED EXCEPT ON DRUG ID CASES
PLEASE PRINT LEGIBLY

INSTRUCTIONS FOR COMPLETION OF THIS FORM

I.   Submitting Agency_____   Agency Case #_____

       County of Incident_____   Date of Incident_____

II.   (Check responses)   Is *Subject/Victim* a juvenile? YES ☐ NO ☐   Is *Subject/Victim* deceased? YES ☐ NO ☐

VICTIM:_____ DOB:_____ Race:_____ Sex:____
       Last Name   First Name   Middle

SUSPECT:_____ DOB:_____ Race:_____ Sex:____
       Last Name   First Name   Middle

SUSPECT:_____ DOB:_____ Race:_____ Sex:____
       Last Name   First Name   Middle

III.   Delivering Officer: _____
                          Last Name   First Name   Title

       Case Officer to receive report:_____Pager#_____
                                      Last Name   First Name   Title

       Phone No._____Email Address:_____GSP Post No. or GBI Region No._____

       Other Officer and/or Agency to Receive Lab Report_____Agency Case #_____

IV.   (Check all that are appropriate)
       Type of Case: Death Case ☐ Homicide ☐ Arson ☐ Assault ☐ Sexual Assault ☐ Suicide ☐ Hit & Run ☐ VGCSA   Other_____

       Manner of Death: Homicide ☐   Suicide ☐   Accidental ☐   Natural ☐   Undetermined ☐

                          MVA/driver ☐   MVA/passenger ☐ MVA/pedestrian ☐   Fire or CO ☐

       Delayed death?   Suspected drugs/poisons?_____

       Cause of Death:_____

Brief Description of Item Submitted	Examination(s) Requested	Brief Case History

V.   PLEASE ANSWER THE FOLLOWING QUESTIONS FOR EACH LABORATORY SERVICE REQUESTED
            REFER TO SERVICE MENU FOR CONDITIONS/RESTRICTIONS FOR REQUESTED SERVICES AND ANALYSES

TRACE EVIDENCE ANALYSIS:
Is perpetrator known to frequent scene?
How often?_____

SEROLOGY/DNA ANALYSIS:
Who was bleeding? (check) suspect ☐ victim ☐ other_____
Did victim receive blood transfusion?_____
Has victim had sexual relations within the last 3 days?_____
Did perpetrator use a condom?_____
Did ejaculation occur outside the body?_____

(Submitting Agency - Retain bottom copy)   OPS FORM 1 REV:2 4/1/00

FIGURE 7.7

GENERAL INFORMAITON

REFER TO DOFS <u>LABORATORY SERVICES & REQUIREMENTS FOR SUBMITTING EVIDENCE MANUAL</u> FOR COMPLETE CONDITIONS/RESTRICTIONS FOR SERVICES AND ANALYSES.

FAILURE TO FULLY COMPLETE THIS FORM WILL RESULT IN A SIGNIFICANT DELAY IN PROCESSING.

1.   Submit a copy of the incident report unless it is a Drug ID case.
2.   Evidence container contents are not verified at the time of receipt.
3.   If using a computer generated or photo copy of this form, please submit (2) two copies.
4.   All evidence submitted in approved Blood Alcohol or Urine Only Collection Kits have their own Submission Form.

<u>SEROLOGY/DNA ANALYSIS:</u>

If DNA is a request, all known samples must be submitted in purple stoppered tube.
All evidence should be air-dried and packaged in paper bag.

<u>LATENT FINGERPRINTS:</u>

AFIS searches require submission of victim elimination prints.

<u>DRUG IDENTIFICATION:</u>

One item per case will be analyzed.
Quantitative analysis of cocaine shall be performed on trafficking and/or condemnation cases.

<u>TRACE EVIDENCE ANALYSIS:</u>

REMEMBER: Hair and fiber evidence must be collected and preserved in the lab (from clothing & linens) before other examinations are performed. You must request hair and/or fiber examinations at the time of evidence submission. These Trace Evidence examinations cannot be performed after items have been opened for examination by other sections of the lab (i.e. Serology/DNA).

For items that have a request for DNA analysis in addition to the request for Trace Evidence examination (hair, fiber, paint, glass, etc.), the Trace Evidence examinations will not be immediately performed. If the results of the DNA examination do not address the appropriate aspects of your case, please contact the Trace Evidence Section Manager to arrange for the completion of the Trace Evidence examinations.

<u>QUESTIONED DOCUMENT SERVICES:</u>

Only three checks per case will be examined.
Only original checks should be submitted.
Misdemeanor bad check cases will not be examined.

INSTRUCTIONS TO COMPLETE FORM

<u>AUTO DATE STAMP THIS FORM IN BOX LOCATED ON TOP LEFT CORNER</u>
<u>SUBMITTING AGENCY RETAIN BOTTOM COPY FOR YOUR RECORDS</u>

I.   A. Submitting Agency: name of submitting agency
     B. Agency Case #: submitting agency case number
     C. County of Incident: self-explanatory
     D. Date of Incident: self-explanatory

II. **Names on reports will be printed exactly as on Submission Form. Be sure name and spelling are accurate.**
     A. Indicate if subject or victim is juvenile and if subject or victim is deceased.
     B. Victim/Suspect: Print last name, then first name, then middle name/initial.
     C. Print Victim/Suspect's date of birth, Sex & Race.

III. A. Delivering Officer: name and title. This is used for chain of custody purposes.
     B. Case officer to receive report: print name clearly - last name first, then first name, followed by title. Please include Officer's phone number and pager number in order to contact for any needed clarifications.
     C. Indicate GSP Post No. or GBI Region No. if applicable.
     D. Other Officer and/or Agency to receive lab report if applicable.

IV. A. Brief Description of Item Submitted: self-explanatory
     B. Indicate Type of Case: print type of case from list at top of Item IV. Be sure to indicate if homicide or death case.
     C. Examination(s) Requested: print what type of analysis is requested.

V.   Answer applicable questions depending upon service requested.

FIGURE 7.7 *(continued)*

CRIME SCENE RECONSTRUCTION

The crime lab is sometimes asked to reconstruct a crime scene from the physical evidence collected. Examples include the reconstruction of automobile accidents from skid marks and the physical damage to the cars and surroundings (Chapter 5), shooting scenes from bullet holes left behind in windows and other material (Chapter 14), and any case where there is a need to piece together exactly what happened using the physical evidence from the crime scene.

A good example of a **crime scene reconstruction** involves a Florida case in which a police officer was fatally injured during a shootout between the police and a suspect. From an upper-floor window, the suspect exchanged fire with police officers trying to arrest him. Many shots were fired back and forth before the suspect was arrested. Besides other charges, the suspect was charged with murder for shooting the police officer. The defense argued that the officer was not shot by the suspect but by another police officer. The defense hired a forensic scientist to reconstruct the crime scene and trace the bullets fired by the suspect and by the police. This involved the use of lasers to trace the path of the bullets from marks in the suspect's room, through the window, and down to the ground below, including blood splatter from the officer. The flight of each bullet was marked with a string. Photographs of the crime scene showed a myriad of strings indicating that the fatal shot had not come from the suspect and that the death was a case of "friendly fire."

Complete reconstruction of a crime scene is rarely needed and normally does not require as much attention to detail. However, there are cases where the only way to determine what happened is to reconstruct the scene piece by piece to show the jury the true chain of events leading up to the crime (Figure 7.8).

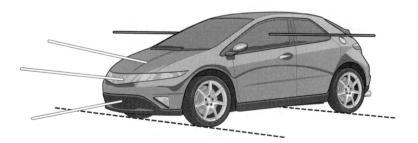

FIGURE 7.8

REVIEW QUESTIONS

1. Which amendment to the U.S. constitution protects citizens from unreasonable search and seizure of their property?

   A. First Amendment   B. Third Amendment
   C. Fourth Amendment   D. Fifth Amendment

2. To search a person's home for evidence the police normally need a

   A. good reason   B. good arrest rate
   C. hunch   D. search warrant

3. A search warrant for a police officer must be obtained from a

   A. police sergeant   B. judge
   C. mayor   D. town clerk

4. To obtain a search warrant a police officer must show

   A. probable cause
   B. the persons or things to be seized
   C. the place to be searched
   D. all of the above

5. Exceptions to requiring a search warrant include

   A. importance of the case   B. emergency
   C. late at night   D. holiday

6. How many exceptions to needing a search warrant are there?

   A. one   B. two
   C. three   D. four

7. Can a police officer search a person subsequent to a lawful arrest?

   A. yes
   B. no
   C. depends on the state
   D. depends on the type of arrest

8. Can a police officer search a person if the person says it is OK?

   A. yes   B. no
   C. depends on the state   D. depends on the time

9. Can a police officer search a person's home if it is a holiday and no judge is available?

A. yes   B. no
C. depends on the state   D. depends on the time

10. If time permits, a police officer should always get

A. backup   B. extra witnesses
C. a written order   D. a search warrant

11. At the crime scene the next step a police must take after obtaining a search warrant is to

A. record the scene
B. search the scene
C. secure and protect the scene
D. collect and package the evidence

12. The most important feature of the search pattern is that it be

A. systematic   B. fast
C. redundant   D. geometric

13. Which search pattern is often used by a single investigator at an outdoor or underwater crime scene?

A. spiral   B. strip
C. grid   D. quadrant

14. Which search pattern is often used to cover a large area?

A. spiral   B. strip
C. grid   D. quadrant

15. Which search pattern searches in one direction and then turns 90° to have the benefit of double-checking the area?

A. spiral   B. strip
C. grid   D. quadrant

16. Which search pattern breaks the area down into smaller sectors?

A. spiral   B. strip
C. grid   D. quadrant

17. To record the crime scene the preferred manner of photographing is

A. digital   B. film
C. video   D. black and white

18. Recording of the crime scene should include photographs, field notes, and a/an

    A. sketch   B. evidence submission list
    C. narration   D. video

19. Blood-soaked clothing should first be _____ before packaging.

    A. cleaned   B. wrapped in plastic
    C. air-dried   D. oven-dried

20. Clothing with bloodstains should be packaged in a/an?

    A. plastic bag   B. paper bag
    C. metal can   D. druggist's fold

21. Soot from an arson scene should be packaged in a/an

    A. plastic bag   B. paper bag
    C. metal can   D. druggist's fold

22. In the absence of any other container an investigator can use a/an _____ to package hair evidence.

    A. envelope   B. old coffee cup
    C. used plastic cup   D. druggist's fold

23. One of the most common mistakes made in collecting evidence is forgetting to collect

    A. enough   B. controls
    C. too much   D. comparisons

24. Most types of evidence can be sent via the U.S. mail except

    A. fingerprints   B. hair
    C. explosives   D. soil

25. What shows that evidence has always been under someone's supervision?

    A. evidence submission list B. chain of custody
    C. mail receipt   D. crime lab receipt

Answers

1. C	10. D	18. A
2. D	11. C	19. C
3. B	12. A	20. B
4. D	13. A	21. C
5. B	14. B	22. D
6. D	15. C	23. B
7. A	16. D	24. C
8. A	17. B	25. B
9. B		

PART III
PHYSICAL EVIDENCE

CHAPTER 8

PHYSICAL EVIDENCE

TERMS YOU SHOULD KNOW

Article VII	percentage
blood type	physical evidence
class characteristic evidence	polygraph
Frye criterion	probability
gatekeeper	rules of evidence
individual characteristic evidence	rules of probability

TYPES OF PHYSICAL EVIDENCE

Anything that is composed of matter (that is, anything that has mass and occupies space) and can be used to determine what happened in a crime is **physical evidence**. It can be as small as a single strand of DNA or as large as a truck. It cannot be guilty of being biased or having a poor memory like testimonial evidence. It can, however, be overlooked at a crime scene. No matter how great the expertise of the crime lab, it can analyze only what the investigators bring in. While almost anything can be physical evidence, it is sometimes helpful to break evidence down into categories to train beginning investigators. This book uses the following categories to classify physical evidence.

Body fluids: Blood, saliva, sweat, and semen

Explosives and incendiaries (arson): Chemicals used to start fires (accelerants) and explosives (oxidizers and reducers), along with the associated debris and devices

Fabrics: Natural, regenerated, and synthetic

Illegal drugs: Narcotics, stimulants, hallucinogens, depressants, club drugs, and steroids

Firearms: Gunshot residue (GSR), handguns, shotguns, rifles, and ammunition

Glass: Fragments and bullet holes

Soil: Whole lumps, from vehicles, from clothing, and from the crime scene

Hair: Animal, human, from individuals, from clothing, and from surfaces

Fingerprints: Latent, visible, and plastic

Impressions: Shoe, tire, teeth, and tool mark

Paint: Chips, lacquers, enamels, and polyurethanes

Liquids: Volatile, viscous, biological, and hazardous

Metals: Filing, fragments, reactive, and poisonous

Questioned documents: Letters, checks, wills, currency, charred, obliterated, and indented

Computer crime: Computers, hard drives, USB drives, floppies, and e-mail

DNA: Blood, semen, saliva, body tissues, and hair.

INDIVIDUAL CHARACTERISTIC EVIDENCE

Physical evidence is normally classified as either individual characteristic or class characteristic evidence. **Individual characteristic evidence** is defined as physical evidence that can be associated with a single, unique source with a high degree of **probability**. There are many examples of individual characteristic evidence such as fingerprints, DNA, striation marks on a bullet, and paint chips (or glass fragments) large enough to be fit back together like pieces of a jigsaw puzzle. The ability to associate a fingerprint with a single individual with a great deal of certainty makes it very easy to show the jury the connection between the defendant and the crime scene and gives the prosecutor a "smoking gun," making it that much easier to get a conviction. The problem is that most of the items sent to the crime lab are not individual characteristic evidence and are much more likely to be associated with a general group rather than an individual.

CLASS CHARACTERISTIC EVIDENCE

Class characteristic evidence is defined as physical evidence that can be associated with a group. The group can be very large or very small. The smaller the group to which the evidence can be connected, the more valuable the evidence. One common example of class characteristic evidence is **blood type**. Human blood can be one of four different blood groups A, O, B, or AB. Let's say a victim is found dead in his apartment and that he has type A blood. There is evidence of a struggle, and scrapings from under his fingernails show traces of skin cells and blood. The blood is typed and found to be type O. A suspect is arrested, and he also has type O blood. How strong a piece of evidence is the blood type? The percentages of the types of blood are well known for various populations, and in the United States are as follows.

Blood type:	A	B	O	AB
Percentage:	40%	11%	45%	4%

If the murder occurred in New York City, with a population of about 8 million, there are about 3.6 million people with type O blood. The number of people with this blood type can be calculated by the following formula.

$$\text{Number with trait} = \text{total number} \times \text{percentage with trait}/100$$

$$= 8{,}000{,}000 \times {}^{45}\!/_{100}$$

$$= 3{,}600{,}000$$

This is a very large group and, like many types of class characteristic evidence, does not really make a very strong connection between the murder and the defendant. Human blood can actually be separated into eight groups because each of the four basic ABO groups can occur as Rh-positive (+) or Rh-negative (–). The percentages for Rh in the population are 86% Rh-positive and 14% Rh-negative (courtesy of the American Red Cross). This results in the following percentages for the U.S. population (courtesy of the American Red Cross).

Blood type:	A+	A–	B+	B–	O+	O–	AB+	AB–
Percentage:	34%	6%	9%	2%	38%	7%	3%	1%

If the blood found under the victim's nails is O+ and the defendant is also O+, this means that there are 3,040,000 people in the Big Apple with the same blood type—still not a very convincing piece of evidence. However, if the trait has a lower percentage or the area has fewer people, the evidence can be of much more value.

Let's say a similar murder occurs in New York, but this time in the small upstate town of Smithville Flats (population 399). In addition, this time the blood type found under the victim's fingernails is AB–

and the chief suspect is also AB–. The number of people in Smithville Flats with blood type AB– can be calculated as

$$\text{Probability} = 399 \times \tfrac{1}{100} = 3.99$$

This means there are probably four people in the town with this blood type. This evidence would be more persuasive in convincing a jury that the suspect is the murderer (in forensic science, it is said that it has more evidentiary value). The probability of a certain piece of evidence existing in the general population is of great importance in determining its evidential value. Since most of the physical evidence received by the crime lab is class characteristic, it is of vital importance that the probability of each type of evidence be established.

RULES OF PROBABILITY

For some types of evidence, such as blood groups, the probabilities are well established. But what if the evidence is a tire track from a Cooper Lifeliner Touring SLE 235/60R16 or red acrylic fiber from a sweater. What percentage of the tires sold in the United States are Cooper Lifeliner Touring SLE 235/60R16 or what percentage of the U.S. population wears red sweaters made from acrylic fibers? Local police departments can contact the FBI for answers to questions like these. The FBI has experts who keep track of the probabilities of finding various types of evidence. If the probabilities are not known, a researcher can just go out into the real world and start counting. This has been done for such types of evidence as the refractive index of glass and the color of paint on cars.

Knowing the probabilities for various types of evidence is important for another reason as well. The rules of probability state that the probability of a chain of independent events is equal to the product of the individual probabilities of each independent event. A simple example can be developed using a deck of playing cards. A normal deck has 52 cards (not counting jokers). The four suits are hearts, clubs, diamonds, and spades. Each suit has 13 cards, 2, 3, 4, 5, 6, 7, 8, 9, 10, jack, queen, king, and ace. Let's calculate the probability of drawing a 5 from a deck of cards. Since there are four 5's in a deck of cards (5 of hearts, 5 of clubs, 5 of diamonds, and 5 of spades) and there are 52 cards in the deck, the probability of drawing a 5 can be calculated as

$$\text{Probability} = \text{selected event/total events}$$

$$= \tfrac{4}{52} = \tfrac{1}{13} = 0.077$$

Now let's calculate the probability of drawing a heart from the deck of cards. There are four suits, so the probability of drawing a heart can be calculated as

$$\text{Probability} = \tfrac{1}{4} = 0.25$$

What is the probability of drawing the 5 of hearts from a deck of cards? Since there is only one 5 of hearts in a deck of 52 cards, the probability of drawing the 5 of hearts can be calculated as

$$\text{Probability} = \tfrac{1}{52} = 0.019$$

The probability of drawing the 5 of hearts can also be calculated using the rules of probability. Since the probability of drawing a 5 is 0.077 and the probability of drawing a heart is 0.25, the overall probability can be calculated as

$$\text{Overall probability} = \begin{array}{l}\text{probability of event } 1 \times \\ \text{probability of event } 2 \times \text{etc.}\end{array}$$

$$= 0.077 \times 0.25 = 0.019$$

This formula is often used to calculate the overall probability for class characteristic evidence analyzed by the crime lab. In the case of blood groups the probability of having type A blood is 0.40 (to convert a percentage to a probability, divide the percentage by 100). The probability of having type Rh-negative blood is 0.14. The overall probability of having A– blood can be calculated as

$$\text{Probability} = 0.40 \times 0.14 = 0.06$$

To convert a probability to a percentage just multiply by 100. So a probability of 0.06 is the same as 6% (0.06×100), which is what the Red Cross reports for the percentage of the population that has type A– blood.

For many cases the probabilities for class characteristic evidence are large enough to render them unimportant by themselves. However, when the individual probabilities are multiplied together, the total probability is small enough to make the evidence very significant. In fact, the total probability for all class characteristic evidence in a case is often small enough to rival that of individual characteristic evidence. A paint chip found at the scene of a hit-and-run homicide scene may match the color of the paint on a suspect's car. This is an example of high-probability class characteristic evidence. If, however, the car was repainted sometime in its past and the layers of color on the paint chip exactly match the layers of color on the car, this becomes very low-probability class characteristic evidence. If the paint chip left behind at the crime scene is large enough to match the damaged paint area of the car (like a piece of a jigsaw puzzle), this can be considered individual characteristic evidence. The exact point at which this occurs is subject to some debate, but sometimes the total probability can be as low as that for fingerprints.

RECOGNITION

Physical evidence can go a long way in showing who committed a crime. However, it must be recognized, collected, and sent to the crime lab for analysis. Part of a forensic scientist's duties includes training investigators to recognize and properly collect various types of evidence. Some types of evidence should always be collected, such as drugs, guns, and ammunition. But an investigator cannot collect everything from a scene that is not nailed down, so some discrimination must be used. The investigator must learn what can be a potentially important piece of evidence and what is of no real value. This takes training and practice and changes with the nature of the case and advances in forensic science.

In the old days hair evidence was of limited use. Forensic scientists could not determine age, sex, or race from hair, and it could not be uniquely associated with a single individual. The best that could be done was a comparison with hair from a suspect and because there is so much natural variation in human hair even this had very limited evidentiary value. Nowadays, with the advent of DNA amplifiers and sensitive matching technologies, a single strand of hair with some blood cells adhering to the root (a follicular tag) can be an individual characteristic piece of evidence.

In the case of the Nicole Brown Simpson and Ronald Goldman double homicide, photographs taken by the police at the crime scene showed drops of blood on Nicole's back that could have been from her assailant. At the time these drops of blood were not recognized and the body was rolled onto its back, put in a body bag, and transported to the morgue. This would have caused Nicole's own blood to mix with the unknown blood spots on her back. Failure to recognize this evidence and collect it appropriately meant that it was forever lost to the investigation.

RULES OF EVIDENCE

When science was first applied to solving crimes, there was always a question about the admissibility of new scientific methods. While some new methods seemed fairly obvious and well grounded in scientific theory, others were more controversial. In the 1920s the police had a new scientific tool to use when questioning a suspect. The **polygraph** is an instrument that records continuously, visually, permanently, and simultaneously changes in cardiovascular, respiratory, and electrodermal patterns as minimum instrumentation standards. It is used, or the results of it are used, for the purpose of rendering a diagnostic opinion regarding the honesty or dishonesty of an individual. While the scientific principles of measuring heart and breathing rates and electrical signals from the skin are well founded, the use of this data to determine if an individual is telling the truth is less certain. The police hooked a suspect up to the polygraph and asked questions. By interpreting the signals from the suspect displayed on the many graphs (hence the name *polygraph*), they could determine whether the suspect was answering the questions truthfully. For this reason, the instruments were often called lie detectors. A polygraph from Lafayette Instruments is shown in Figure 8.1.

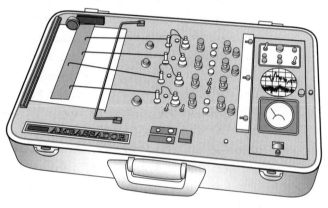

FIGURE 8.1

Five pens record the required information (Table 8.1).

TABLE 8.1

	►O MECH. PNEUMO
	►O ALL-PURPOSE
	►O GSR
	►O MECH. CARDIO
	►O MULTI-FUNCTION

In 1923 the admissibility of polygraph evidence was taken all the way to the U.S. Supreme Court in the case of *Frye* v. *United States*. The court listened to testimony from a number of scientists and scientific organizations and decided that a polygraph lacked the scientific validity to be used as evidence in a court of law. The court stated: "While courts will go a long way in admitting expert testimony deduced from a well-recognized scientific principle or discovery, the thing from which the deduction is made must be sufficiently established to have gained general acceptance in the particular field in which it belongs."

This idea that a new method must have the general acceptance of the scientific field in which it belongs is called the **Frye Criterion**. For many years this was the main criterion used to determine the admissibility of new scientific methods.

Let's say a person wants testify in a murder case. He tells the judge he is an expert in phrenology (the determination of a person's character from the shape of the head). He claims that he can tell whether someone has committed a crime by reading the bumps on their head. A judge could use the Frye criterion to determine if phrenology was accepted as valid by the general scientific community. She could get feedback from the American Medical Association, American Chemical Society, American Association for the Advancement of Science, and American Academy of Forensic Sciences, to name a few, and based on this information, would not allow this person to testify.

In 1993, in the case of *Daubert* v. *Merrell Dow Pharmaceutical, Inc.*, the U.S. Supreme Court decided that the Frye criterion was not the absolute standard for the acceptance of forensic evidence. It decided that it would be more consistent to include forensic evidence in the Federal Rules of Evidence. Article VII of the Federal Rules of Evidence lists the rules for admissibility of opinions and expert witness testimony. Of particular importance to the forensic community are Rules 702 through 706, which govern expert witness testimony:

Article VII: Opinions and Expert Testimony

Rule 701: Opinion Testimony by Lay Witnesses

If the witness is not testifying as an expert, the witness' testimony in the form of opinions or inferences is limited to those opinions or inferences which are (a) rationally based on the perception of the witness, and (b) helpful to a clear understanding of the witness' testimony or the determination of a fact in issue, and (c) not based on scientific, technical, or other specialized knowledge within the scope of Rule 702.

Rule 702: Testimony by Experts

If scientific, technical, or other specialized knowledge will assist the trier of fact to understand the evidence or to determine a fact in issue, a witness qualified as an expert by knowledge, skill, experience, training, or education, may testify thereto in the form of an opinion or otherwise, if (1) the testimony is based upon sufficient facts or data, (2) the testimony is the product of reliable principles and methods, and (3) the witness has applied the principles and methods reliably to the facts of the case.

Rule 703: Bases of Opinion Testimony by Experts

The facts or data in the particular case upon which an expert bases an opinion or inference may be those perceived by or made known to the expert at or before the hearing. If of a type reasonably relied upon by experts in the particular field in forming opinions or inferences upon the subject, the facts or data need not be admissible in evidence in order for the opinion or inference to be admitted. Facts or data that are otherwise inadmissible shall not be disclosed to the jury by the proponent of the opinion or inference unless the court determines that their probative value in assisting the jury to evaluate the expert's opinion substantially outweighs their prejudicial effect.

Rule 704: Opinion on Ultimate Issue

(a) Except as provided in subdivision (b), testimony in the form of an opinion or inference otherwise admissible is not objectionable because it embraces an ultimate issue to be decided by the trier of fact.

(b) No expert witness testifying with respect to the mental state or condition of a defendant in a criminal case may state an opinion or inference as to whether the defendant did or did not have the mental state or condition constituting an element of the crime charged or of a defense thereto. Such ultimate issues are matters for the trier of fact alone.

Rule 705: Disclosure of Facts or Data Underlying Expert Opinion

The expert may testify in terms of opinion or inference and give reasons therefore without first testifying to the underlying facts or data, unless the court requires otherwise. The expert may in any event be required to disclose the underlying facts or data on cross-examination.

Rule 706: Court Appointed Experts

(a) Appointment.

The court may on its own motion or on the motion of any party enter an order to show cause why expert witnesses should not be appointed, and may request the parties to submit nominations. The court may appoint any expert witnesses agreed upon by the parties, and may appoint expert witnesses of its own selection. An expert witness shall not be appointed by the court unless the witness consents to act. A witness so appointed shall be informed of the witness' duties by the court in writing, a copy of which shall be filed with the clerk, or at a conference in which the parties shall have opportunity to participate. A witness so appointed shall advise the parties of the witness' findings, if any; the witness' deposition may be taken by any party; and the witness may be called to testify by the court or any party. The witness shall be subject to cross-examination by each party, including a party calling the witness.

(b) Compensation.

Expert witnesses so appointed are entitled to reasonable compensation in whatever sum the court may allow. The compensation thus fixed is payable from funds which may be provided by law in criminal cases and civil actions and proceedings involving just compensation under the fifth amendment. In other civil actions and proceedings the compensation shall be paid by the parties in such proportion and at such time as the court directs, and thereafter charged in like manner as other costs.

(c) Disclosure of appointment.

In the exercise of its discretion, the court may authorize disclosure to the jury of the fact that the court appointed the expert witness.

(d) Parties' experts of own selection.

Nothing in this rule limits the parties in calling expert witnesses of their own selection.

In essence this reinforced the role of the judge as the **gatekeeper** deciding what was allowed as evidence in a court case and what was inadmissible. Judges still often use the Frye criterion for themselves to determine if a scientific method is reliable enough to be used as evidence, but the Federal Rules of Evidence give a judge a great deal of latitude in determining what should be allowed and what should be excluded. It should be noted that while most states and federal laws do not allow prosecutors or police to request or require anyone to take a polygraph test, 18 states allow defendants to present polygraph results if they want to. Federal agencies can also use polygraphs in cases involving national security.

REVIEW QUESTIONS

1. Evidence that has mass and occupies space is called

   A. circumstantial   B. testimonial
   C. physical   D. hearsay

2. Evidence that can be associated with a single, unique source is called

   A. individual characteristic   B. class characteristic
   C. physical   D. testimonial

3. Evidence that can be associated with a group is called

   A. individual characteristic   B. class characteristic
   C. physical   D. testimonial

4. Type A+ blood is considered _____ evidence.

   A. individual characteristic   B. class characteristic
   C. physical   D. testimonial

5. Fingerprints are considered _____ evidence.

   A. individual characteristic   B. class characteristic
   C. physical   D. testimonial

6. What is the most common blood group in the United States?

   A. A   B. B
   C. O   D. AB

7. What percentage of the U.S. population is Rh-positive?

   A. 16%   B. 42%
   C. 84%   D. 95%

8. How many people in a town of 10,000 are likely to have type O+ blood?

   A. 3800   B. 5000
   C. 8500   D. 9500

9. The probability of a suspect having a particular fiber is 0.01, and the probability of wearing a certain brand of sneaker is 0.05. What is the overall probability of the suspect being in possession of these two pieces of evidence?

   A. 0.05   B. 0.005
   C. 0.0005   D. 0.00005

10. The probability 0.05 is the same as

    A. 0.05%
    B. 0.5%
    C. 5%
    D. 50%

11. Most evidence analyzed by the crime lab is

    A. individual characteristic
    B. class characteristic
    C. physical
    D. testimonial

12. The requirement that a new scientific method be generally accepted by the scientific community to be admissible in court is called

    A. the Federal Rules of Evidence
    B. the Frye criterion
    C. Rule 702
    D. Rule 703

13. Which case determined the inadmissibility of polygraph evidence in a court case?

    A. *Frye* v. *United States*
    B. *Daubert* v. *Merrell*
    C. *Lafayette* v. *United States*
    D. American Polygraph Association

14. Nowadays the admissibility of forensic evidence falls under the

    A. U.S. Constitution
    B. Bill of Rights
    C. Federal Rules of Evidence
    D. Frye criterion

15. The case of *Daubert* v. *Merrell Dow Pharmaceutical, Inc.*, established the judge as the _____ for all evidence presented in a case.

    A. advocate
    B. gatekeeper
    C. grid
    D. quadrant

16. Which of the Federal Rules of Evidence covers the testimony of experts?

    A. Rule 701
    B. Rule 702
    C. Rule 703
    D. Rule 704

17. A polygraph records the following signals

    A. cardiovascular
    B. respiratory
    C. electrodermal
    D. all of the above

18. Which article of the Federal Rules of Evidence covers opinions and expert testimony

    A. Article III
    B. Article V
    C. Article VII
    D. Article IX

19. What percentage of the U.S. population is A–?

    A. 6%   B. 7%
    C. 34%   D. 40%

20. If the _____ is low enough, class characteristic evidence can become individual characteristic evidence.

    A. contamination   B. probability
    C. quantity   D. recognition

21. Part of a forensic scientist's duty is to train investigators in the _____ of evidence.

    A. recognition   B. analysis
    C. cataloging   D. interpretation

22. A good source of information on the probabilities of physical evidence is the

    A. local police   B. Internet
    C. FBI   D. DOJ

23. The lower the probability, the greater the

    A. evidentiary value   B. cost
    C. percentage   D. recognition

24. The final decision on the admissibility of evidence is up to the

    A. jury   B. judge
    C. district attorney   D. defense

25. A paint chip large enough to be fit like a jigsaw puzzle piece into a missing section of paint on a suspect's car is considered

    A. individual characteristic   B. class characteristic
    C. hearsay   D. testimonial

Answers

1. C	10. C	18. C
2. A	11. B	19. A
3. B	12. B	20. B
4. B	13. A	21. A
5. A	14. C	22. C
6. C	15. B	23. A
7. C	16. B	24. B
8. A	17. D	25. A
9. C		

CHAPTER 9

BODY FLUIDS

TERMS YOU SHOULD KNOW

ABO blood groups	EMIT	p30
absorption–elution	erythrocytes	phenotype
acid phosphatase	genotype	plasma
agglutination	heterozygous	platelets
allele	homozygous	precipitin test
antibodies	indirect typing	PSA
antigens	Leone Lattes	Punnet square
aspermia	leukocytes	Rh factor
benzidine	luminol	secretor
direct blood typing	metabolites	thrombocytes
EDTA	oligospermia	toxicology

BLOOD AND THE ABO BLOOD GROUPS

About 8% by weight of the average human body is blood. This corresponds to about 5 L in the average person. Blood has five main functions in the human body. First, it is the main transportation system, carrying oxygen from the lungs to all the cells in the body and carbon dioxide back to the lungs. It also transports various chemical messengers released by the body, as well as nutrients and waste material. Second, the circulation of blood helps maintain the body's temperature. Third, the blood also maintains the body's pH at about 7.4 by using carbon dioxide to buffer the system. Fourth, the blood transports toxins to the kidneys where enzymes break them down into chemicals, which are excreted from the body in urine or sweat. The kidneys filter the entire volume of the blood about 1.5 times per hour. Fifth, the blood helps control the balance of the body's electrolytes, such as salt.

Human blood can be described as being mostly water with three different types of cells suspended in it. The three types of cells are **erythrocytes** (red blood cells, RBC), **leukocytes** (white blood cells), and **thrombocytes** (blood **platelets**). When human blood is put in a test tube and centrifuged (spun around in a circle at a very high speed), it separates into three layers. The top layer is a straw-colored liquid called **plasma**. Plasma is about 92% water and represents about 55% of the volume of the blood. Next comes a very thin, cream-colored layer called the buffy coat. It is composed mainly of white blood cells and platelets. The densest layer, at the bottom of the tube, consists of red blood cells. They constitute about 45% of the blood by volume.

Red blood cells contain hemoglobin, which transports oxygen from the lungs to the cells. White blood cells are a major part of the body's immune system. The body uses tags made out of proteins to identify its own cells to keep the immune system from mistaking them for invading organisms and attacking them. Human red blood cells can have A or B protein tags, called **antigens**, on them for identification. Red blood cells with A antigens are type A, and red blood cells with B antigens are type B. Red blood cells with no antigens are called type O, and red blood cells with both A and B antigens are called type AB. There is also a D antigen that controls the **Rh factor**. If the D antigen is present, the person is Rh-positive. If the antigen is absent, the person is Rh-negative. Table 9.1 summarizes this information.

TABLE 9.1

Blood Type	Antigen Present on Red Blood Cells
A+	A, D
A–	A
B+	B, D
B–	B
AB+	A, B, D
AB–	A, B
O+	D
O–	None

There are specific substances called **antibodies**, that recognize and bind to antigens. The body produces specific antibodies for specific antigens, and an antibody is normally named for the specific antigen that it binds to. For example, an antibody that specifically binds to an A antigen is called an anti-A antibody. An antibody is bifunctional, which means that one antibody can bind to two different antigens on two separate cells. This leads to a large clumping together of cells called **agglutination**, which can be used to type blood. When a few drops of an anti-A antibody solution are mixed with a few drops of type A blood, agglutination occurs. It can be seen quite easily with the unaided eye or using a low-power microscope. A person with type A blood never has anti-A antibodies in their blood serum since this would cause the blood in their veins and arteries to clot and that would be fatal.

For a long time doctors tried to transfer blood from one person to another to replace blood lost through an accident or an operation. Transfusions sometimes worked but sometimes were almost instantly fatal. In 1901 Karl Landsteiner discovered the **ABO blood groups**, for which he received the Nobel Prize in 1930. Armed with this knowledge doctors could successfully transfer blood between people without killing them. Table 9.2 lists the different antigens and antibodies present in human blood.

TABLE 9.2

Blood Type	Antigen on RBC	Antibody Present in Serum
A	A	Anti-B
B	B	Anti-A
O	None	Anti-A, anti-B
AB	A, B	None

People with type O blood are sometimes referred to as universal donors. Since their red blood cells have no A or B antigens on the surface, they do not cause agglutination when given to someone else. People with type AB blood are sometimes called universal receivers. Since they don't have anti-A or anti-B antibodies in their blood serum, they can receive any type of blood in a transfusion.

This method of **direct blood typing** by adding drops of known antibodies works only on whole, liquid blood. Agglutination or clotting of blood cannot be used on a sample of blood that is already clotted and dry. Unfortunately, most blood sent to the crime lab is dried, not whole. In 1915 the Italian forensic scientist **Leone Lattes** developed a method of typing dried bloodstains. This **indirect blood typing** is so sensitive that it has successfully been used to type the blood of Egyptian mummies thousands of years old. The procedure, often referred to as the **absorption–elution** method, is based on the following techniques. Let's say a piece of fabric is found with a bloodstain on it. A small piece of the fabric is cut off, and the fabric threads are teased apart. The fabric is then put in a small container of normal saline (a water solution with the same salt concentration as the human body), and a few drops of anti-A and anti-B antibodies are added. The antibodies bind to the corresponding antigens on the surface of the dried blood cells. The fabric is then removed and washed with normal saline, removing any antibodies not attached to the bloodstained fabric. It is then placed in a container of fresh saline and heated to a temperature of 54°C for about 5 min. This temperature is high enough to break the antibody–antigen bonds, and the antibodies are released into the saline solution. The fabric is then removed from the container, and the solution is tested with known blood cells. If the bloodstain was originally type A blood, then only anti-A antibodies would have stuck to the bloodstain on the fabric. They would have been carried over to the second saline solution and released at the higher temperature. Adding type A blood cells to the solution would cause agglutination. A summary of the results from a Lattes test is shown in Table 9.3. The plus sign indicates agglutination (clotting), and the minus sign indicates no reaction.

TABLE 9.3

Addition of A Blood Cells	Addition of B Blood Cells	Type of Original Bloodstain
+	−	A
−	+	B
+	+	AB
−	−	O

When a sample of suspected blood is found at the crime scene, there are some basic questions that must be answered:

1. Is it blood?

2. Is it human blood?

3. What type of blood is it?

The first question is an obvious one. A rust stain can look very much like a dried bloodstain, so some sort of screening test should be applied. Blood contains an enzyme called peroxidase that makes its identification easier. Many chemicals react with peroxidase to give a visible color change indicating that the stain is blood. Two older tests involved **benzidine** and phenolphthalein. In the case of benzidine the presence of peroxidase makes the chemical turn blue, and in the case of phenolphthalein it turns red. A more sensitive chemical test used nowadays involves **luminol** (3-aminophthalhydrazide). It has the added advantage that it glows in the dark. Luminol comes in aerosol cans and can be sprayed over the crime scene. When the lights are turned off, even minute traces of blood glow. The luminol test is the most sensitive of the three tests (it can detect a blood dilution of 1:5,000,000). There are certain compounds that have been known to cause false positives; these include horseradishes, radishes, oranges, lemons, and grapefruits.

Once a spot has been confirmed as blood, the next question is whether it is human blood. The suspect may claim that the bloodstain on his shirt came from a very rare steak he had been carving the night before. The standard test to determine if a bloodstain is human is called a **precipitin test**. Human blood cells are injected into a laboratory animal, and the animal's immune system creates antibodies that specifically bind to human blood cells. These anti-human blood antibodies can be collected from the animals and used to test for the presence of human blood. There are many ways to carry out the precipitin test. It can be performed using a simple test tube. A small volume of anti-human blood antibody solution is first introduced into the test tube. Next, a solution of suspected human blood is added on top. The formation of a dark ring at the interface indicates the blood is human.

The precipitin test can also be done using an agar gel plate. The anti-human antibody is put in one well, and the suspected human blood solution is put in another. The antigens and antibodies diffuse toward one another, and the formation of a dark line between the two wells indicates the blood is human. The reaction can be intensified and made more sensitive by applying a voltage to the plate. Once the blood has been shown to be human, the Lattes method can be used to determine the blood type.

Bloodstained evidence should first be air-dried. Garments should be folded around the bloodstain and placed in a nonairtight container such as a paper bag. Try to preserve bloodstain patterns during the packaging and shipping. Bloodstains from immovable objects can be collected with a clean cotton swab moistened with distilled water. The swab can then be air-dried and packaged in clean paper or in an envelope with sealed corners. Control and known samples should also be collected. The use of special tubes for collecting blood is recommended. Collect two 5-mL samples using purple-topped tubes (these are preevacuated and have the anticoagulant ethylenediaminetetraacetic acid [EDTA] already added to keep the blood in liquid form). For a test for drugs or alcohol collect samples using gray-topped tubes (these use sodium fluoride as the anticoagulant). These tubes should be kept refrigerated at 4°C.

THE PUNNET SQUARE AND PATERNITY TESTING

Characteristics such as blood type are inherited as genes from our parents. The gene for blood type is composed of two **alleles** (one from each parent), which can be dominant, codominant, or recessive. When an allele is dominant, it is always expressed, when two alleles are codominant they are both expressed, and when an allele is recessive it is expressed only when the other allele is the same. The pair of alleles is known as the **genotype**, and the expressed trait (like blood type) is known as the **phenotype**. The allele for type A blood has the symbol A; B is for B; and O is for O. Table 9.4 lists the genotypes and phenotypes for blood.

TABLE 9.4

Genotype	Phenotype
AA	Type A blood
AO	Type A blood
BB	Type B blood
BO	Type B blood
AB	Type AB blood
OO	Type O blood

When both alleles for a given genotype are the same, it is called **homozygous**, and when both alleles are different, it is called **heterozygous**. Note that a person can have type A blood and be either homozygous or heterozygous. The only way to know for sure is to know the blood type of the previous generations or offspring. There are two blood types where the person must be homozygous, and they are AB and O. The genotypes of offspring can be determined using a device known as a **Punnet square**. It is often used in paternity cases. The alleles for the mother's genotype are put on one side, and the suspected father's alleles are put on the other. All the possible combinations and their probabilities can then be determined. Let's say the mother is type AB and the suspected father is type O. The Punnet square is set up as follows:

		Mother's genotype	
		A	B
Father's	O	AO	BO
genotype	O	AO	BO

In this case 50% of the offspring would be expected to be AO genotype (type A blood) and 50% of the offspring would be expected to be BO genotype (type B blood). If the child in question has type AB blood, then the suspect could not be the father. While just ABO blood types have been mentioned, there are many other inherited blood factors that can be analyzed. Using these, a probability of more than 90% can be established. Nowadays, the use of DNA typing can raise the probability to more than 99% certainty.

SALIVA

Saliva is becoming more and more useful as physical evidence. In the past, it was mostly used to determine blood type. About 80% of the population is classified as secretors. A **secretor** is a person who expresses their blood antigens in their body fluids. This means that the saliva from a secretor can be used to determine their blood type. A cigarette butt or the flap of an envelope has been used to connect a suspect to a crime scene. However, the various blood types have very high probabilities of occurrence in the general population, which makes this type of evidence relatively weak. The advent of DNA typing has led to a search for physical evidence that can be used for this individual characteristic type of connection. It turns out that saliva is an excellent source of DNA, and quantities as small as that left on the back of a stamp have been used to positively identify perpetrators.

Saliva evidence is collected in much the same way as blood evidence. It is important to prevent any contamination, so gloves should always be worn. Evidence such as cigarette butts, chewing gum, bite marks, envelopes, and stamps should be packaged in clean paper or a paper bag. Like any biological fluid, the evidence should be packaged in a nonairtight container. If the evidence is damp, it should be air-dried before packaging. Saliva residues can be removed from immovable objects using a moistened cotton swab.

SEMEN

In the case of sexual crimes one of the most important pieces of physical evidence for the investigator to discover is the presence of seminal fluid (semen). Semen is the liquid portion of the male ejaculation. It is composed of about 95% seminal fluid and about 5% spermatozoa. Spermatozoa, or sperm, are the vehicles that transport the genetic material of the male to the female egg. In the past, the presence of sperm was used to determine if a stain was seminal in nature. The average male ejaculation is less than a teaspoon (about 4 mL), but it contains about 200 million spermatozoa (Figure 9.1). These can be easily identified under a microscope.

FIGURE 9.1

However, once the seminal fluid dries out, the sperm become quite brittle and can disintegrate with handling. Their fragile nature makes it much more difficult to locate sperm on a dried stain. In addition, some males have no sperm (**aspermia**) or very few sperm (**oligospermia**) in their seminal fluid. For a long time forensic scientists have looked for a method to determine whether a stain is seminal in nature without relying on the presence of spermatozoa. The majority of the seminal fluid is generated by the prostate gland (Figure 9.2). The testes are responsible for the production of spermatozoa.

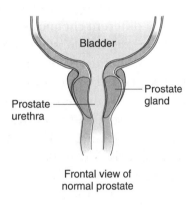

FIGURE 9.2

The enzyme **acid phosphatase** is present throughout the body. However, its concentration is much higher (about 100 times) in the prostate gland than anywhere else. This makes it an excellent screening tool for the presence of seminal fluid (since it is also present in other body fluids, it cannot be used to positively prove the stain is seminal in nature).

When the scene of a sexual crime is searched, it is customary to first try to locate any seminal stains. This can be accomplished using ultraviolet (UV) light since seminal stains fluoresce under UV light. Suspected stains can be tested using a piece of filter paper moistened with a solution of sodium naphthol phosphate or Fast Blue B. Both these chemicals change color on reacting with the acid phosphatase present in the seminal fluid.

The article carrying the seminal stain (bed sheet, undergarment, clothing, or rug) should be air-dried and packaged in a nonairtight container such as a paper bag. Once it is delivered to the crime lab, scientists look for the presence of a protein known as p30.

It has been mentioned before that forensic scientists had been looking for a substance that would positively prove that a stain is semen. What was needed was a chemical that is present in semen and in no other body fluid. That substance turned out to be a protein that is produced only in the prostate. It is called **p30** or **prostate specific antigen (PSA)**. Detection of the p30 protein is positive proof of the presence of semen.

TOXICOLOGY

The word *toxicology* comes from the Greek term *toxon*, which means "bow." The tips of bows were sometimes dipped in poison to make them more deadly. **Toxicology** is the study of body fluids, tissue, and organs for the presence of drugs or poisons. A toxicologist must have a minimum of a baccalaureate degree, a master's degree, or a Ph.D. in the physical or biological sciences. At least 2 years of work in toxicology is normally required after graduation (the actual number of years varies among certification boards). There are literally thousands of different chemicals that can be present in a person. In addition, the original substances are often changed to new chemicals called **metabolites** by reactions inside the body. Marijuana, cocaine, opiates, phencyclidine (PCP), and amphetamines are all turned into **metabolites** by the human body. Heroin is changed to morphine by body chemistry, and tetrahydrocannabinol (THC), the active ingredient in marijuana, is changed to five different metabolites.

The analysis of drugs or poisons is usually a two-step process. The first step is called the presumptory or screening test. It is a fast, easy test to check for the presence of a drug or poison. One of the most common screening tests is an immunoassay. This technique involves attaching a drug to a protein carrier and injecting it into a laboratory animal. The animal's immune system develops antibodies that bind specifically to the drug in question. There are three different types of immunoassays used in testing for drugs or poisons, with the enzyme multiplied immunoassay technique (EMIT) being the most popular. EMIT is manufactured by Syva Laboratories, and it uses an enzyme as the detection mechanism. A test strip with several different EMIT tests on it can be dipped into a suspect's urine, and color changes indicate the presence of specific drugs (in laboratories it is sometimes referred to as the hipty dipty stick test). A radio immunoassay (RIA) is a test produced by many manufacturers such as Roche Diagnostics. While similar to EMIT, it uses a radioactive isotope to detect the drug. The use of radioactive substances makes it less popular than EMIT. A fluorescence polarization immunoassay (FPIA) is manufactured by Abbott Laboratories. Fluorescent compounds are chemically linked to the binding of antibodies to specific drugs and their metabolites. The use of screening techniques such as immunoassays makes the detection of drugs and poisons fast and easy; however, they sometimes yield false positives. For that reason a test that positively identifies a drug or poison is required.

Once the presence of a drug or poison is indicated, a confirmatory test is used. The confirmatory test of choice is gas chromatograph–mass spectrometry (GC/MS). As mentioned in Chapter 4, GC/MS can unequivocally identify any organic chemical (drug or poison). The main sources of evidence for toxicologists are urine, blood, hair, saliva, and sweat. The time required to detect drugs using blood, urine, saliva, or sweat varies from about 1 to 5 days. In the case of hair testing it takes about 5 days for a drug or its **metabolites** to appear in the hair, but its presence can be detected for 6 months or more.

Many types of poisons can be present in a victim. In general, poisons can be put into the following groups: gases, corrosives, organic compounds, inorganic compounds, and metals. The following list is not complete but mentions some of the more common examples in each category.

The victim can inhale gases that can pass from the lungs directly into the bloodstream. Carbon monoxide is a colorless, odorless gas that kills by preventing the hemoglobin in the blood from carrying oxygen. A person can literally suffocate in a room full of air. Carbon dioxide remains in the blood for up to 6 months after a person dies. Hydrogen sulfide smells like rotten eggs at low levels but at higher concentrations cannot be detected by smell and is quite lethal. Arsine is the hydride of arsenic and forms a colorless gas with an odor of garlic. Phosgene gas was used in World War I and is also known as carbonyl chloride. Hydrogen cyanide is formed when an acid reacts with a salt of cyanide. The resulting gas is very poisonous and smells of bitter almonds. Some pathologists can detect cyanide poisoning from the odor during the autopsy. About 50 mg of cyanide is considered a lethal dose. Cyanide works by inactivating the enzyme cytochrome oxidase and blocking the oxidation of glucose inside cells. The person dies in a matter of minutes. Chlorine gas can also be very poisonous, but it is usually formed by accident when household chemicals such as bleach (sodium hypochlorite) and toilet bowl cleaner (hydrochloric acid) are mixed.

$$\text{Bleach} + \text{acid} \rightarrow \text{chlorine gas} + \text{water} + \text{salt}$$

$$NaClO + 2HCl \rightarrow Cl_2(g) + H_2O + NaCl$$

Corrosives work by destroying and dissolving bone and tissue. Death is normally due to extensive damage to the throat, esophagus, and stomach. Corrosives are usually acids or bases. Acids include hydrochloric acid, nitric acid, sulfuric acid, and perchloric acid. In their concentrated form, any of these, are extremely corrosive. Bases include sodium hydroxide, potassium hydroxide (potash), calcium hydroxide, and calcium oxide (lime).

There are many organic poisons, both naturally occurring (produced in nature) and synthetic (made in a laboratory). Organic poisons include alkaloids, barbiturates, glycosides, ricin, botulin, curare, and various venoms. Alkaloids are nitrogen-containing compounds extracted from plants. Curare, an extract from the bark of the tree *Strychnos toxifera*, is an example of an alkaloid. Certain South American tribes prepared the poison by boiling the bark and a mixture of other ingredients for about 2 days. The solution was then strained and left to evaporate into a dark, viscous liquid. Darts dipped into the liquid could be fired through blowguns to bring down birds or mammals. Curare causes the paralysis of skeletal muscles, which can lead to death by suffocation. The person is awake and aware of the paralysis until unconsciousness sets in. Strychnine is another related alkaloid that can be extracted from the tree *Strychnos nux-vomica.* Strychnine is a convulsive and causes the victim to suffer convulsions of all their voluntary muscles before death by asphyxia sets in. Africa has poisons for arrows as well, and one of the deadliest is obtained from the **Acokanthera** plant. This extract contains the cardiac glycoside ouabain, which can be lethal at a dose of 0.002 g. Cardiac glycosides work by slowing down the heart and decreasing the venous blood pressure. Ricin is a highly toxic, white protein produced from castor beans. It enters the cells of the body and prevents them from making proteins necessary to sustain life. Botulinal toxin, produced by the bacterium *Clostridium botulinum,* is the most toxic poison known. As little as 1 g of this toxin could kill 1 million people.

Inorganic and metallic poisons include antimony, arsenic, barium, lead, mercury, phosphorus, and thallium. Poisoning by the heavy metals mercury and lead occurs when these metals react with enzymes in the body and inactivate them. Symptoms of heavy metal poisoning often include stomach pains, coma, and then death.

REVIEW QUESTIONS

1. A 200-lb man would be expected to have how many pounds of blood?

   A. 5   B. 8
   C. 16   D. 20

2. Another name for white blood cells is

   A. erythrocytes   B. leukocytes
   C. thrombocytes   D. granulocytes

3. Another name for red blood cells is

   A. erythrocytes   B. leukocytes
   C. thrombocytes   D. granulocytes

4. Another name for platelets is

   A. erythrocytes   B. leukocytes
   C. thrombocytes   D. granulocytes

5. The straw-colored watery component of blood is called

    A. plasma   B. the buffy coat
    C. platelets   D. hemoglobin

6. Red blood cells are what percentage of the blood?

    A. 10%   B. 25%
    C. 45%   D. 55%

7. A person with type A blood has which antigens on their RBC?

    A. A   B. B
    C. AB   D. none

8. A person with type B blood has which antigen on their RBC?

    A. A   B. B
    C. AB   D. none

9. A person with type O+ blood has which antigen on their RBC?

    A. A   B. B
    C. AB   D. D

10. A person with type A+ blood has which type of antibodies in their blood serum?

    A. anti-A   B. anti-B
    C. anti-D   D. none

11. A person with type AB blood has which type of antibodies in their blood serum?

    A. anti-A   B. anti-B
    C. anti-D   D. none

12. What temperature is used to break the antibody–antigen bond?

    A. 25°C   B. 37°C
    C. 54°C   D. 100°C

13. In the last step of the absorption–elution method only type B cells cause an agglutination reaction. What type of blood was the original stain?

    A. A   B. B
    C. O   D. AB

14. An inherited characteristic is

    A. a gene   B. an allele
    C. homozygous   D. heterogeneous

15. A mother who is homozygous type A and a father who is homozygous type B will have a child with what blood type?

A. A   B. B
C. AB   D. O

16. Can a type AB mother and a type O father have a type B baby?

A. yes (50% chance)   B. no
C. can't be determined   D. yes (25% chance)

17. What percentage of the population are secretors?

A. 20%   B. 50%
C. 80%   D. 100%

18. What is a good source of saliva evidence?

A. chewing gum   B. cigarette butts
C. envelopes and stamps   D. all of the above

19. Biological fluids should always be packaged in _____ containers.

A. airtight   B. plastic
C. metal   D. nonairtight

20. A dried blood spot can be collected using a cotton swab moistened with

A. EDTA   B. alcohol
C. distilled water   D. sodium fluoride

21. The condition in which no spermatozoa are present in the seminal fluid is called

A. aspermia   B. oligiospermia
C. homozygous   D. heterozygous

22. An easy way to screen for the presence of seminal fluid in a large area is to use

A. visible light   B. X-rays
C. UV light   D. infrared light

23. The study of body fluids for the presence of drugs and poisons is called

A. pathology   B. toxicology
C. virology   D. urology

24. Most screening tests for drugs are based on

A. EMIT   B. RIA
C. FPIA   D. GC/MS

25. The most popular confirmatory test for the presence of drugs is

A. EMIT	B. RIA
C. FPIA	D. GC/MS

Answers

1. C	10. B	18. D
2. B	11. D	19. D
3. A	12. C	20. C
4. C	13. B	21. A
5. A	14. A	22. C
6. C	15. C	23. B
7. A	16. A	24. A
8. B	17. C	25. D
9. D		

CHAPTER 10

EXPLOSIVES AND INCENDIARIES (ARSON)

TERMS YOU SHOULD KNOW

ANFO	headspace	primary explosives
binaries	high explosives	reducing agent
EGIS	ignition	seat of the blast
explosion limit	temperature	secondary
fire triangle	low explosives	explosives
flammable range	modus operandi	sniffer
flash point	oxidizing agent	taggant
fuel	point of origin	vapor concentration

THE CHEMISTRY OF FIRE

While there are literally millions of different chemical reactions, chemists tend to combine them into three or four groups to make them easier to understand. One system groups chemical reactions into three major classes: precipitation, acid–base, and oxidation–reduction. Fire is an example of an oxidation–reduction reaction (sometimes called a combustion reaction). In an oxidation–reduction reaction there is a transfer of electrons from one chemical, called the **reducing agent**, to another chemical, called the **oxidizing agent**. The reducing agent in a combustion reaction or fire is often called the **fuel**. The oxidizing agent in most fires is oxygen from the air (oxygen is the most common oxidizing agent, hence the name) is often called the oxidant. The transfer of electrons from the fuel to the oxygen in the air is very energetic, and this energy is given off as heat and light.

The following equation below illustrates the room temperature oxidation–reduction reaction between octane (a component of gasoline) and oxygen from the air.

$$2C_8H_{18}(l) + 25O_2(g) \rightarrow 16CO_2(g) + 18H_2O(l)$$

Reducing agent   Oxydizing agent
(fuel)   (oxidizer)

134

Octane combines chemically with oxygen to form carbon dioxide and water (the combustion of all hydrocarbons produces carbon dioxide and water as products). Another product formed by this reaction is energy, which is released as both heat and light.

This reaction can occur about 50 times a second in your car's engine. The heat from the reaction drives the pistons up and down and powers your car. When you fill up your car with gasoline, it comes in contact with the oxygen in the air but does not undergo combustion because a combination of gasoline and air is stable at room temperature. The gasoline molecules must collide at higher speeds with the oxygen molecules to produce carbon dioxide, water, and heat. Temperature is a measure of the speed at which molecules travel. For a combustion reaction to occur, the temperature must be raised to what is known as the **ignition temperature** (sometimes called the autoignition temperature). For gasoline the ignition temperature is about 536°F (280°C). This temperature is provided by the spark plugs in your car's engine. Each time the engine needs the reaction to start, a spark from the spark plug provides the ignition temperature for the mixture of gasoline and air. The heat from the reaction is enough to keep the reaction going in a process known as a chain reaction. The fire keeps on going until it runs out of fuel or oxidizer. The ignition temperatures of some common materials are listed in Table 10.1.

TABLE 10.1

Material	Ignition Temperature	
	°F	°C
Gasoline	536	280
Kerosene	410	210
Turpentine	488	253
Paper	842	450
Wood	489	254
Coal	750	400

Another example of an oxidation–reduction reaction that can produce a great deal of heat is the thermite reaction. In the thermite reaction, powdered aluminum and iron oxide are mixed together and heated to their ignition temperature. Once the reaction is started, aluminum oxide and iron metal are produced. The reaction gets so hot that the iron produced is molten. This reaction was used in the past to melt iron and weld metals together. The author has been once called to a crime scene in Syracuse, NY, where a bag of thermite had been placed on a man's car and ignited. The reaction burned so hot that the molten iron melted the hood of the car, part of the engine, and right through the floor beneath the car which was parked in a multilevel garage.

The three things needed to keep a fire going are fuel, oxidizer, and heat. This is often referred to as the **fire triangle** (Figure 10.1). If you remove any side of the fire triangle, the fire will go out.

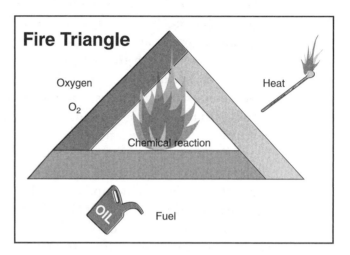

FIGURE 10.1

A combustion reaction produces a flame only if both the fuel and the oxidizer are in a gaseous state. The oxygen from the air is always in a gaseous state, and the fuel must also be in a gaseous state to produce a flame. Wood burns with a flame because the heat from the reaction breaks down the solid molecules of the wood (mostly cellulose) into smaller gaseous molecules in a process called pyrolysis. These small, gaseous molecules from the breakdown of the cellulose mix with the oxygen from the air and produce the flame.

Another temperature that is important is the **flash point**. This is the temperature at which the fuel produces enough vapor to support combustion. The flash point is always much lower than the ignition temperature for a substance. While the ignition temperature of gasoline is 536°F, its flash point is –50°F. If the temperature of gasoline is –55°F and a match is held over the gasoline, it does not combust. At this temperature the gasoline cannot produce enough vapor to support combustion.

There is only a narrow range over which a mixture of fuel vapor and air burns. This is known as the **flammable range** and is normally reported as the ratio between the volume of fuel vapor and the volume of air expressed as a percentage. The flammable range for gasoline (regular unleaded) is about 1.5% to 7.6% fuel vapor to air. The lower limit of the flammable range (LLF) is referred to as a lean mixture, and the upper limit is referred to as a rich mixture. Lean mixtures are much more fuel-efficient but burn hotter. Rich mixtures burn much cooler. Before gas prices went up, cars used to use rich mixtures. Nowadays, to improve on gas mileage, cars burn a leaner mixture that produces much more heat. This is of great concern to firefighters responding to car accidents.

The flammable range is also known as the **explosion limit**. When a gasoline air mixture reaches the explosion limit from the lower end (LEL) and an ignition source is present, the mixture instantaneously combusts. If the gas mixture is contained, an explosion will result. Mixtures that reach the explosion limit from the upper end (UEL) tend to produce both an explosion and a fireball. These tend to be less survivable than gas explosions occurring at the lower explosion limit.

An example is an explosion that occurred many years ago at the YWCA in Binghamton, NY. A person went into a room, turned on a gas stove, and sat down on the bed with a lit cigarette. As the concentration of the gas in the room reached the lower explosion limit, the cigarette acted as an ignition source and there was an explosion. A section of an outside wall of the building that ran along the sidewalk was pushed into the street. Passersby looked through the gaping hole in the wall and saw a startled, but unhurt, person still sitting on the bed. This is an example of an explosion at the lower explosion limit.

ARSON INVESTIGATION

The phrase *modus operandi* (MO) is Latin for "mode of operation." It is used frequently in forensic science to describe a distinct pattern or method of operation, especially one that indicates or suggests that a single criminal has carried out more than one crime. Crime scenes involving explosions and arson cases are among the most difficult for an investigator. These are scenes of massive destruction and the nature of the crime depends on planning on the part of the criminal. These crimes require a higher degree of sophistication than many other types of crime. The planning and the extensive destruction, combined with the large number of people who are called to the scene, make it difficult to collect good evidence. In general, the investigator of a suspected arson scene has three main avenues of investigation.

1. Modus operandi

2. Owner of the building

3. Revenge.

There are many different ways of starting a fire. An arsonist can use an accelerant (a liquid like gasoline or kerosene), an active metal, a chemical igniter, a mechanical timer, or a hundred other means to start a fire. Once the arsonist has success and perfects a certain technique, they normally keep using the same method. By determining the way the fire was started, the modus operandi of the arsonist can be determined. Knowing the MO can help the investigator tie together a series of seemingly unrelated fires or generate a list of suspects based on known arsonists.

The owner of the building, or whoever receives insurance payments for the loss of the building or its contents, is always a good suspect. Besides checking alibis, clothing can be collected for traces of accelerants, and the suspect's car and garage can be searched for containers.

The first priority at any fire scene is rescuing any victims and putting out the fire. Once the fire is out, it is the duty of the fire investigators to determine its cause. A fire investigation should center on the **point of origin** of the fire. There are many different methods of determining the point of origin of the fire, and different investigators have their own personal preferences.

Fires burn upward and outward. By tracing the damage from the fire, the investigator can extrapolate back to the point of origin. This can be more difficult than it sounds since winds, firewalls, hallways, and the construction details of the building can force the fire to take different pathways.

Many investigators use a portable combustion meter (sometimes called a **sniffer**) to determine the point of origin of the fire. A sniffer has a wand that draws air in with an internal pump. The air is then pumped over a catalyst-coated resistance element. The resistance of the resistor depends on heat. When the air contains any combustible vaporlike gasoline, it burns as it passes over the catalyst-coated resistance element. This raises its resistance, altering the electrical balance with a reference resistor. This imbalance sounds an audible alarm and produces a reading on the dial. An example of a portable combustion meter is the TLV sniffer sold by Scott Instruments (Figure 10.2).

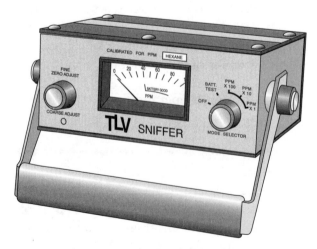

FIGURE 10.2

Some investigators prefer to use dogs trained to detect accelerants. They can cover large areas quickly and have an extremely sensitive sense of smell. It does take a certain amount of time to train a dog as well as a commitment from the dog's handler.

A search of the questioned crime scene should include a search for the following items: candles, cigarettes, matches, Molotov cocktails, chemicals, and any electrical or mechanical devices that may have been used to start the fire. The investigator should also look for the presence of streamers. Streamers are burn trails left behind on carpeted or hardwood floors where the arsonist has laid down accelerant to aid in the spreading of the fire.

Once the point of origin of the fire has been located, the investigator collects a few quarts of soot and debris from the point of origin of the fire. Even though the destruction of the building might be quite complete, some of the accelerant often soaks into various materials and is not burned in the fire. The debris should be collected in a metal can or glass jar and sealed airtight to prevent the evaporation of potential evidence.

Then the investigator checks objects around the point of origin to see if they belong in the place where they are found. Any soot or ashes that are unusual in color should be collected. The normal fire protection equipment, such as sprinklers and alarms, should also be checked to see if it has been tampered with or altered. If the fire was set with the use of an accelerant, it is likely that a container is still at the crime scene or has been disposed of nearby. All possible entry points should be checked for forced entry.

HEADSPACE GAS CHROMATOGRAPHY

Once the crime lab receives the sealed container with the soot and debris inside, it is subjected to headspace gas chromatography. In this technique a small amount of the sample is heated in a sealed container. Any accelerants that may be present in the sample collected at the arson scene are vaporized by the heat. A needle is inserted into the container, and the vapor above the soot and debris (called the **headspace**) is sampled. The sampled headspace is then injected into a gas chromatograph. The gas chromatograph separates any compounds present in the headspace, and the results are presented as a gas chromatogram. The forensic scientist can tell what chemicals, if any, were present in the soot and debris taken from the suspected crime scene by analyzing the gas chromatogram.

There are modifications of the basic headspace gas chromatography technique with much greater sensitivity. Most of these methods are based on vapor concentration. The vapor from the headspace is concentrated on activated charcoal. In one method an inert gas such as nitrogen or helium is pumped through the container with the soot and debris as it is heated. The inert gas passes though a tube filled with activated charcoal, which traps any organic substances. When the process is complete, the organic substances are driven off the charcoal by heating (called thermal desorption) or washed off with carbon disulfide (called elution) and introduced into a gas chromatograph. **Vapor concentration** headspace gas chromatography is about 100 times more sensitive then regular headspace gas chromatography. It has been used to detect the presence of accelerants from the clothing of an arsonist although no gasoline had been spilled by the arsonist onto their clothing. The mere process of pouring gasoline allowed the fabric of the clothing to absorb enough vapors to be detected by vapor concentration gas chromatography.

When responding to a fire, the fire department does not require a search warrant since it is responding to an emergency situation. Once the fire has been extinguished, the fire investigators can stay at the scene and collect evidence without a search warrant since the evidence is volatile in nature and would quickly be lost or destroyed. However, once the fire department or police leave the scene, and time permits, a search warrant must be obtained to search the area further or collect any more evidence. This is clearly spelled out in the Michigan Supreme Court decision in the case of *Michigan* v. *Tyler.* The text of the supreme court decision is as follows.

Michigan v. *Tyler*, **436 United States 499 (1978)**
Michigan v. *Tyler et al.*
Certiorari to the Supreme Court of Michigan
No. 76–1608.
Argued January 10, 1978
Decided May 31, 1978

Shortly before midnight on January 21, 1970, a fire broke out in respondents' furniture store, to which the local fire department responded. When the fire chief arrived at about 2 A.M., as the smoldering embers were being doused, the discovery of plastic containers of flammable liquid was reported to him, and after he had entered the building to examine the containers, he summoned a police detective to investigate possible arson. The detective took several pictures but ceased further investigation because of the smoke and steam. By 4 A.M. the fire had been extinguished and the firefighters departed. The fire chief and detective removed the containers and left. At 8 A.M. the chief and his assistant returned for a cursory examination of the building.

About an hour later the assistant and the detective made another examination and removed pieces of evidence. On February 16 a member of the state police arson section took photographs at the store and made an inspection, which was followed by several other visits, at which time additional evidence and information were obtained. Respondents were subsequently charged with conspiracy to burn real property and other offenses. Evidence secured from the building and the testimony of the arson specialist were used at respondents' trial, which resulted in their convictions, notwithstanding their objections that no warrants or consent had been obtained for entries and inspection of the building and seizure of evidentiary items. The State Supreme Court reversed the respondents' convictions and remanded the case for a new trial, concluding that "[once] the blaze [has been] extinguished and the firefighters have left the premises, a warrant is required to re-enter and search the premises, unless there is consent or the premises have been abandoned."

While the initial entry, search, and collection of evidence without a search warrant was deemed legal, the subsequent searches violated the defendant's Fourth Amendment rights. The court stated:

1. Official entries to investigate the cause of a fire must adhere to the warrant procedures of the Fourth Amendment as made applicable to the States by the Fourteenth Amendment. Since all the entries in this case were "without proper consent" and were not "authorized by a valid search warrant," each one is illegal unless it falls within one of the "certain carefully defined classes of cases" for which warrants are not mandatory.

(a) There is no diminution in a person's reasonable expectation of privacy or in the protection of the Fourth Amendment simply because the official conducting the search is a firefighter rather than a policeman, or because his purpose is to ascertain the cause of a fire rather than to look for evidence of a crime. Searches for administrative purposes, like searches for evidence of crime, are encompassed by the Fourth Amendment. The showing of probable cause necessary to secure a warrant may vary with the object and intrusiveness of the search, but the necessity for the warrant persists.

(b) To secure a warrant to investigate the cause of a fire, an official must show more than the bare fact that a fire occurred. The magistrate's duty is to assure that the proposed search will be reasonable, a determination that requires inquiry into the need for the intrusion, on the one hand, and the threat of disruption to the occupant, on the other.

2. A burning building clearly presents an exigency of sufficient proportions to render a warrantless entry "reasonable," and, once in the building to extinguish a blaze, and for a reasonable time thereafter, firefighters may seize evidence of arson that is in plain view and investigate the causes of the fire. Thus no Fourth and Fourteenth Amendment violations were committed by the firemen's entry to extinguish the blaze at the respondents' store, nor by the fire chief's removal of the plastic containers.

3. On the facts of this case, moreover, no warrant was necessary for the morning re-entries of the building and seizure of evidence on January 22 after the 4 A.M. departure of the fire chief and other personnel since these were a continuation of the first entry, which was temporarily interrupted by poor visibility.

4. The post-January 22 entries were clearly detached from the initial exigency, and since these entries were made without warrants and without consent, they violated the Fourth and Fourteenth Amendments. Evidence obtained from such entries must be excluded at respondents' retrial.

The case was appealed to the U.S. Supreme Court, which upheld the decision of the Michigan Supreme Court. The findings of the U.S. Supreme Court were as follows.

Michigan v. *Tyler*
United States Supreme Court
May 31, 1978
436 United States 499

(Here, in a 7–1 decision, with one justice not participating, the Supreme Court says firefighters, and/or police and arson investigators, may seize arson evidence at a fire without warrant or consent, on the basis of exigent circumstances and/or plain view. The seizures, however, must occur during the firefighting operation or soon after the flames have been extinguished. Subsequent re-entries to search must be based on a search warrant or consent.)

A fire breaks out in defendant's furniture store shortly before midnight and the fire department responds and is "just watering down smoldering embers" when the fire chief arrives at 2:00 A.M. He is informed by his assistant that two plastic containers of flammable liquid had been found in the building.

The two then use portable lights and enter the gutted store, which was still filled with smoke and steam, to examine the containers. (No warrant or consent.)

The chief concludes there is an arson possibility and he calls a police detective who arrives about 3:30 A.M. The detective takes some photos and he and the chief look around briefly. The steam and smoke make it impossible, however, and they and the firefighters leave at 4:00 A.M. At 8:00 A.M. the chief and his assistant return and look around briefly. The assistant and the detective return at 9:00 A.M. They find evidence not previously visible, due to the smoke and steam, burned carpet and tape, and remove those items in a brief search. (Still no warrant or consent.)

On three subsequent occasions, four days after the fire, seven days after the fire, and twenty-five days after the fire, other investigators, without warrant or consent, return to the scene, search and remove arson evidence. The defense objects to the admission of all the evidence, but the defendants are convicted. The Michigan Court of Appeals agrees, but the Michigan Supreme Court reverses the conviction and orders a new trial, holding that all entries after the fire was extinguished at 4:00 A.M. were unconstitutional, without warrant or consent.

The Supreme Court affirms the Michigan Supreme Court's decision as to all re-entries after the 9:00 A.M. search, those four days, seven days, and twenty-five days after the fire, but permits the use of the evidence found during the fighting of the fire and through the 9:00 A.M. search.

"A burning building clearly presents an exigency of sufficient proportions to render a warrantless entry reasonable. Indeed, it would defy reason to suppose that firemen must secure a warrant or consent before entering a burning structure to put out the blaze. And once in a building for this purpose, firefighters may seize evidence of arson that is in plain view."

Furthermore, the Court said, *"... officials need no warrant to remain in a building for a reasonable time to investigate the cause of a blaze after it has been extinguished."*

Here, the Court noted, the 8:00 A.M. and 9:00 A.M. searches were mere continuations of the initial search, put off necessarily by darkness, smoke, and steam.

The message from the courts is very clear. If there is time to obtain a search warrant, do so.

EXPLOSIVES

The difference between fires and explosions is the speed at which the oxidation–reduction reaction occurs. In the case of fires the rate-controlling step is the speed at which oxygen from the air can reach the fuel. In the case of explosions the fuel is intimately premixed with the oxidizer, so the reaction can occur much faster. The speed of this reaction is used to separate explosives into two main categories, low and high. **Low explosives** generally burn at subsonic speeds (<345 m/s or 776 mph) called the speed of deflagration. For this reason low explosives burn rather than detonate and are often used as propellants. In order to explode, low explosives must be contained, as in a pipe bomb. Most explosives use a chemical oxidizer instead of relying on oxygen from the air. Some examples of low explosives are as follows.

Gas mixtures: Mixtures of a fuel and air can be explosive if contained and the mixture is within the explosion limit.

Black powder: One of the first explosive mixtures discovered was black powder. It is a mixture of 75% potassium nitrate, 15% charcoal, and 10% sulfur.

Smokeless powder: Single-base smokeless powder is made of nitrocellulose. Double-base smokeless powder is made of nitrocellulose mixed with nitroglycerin.

In fact almost any fuel can be mixed with any oxidizer to produce a low explosive. Examples of common fuels and oxidizers are listed in Table 10.3. A simple example of a bomb made from a low explosive is a pipe bomb. A low explosive needs to be confined to explode, so it is packed into a threaded metal pipe and metal caps are screwed onto each end. Black powder, smokeless powder, and sugar and perchlorate mixtures have all been used in pipe bombs. There have even been examples of chlorate and pancake mix used in a pipe bomb.

TABLE 10.3

Fuel	Oxidizer
Sulfur	Sodium nitrate
Charcoal	Sodium chlorate
Aluminum	Ammonium nitrate
Magnesium	Potassium chlorate
Titanium	Potassium permanganate

Black powder can be purchased at many sporting goods stores with a driver license. A container of black powder obtained at a sporting goods store is shown in Figure 10.3.

FIGURE 10.3

High explosives detonate rather than burn. The whole mixture reacts almost instantaneously at supersonic speeds. The speed of the decomposition is called the speed of detonation. Most explosive experts set an arbitrary speed of 1000 m/s as the dividing point between low and high explosives. Because the speed of detonation is supersonic, high explosives do not need to be contained to explode.

High explosives are normally separated into two categories, primary and secondary high explosives. **Primary explosives** are sensitive to shock, friction, heat, static electricity, and electromagnetic radiation. They detonate rather than burn, and small quantities are used as blasting caps and primers. Some examples of primary explosives are as follows.

Nitroglycerin

Lead styphnate

Lead azide

Mercury fulminate

Tetryl

Tetrazene

Nitroglycerin is so shock-sensitive that it is generally considered too dangerous to handle. It is interesting to note that it is probably the most powerful explosive known and that it is used as a standard in comparing the strengths of other explosives. Nitroglycerin was used extensively in mining operations and with many fatalities. In 1867 Alfred Nobel discovered a way to stabilize nitroglycerin. He found that if he mixed it with diatomaceous earth, the resulting substance was not shock-sensitive. He called the mixture dynamite. Nowadays dynamite uses sawdust as the stabilizing agent.

Alfred Nobel also invented the blasting cap. Blasting caps are primary explosives used to set off **secondary explosives**. There are two main types of blasting caps, electrical and nonelectrical. Electrical caps have two wires coming out of them and are set off by passing an electrical current through the wires. For safety reasons, it is important to keep the electrical leads shunted when not in use. Nonelectrical caps have a safety fuse that burns at a defined rate. This means that the time delay from lighting the fuse to setting off the charge can be calculated from the length of the fuse.

While Alfred Nobel made the first blasting caps out of mercury fulminate, most caps nowadays use lead styphnate (Figure 10.4). Mercury fulminate crystallizes with age, and the crystals are very sensitive. Lead azide can also form copper crystals when exposed to moisture in copper shells. Any caps that show signs of deterioration or signs of crystallization are considered extremely dangerous.

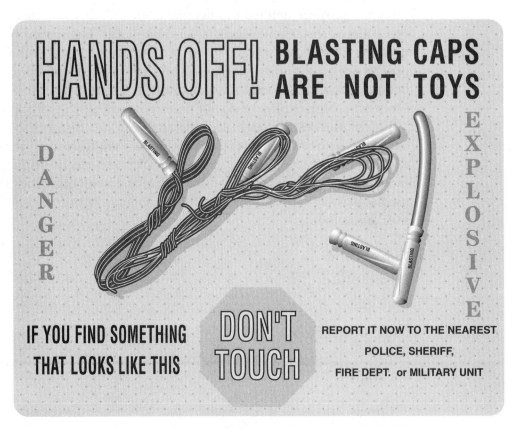

FIGURE 10.4

Secondary high explosives need a primary explosive to detonate them. Some examples of secondary high explosives are as follows.

Dynamite: A mixture of wood pulp and nitroglycerin

TNT: Trinitrotoluene, also the explosive in military dynamite

RDX: Cyclotrimethylenetrinitramine, also called Cyclonite (RDX= research department explosive) in the form of a plastic it carries the military designation C-4

HMX: Cyclotetramethylenetetranitramine, often used in plastic-bonded explosives

PBX: Plastic-bonded explosive, a mixture of HMX and plastic binder

PETN: Pentarythritoltetranitrate, used in the military for hand grenades and primacord

ANFO: Ammonium nitrate fuel oil

Binaries: Explosives made from two chemicals that are not explosive on their own but form a highly explosive substance when mixed together.

At one time dynamite was one of the principal explosives used. The problem with it was that when it was stored for long periods of time or subjected to heat, the nitroglycerin could "sweat" out of the dynamite, making the sticks very dangerous. Dynamite was usually sold based on the weight of the nitroglycerin to the weight of the dynamite. Dynamite labeled 40 was 40% nitroglycerin by weight. Nowadays military dynamite is made from TNT and does not contain nitroglycerin. When military dynamite is thrown on a fire, it simply burns. Being a secondary explosive, it needs a primary explosive to detonate it. Therefore military dynamite is safe to handle until a blasting cap is inserted into it.

In the commercial market ammonium nitrate-based explosives have mostly replaced dynamite. Ammonium nitrate is the oxidizer, and it is mixed with a fuel such as fuel oil or a carbohydrate such as guar gum. The mixture forms an emulsion with a gellike consistency and is inexpensive and safe to handle. It is used in many commercial blasting operations and was used in the Oklahoma Federal Building bombing in 1995 and in the World Trade Center bombing in 1993. An ANFO bomb carried in a Ryder truck caused the damage shown in Figure 10.5.

FIGURE 10.5

DETONATORS

Detonators can be electrical, mechanical, chemical, or fused. They work by releasing a great amount of heat and energy into a secondary explosive, causing it to detonate. For most applications the detonator is a blasting cap with some type of timing or electrical device attached to it. Three main types of detonators can be used: electrical, mechanical, and chemical.

Electrical detonators are the most sophisticated. They can employ timing circuits, remote control radios, cell phones, and computers, to name a few. They can send an electrical signal to a relay, which can then send a signal to an electrical blasting cap.

Mechanical detonators can use a mechanical device such as a wind-up alarm clock. The striker-bell combination can be wired to a battery, so it is really a combination mechanical electrical detonator.

The bomb set off in Centennial Olympic Park on July 27, 1996, used a Big Ben alarm clock as a timing device to relay the current from a 12-V battery to detonate smokeless powder. A press release from the FBI in connection with the bombing is shown in Figure 10.6.

WANTED BY THE ATLANTA BOMB TASK FORCE

Information Regarding Anyone Seen With the Components
Used in the Recent Bombings in Atlanta, Georgia
1-888-283-2662

Statement of FBI SAC Jack A. Daulton and Inspector Woody R. Euderson

- Accrate Arms #7 or #9 smokeless powder, as much as 3-4 pounds
- Olive green military-style ALICE backpack, medium size, black tape used on front buckles, no internal frame, wooden rod used as handle
- Three 12" long, 2" diameter metal pipes, with six 2" diameter metal end caps
- One steel plate, 1/8" thick (11-gauge), about 15" long and 8" wide, cut to size with an oxy-acetylene torch
- Olive green foam padding, two 3/8" thick sheets laminated together, about 15" long and 8" wide
- Cut masonry nails, size 8d (2-1/2" long), about 6 pounds
- Blue Everready brand Model 732 12-volt lantern battery
- Westclox brand Big Ben wind-up alarm clock
- Gray duct tape
- Black plastic electrical tape

FIGURE 10.6

Chemical detonators make use of a chemical reaction to set off the explosive. A safety fuse on a blasting cap is an example of a chemical detonator, as well as a lit cigarette or candle used to time an explosion. On occasion sulfuric acid has been used to detonate a pipe bomb. The sulfuric acid reacts slowly with the sugar and produces heat. Eventually the heat becomes sufficient to set off the explosive.

Detonators often employ metal pieces that often survive the explosion. Tool marks from wire cutters and pieces of timing mechanisms can be used to connect the bomb with the criminal.

BOMBING INVESTIGATIONS

The scene should first be searched by experts to determine if there is a second bomb set as an entrapment device. Once it is determined that there is no danger of a second explosion and the building is deemed structurally safe, a search of the scene should be conducted to locate the **seat of the blast**. This is usually easy to find since the explosion leaves a big crater. The search should start at the crater and spiral outward in ever-widening circles. The investigators should sift through the dirt and rubble looking for bits of metal or pieces of explosive wrapping that may contain date-shift codes traceable to the manufacturer.

The first $\frac{1}{2}$ in of soil or debris from the seat of the blast should be removed and collected. In addition, any objects in close proximity to the blast should also be collected. Soft materials often attract explosive residue and should also be collected. Small samples of actual explosives can be taken (not mailed) to the crime lab in sealed glass or metal containers. Only a small quantity (~$\frac{1}{8}$ teaspoon) is needed. Immovable objects can be wiped with a cotton swab moistened with acetone.

Once the crime lab has received the material, several different methods can be used to determine the identity of the explosive. In the past, color tests involving spot plates and high-performance liquid chromatography were carried out on the debris and on acetone washings. Nowadays the preferred method for determining the presence of explosive residue is the use of ion mobility spectrometry, X-ray and gamma-ray methods, and gas chromatography combined with a chemiluminescence detector that is very specific for the nitrogen present in most explosives. The ATF uses the **EGIS** explosives trace detection system to check residue for the presence of explosives. This was the system used to detect the ANFO used in the Oklahoma Federal Building bombing. Thermo Electron, the company that makes the EGIS, describes it as follows.

The EGIS Explosives Detection Systems, EGIS II and EGIS III, are highly sensitive devices developed to detect various types of commercial and military explosives, including dynamite, Semtex, C4, and TNT. EGIS Systems are designed to be used in conjunction with other techniques in order to provide a comprehensive program to screen for explosives. The EGIS System utilizes identical separation and detection technologies used in advanced forensic laboratories worldwide: gas chromatography combined with chemiluminescent detection, providing the EGIS with the ultimate in speed, accuracy, and sensitivity—without compromise. Gas chromatography is the most widely used scientific technique for the positive separation and identification of explosive compounds in a complex mixture. The sample material is heated into a gaseous form, added to a carrier gas, and introduced into the "separation column" where the mixture is separated into its individual component compounds by precisely controlled temperature cycling. These components are passed to the chemiluminescent detector in the carrier gas.

Unlike other detectors which respond to the thousands of nonnitro compounds in a sample, the chemiluminescent detector of the EGIS will only respond to nitro-based compounds of certain structures in the sample, making the EGIS more selective with less false positives. As all nitrogen-based high explosives contain nitro groups, the nitro-selective chemiluminescent detector of EGIS is ideal due to its unique selectivity.

The EGIS detection system utilizes specially designed sample wipes to obtain its sample. The EGIS operator rubs a sample wipe on the surfaces of objects, areas, vehicles, or people to collect any explosive residue present. The amount of sampling time varies from a few seconds to a few minutes depending on the size of the object, the security risk involved, and the amount of time that is available to conduct the sampling. When done, the operator immediately inserts the sample wipe into the sample inlet port on the EGIS, which automatically initiates an analysis cycle.

Within 16 seconds or less, the analysis is complete, and EGIS displays either a Clear or Alarm message. If the Alarm message displays, one or more explosives have been detected. The type(s) of explosive(s) found will be displayed. If the Clear message displays, no explosives were detected

The EGIS II is shown in Figure 10.7.

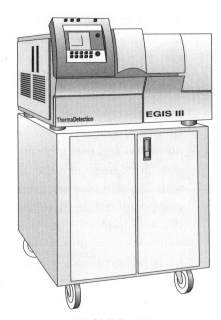

FIGURE 10.7

Investigators often search the blast crater with an ultraviolet light and a magnetic probe in the hope of finding small particles called taggants that are sometimes put in explosives by manufacturers. The purpose of a **taggant** is postdetonation identification of the explosive, manufacturer, and lot number. Taggants (Figure 10.8) are small particles, about the size of a grain of pepper, that are magnetic, fluorescent, and contain minislabs of color that can be read using a microscope. They were invented in the 1970s by Richard G. Livesay of 3M. In 1985 Livesay set up his own company, Microtrace, to sell taggants for many types of applications. A U.S. government grant tested the practicality of putting taggants in commercial explosives. Between 1977 and 1980 three major explosives manufacturers (Dupont, Hercules, and Atlas Powder Company) successfully added taggants to about 3200 tons of explosives. When the grant ran out, the taggant program was stopped. Countries such as Switzerland require all explosive manufacturers to put taggants in their products. Because of the increased concern with terrorism, the U.S. government is once again looking at requirements to put these devices in explosives.

FIGURE 10.8

REVIEW QUESTIONS

1. Fire is an example of what type of chemical reaction?

   A. precipitation   B. acid–base
   C. oxidation–reduction   D. none of the above

2. Oxygen is the most common example of a/an

   A. oxidizing agent   B. reducing agent
   C. precipitate   D. fuel

3. In a combustion reaction, isooctane is the

   A. oxidizer   B. fuel
   C. oxidizing agent   D. acid

4. The temperature required to initiate a combustion reaction is called the

   A. ignition temperature   B. flash point
   C. critical temperature   D. triple point

5. The temperature required to make fuel produce enough vapor to support combustion is called the

   A. ignition temperature   B. flash point
   C. critical temperature   D. triple point

6. Temperature is a measure of a molecule's

   A. size   B. volume
   C. speed   D. identity

7. At –60°F gasoline

   A. freezes
   B. burns
   C. vaporizes
   D. cannot support combustion

8. A 2% mixture of gasoline vapor in air is considered

   A. rich   B. noncombustible
   C. saturated   D. lean

9. A pattern that indicates the work of a single criminal is referred to as a/an

   A. MO   B. ABO
   C. EGIS   D. TLV

10. A chemical used to start a fire is known as a/an

    A. initiator   B. accelerant
    C. oxidizer   D. blasting cap

11. The search of a potential arson scene must center on the

    A. seat of the blast   B. entrances
    C. exits   D. point of origin

12. Soot and debris collected from a suspected arson scene must be packaged in a/an

    A. plastic bag   B. paper bag
    C. metal can   D. envelope

13. Forensic scientists use which technique to determine the presence of an accelerant in soot and debris?

    A. HPLC   B. headspace GC
    C. AAS   D. IR

14. The use of vapor concentration makes the detection of accelerants about how many more times sensitive?

    A. 10 times   B. 100 times
    C. 1000 times   D. 1 million times

15. Which case reestablished the Fourth Amendment rights of individuals with respect to the collection of arson evidence?

    A. *Frye* v. *United States* B. *Mincey* v. *Arizona*
    C. *Michigan* v. *Tyler*   D. *Daubert* v. *Merrell*

16. The blast effect of low explosives is

    A. subsonic   B. supersonic
    C. really loud   D. really powerful

17. Explosives differ from fires based on the _____ of the reaction.

    A. strength   B. completeness
    C. speed   D. reversibility

18. Smokeless powder is an example which type of explosive?

    A. low   B. primary
    C. secondary   D. binary

19. TNT is an example of which type of explosive?

    A. low   B. primary
    C. secondary   D. binary

20. The detonation of a secondary explosive requires a

    A. fuse   B. heat source
    C. blasting cap   D. shock

21. Military dynamite contains

    A. TNT   B. nitroglycerin
    C. RDX   D. smokeless powder

22. Dynamite used in commercial blasting has been largely replaced by cheaper explosives such as fuel oil mixed with

    A. aluminum   B. charcoal
    C. sugar   D. ammonium nitrate

23. EGIS instruments combine gas chromatography with which detector?

    A. thermal   B. ECD
    C. chemiluminescence   D. FID

24. The search of a bomb scene should always center on the

    A. seat of the blast   B. entrances
    C. exits   D. point of origin

25. Small devices added to explosives to allow identification in postexplosion investigations are called

    A. markers   B. taggants
    C. IDs   D. tracers

Answers

1. C	10. B	18. A
2. A	11. D	19. C
3. B	12. C	20. C
4. A	13. B	21. A
5. B	14. B	22. D
6. C	15. C	23. C
7. D	16. A	24. A
8. D	17. C	25. B
9. A		

CHAPTER 11

FABRICS

TERMS YOU SHOULD KNOW

allistic or threat	cotton	pyrogram
levels	Kevlar	pyrolysis GC
angora wool	linen	regenerated fibers
ballistic or threat	manufactured fibers	silk
levels	mohair	synthetic fibers
birefringence	natural fibers	vacuum filter
cashmere	nylon	wool

NATURAL FIBERS

Fabrics are both a good source of fibers and excellent carriers of fiber evidence. Fibers are transferred between individuals and objects when they come in contact. Locard's principle states that every contact leaves a trace. It makes sense, therefore, that the more violent the contact, the greater the transfer of fiber evidence. Fibers are lost with time as well. In general, fibers found on a suspect tend to show contacts that occurred within the last 24 h. This is an important source of information for the investigator, and the collection of fiber evidence is crucial in many criminal investigations. Fibers are divided into two main categories, natural and manufactured.

Natural fibers come from the fur of animals, silkworms, and plants. Some examples of natural fibers are listed below.

Wool: Fibers from the fur of animals such as sheep, goats, mink, alpacas, and llamas, to name a few. **Mohair** comes from the Angora goat. Angora wool comes from the Angora rabbit. **Cashmere** comes from the Kashmir goat.

Cotton: Cotton comes from the seedpod of the cotton plant. It is the principal clothing fiber of the world. The fiber is hollow, and under a microscope looks like a twisted ribbon.

Silk: Silk fibers come from silkworm cocoons. For its size it is stronger than steel.

Linen: Linen is a vegetable fiber that is 2 to 3 times stronger than cotton. It comes from the stalk fibers of the flax plant.

Hemp: Hemp is a vegetable fiber taken from the stem of the *Cannabis* plant. It is very strong and can be used to make rope or woven into a fabric.

MANUFACTURED FIBERS

Manufactured fibers can be produced from natural fibers, in which case they are called **regenerated fibers,** or they can be made from totally new substances created in a laboratory and called **synthetic fibers.** Manufactured fibers are normally formed by extruding liquids into filaments. Some examples of regenerated fibers are acetate, triacetate, and rayon. They are all formed from regenerated cellulose obtained by dissolving cotton in the appropriate solvent.

Some examples of synthetic fibers are **nylon**, polyester, acrylic, olefin, and aramid. Aramid is sold by Dupont under the trade name **Kevlar.** It has great strength and great resistance to stretching and when properly woven into a thick enough material, it can be used as a bulletproof garment. A large number of companies sell Kevlar vests to police agencies as protective body armor (most companies do not like to use the term *bulletproof vest* because some types of bullets can penetrate any Kevlar vest on the market). The Kevlar fabric used by these companies to make body armor for police officers is shown in Figure 11.1.

Different thicknesses of body armor can withstand different types of ammunition. The industry sets four **ballistic** or **threat levels** for concealable vests through what are known as NIJ standards.

Level I offers the most basic protection, and it is the same as the ballistic vest issued during the NIJ demonstration project in the 1970s.

Level IIA offers greater protection from lower-velocity 9-mm and 40 S&W ammunition.

Level II offers even greater protection like higher-velocity 357-caliber Magnum and 9-mm ammunition.

Level IIIA is the highest protection available for concealable ballistic vests. It protects against most handguns and against all the weapons from the previous three levels.

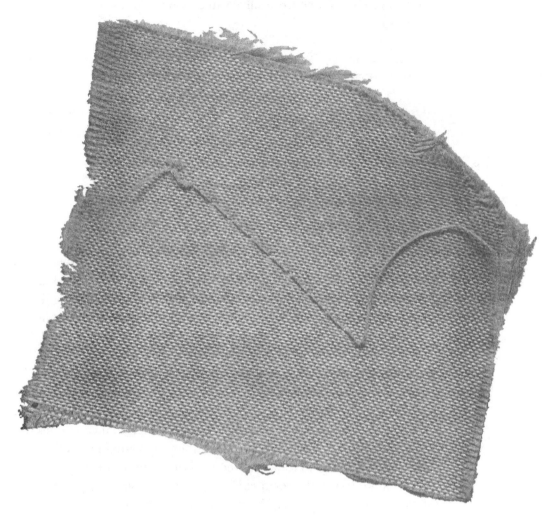

FIGURE 11.1

IDENTIFICATION

Fibers can be identified under a microscope based on their shape, size, and optical properties. Measurement of a fiber's **birefringence** (Chapter 5) using a polarizing light microscope is one method of determining the identity of the fiber. A microspectrophotometer can also be used to analyze the chemical identity of the fiber and any dye used to color it. However, the most common means of discovering the chemical identity of a fiber is the use of **pyrolysis gas chromatography (GC)**. Pyrolysis GC is based on the thermal decomposition of a substance into smaller gaseous molecules that are then analyzed by GC. An example of a pyrolyzer manufactured by Shimatzu is shown in Figure 11.2.

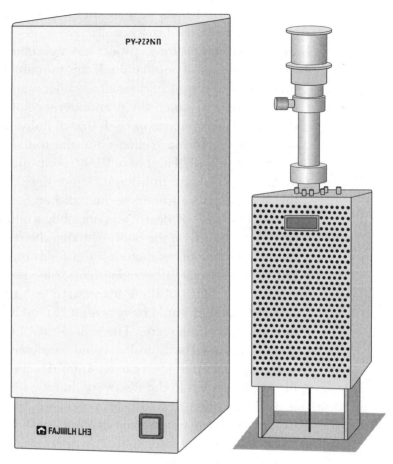

FIGURE 11.2

The fiber is inserted into the pyrolysis unit, which it heats to a high enough temperature to thermally decompose the sample. The GC separates the gases produced, and the results are recorded as a **pyrogram**. A computer can match the pyrogram to thousands stored on the computer's hard drive and identify the fiber.

Any fabric found near the scene of a crime may be important to the investigation. All items collected may be carriers of trace evidence and must be packaged separately. Do not overlook fibers that may be present on the victim's mouth, hands, or feet. Also remember to collect comparison standards. These are fabric items that can later be compared to fabric items found on the victim or the suspect. Whole pieces of fabric can sometimes be individual characteristic evidence if there is a tear that can be matched.

Once received by the crime lab, fabrics and carriers of fiber evidence can be analyzed. Fibers adhering to fabrics can be removed by hanging the article over a piece of white paper and combing it with a stiff brush. The fibers fall onto the white paper where they can be collected with tweezers. This process can also be carried out using a specially constructed vacuum cleaner (a **vacuum filter**) that deposits all the fibers removed onto a white disk of filter paper. On some occasions rollers with an adhesive covering (or some form of tape) have been used successfully.

Each fiber found on a suspect has a certain probability of occurring in the general population. If this probability is known, then the overall probability of finding all the fibers can be calculated.

An example in which the preponderance of fiber evidence made the overall probability approach that of individual characteristic evidence was the Wayne Williams' murder trial.

Between July 1979 and May 1981, twenty-nine children in the city of Atlanta, GA, were murdered. There were details of the murders that led the police to believe that all had been committed by one man. The cause of death was normally asphyxiation, and certain fibers were found on the bodies, linking them together. Some of the most important fibers included the following: yellow–green nylon fibers, violet acetate fibers, dog hairs, blue rayon fibers, and yellow nylon fibers. Many of these fibers were very unusual, and so it was thought that they would be very useful in linking a suspect to the victims and the crime scene. The yellow–green nylon fibers had a triangular cross section, and it could be determined that they had been manufactured for a carpet. Inquiries sent by the police to textile producers led to the discovery that the fiber was from the Wellman Corporation. It had been purchased by West Point Pepperell Corporation to manufacture Luxaire English Olive carpet. It is interesting to note that after the newspapers printed a story about the police's interest in fibers found on the bodies, all subsequent victims were discovered either nude or with their outer clothing missing, and many were dumped in a river. The murderer had obviously read the story and was trying to remove any evidence before disposing of the bodies. This illustrates the danger of disclosing the details of an ongoing investigation.

The Atlanta police and the FBI conducted stakeouts at access points to the river, wooded areas, and other potential sites where a body could be disposed of. At 2 A.M. on May 22, 1981, a stakeout team heard a loud splash and noticed a car slowly driving across the James Jackson Parkway Bridge over the Chattahoochee River. The driver, Wayne Williams, was stopped, questioned, and allowed to proceed.

Two days later the body of Nathaniel Carter was found in the Chattahoochee River about 1 mi downstream from the James Jackson Parkway Bridge. The same yellow–green nylon carpet fibers were present on the body. When Wayne Williams' story did not check out, the police obtained a search warrant for his home and cars. When the investigators searched Wayne Williams' home, they discovered that the floors were covered with Luxaire English Olive carpet. They also discovered dog hairs and other fibers in his home that matched those found on the victims. In addition, other fibers matched the carpeting in cars that Wayne Williams had access to. The probability of Luxaire English Olive carpet fiber being present at random in a residence in Atlanta was estimated to be 0.00013. There were 28 different types of fibers that were used to associate Wayne Williams, with the victims and the crime scene. When the individual probabilities of each fiber are multiplied together, the overall probability approaches that of a fingerprint. Wayne Williams was convicted of the murders of Nathaniel Carter and Jimmy Payne and during the trial was linked to the murder of ten other boys or young men. It is not uncommon for prosecutors to charge a suspect in serial cases with just two murders. It is sometimes wise to use the two strongest cases and not let any weaker ones introduce doubt into a jury's mind.

REVIEW QUESTIONS

1. Fibers collected from a victim tend to indicate contacts in the last

   A. 1 h   B. 24 h
   C. 1 week   D. 1 month

2. Cotton is an example of which type of fiber?

   A. natural   B. synthetic
   C. regenerated   D. none of the above

3. Rayon is an example of which type of fiber?

   A. natural   B. synthetic
   C. regenerated   D. none of the above

4. Nylon is an example of which type of fiber?

   A. natural   B. synthetic
   C. regenerated   D. none of the above

5. Kevlar can be woven to produce

   A. neckties   B. shirts
   C. curtains   D. body armor

6. Angora wool comes from a/an?

   A. Kashmir goat   B. Angora goat
   C. worm cocoon   D. Angora rabbit

7. Mohair comes from a/an?

   A. Kashmir goat   B. Angora goat
   C. worm cocoon   D. Angora rabbit

8. Silk comes from a/an?

   A. Kashmir goat   B. Angora goat
   C. worm cocoon   D. Angora rabbit

9. Linen is an example of a fiber that comes from a/an?

   A. plant   B. animal
   C. worm   D. synthetic

10. A manufactured fiber made from chemicals from the laboratory is called

    A. natural   B. synthetic
    C. regenerated   D. none of the above

11. The group responsible for setting standards for protective vests is the

    A. FBI   B. PBA
    C. NIJ   D. ATF

12. The highest level of protection for a concealed protective vest is

    A. level I   B. level IIA
    C. level II   D. level III

13. The most common method used to identify fibers is

    A. pyrolysis GC   B. HPLC
    C. AAS   D. IR

14. A fiber that is hollow and looks like a twisted ribbon under the microscope is probably

    A. nylon   B. wool
    C. cotton   D. silk

15. The process of breaking a larger molecule into smaller ones using heat is called

    A. birefringence   B. chemiluminescence
    C. pyrolysis   D. combustion

16. An optical property that allows fibers to be identified under a microscope is called

    A. birefringence   B. chemiluminescence
    C. pyrolysis   D. combustion

17. The resulting output of a pyrolysis GC analysis of a fiber is called a/an

    A. pyrogram   B. chromatogram
    C. mass spectrum   D. IR spectrum

18. All articles of clothing collected from a victim and a suspect must be packaged

    A. together   B. separately
    C. in airtight containers D. in metal containers

19. When fibers are found in a victim's mouth, the investigator should also collect

    A. lipstick   B. toothbrushes
    C. dental records   D. comparison standards

20. If a piece of torn fabric can be fitted to the original fabric, the evidence is probably

    A. class characteristic   B. individual characteristic
    C. common   D. of low evidentiary value

21. One of the most important fibers in the Wayne Williams' murder trial was a yellow–green nylon fiber from a/an

    A. Ford trunk liner   B. sweater
    C. Luxaire carpet   D. bedspread

22. Wayne Williams was convicted of how many murders?

    A. 2   B. 10
    C. 12   D. 29

23. Wayne Williams became a suspect when he was spotted

    A. on a highway   B. in the woods
    C. on a bridge   D. by a cemetery

24. The probability of Wayne Williams' home having the same carpet fiber as that found on the victims was

    A. very small   B. very great
    C. about average   D. impossible to calculate

25. Fiber evidence can be collected from fabrics by

    A. brushing   B. vacuuming
    C. adhesive tape rolling D. all of the above

Answers

1. B	10. B	18. B
2. A	11. C	19. D
3. C	12. D	20. B
4. B	13. A	21. C
5. D	14. C	22. A
6. D	15. C	23. C
7. B	16. A	24. A
8. C	17. A	25. D
9. A		

CHAPTER 12

ILLEGAL DRUGS

TERMS YOU SHOULD KNOW

alveolar sacs	fuel cell	narcotic
BAC	GHB	NHTSA
club drugs	heroin	OLS
cocaine	HGN	opium
confirmatory test	implied consent	PCP
controlled	IR	pharmaceuticals
substances	ketamine	presumptory test
dronabinol	LSD	psilocybin
drug	marijuana	pseudoephedrine
Ecstasy	marinol	Rohypnol
ephedrine	MDMA	SFST
euphoria	methamphetamine	WAT

COCAINE, METHAMPHETAMINE, MARIJUANA, HEROIN, MDMA, PHARMACEUTICALS, CLUB DRUGS, AND INHALANTS

Illegal drugs and related materials are the largest class of physical evidence received by crime labs. In fact, the sheer quantity of illegal drug-related physical evidence has been the main driving force for the expansion of crime laboratories across the United States. When the term *drug* is used in this chapter, it refers to an illegal drug. A **drug** is a chemical that causes a physiological or psychological action in the body. Normally, illegal drugs are abused because they produce a euphoric effect. **Euphoria** is a deep sense of well-being, and many people take illegal drugs because it makes them feel good.

This sense of euphoria comes at a price. The abuse of drugs can result in tolerance and dependency. Tolerance occurs when, over time, an ever-increasing dose of a drug is required. Dependency can be physical or mental. Physical dependency results when the body becomes accustomed to the regular intake of a drug. This can happen if the drug user takes a new dose before the effects of the previous dose have worn off. Once a person develops a physical dependency, the body expects a regular intake of the drug. If the person stops taking the drug, they will develop withdrawal sickness (sometimes called abstinence syndrome). Withdrawal sickness has many symptoms including cramps, nausea, chills, vomiting, insomnia, convulsions, pain, and hallucinations.

Psychological dependence occurs when a deep need for the continued intake of a drug occurs in an individual and can be a very powerful force. A famous experiment was conducted by the New York City Department of Health in which a laboratory rat was hooked up to a tube that delivered cocaine doses directly to its brain each time it depressed a small lever. Another lever was set up to deliver a pellet of food each time it was depressed by the rat. While cocaine is not physically addictive, there was such a strong degree of psychological addiction that the rat kept pushing the cocaine lever until it eventually starved to death.

The federal government keeps track of illegal drugs that are showing up in arrests on the street. The most used illegal drugs are listed in a threat matrix published by the National Drug Intelligence Center of the U.S. Department of Justice. A threat matrix chart from 2004 is shown in Figure 12.1.

Nationally 37% of state and local police agencies identify cocaine as the major drug threat. Next are methamphetamine at 36%, marijuana at 13%, heroin at 9%, and 3,4-methylenedioxymethamphetamine (MDMA) at 1%. Drug abuse also leads to many associated crimes. State and local police agencies estimate that cocaine abuse contributes the most to violent crime, about 50%, and to property crime, about 42%. Methamphetamine contributes about 32% to violent crime and 30% to property crime. For marijuana the contribution to violent crime is about 5%, and to property crime about 11%. For heroin the contribution to violent crime is 5%, and to property crime 11%. The availability and threat of the four major illegal drugs vary from region to region within the United States. In the Pacific, southwestern, and west central United States, methamphetamine is the drug of greatest concern. In the Great Lakes, northeastern, mid-Atlantic, and southeastern United States, cocaine is the drug of greatest concern. The primary markets for cocaine include New York, Chicago, Atlanta, Miami, Houston, and Los Angeles. The primary markets for methamphetamine include Los Angeles, San Francisco, and Phoenix.

The leaves of the coca plant, *Erythroxylon coca,* were given to Inca royalty in keeping with their religious and cultural beliefs. The South American Indians chewed on the leaves to get additional strength and endurance. In the 1880s Sigmund Freud considered cocaine a miracle drug that led to clarity of the mind. He prescribed it to many of his patients before its addictive properties became known.

National Drug Threat Assessment 2004: Threat Matrix

Illicit Drug	Source Locations	Seized en route/within U.S. in 2002	Transit Countries	Entry Points into U.S.	Primary Markets and Principal Suppliers	Wholesale Price Range in the U.S.	Retail Price Range in the U.S.	Retailers	Key Developments	Projections
Cocaine	Foreign: Colombia, Peru, Bolivia. Domestic: None	101,877.8 kg (352,000 kg reportedly available to U.S. markets)	Mexico, Central American countries, Caribbean island nations	SWB states (Texas, California, Arizona, New Mexico), Miami/S Florida, New York	Atlanta: Mexican, Dominican Chicago: Mexican, Colombian, Dominican Houston: Mexican, Colombian Los Angeles: Mexican, Colombian Miami: Colombian New York: Colombian, Mexican, Dominican (also Mexican, Dominican) Jamaican, Puerto Rican, and Traditional Organized Crime groups)	$10,000-$38,000 per kg (powder)	$20-$200 per gram (powder) $5-$100 per rock (crack)	African American and Hispanic criminal groups and street gangs; Caucasian local independent dealers; Dominican, Haitian, Jamaican, Mexican, Native American, and Puerto Rican criminal groups	DEA Cocaine Signature Program data indicate that average wholesale cocaine purity may be increasing after previous decreases each year between 1999 and 2002.	Potential worldwide cocaine production will likely decrease slightly due to increases in eradication and coca spray operations as well as a resumption of the Airbridge Denial Program. This may result in a decrease in cocaine availability in the United States.
Methamphetamine	Foreign: Mexico and, to a much lesser extent, Southeast Asia (Burma) Domestic: California, Central States (Arkansas, Illinois, Indiana, Iowa, Missouri)	2,512.6 kg	Mexican: Direct from source SE Asian: Direct from source	Mexican: SWB states (primarily California) followed by Texas, Arizona, and New Mexico) SE Asian: San Francisco	Central States: Caucasian, Mexican Los Angeles: Mexican Phoenix: Mexican San Diego: Mexican San Francisco: Mexican	$6,600-$28,600 per kg* (powdered) $8,500-$200,000 per kg* (ice-high purity crystal methamphetamine) *normally sold in lb quantities $3,000-$13,000 per lb (powdered)	$40-$125 per gram (powdered) $120-$500 per gram (ice)	Mexican, Caucasian, and Asian criminal groups; Caucasian local independent dealers; Asian and Hispanic street gangs; OMGs	The availability of high purity crystal methamphetamine (ice) increased sharply over the past year, primarily because of a significant increase in ice production by Mexican criminal groups, who appear to have supplanted Asian criminal groups as the predominant producers of ice in the country.	The number of low capacity methamphetamine laboratories likely will increase significantly in the Great Lakes and Southeast regions.
Marijuana	Foreign: Mexico, Colombia, Canada, Jamaica Domestic: California, Appalachia (Kentucky, Tennessee), Hawaii, Pacific Northwest (Washington, Oregon)	1,098,703.5 kg	Mexican: Direct from source Colombian: Mexico, Caribbean island nations Canadian: Direct from source Jamaican: Caribbean island nations	Mexican: SWB states, (primarily Texas followed by California, Arizona, and New Mexico), New York Colombian: Miami/S Florida, SWB states (Texas, California, Arizona, and New Mexico) Canadian: Northern border states Jamaican: Miami/S Florida, New York	Chicago: Mexican Dallas/Houston: Mexican Los Angeles/San Diego: Caucasian, Mexican, Jamaican Miami: Jamaican, Bahamian New York: Jamaican, Mexican, Colombian, Caucasian Phoenix/Tucson: Mexican, Jamaican Seattle: Caucasian, Asian, Mexican, Outlaw Motorcycle Gangs (OMGs)	$660-$2,640 per kg* (commercial-grade) $1,320-$13,200 (sinsemilla) *normally sold in lb quantities $300-$1,200 per lb (commercial-grade) $600-$6,000 per lb (sinsemilla)	$5-$50 per gram $2-$5 per joint	Mexican, African American, Asian, Caucasian, and Jamaican criminal groups; African American and Hispanic street gangs; prison gangs; local independent dealers (Caucasian, Asian, African American, and Mexican); OMGs	Texas POEs surpassed California POEs in marijuana seizures in 2002, reflecting a possible shift in either transportation routes or transportation methods used.	Continued high demand for high potency marijuana may fuel increased indoor cultivation.
Heroin	Foreign: Mexico, South America (primarily Colombia), Southeast Asia (primarily Burma), Southwest Asia (primarily Afghanistan) Domestic: None	2,799.4 kg	Mexican: Direct from source South American: Direct from source, Mexico, Central/South American countries Southeast Asian: China, SE Asian countries, Taiwan, Hong Kong, Canada Southwest Asian: African, European, and Central Asian countries	MX: SWB states (primarily Texas and California followed by Arizona and New Mexico) SA: International Airports (Miami, JFK); Atlanta, Boston, Houston, Newark, and San Juan; SWB states SEA: Los Angeles, Portland, Seattle, San Francisco, Baltimore, Buffalo, Chicago, Detroit, New York, Washington, D.C. SWA: New York, Chicago, Detroit, Los Angeles	Boston: Colombian (S.A.), Dominican (S.A) Chicago: Colombian (S.A), Mexican (MX), Los Angeles: Mexican (MX) New York: Colombian (S.A), Dominican (S.A), Chinese (SEA), Nigerian (SEA), Pakistani (SWA), Russian (SWA)	$15,000-$65,000 per kg (MX) $35,000-$115,000 per kg (SWA) $60,000-$125,000 per kg (SA) $90,000-$120,000 per kg (SEA)	$10 per dose (approximately 50-100 mg)	African American, Asian, Caucasian, Cuban, and Puerto Rican criminal groups; African American and Hispanic street gangs; local independent dealers	Potential heroin production estimates for Colombia were revised upward for 2002 and previous years. Worldwide potential heroin production increased significantly in 2002 primarily due to increases in Afghanistan.	Heroin traffickers will continue to make sporadic attempts to increase the market share of South American heroin in the western United States and that of Mexican heroin in eastern states; however, the success of such attempts likely will be limited.
MDMA	Foreign: Netherlands, Belgium and, to a much lesser extent, Germany, Poland, Latin America, and Canada Domestic: Limited	3,495,960 du (dosage unit) (e.g., tablets and capsules) (seized at POEs)	Canada, Dominican Republic, Mexico, Western European countries	International Airports: New York, Miami, Newark	Los Angeles: Israeli, Russian Miami: Israeli, Russian (also Colombian, Dominican) New York: Israeli, Russian (also Asian, Colombian, Dominican, and Traditional Organized Crime groups)	$5-$17 per du (1,000 du lots)	$10-$75 per du	Caucasian local independent dealers; Asian, African American, and Hispanic street gangs; OMGs	Asian criminal groups and street gangs increasingly are distributing MDMA at the wholesale and retail levels.	Overall demand for MDMA likely will remain stable or decline.

April 2004

FIGURE 12.1

In 1886 the Coca Cola Company marketed its new soft drink, made from the same coca leaves, as an alternative to alcoholic drinks. A bottle of Coca Cola contained about 60 mg of cocaine. Things really did go better with Coke. In 1903 the company was forced to remove cocaine from its beverage, but it uses the leaves (cocaine-free) for flavor to this very day.

The leaves of the coca plant contain about 0.5% cocaine by weight. When they are soaked mashed together, the cocaine can be extracted with the aid of a solvent. The resulting extract is about 70% cocaine hydrochloride by weight. Cocaine hydrochloride is a salt, and a user can either inject it intravenously or inhale (snort) it through their nose. Since heating cocaine hydrochloride makes it decompose before it vaporizes, it cannot be smoked as is. The base form of cocaine, which can be smoked, can be freed by extraction with a solvent (this is called free-base cocaine) such as ether, but this is very dangerous. However, a more convenient method of making a form of cocaine that can be smoked was soon discovered. When cocaine hydrochloride is mixed with an aqueous solution of baking soda and heated, the basic form of the drug is obtained. As the mixture is heated, a cracking sound is produced, hence the name crack cocaine.

Methamphetamine is structurally related to **ephedrine**, a natural stimulant found in the *Ephedra* plant. It is a stimulant and causes a euphoric effect in the user. Methamphetamine is sold on the street in three main forms, powdered methamphetamine, ice methamphetamine, and methamphetamine tablets.

Powdered methamphetamine, also called crystal or crank, is the most common of the forms found in the United States. It is produced in secret, illegal laboratories (called clandestine laboratories) and can be injected, snorted, ingested, or smoked.

Ice methamphetamine gets its name from the fact that it looks like tiny pieces of ice. It is also know as glass, batu, or shabu. It can be made in clandestine laboratories by recrystallizing powdered methamphetamine in a solvent such as water, alcohol, or acetone. Ice methamphetamine is usually smoked.

Methamphetamine tablets are normally manufactured abroad (most in Burma). They can be flavored and taken by mouth, or they can be smoked. The tablets are often imprinted with an R or a WY.

Methamphetamine is manufactured in clandestine laboratories using ephedrine or **pseudoephedrine** as a starting ingredient. Both ephedrine and pseudoephedrine are commonly found in over-the-counter cold remedies because of their ability to act as decongestants. Pseudoephedrine, for example, is found in the over-the-counter cold remedies Sudafed and Afrin. There are five main methods that clandestine laboratories use to manufacture methamphetamine.

The first method uses ephedrine or pseudoephedrine as the starting material along with hydroiodic acid and red phosphorus. This process yields a very high-quality methamphetamine and is a preferred method of clandestine Mexican labs.

A second method involves the same ingredients as the first method but uses iodine instead of hydroiodic acid. Since hydroiodic acid is more difficult to obtain than iodine, this method is used when hydroiodic acid is in short supply. The reaction of the iodine with the red phosphorus in water creates hydriodic acid.

A third method uses ephedrine or pseudoephedrine with iodine and hypophosphorous acid. This method is useful when it is difficult to obtain red phosphorus, however, it can be very dangerous since one of the waste products is phosphine gas.

A fourth method uses ephedrine or pseudoephedrine along with ammonia and sodium metal.

A fifth method uses mercuric acid, methylamine, phenyl-2-propanone, and aluminum and is often called the P2P method.

As noted above, many chemicals are used in the production of methamphetamine. Police and government agencies are growing more concerned with the toxic chemicals left behind in clandestine laboratories. For every pound of methamphetamine manufactured, about 6 lb of toxic waste chemicals are produced. A methamphetamine lab cleanup bill has been introduced into Congress that would authorize the Environmental Protection Agency (EPA) to set cleanup guidelines and standards for the nation.

Marijuana is the most commonly used illegal drug in the United States. It is estimated that more than 12 million Americans above the age of 12 use marijuana at least once a month. It is also estimated that about 54% of the population between the ages of 18 and 25 have tried marijuana. Its usage can be traced back thousands of years to China and it has been described in a Chinese medical compendium dating back to 2737 B.C. It spread from China to India to North Africa and finally showed up in Europe in 500 A.D. References to marijuana appeared in the *United States Pharmacopeia* from 1850 to 1942 where it was recommended for the treatment of rheumatism, nausea, and labor pains.

Marijuana is a greenish-brown mixture of the leaves, flowers, stems, and seeds of the plant *Cannabis*. There are two forms of the plant: *Cannabis sativa* grows in most parts of the world, and a more potent form, *Cannabis inca*, is grown in Afghanistan where it is used to make hashish. Nowadays, most of the marijuana grown in the United States is a hybrid of the two varieties. The active ingredient in marijuana is tetrahydrocannabinol (THC). The concentration of THC is greatest in the resin found on the flowers and leaves of the female plant. The flowers themselves and then the leaves have the next highest concentration of THC. Very little of the active ingredient, THC, exists in the stems and seeds of the plant. Sinsemilla is the bud of the female plant and is the part of the plant most often smoked. There are specific receptor sites in the human brain to which THC can bind. Once bound, the receptors trigger the euphoric effect for which the drug is taken.

There are presently two medical conditions for which marijuana is used: (1) to decrease the intraocular pressure in people suffering from glaucoma, a condition where the pressure builds up to a dangerous level and can cause blindness, and (2) to lessen the nausea caused by some anticancer drugs and by AIDS treatment. In 1966 chemists were able to synthesize THC, and in 1985 the synthetic form was called **dronabinol** or **marinol.**

Heroin is a derivative of the narcotic morphine. A **narcotic** is a drug that reduces pain and causes sleep. Morphine is the active ingredient of **opium,** the juice of the unripe poppy plant (*Papaver somniferum*). This juice contains about 12% morphine by weight. There is a famous scene in the Wizard of Oz where the witch says, "Poppies will make them sleep." In 3400 B.C. the Sumerians cultivated the poppy in Lower Mesopotamia. They called it Hul Gil, which meant "joy plant." The growing of poppies for opium spread to the Assyrians, Babylonians, and Egyptians, and in about 400 A.D. Arab and Turkish traders introduced opium to the Chinese. The use of this drug became so widespread that the Chinese emperor made it illegal. A mixture of opium, alcohol (like sherry wine), and herbs was sold to the public as laudanum. In 1898 Bayer marketed a new wonder drug designed to cure all sorts of ailments. If you had a pain, you could go to the local drugstore and buy Bayer heroin over the counter. After it became illegal to sell heroin in the United States, Bayer switched to its next miracle drug, aspirin.

Heroin is manufactured by reacting morphine with acetic anhydride. It is more potent than morphine or codeine and creates a greater euphoric effect. Heroin is normally sold on the street as a mixture of heroin and various cutting agents, which can include quinine, mannitol, lactose, starch, and even arsenic. The user takes heroin as an intravenous injection. A typical method of administration involves a small portion of heroin, the hydrochloride salt of diacetylmorphine, with water in a spoon. Heroin is not very soluble in cold water, so the mixture in the spoon is held over a candle and warmed until dissolved. The use of a spoon became a cultural statement in the 1970s: Spoons were sometimes worn as jewelry, and a popular 1970s music group was called the Lovin' Spoonful.

MDMA, also known as **Ecstasy,** is a hallucinogen that is also a member of a group of synthetic drugs used at nightclubs and referred to as **club drugs.** Merck Pharmaceutical synthesized MDMA back in 1912. At first its use was limited to animals, but in 1976 Alexander Shulgin of San Francisco synthesized and taste-tested MDMA. He described the effect as follows.

I feel absolutely clean inside, and there is nothing but pure euphoria. I have never felt so great or believed this to be possible. The cleanliness, clarity, and marvelous feeling of solid inner strength continued throughout the rest of the day and evening. I am overcome by the profundity of the experience.

MDMA is classified as a moderate threat by the U.S. Department of Justice. It was used by psychotherapists in the 1980s but has since been banned altogether by the DEA. About 90% of MDMA is synthesized in Belgium and the Netherlands. Pure MDMA is a white crystalline solid. A typical dose is about 125 mg, and it is normally taken orally as a tablet, a capsule, or powder.

Pharmaceuticals are a class of abused substances that are available legally by prescription. They are obtained illegally by improper prescribing, forging prescriptions, theft, or going to multiple doctors for prescriptions. A new source of these drugs can be Internet pharmacies. Pharmaceuticals include the following drugs: narcotics such as hydrocodone (Vicodin), oxycodone (Oxycontin), hydromorphone (Dilaudid), and codeine; depressants such as barbiturates and tranquilizers, of which Alprazolam and diazepam (Valium) are the most widely abused; and stimulants such as dextroamphetamine (Adderall) and methylphenidate (Ritalin). The use of pharmaceuticals is on the rise.

Club drugs are often used at all-night dance parties called raves. The term applies to all drugs used at these parties, including (gamma-hydroxybutyrate) (GHB), ketamine, Rohypnol, MDMA, and the hallucinogens lysergic acid diethylamide (LSD), phencyclidine (PCP), and psilocybin. GHB and Rohypnol are depressants. Since they are tasteless and odorless, they can be slipped into a person's drink without their knowledge. For this reason GHB, Rohypnol, and ketamine are often referred to as date rape drugs. In 1996 the U.S. Congress increased the penalties for the use of any controlled substance in a sexual crime.

GHB was available over the counter at health food stores in the 1980s. It was used by body builders to help increase muscle mass and reduce fat. **Rohypnol** can cause a condition known as anterograde amnesia. In this state a person may not remember any of the events that occur when they are incapacitated. This effect is greatly increased when the drug is mixed with alcohol. **Ketamine** is legally used mostly as an animal anesthetic. It has also been approved for use as an anesthetic in humans. At normal usage levels ketamine causes a dreamy state and hallucinations.

The Swiss chemist Albert Hoffmann first synthesized LSD in 1943. It is a derivative of lysergic acid, which is produced by ergot fungus. It is a powerful drug that can be active in as small a dose as 25 μg. Albert Hoffmann accidentally ingested some LSD and experienced the first "acid trip." People who use LSD can sometimes experience flashbacks, which are hallucinogenic episodes that can occur even after a person has stopped using the drug. LSD is available in the form of tablets, capsules, liquid, gelatin squares, and sugar cubes.

PCP can be snorted, smoked, or eaten. It was developed in the 1950s as an intravenous anesthetic but was never actually approved for use in humans because of its adverse psychological effects. PCP can be manufactured in clandestine laboratories using a simple chemical process. It is often mixed with other drugs or used to lace cigarettes, cigars, and marijuana joints. It can cause a feeling of invincibility in the user, which can cause problems for police trying to subdue a suspect who is on PCP. The individual can exhibit great feats of strength because they feel no pain. Pain normally limits the force a person can apply. If a person tries to lift up a car, their body will tell them to stop by the use of pain. A person on PCP does not have the benefit of this feedback mechanism and can perform extraordinary feats only to find out, when the PCP wears off, that they have torn muscles, ligaments, and tendons and broken bones.

Psilocybin is the active ingredient in hallucinogenic mushrooms. In some states the police have reported finding chocolates filled with ground-up hallucinogenic mushrooms. It is interesting to note that the use of hallucinogenic mushrooms is part of the religious practices of some American Indians. Even though psilocybin is illegal, the U.S. Supreme Court has decided that it is legal for Native Americans to use it as part of their religious practices. This right, however, does not extend beyond the boundaries of their territories.

Inhalants are solvent vapors that cause a euphoric effect. These solvents can be found in thousands of household products and include volatile solvents, aerosols, gases, and nitrates. Spray paint, glue, nail polish remover, and cleaning fluid are some of the most common sources of these materials. Abuse of these drugs can cause dizziness, withdrawal, nausea, vomiting, and seizures. These chemicals can cause damage to the user's heart, lungs, brain, kidneys, and liver.

There are many terms used in conjunction with street drugs. Appendix A contains a glossary of street drug terms from the Executive Office of the President, Office of National Drug Control Policy, February 2004 (http://www.whitehousedrugpolicy.gov).

THE CONTROLLED SUBSTANCES ACT

In 1970 the federal government decided to combine all the laws governing the manufacture, sale, and use of drugs that were considered dangerous and passed the Controlled Substance Act. This act established five categories, or schedules, which listed drugs based mainly on two criteria: their established medical use and their potential for abuse. The potential for abuse is determined by a drug's potential for causing physical and psychological dependence. Drugs placed in schedules are called **controlled substances** and cannot be obtained legally without a prescription. A description of the five schedules is as follows.

Schedule I

Drugs in this schedule have no accepted medical use and have a high potential for abuse. Since there is no accepted medical use, drugs in schedule I cannot be prescribed by physicians. Drugs included in schedule I include heroin, marijuana, LSD, MDMA, peyote, mescaline, psilocybin, N-ethylamphetamine, acetylmethadol, fenethylline, tilidine, dihydromorphine, and methaqualone.

Schedule II

Drugs in this schedule have accepted medical use and have a high potential for abuse. Drugs in schedule II can be prescribed by physicians only with strict controls. Many of these drugs include narcotics. Drugs included in schedule II include opium, morphine, codeine, hydromorphone (Dilaudid), methadone, pantopon, meperidine (Demerol), cocaine, oxycodone (Percodan), oxymorphone (Numorphan), amphetamine (Dexedrine), methamphetamine (Desoxyn), phemnetrazine (Preludin), methylphenidate (Ritalin), amobarbital, pentobarbital, secobarbital, fentanyl (Sublimaze), sufentanil, etorphine hydrochloride, phenylacetone, dronabinol, and nabilone.

Schedule III

Drugs in this schedule have accepted medical use and have a medium potential for abuse. Drugs in schedule III include derivatives of barbituric acid, glutethimide (Doriden), nalorphine, benzphetamine, chlorphentermine, clortermine, phendimetrazine, paregoric, and any compound, mixture, preparation or suppository dose form containing amobarbital, secobarbital, or pentobarbital.

Schedule IV

Drugs in this schedule have accepted medical use and have a lower potential for abuse. Drugs in schedule IV include barbital, phenobarbital, methylphenobarbital, chloral hydrate, ethchlorvynol (Placidyl), meprobamate, (Equanfl, Miltown), paraldehyde, methohexital, fenfluramine, diethylpropion, phentermine, chlordiazepoxide (Librium), diazepam (Valium), oxazepam (Serax), clorazepate (Tranxene), flurazepam (Dairnane), clonazepam (Clonopin), prazepam (Verstran), alprazolam (Xanax), halazepam (Paxipam), temazepam (Restoril), triazolam (Ralcion), lorazepam (Ativan), midazolam (Versed), quazepam (Do), mebutamate, and dextropropoxyphene (Darvon).

Schedule V

Drugs in this schedule have accepted medical use and have the lowest potential for abuse. Drugs in schedule V include buprenorphine and propylhexedrine. Sometimes the difference between some schedule V preparations and over-the-counter products is just the concentration of the active ingredient.

ANALYSIS OF DRUG EVIDENCE

The collection of drug evidence must be done with great care. Many drugs are so potent that they can cause an effect through inhalation or absorption through the skin. Just touching a drug like fentanyl causes enough to be absorbed through the skin to produce an effect. For this reason it is important for the investigator to use gloves and sometimes a mask when collecting drug evidence. Often investigators use for packaging whatever container the drug is already in.

Drug analysis is done in two steps. The first step is a quick and easy screening to determine if a drug is probably present and is called the **presumptory test**. The second step is a more thorough, accurate test to positively prove the presence of a drug and is called the **confirmatory test**.

An officer normally carries out the presumptory test in the field. The most common of these presumptory drug tests are based on color. A small plastic pouch contains a series of chemicals in sealed plastic capsules. The officer takes a small amount of the drug in question, about the size of a match head, and places it in the plastic pouch. The officer then squeezes the glass ampoules within the pouch until they break and release the chemical reagent. Specific color changes indicate the possible presence of a drug. This information can be used by the officer as probable cause for an arrest. Examples of these pouches manufactured by NIK are shown in Figure 12.2. NIK produces presumptory test kits for the following drugs in the NIK system of narcotic identification.

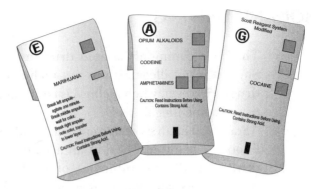

FIGURE 12.2

A. Opiates and amphetamine screening

B. Heroin and opium alkaloids screening

C. Barbiturates

D. LSD

E. Cannabis—marijuana, hashish, hash oil

F. Acid neutralizer

G. Cocaine, rock cocaine, crack, HCL, free base

H. Methadone

J. PCP special opiates

K. Opiates

L. Heroin

M. Methaqualone

N. Pentazocine

P. Propoxyphene

Q. Ephedrine

R. Methcathinone, Valium, and Rohypnol

U. Methamphetamine/Ecstasy (MDMA)

Presumptory tests can yield false positives and for this reason cannot be used in court to positively prove the presence of a drug. The identity of a drug can be positively determined using a mass or infrared spectrum. Most forensic laboratories use a gas chromatograph–mass spectrometer (GC/MS) as the preferred confirmatory method for drug identification (Chapter 4). It is a convenient method for dealing with the mixtures of drugs that often appear on the street. A new technique is to include an infrared spectrometer so that both the infrared and mass spectra can be presented in court. This method is known as GC/MS-FTIR.

ALCOHOL AND DRIVING

The most commonly abused drug in the United States is alcohol. Since it is not illegal, it was not included with the aforementioned drugs. However, when alcohol is combined with the act of driving, it can become illegal.

Statistical analysis of automobile accidents has shown that the likelihood of being involved in an accident increases greatly when the driver is under the influence of alcohol. This has led the government to pass laws against driving while intoxicated (DWI). At first, the problem was that it was very difficult to prove that a person was intoxicated. In 1939 Indiana passed the first per se alcohol laws. *Per se* is a Latin term meaning "in itself." The Indiana law defined driving while intoxicated as having a blood alcohol content (BAC) above a specific value. Nowadays the limit for DWI has been set at the federal level at 0.08%. New York State, for instance, uses the following criteria.

BAC: Blood alcohol content or concentration

DWI: Driving while intoxicated; 0.08 BAC or higher or other evidence of intoxication

DWAI: Driving while ability-Impaired (by alcohol); .05 BAC to .07 BAC, or other evidence of impairment

DWAI/Drugs: Driving while ability-impaired (by a drug that is not alcohol)

Chemical test refusal: A driver who refuses to take a chemical test (normally a test of breath, blood, or urine) can receive a driver license revocation and must pay a $300 civil penalty ($350 for a driver of commercial vehicles) to apply for a new driver license. A driver who refuses a chemical test during the 5 years after a DWI-related charge will have their driver license revoked for 1 year and must pay a $750 civil penalty to apply for a new driver license.

Zero tolerance law: A driver who is less than 21 years of age and who drives with a 0.02 BAC to 0.07 BAC violates the zero tolerance law.

The penalties in New York State are listed in Table 12.1.

TABLE 12.1   *Penalties for Alcohol-Related and Drug-Related Violations*

Violation	Mandatory Fine[a]	Maximum Jail Term	Mandatory Driver License Action (2)
Driving while intoxicated (DWI)	$500–$1,000	1 year	Revoked for at least 6 months
Second DWI violation in 10 years (E felony)	$1,000–$5,000	4 years	Revoked for at least 1 year
Third DWI violation in 10 years (D felony)	$2,000–$10,000	7 years	Revoked for at least 1 year
Driving while ability-impaired (DWAI)	$300–$500	15 days	Suspended for 90 days
Second DWAI violation in 5 years	$500–$750	30 days	Revoked for at least 6 months
Zero tolerance law	$125 civil penalty and $100 fee to terminate suspension	None	Suspended for 6 months
Second zero tolerance law	$125 civil penalty and $100 reapplication fee	None	Revoked for 1 year or until age 21
Chemical test refusal	$300 civil penalty ($350 for commercial drivers)	None	Revoked for at least 6 months
Chemical test refusal within 5 years of a previous DWI-related charge	$750 civil penalty	None	Revoked for at least 1 year

TABLE 12.1 *(continued)*

Violation	Mandatory Fine[a]	Maximum Jail Term	Mandatory Driver License Action (2)
Chemical test refusal Zero tolerance law	$300 civil penalty and $50 reapplication fee	None	Revoked for at least 1 year
Chemical test refusal Second or subsequent zero tolerance law	$750 civil penalty and $50 reapplication fee	None	Revoked for at least 1 year
Driving under the influence (out-of-state)	N/A	N/A	Revoked for at least 90 days; if less than 21 years of age, revoked at least 1 year
Driving under the influence (out-of-state) with any previous alcohol-drug violation	N/A	N/A	Revoked at least 90 days; if less than 21 years of age, revoked at least 1 year or until age 21 (longest term)

[a] Surcharges are added to misdemeanors ($160) and felonies ($270).

[b] The driver license penalties for drivers under the age of 21 and for professional drivers are different.

The value of 0.08% was determined by analyzing the BAC of drivers involved in automobile accidents. At a level of 0.08% a driver is 4 times as likely to be involved in an automobile accident. A graph from the U.S. Department of Transportation is shown in Figure 12.3.

A blood sample can be withdrawn from a suspected drunk driver and analyzed by gas chromatography to determine their BAC. Does the removal of blood from a person for BAC analysis violate their Fifth Amendment rights? The Fifth Amendment states:

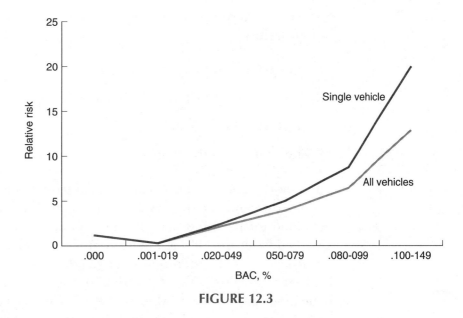

FIGURE 12.3

Article [V.]: No person shall be held to answer for a capital, or otherwise infamous crime, unless on a presentment or indictment of a Grand Jury, except in cases arising in the land or naval forces, or in the Militia, when in actual service in time of War or public danger; nor shall any person be subject for the same offence to be twice put in jeopardy of life or limb; nor shall be compelled in any criminal case to be a witness against himself, nor be deprived of life, liberty, or property, without due process of law; nor shall private property be taken for public use, without just compensation.

In the case of *Schmerber* v. *California* the U.S. Supreme Court considered the case of an individual who had been arrested for drunk driving while receiving treatment for injuries in a hospital. During his treatment, a police officer ordered a doctor to take a blood sample, which indicated that Schmerber had been drunk while driving. The blood test was introduced as evidence in court, and Schmerber was convicted. The U.S. Supreme Court decided that the Fifth Amendment referred only to testimonial evidence. A defendant cannot be required to testify against himself. However, taking a blood sample is not always convenient. In addition, the BAC in the arterial system is much greater then that in the venous system while alcohol is still being absorbed by the body. This absorption can take between 30 and 90 min, and during this time the BAC in the arterial system can be more than 40% greater than that in the venous system. Since blood is withdrawn from the venous system, this can result in an incorrectly low BAC value.

The rate of absorption of alcohol by the human body is controlled by four factors:

1. The quantity of alcohol consumed

2. The time over which the alcohol was consumed

3. The form of the alcohol

4. The contents of the stomach.

The more alcohol a person consumes, the faster it is absorbed into the bloodstream; also, the faster it is consumed, the faster it enters the bloodstream. If the alcohol is in a purer form, like vodka, it is absorbed faster than if it is a more complicated mixture, like beer.

The contents of the stomach are one of the most important factors in determining the rate of absorption and what maximum BAC value a person will reach. Most of the absorption of alcohol by the body occurs in the small intestine. The presence of food causes the stomach to delay emptying its contents into the small intestine, which can significantly increase the time it takes for the blood to reach its maximum BAC value.

The body eliminates alcohol by excretion and oxidation. Excretion occurs by breathing, sweating, and urination, and oxidation occurs in the liver. About 98% of the alcohol in the body is turned into carbon dioxide and water by the liver. The rate of elimination is constant and can be calculated by the formula

$$\text{Rate of elimination} = 0.01 + 0.014(\text{weight}/300\text{ lb})$$

This works out to about 0.015% per hour. Standard tables are used to calculate what your maximum BAC will be based on your body weight and the number of drinks (quantity of alcohol) you have consumed.

One drink is defined as having ½ oz of pure ethyl alcohol; each of the following is considered one drink.

10 oz to 12 oz of beer at 4% to 5% alcohol, or

8 oz to 12 oz of wine cooler at 4% to 6% alcohol, or

4 oz to 5 oz of table wine at 9% to 12% alcohol, or

2.5 oz of fortified wine at 20% alcohol, or

1.25 oz of 80 proof distilled spirits at 40% alcohol, or

1 oz of 100 proof distilled spirits at 50% alcohol.

After 1 h of drinking

TABLE 12.2

Number of Drinks	Body Weight for Males							
	100	120	140	160	180	200	220	240
1	.021	.015	.010	.007	.004	.002	.001	.000
2	.058	.046	.036	.030	.024	.020	.018	.014
3	.095	.077	.062	.053	.044	.038	.035	.029
4	.132	.108	.088	.076	.064	.056	.052	.044
5	.169	.139	.114	.099	.084	.074	.069	.059
6	.206	.170	.140	.122	.104	.092	.086	.074
7	.243	.201	.166	.145	.124	.110	.103	.089
8	.208	.232	.192	.168	.144	.128	.120	.104
9	.317	.263	.218	.191	.164	.146	.137	.119
10	.354	.294	.244	.214	.184	.164	.154	.134
11	.391	.325	.270	.237	.204	.182	.171	.149
12	.428	.356	.296	.260	.224	.200	.188	.164

Number of drinks	Body Weight for Females							
	100	120	140	160	180	200	220	240
1	.029	.021	.016	.012	.009	.006	.004	.002
2	.074	.058	.048	.040	.034	.028	.024	.020
3	.119	.095	.080	.068	.059	.050	.044	.038
4	.164	.132	.112	.096	.084	.072	.064	.056
5	.209	.169	.144	.124	.109	.094	.084	.074
6	.253	.206	.176	.152	.134	.116	.104	.092
7	.299	.243	.208	.180	.159	.138	.124	.110
8	.344	.280	.240	.208	.184	.160	.144	.128
9	.389	.317	.272	.236	.209	.182	.164	.145
10	.434	.354	.304	.264	.234	.204	.184	.164
11	.479	.391	.336	.292	.259	.226	.204	.182
12	.524	.428	.368	.320	.284	.248	.224	.200

When alcohol enters the body, it dissolves in all the body fluids. Based on this fact, a more exact formula for calculating the blood alcohol content of an individual is

$$\% \text{ BAC (g/100 mL)} = 0.10 \times M_A/(V_D \times M_B)$$

where M_A = mass of alcohol (g), V_D = volume of distribution (L/kg), and M_B = body mass (kg).

The mass of alcohol (M_A) can be calculated from the number of grams of alcohol in an actual drink. This is a function of the volume of the alcohol in the drink, the proof (twice the percent) of the alcohol, and the density of the alcohol (about 0.80 g/mL). A convenient formula for calculating the grams of alcohol in a drink made from liquor is

$$M_A = \text{ounces of liquor} \times \text{proof}/200 \times 28.4 \text{ g/oz} \times 0.80 \text{ g/mL}$$
or
$$= 0.11 \times \text{ounces of liquor} \times \text{proof}$$

In the case of wine and beer, which don't use proof, the formula is

$$M_A = \text{ounces of liquor} \times \text{percent}/100 \times 28.4 \text{ g/oz} \times 0.80 \text{ g/mL}$$
$$= 0.23 \times \text{ounces of liquor} \times \text{percent}$$

The volume of distribution (V_D) takes into account how much of a person's body mass is fluid in which the alcohol can dissolve. V_D is equal to 0.7 L/kg for men and 0.6 L/kg for women.

The mass of the body (M_B) in kilograms can be calculated by dividing a person's body weight in pounds by 2.2 lb/kg.

$$M_B = \text{body weight in pounds}/2.2$$

CASE I: A 120-lb woman consumes three drinks, each containing one shot of 80 proof vodka. What is her BAC? (Each mixed drink is assumed to contain 1 jigger or 1.5 oz of vodka.)

$$\text{Three drinks} = 3 \times 1.5 \text{ oz} = 4.5 \text{ oz}$$
$$M_A = 0.11 \times \text{ounces of liquor} \times \text{proof}$$
$$= 0.11 \times 4.5 \text{ oz} \times 80$$
$$= 39.6 \text{ g}$$
$$V_D = 0.6 \text{ L/kg (for women)}$$
$$M_B = 120 \text{ lb}/2.2 \text{ lb/kg} = 55 \text{ kg}$$
$$\% \text{ BAC (g/100 mL)} = 0.10 \times M_A/(V_D \times M_B)$$
$$\text{BAC} = 0.10 \times 39.6 \text{ g}/(0.6 \text{ L/kg} \times 55 \text{ kg})$$
$$= 0.12\%$$

CASE II: A 180-lb man has four beers (4.0% alcohol, 12 oz each) in 1 h. What is his BAC?

$$\text{Four beers} = 4 \times 12 \text{ oz} = 48 \text{ oz}$$
$$M_A = 0.23 \times \text{ounces of liquor} \times \text{percent}$$
$$= 0.23 \times 48 \text{ oz} \times 4.0\% = 44.2 \text{ g}$$
$$V_D = 0.7 \text{ (for men)}$$
$$M_B = 180 \text{ lb}/2.2 \text{ lb/kg} = 81.8 \text{ kg}$$
$$\% \text{ BAC (g/100 mL)} = 0.10 \times M_A/(V_D \times M_B)$$
$$\text{BAC} = 0.10 \times 44.2 \text{ g}/(0.7 \text{ L/kg} \times 81.8 \text{ kg})$$
$$= 0.077\%$$

The determination of DWI is a two-step process. The first step is a field evaluation of a suspected drunk driver. This can be initiated by observing the erratic behavior of an automobile or by stopping a car for a traffic infraction or at a checkpoint. The first step requires some probable cause for the police officer to arrest the driver and take them to the police station. The police officer can use several techniques to establish probable cause for DWI such as alcohol-sniffing devices, but the most common are field sobriety tests. There are various portable devices that can sense alcohol from the breath of a person, but the readings are normally not reliable enough to be used in court, hence they are used only to show probable cause.

The use of field sobriety tests is somewhat controversial. While there are many different types of tests, they are all designed to indicate to the officer conducting the test the degree of intoxication of the subject. Some tests, like reciting the alphabet backward, are very difficult for most sober people. The **National Highway Traffic Safety Administration (NHTSA)**, which is part of the U.S. Department of Transportation, officially recommends only three field sobriety tests, **horizontal gaze nystagmus (HGN)**, **walk-and-turn (WAT)**, and **one-leg stand (OLS)**. In random tests on individuals who were either sober or had a blood alcohol content of 0.10% or greater, the police correctly identified the intoxicated individuals 88% of the time using the HGN, 79% of the time using the WAT, and 83% of the time using the OLS. The use of field sobriety tests is voluntary in most states.

The NHTSA provides a training manual for the **standardized field sobriety tests (SFST)**. They are described by the NHTSA manual as follows.

HGN Testing

Horizontal Gaze Nystagmus is an involuntary jerking of the eye that occurs naturally as the eyes gaze to the side. Under normal circumstances, nystagmus occurs when the eyes are rotated at high peripheral angles. However, when a person is impaired by alcohol, nystagmus is exaggerated and may occur at lesser angles. An alcohol-impaired person will also often have difficulty smoothly tracking a moving object. In the HGN test, the officer observes the eyes of a suspect as the suspect follows a slowly moving object, such as a pen or small flashlight, horizontally with his or her eyes. The examiner looks for three indicators of impairment in each eye: if the eye cannot follow a moving object smoothly, if jerking is distinct when the eye is at maximum deviation, and if the angle of onset of jerking is within 45 degrees of center. If, between the two eyes, four or more clues appear, the suspect likely has a BAC of 0.08 or greater. NHTSA research found that this test allows proper classification of approximately 88 percent of suspects. HGN may also indicate consumption of seizure medications, phencyclidine, a variety of inhalants, barbiturates, and other depressants.

Walk and Turn

The Walk-and-Turn test and One-Leg Stand test are "divided attention" tests that are easily performed by most unimpaired people. They require a suspect to listen to and follow instructions while performing simple physical movements. Impaired persons have difficulty with tasks requiring their attention to be divided between simple mental and physical exercises.

In the Walk-and-Turn test, the subject is directed to take nine steps, heel-to-toe, along a straight line. After taking the steps, the suspect must turn on one foot and return in the same manner in the opposite direction. The examiner looks for eight indicators of impairment: if the suspect cannot keep balance while listening to the instructions, begins before the instructions are finished, stops while walking to regain balance, does not touch heel-to-toe, steps off the line, uses arms to balance, makes an improper turn, or takes an incorrect number of steps. NHTSA research indicates that 79% of individuals who exhibit two or more indicators in the performance of the test will have a BAC of 0.08 or greater.

One-Leg Stand

In the One-Leg Stand test, the suspect is instructed to stand with one foot approximately six inches off the ground and count aloud by thousands (One thousand-one, one thousand-two, etc.) until told to put the foot down. The officer times the subject for 30 seconds. The officer looks for four indicators of impairment, including swaying while balancing, using arms to balance, hopping to maintain balance, and putting the foot down. NHTSA research indicates that 83% of individuals who exhibit two or more such indicators in the performance of the test will have a BAC of 0.08 of greater.

Most police officers find the HGN test the most reliable. It is based on involuntary muscle movement that is directly related to the BAC of the subject. The other tests, based on physical or cognitive skills, can be passed by a person with a high BAC and can be failed by a sober person with poor physical or cognitive skills. Since there is a lot of natural variation in people's physical and cognitive skills, it is very difficult for an officer to evaluate the results. People do not have control over their involuntary motions, so HGN is considered more reliable. The findings of the NHTSA support this observation.

Most states, including New York, have an **implied consent** law. When a police officer requests a driver to submit to a chemical test, state law provides that anyone who operates a motor vehicle in that state has given their implied consent to taking a chemical test on their breath, blood, urine, or saliva for the purpose of determining their BAC. Refusal to take the test carries an automatic loss of driving privileges and a civil fine. The police may also request a court order for the chemical test.

BREATHALYZER, INTOXILYZER, AND ELECTROCHEMICAL INSTRUMENTS

The blood in a person's body is pumped from the right ventricle to the lungs via the pulmonary artery (the only artery in the body that carries unoxygenated blood). Once in the lungs, the blood picks up oxygen and releases carbon dioxide and any other waste gases such as alcohol. This exchange of gases takes place across the very fine membranes of the **alveolar sacs**. The lungs are made up of about 250 million alveolar sacs. The alcohol in a person's blood is about 2100 times more concentrated than the alcohol in a person's breath. This ratio is controlled by body temperature, so it is the same for each person. In the 1930s a device was invented by Rolla Harger of the Indiana University School of Medicine known as the Harger Drunkometer. The instrument was used for many years until the Breathalyzer, which was designed by Robert Borkenstein in 1954, replaced it. It measured the alcohol content of a person's breath, multiplied it by 2100, and calculated the BAC. This system collects a fixed volume of alveolar air and passes it through an alcohol-sensitive chemical reagent. Alcohol in the sample produces a color change in the reagent that is measured by a photometric system and yields the BAC.

The Breathalyzer was quite reliable but required more operator training and required the operator to change the ampoules filled with a mixture of sulfuric acid, potassium dichromate, silver nitrate, and water. The instrument also had no printed output. In an effort to simplify the operator's work and remove the chemicals, an optical approach was developed. This new breed of instrument used spectrophotometry (Chapter 4) to measure the alcohol content in a person's breath. The Intoxilyzer 5000, for example, uses the absorption of **infrared (IR)** radiation from the alcohol in a person's breath to determine BAC. A person is given three chances to blow sufficient breath into a disposable mouthpiece. If the subject fails to provide enough breath, it is considered a refusal. Once the breath is trapped within a transparent chamber, an infrared beam of light is passed through it. The instrument measures the absorption of infrared light by the alcohol in the breath and uses this to calculate the BAC. A schematic of an Intoxilyzer is shown in Figure 12.4.

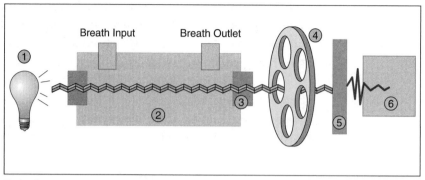

Breath Input   Breath Outlet

The Intoxilyzer 5000 measures the degree alcohol absorbs infrared energy...the more alcohol present, the greater the absorption. As shown, a quartz lamp (1) generates IR energy which travels through a sample chamber (2) containing the subject's breath. Upon leaving the chamber, a lens (3) focuses the energy onto the chopper wheel (4) containing three or five narrowband IR filters. The IR energy passed by the filters is focused on a highly sensitive photo detector (5) which converts the IR pulses into electrical pulses. The microprocessor (6) interprets the pulses and calculates the Blood Alcohol Concentration which is then displayed.

FIGURE 12.4

An Intoxilyzer 5000 is shown in Figure 12.5.

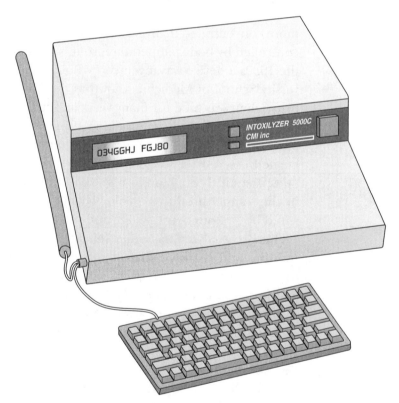

FIGURE 12.5

Notice that it uses no chemicals and has a keyboard that allows the operator to type in pertinent information like time, data, and the subject's name. The instrument also produces a multicopy printed output that can be used in court.

The newest type of Breathalyzer combines infrared detection with fuel cell technology. A **fuel cell** is a device that can act like a battery when a fuel and an oxidant are pumped through it. There is always oxygen in the air, so Breathalyzers use the alcohol in a person's breath as a source fuel. The current produced by the fuel cell is proportional to the alcohol in the person's breath. Figure 12.6 is a schematic of this type of instrument.

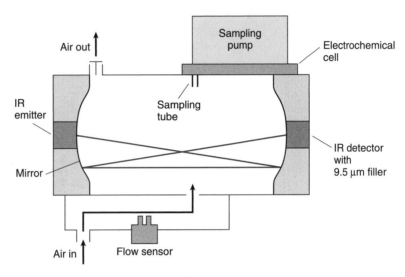

FIGURE 12.6

The New York State Police use the Alcotest 7100 MK III. A description of this instrument from Draeger Safety, Inc., is as follows.

> The Alcotest 7110 MK III-C offers undisputedly the most advanced Evidential Breath alcohol testing technology available today. Two different and independent measuring systems, infrared spectroscopy and electrochemical cell technology, are used to analyze and display breath alcohol results, therefore, providing the highest possible level of forensic and legal integrity. The superior quality of the Infrared system operates at a higher wavelength of 9.5 μm, is virtually nonsensitive to any potentially interfering substances allowing the elimination of a problematic chopper wheel with multiple optical filters. The Draeger temperature controlled fuel cell prevents condensation and provides an extended lifetime sensor, while guaranteeing exceptional accuracy even at extreme ambient temperatures. The built-in communication firmware provides the capability of networking with a host computer allowing remote system diagnosis and software updating.

This instrument is shown in Figure 12.7. It has containers representing 0.00% BAC and 0.08% BAC, which are connected to the instrument and are run just prior to determining a suspect's BAC. The results for the calibration and the suspect's BAC are printed at the end of the analysis.

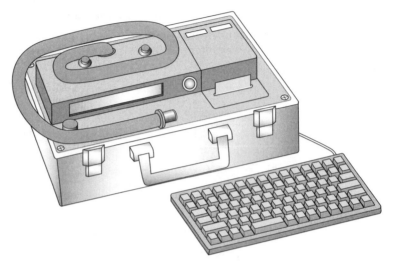

FIGURE 12.7

If a suspect refuses to take a chemical test (most states still refer to the modern Breathalyzer tests as chemical even though they haven't used chemicals in years), the police can still charge the suspect with DWI. While at the police station the officers normally have the suspect take another series of field sobriety tests. This is normally done for three reasons: (1) to give any alcohol in the mouth a chance to be absorbed, (2) to allow any alcohol in the stomach to make its way into the small intestine to be absorbed, and (3) to videotape the actions of the suspect. If the suspect refuses to take the chemical test, the police can still charge the suspect with DWI, and the videotape, as well as the officer's testimony, can be presented to a jury as evidence of intoxication.

REVIEW QUESTIONS

1. The largest volume of evidence received by crime labs is related to

   A. counterfeiting   B. drugs
   C. murder   D. firearms

2. Euphoria describes a state of

   A. exhaustion   B. sleep
   C. well being   D. hallucination

3. The need for more and more of a drug to achieve the same effect is called

   A. tolerance   B. physical dependency
   C. psychological dependency D. toxicity

4. Withdrawal sickness is a sign of

   A. tolerance   B. physical dependency
   C. psychological dependency D. toxicity

5. A deep need to keep taking a drug is called

   A. tolerance   B. physical dependency
   C. psychological dependency D. toxicity

6. The two greatest drug threats in the United States are cocaine and

   A. methamphetamine B. marijuana
   C. heroin   D. MDMA

7. Coca Cola once contained the drug

   A. methamphetamine B. marijuana
   C. heroin   D. cocaine

8. Bayer first marketed which drug as its new wonder medicine?

   A. methamphetamine B. marijuana
   C. heroin   D. cocaine

9. Which drug is related to ephedrine?

   A. methamphetamine B. marijuana
   C. heroin   D. cocaine

10. Ice is a form of which drug?

   A. methamphetamine B. marijuana
   C. heroin   D. cocaine

11. The production of 1 lb of methamphetamine produces how many pounds of toxic waste?

   A. 2   B. 4
   C. 6   D. 8

12. The concentration of THC in the marijuana plant is greatest in the

   A. leaves   B. stem
   C. seeds   D. resin

13. An example of a club drug is

   A. GHB   B. ketamine
   C. Rohypnol   D. all of the above

14. LSD has no accepted medical use and a high potential for abuse. LSD is in which schedule?

   A. schedule I   B. schedule II
   C. schedule III   D. schedule IV

15. Morphine has an accepted medical use and a very high potential for abuse. Morphine is in which schedule?

   A. schedule I   B. schedule II
   C. schedule III   D. schedule IV

16. A color test for drugs is known as

   A. presumptory   B. confirmatory
   C. absolute   D. none of the above

17. A color test for drugs is often used for

   A. evidence   B. proof
   C. probable cause   D. show

18. The collection of blood, breath, saliva, or urine to determine a suspect's BAC does not violate the suspect's Fifth Amendment rights. This was finding of which Supreme Court case?

   A. *Mincey* v. *Arizona*   B. *Michigan* v. *Tyler*
   C. *Schmerber* v. *California*   D. *Daubert* v. *Merrell*

19. The BAC of a 140-lb woman who consumed three drinks in 1 h is

   A. 0.02%   B. 0.05%
   C. 0.08%   D. 0.10%

20. A 150-lb person eliminates alcohol from their body at a rate of _____ per hour.

   A. 0.010%   B. 0.017%
   C. 0.020%   D. 0.025%

21. The most reliable field sobriety test is the

   A. walk and turn   B. one-leg stand
   C. horizontal gaze nystagmus   D. backward alphabet

22. In most states driving a car means that you have already given _____ to a chemical test.

   A. implied consent   B. written consent
   C. verbal consent   D. no consent

23. The Alcotest 7100 series uses both an infrared light and a
    _____ for the detection of alcohol.

    A. chemical reaction   B. spectrophotometer
    C. color change   D. fuel cell

24. The ratio of alcohol in the breath to alcohol in the blood
    is

    A. 1:100   B. 1:200
    C. 1:2100   D. 1:250,000,000

25. If a person cannot produce enough breath for the Alcotest
    7100 in three attempts, it is considered a/an

    A. proof of DWI   B. proof of DWAI
    C. refusal   D. inconclusive result

Answers

1. B	10. A	18. C
2. C	11. C	19. C
3. A	12. D	20. B
4. B	13. D	21. C
5. C	14. A	22. A
6. A	15. B	23. D
7. D	16. A	24. C
8. C	17. C	25. C
9. A		

CHAPTER 13

FIREARMS

TERMS YOU SHOULD KNOW

breechblock	grains	rate of twist
broach cutter	groove	revolver
button cutter	GSR	rifling
caliber	handgun	rim fire
choke	inverted	RN
contact shot	JHP	rule of sixes
ejector	land	SEM/EDX
everted	long gun	semiautomatic
extractor	mandrel cutter	SJHP
firing pin	muzzleloader	SP
FMC	NIBIN	SWC
FMJ	pistol	WC
gauge		

HISTORY OF FIREARMS

Black powder was discovered more than 1000 years ago in China. However, it wasn't until the fourteenth century that it was used in guns. The first guns were cannons—large, fixed, metal devices that were better at making noise than anything else. Eventually cannons became more accurate and useful, and the idea of pushing a projectile out of a metal barrel using gunpowder became part of modern warfare. The next big step in the evolution of firearms occurred when cannons were made small enough for one person to handle. Guns that needed two hands, and often a wooden support, to fire were called **long guns**. Guns that could be held in one hand were called **handguns**. All these weapons were loaded by putting the powder and the lead ball into the barrel through the firing end or muzzle of the gun. For this reason they were known as **muzzleloaders**. Figure 13.1 shows a flintlock muzzleloader. A flint held in a vise strikes metal, creating hot sparks of metal that ignite black powder in the flash pan.

FIGURE 13.1

Early handguns were not very accurate or practical for battle. Once the round ball came out of the barrel, it started to spin in a random direction. The spin made its trajectory curve in a random direction as well. Actually, this was not as great a drawback as it might seem. Most early handguns were used by noblemen to settle matters of honor. Since the duelers were among the wealthiest of the population, they had everything to live for. The ability to miss the other person while still proving one's courage by dueling had its advantages. These early handguns were first invented in Pistoja, a town in Tuscany, Italy. The ornately decorated dueling handguns often had the name of the town where they were made, Pistoja, inscribed on them, and from this we get the modern name for the handgun, **pistol**.

Many attempts were made to improve the accuracy of long guns. At first, longer and longer barrels were used, but this made the weapons quite awkward to handle or carry. The ability to hit an object at a greater distance took the long gun on two separate paths.

On one hand, discharging multiple projectiles out of the barrel of a gun meant that there was a greater probability of hitting a target. This was the principle behind the shotgun. The pellets from a shotgun begin to deviate from a straight line as soon as they leave the barrel of the gun. Since they are all spinning randomly, the pattern of shot forms an ever-widening circle. The size (diameter) of the shotgun barrel is measured using a rather archaic measurement system called gauge. The gauge was once measured by how many lead balls weighing a total of 1 lb could fit into the diameter of the shotgun barrel. For example, a lead ball could fit into the diameter of a 12-gauge shotgun barrel weighing $\frac{1}{12}$ of a pound. The actual diameter of a shotgun barrel actually decreases as the gauge increases. A list of shotgun gauges and their corresponding barrel diameters appears in Table 13.1.

TABLE 13.1

Gauge	Diameter (in)
10	0.775
12	0.729
16	0.662
20	0.615
28	0.550
410[a]	0.410

[a]This is not really a gauge but a caliber.

Figure 13.2 shows a 12-gauge shotgun. It has a variable **choke** that adjusts to different constriction simply by turning. The choke affects the pattern of the shot as it leaves the barrel.

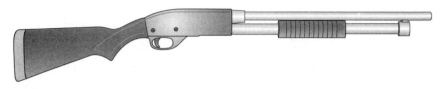

FIGURE 13.2

On the other hand, it was known that spinning a projectile in a direction perpendicular to the flight path (like the spiral of a football) causes it to travel in a straight line. Archers turned the feathers on their arrows to make them more accurate. Sometime in the fifteenth century gun manufacturers started putting grooves in the smooth bores of musket barrels. These grooves twist as they run the length of the barrel and are called **rifling**. It is the rifling of the barrel that distinguishes a modern rifle from a musket. It took about 350 years before this improvement was accepted by the military.

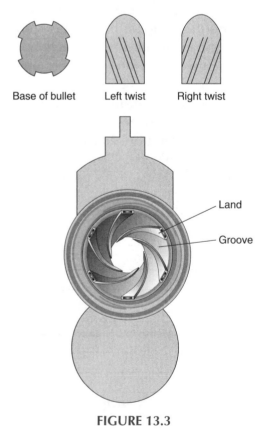

FIGURE 13.3

The **caliber** of a rifle is the diameter of the original barrel before the rifling is added. The original surface is referred to as the **land**, and the surface that has had metal scraped off it is called the **groove** (Figure 13.3). So the caliber is the inside diameter of a gun barrel from land to land. The diameter of U.S. rifles is in inches, and the decimal point is omitted. The diameter of metric barrels is in millimeters. Some examples are given in Table 13.2.

TABLE 13.2

Land-to-Land Diameter	Caliber
0.22 in	22
0.357 in	357
0.44 in	44
0.45 in	45
9 mm	9 mm
10 mm	10 mm

Some calibers also have a historical basis. The 30–06 rifle caliber is based on a 0.30-in-diameter bullet seated in a case designed in 1906. Figure 13.4 shows a 22-caliber bullet, a 9-mm bullet, a 357-caliber bullet, and a 12-gauge shotgun shell.

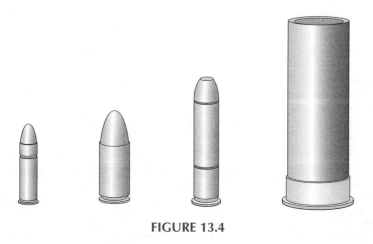

FIGURE 13.4

When handguns began to be used for military purposes and self-defense, rifling was put into the barrel to increase the accuracy. There are basically two types of handguns, semiautomatic and revolver (there are single-shot handguns, but they are not common). A **semiautomatic** handgun has a magazine filled with ammunition. As one round is fired, it uses the expelled gases to push the slide back and load another round. If the gun keeps firing when the trigger is pulled, it is considered an automatic or machine gun. Figure 13.5 is an exploded diagram of a semiautomatic handgun.

FIGURE 13.5

FIGURE 13.6

A **revolver** uses a cylinder or wheel to hold the ammunition. Each time the trigger is pulled, a new round is rotated into the firing position. A single-action revolver needs to have the hammer pulled back each time it is fired. In the case of a double-action revolver (the most common variety) the hammer is pulled back automatically when the trigger is pulled. Some police officers prefer to have the revolver rotate a fresh round into the firing position each time the trigger is pulled. However, the advent of more reliable ammunition and the greater firepower (more rounds in a magazine and quicker reload times) has made semiautomatic handguns the new standard for police officers. Figure 13.6 is an exploded diagram of a revolver.

MANUFACTURING OF MODERN FIREARMS

The process of putting the grooves into a modern rifle or handgun barrel requires a hardened metal tool known as a cutter. Today there are two commonly used cutters, button and mandrel. They are normally made of a very hard material, like tungsten carbide, and are twisted at a predetermined rate to make the grooves spiral down the length of the barrel.

The first cutters were simple hook cutters. A gunsmith twisted the hook as he pulled it through the gun barrel. Each groove needed to be made separately, and this was a very labor-intensive process. A **broach cutter** was an improvement in that all the grooves are cut at once. As the cutter is pulled through a barrel, it is rotated. The hardened tungsten carbide cutter leaves microscopic scratches (striation marks) in the barrel, and these striation marks make every barrel unique. When the soft lead of the bullet moves through the barrel, it picks up these striation marks. This allows the forensic investigator to identify a weapon from the bullets fired from it. Agents from the Federal Bureau of Investigation (FBI) actually collected successive gun barrels from the Smith & Wesson production line that had been cut by the same cutter; they test-fired the assembled weapons and found that the striation marks were unique for each gun. Figure 13.7 shows a broach cutter.

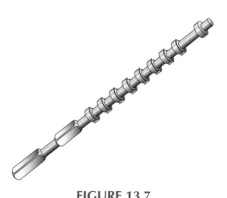

FIGURE 13.7

The cutting can be twisted to the right or left; it can have different numbers of lands and grooves (from 4 to 32); and it can have different rates of twist. This makes every gun barrel unique, which makes the bullets fired from every gun unique. Figure 13.8 shows a broach-cut barrel with six lands and grooves twisted to the left.

Broach cut
6-left rifling pattern

Land   Groove

FIGURE 13.8

A **button cutter** produces the most accurate gun barrels. This cutter is slightly larger than the gun barrel, so when it is pulled through, it compresses the metal to the correct size. This results in a more uniform barrel and generally the most accurate grouping of fired bullets. Since a button cutter (Figure 13.9) compresses the metal of the barrel instead of cutting it, it isn't really a cutter.

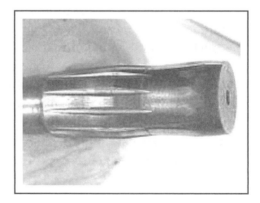

FIGURE 13.9

The tool most commonly used to put grooves in a gun barrel is a **mandrel cutter**. This cutter uses a process called hammer forging in which the barrel of the gun is squeezed around the mandrel using high pressure (there is no hammer involved). Mandrel cutters provide a very quick, efficient method for putting grooves in gun barrels. Most manufacturers use mandrel cutters for high-volume gun barrel production.

BULLET COMPARISON

The forensic scientist has several methods of analysis for any questioned bullet. First, an overall observation of the bullet indicates its general characteristics. A list of these characteristics is given in Table 13.3.

TABLE 13.3

Bullet Type	Meaning	Purpose
FMJ	Full metal jacket	Deep penetration, general purpose, military
JHP	Jacketed hollow point	Controlled expansion, good accuracy, hunting
SJHP	Semijacketed hollow point	Greater expansion, good accuracy, hunting
FMC	Full metal case	Light metal jacket
SP	Soft point	Greater penetration than hollow point
WC	Wad cutter	Leaves round hole in paper, target practice
SWC	Semi-wad cutter	Target practice and general purpose
RN	Round nose	General purpose

The diameter and total mass of the bullet are also measured. The diameter indicates the caliber of the bullet and the type of weapon that fired it. The mass of the bullet indicates the particular class of ammunition it belongs to. Bullet masses are specified by manufacturers using the archaic system of **grains**. There are 7000 gr in 1 lb. Since forensic scientists use the metric system, bullet mass is measured in grams and then converted to grains by the formula

$$\text{Grains} = 15.4 \times \text{grams}$$

The striation marks on the bullet are examined next. The number of lands and grooves are noted, along with the direction of twist. The widths of the lands and grooves are then recorded (using a optical microscope with a calibrated eyepiece or video output tied to a computer). The rate of twist is also measured. The **rate of twist** refers to the pitch or angle the striation marks make with the longitudinal axis of the bullet. This rate is often given as a ratio, such as 1 in 10, which means the bullet makes one complete rotation for every 10 in it travels down the gun barrel. There is an optimum rate of twist for each type of bullet, which can be calculated using the formula

$$\text{Rate of twist} = \frac{150(\text{diameter of bullet})^2}{\text{length of bullet}}$$

(If the muzzle velocity of the bullet is greater than 2800 ft/s, a value of 180 is used instead of 150.)

For example, a bullet with a diameter of 0.357 (a 357 Magnum handgun caliber) has a length of 1.000 in. What is the optimum rate of twist?

$$\text{Rate of twist} = \frac{150(0.357)^2}{1.000} = 19$$

This bullet would be expected to be fired from a gun with a rate of twist of 1 in 19 (one complete twist of the bullet for every 19 in of travel).

This formula can be useful in estimating the length of a bullet that has been crushed on impact (Figure 13.10).

FIGURE 13.10

All these characteristics help the forensic scientist determine the caliber, manufacturer, and type of ammunition of the questioned bullet. There are charts of this type of information called general rifling characteristics (GRC). Table 13.4 is an example of a chart (based on one) from www.firearmsid.com for a 9-mm Luger revolver.

TABLE 13.4

Manufacturer	Twist	Lands and Grooves	Land	Groove
AA Arms, Inc.	R	6	0.055	0.120
Astra	R	6	0.053	0.128
Beretta	R	6	0.055	0.130
Hi-Point Firearms	R	6	0.055	0.120
Interdynamic	R	6	0.055	0.124
Llama	R	6	0.054	0.120
Mauser	R	6	0.054	0.128
Smith & Wesson	R	6	0.056	0.122
Star	R	6	0.054	0.126
Swd, Inc.	R	6	0.055	0.120

This type of information is class characteristic. The next step in the process is a comparison of the questioned bullet with a bullet test-fired from a suspect's weapon. One can never match a bullet to the barrel of a questioned gun. The gun must be test-fired and a side-by-side match of the two bullets made using a comparison microscope. The striation marks caused by each gun barrel are unique and can be used to identify from which gun barrel a bullet was fired. The guns are test-fired into a large metal tank, about 2 ft by 5 ft by 8 ft, filled with water. The water stops the bullet, fired at an angle of about 30° into the surface of the water, without causing any damage. After test-firing, the lid of the tank is removed and the bullet is collected. A bullet recovery tank is shown in Figure 13.11.

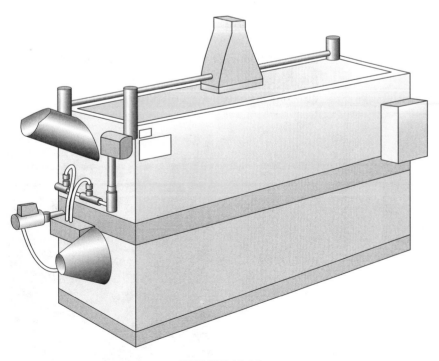

FIGURE 13.11

The bullet recovered from the tank and the questioned bullet are put under the two stages of a comparison microscope and rotated until the lands and grooves match (if they don't match, the bullets obviously were not fired from the same weapon. The forensic scientist then looks to see if the striation marks on the bullets match. If they do (forensic scientists like to see about 12 marks that match, but this is subjective), then the bullets were fired from the same gun; if they do not, one is rotated until the lands match up again and the striation marks are checked. The bullet may need to be rotated as many times as there are lands (for example, a Beretta 9-mm Luger with six lands and grooves may need to be rotated six times to check for all possible orientations). Two bullets fired from the same gun are shown in Figure 13.12.

FIGURE 13.12

Sometimes a criminal dismantles or destroys parts of a weapon in an attempt to keep the police from being able to test-fire it. In most states the central police laboratory has a huge inventory of all different types of weapons that can be used to reconstruct any missing or broken parts of a gun that must be test-fired. In New York State the reference firearm collection (RFC) is kept in Albany. The FBI also has an extensive collection, which is shown in Figure 13.13.

FIGURE 13.13

CARTRIDGE CASE MARKINGS

Sometimes all that is recovered at the crime scene are spent cartridge cases. A cartridge case can also pick up markings from the weapon that fired it that allow positive identification. Cartridge case marking are produced when the hardened steel of the gun comes to contact with the softer brass or nickel of the case. These markings include ejector, extractor, firing pin, breechblock, chamber, shear, and firing pin drag impressions. A cartridge is shown in Figure 13.14.

Bullet ①
Smokeless powder ②
Cartridge case ③
Primer ④

FIGURE 13.14

The **firing pin** of a gun is pushed forward by the hammer and strikes the primer (4 in Figure 13.14). The primer contains a primary explosive such as lead styphnate mixed with barium nitrate and antimony sulfide. This mixture detonates when struck by the firing pin and sets off the smokeless powder. Deflagration of the smokeless powder creates gases under high pressure that push the bullet out of the barrel. The primer cup is made from a soft metal that records an excellent impression of the firing pin. The firing pin mark from a comparison microscope is shown in Figure 13.15.

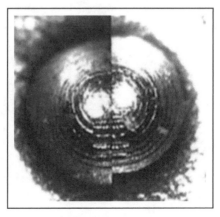

FIGURE 13.15

The primer also records an excellent impression of the metal part of the gun behind the bullet called the **breechblock**. This can be used to positively identify a cartridge case as having been fired from a questioned weapon. Two primers with the same breechblock striations are shown in Figure 13.16.

Extractor marks are made by whatever mechanism is used to remove the bullet from a semiautomatic, pump, lever, bolt, or other autoloading weapon. The **extractor** is normally a hook made from hardened metal, which scratches the metal case near the base. These striation marks can be used to identify the gun. Figure 13.17 shows two cases with the same extractor striations.

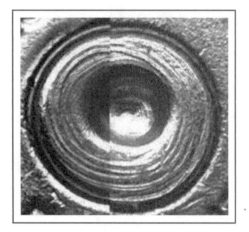

FIGURE 13.16

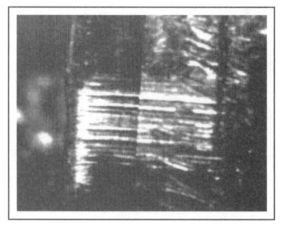

FIGURE 13.17

The **ejector** is a device for pushing the fired cartridge case out of a weapon. Two cases with the same ejector striations are shown in Figure 13.18.

Chamber marks are caused by expanding gases under high pressure forcing the sides of the cartridge case against the walls of the chamber. As the expanded case is dragged out of the chamber, it is scratched. Figure 13.19 shows two cases with the same chamber striations.

FIGURE 13.18

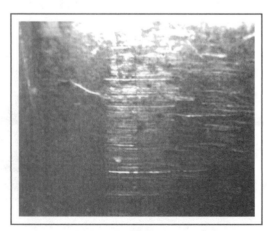

FIGURE 13.19

Shear marks occur when the back of the cartridge case slams up against the breechblock of a weapon. The hole where the firing pin comes out can produce an impression in the primer. Often, perpendicular motion of the barrel, and hence the cartridge case, produces a shear mark. Two primers with the same shear marks are shown Figure 13.20.

Firing pin drag occurs when there is relative motion of the cartridge and the firing pin drags as it retracts from the primer. This dragging action causes striation marks to be left on the primer. Figure 13.21 shows two primers with the same firing pin drag marks.

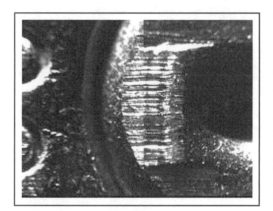

FIGURE 13.20   **FIGURE 13.21**

The pellets from shotguns do not come in contact with the barrel of the shotgun. They are held in a plastic cup until they exit the gun barrel (Figure 13.22). These pellets do not pick up any striations that can be used to tell from which barrel they were fired. The diameter of a pellet can be measured to determine the type of shotgun ammunition used (Table 13.5).

TABLE 13.5   *Regular Ammunition*

Shot Sizes

	F	T	BBB	BB	1	2	3	4	5	6	7	7¹/₂	8	8¹/₂	9
Pellet Diameter	●	●	●	●	●	●	●	●	●	●	●	●	●	●	●
Inches	.22	.20	.19	.18	.16	.15	.14	.13	.12	.11	.10	.095	.09	.085	.08
Millimeters	5.59	5.08	4.83	4.57	4.06	3.18	3.56	3.30	3.05	2.79	2.54	2.41	2.29	2.16	2.03

Buckshot Sizes

	No. 000	No. 00	No. 0	No. 1	No. 2	No. 3	No. 4
Pellet Diameter	●	●	●	●	●	●	●
Inches	.36	.33	.32	.30	.27	.25	.24
Millimeters	9.14	8.38	8.13	7.62	6.86	6.35	6.10

Slugs

Sabot Slug	Rifled Slug (Foster)

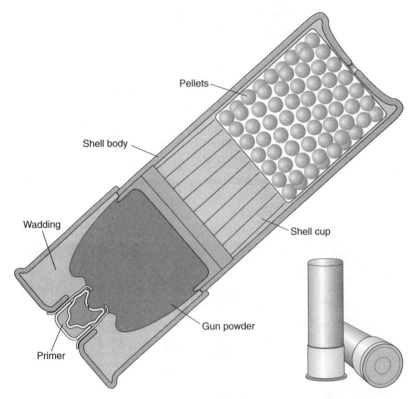

FIGURE 13.22

A handy rule of thumb is that pellets from the average shotgun spread about 1 in per yard of travel. A pattern of pellets from a shotgun that has formed a circle about 5 in diameter must have been fired from about 5 yd (15 ft) away. While the pellets cannot be matched to the barrel, the cartridge case markings can be matched to the weapon.

Some investigators prefer to use the **rule of sixes** in estimating the distance in the case of a shotgun wound. At a distance of 6 ft or less the wound appears as a single, round hole. At a distance of up to 6 yd it appears as a central hole with many small pellet holes around it. At a distance greater than 6 yd it is a series of small pellet holes. Figure 13.23 shows pellet spread in an X-ray.

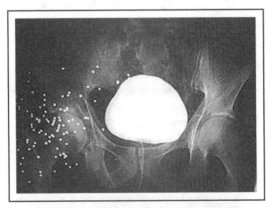

FIGURE 13.23

NATIONAL INTEGRATED BALLISTIC IDENTIFICATION NETWORK

The **National Integrated Ballistics Information Network (NIBIN)** was developed by a partnership between the FBI and the Bureau of Alcohol, Tobacco, and Firearms. It is a computer system that allows forensic scientists to enter digitally captured images of fired bullets and fired cartridge cases from crime scenes and test-fired firearms. This network allows the user to scan all the images in the database to see if there are any matches. The computer alerts the NIBIN user of any hits. A hit is defined as a linkage between at least two different crime investigations where there had previously been no known connection. Examples of some digital NIBIN images are shown in Figure 13.24.

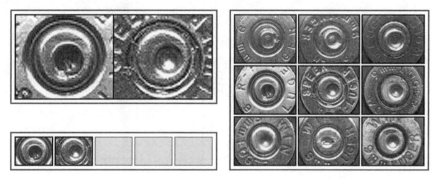

FIGURE 13.24

GUNSHOT RESIDUE

The detection of **gunshot residue (GSR)** on both the victim and the perpetrator of a crime involving a firearm is of great importance in criminal investigations. The presence of GSR on the victim can be used to estimate the distance between the victim and the gun, which can be very important in establishing whether the shooting was a case of suicide, self-defense, or murder. Blast distances can be estimated by reproducing the GSR patterns using identical weapons and ammunition. If the weapon is unknown, an estimate of the distance can be made from the wound and the GSR particles. Distances are described as contact, near contact, or intermediate contact. Beyond about 3 ft, the distance is difficult to determine.

A **contact shot** (often used in execution shootings or suicides) causes a star-shaped tear in any fabric (or skin over bone) because of the hot expanding gases. A circular bruise normally develops over the skin as a result of the pressure of the gases. Burning of fabric or skin due to the heat of the expanding gases is also seen.

A near-contact shot shows a very heavy concentration of GSR and considerable stippling (the presence of small abrasions caused by unburned powder and small metal fragments striking the skin).

An intermediate shot shows a wider, lighter GSR pattern. The bullet hole also tends to be more irregular as the bullet begins to tumble in flight.

An entrance wound is always smaller and has **inverted** margins (skin bent into the body). There is also bullet wipe around the entrance hole. An exit wound is larger and has **everted** margins (skin bent outward); it is also more irregular. Two examples from the same bullet wound, caused by a 9-mm handgun, show the entrance wound (Figure 13.25) and the exit wound (Figure 13.26).

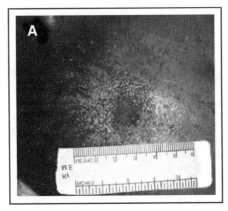

FIGURE 13.25

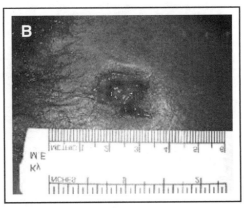

FIGURE 13.26

For shooting suspects two tests are commonly used to determine if a person has recently fired a weapon. The first is atomic absorption spectroscopy (AAS) (Chapter 4). When the primer at the back of the bullet is detonated by the strike of the firing pin, some of the blast goes backward and covers the hand of the shooter. The elements of the primer, lead, barium, and antimony, are very prominent in the particles of primer blast. In AAS analysis, the backs of the suspect's hands are rubbed with a cotton swab moistened with a dilute solution of nitric acid. The backs of both hands are swabbed, and the swabs are collected in separate packages. Alternatively, the hands of the suspect are dipped into separate packages filled with dilute nitric acid. The samples are then introduced into the AAS, and the presence of lead, barium, or antimony is determined.

The use of a **scanning electron microscope** with an **energy-dispersive X-ray** attachment **(SEM/EDX)** (Chapter 4) is becoming more popular because its increased sensitivity allows for the detection of GSR on a shooter's hand for a longer time after the firing. A metal stud is pressed against the hand of the suspect, and adhesive on the end of the stub picks up any GSR particles from the primer blast embedded in the skin. The particles are of a characteristic size and shape, and the elements lead, barium, and antimony can be determined from the EDX spectrum.

It should be noted that one type of weapon that does not produce a primer blast is a 22-caliber gun. This type of ammunition is called a **rim fire** cartridge because it has no central primer that is pressed into the bottom. Rim fire cartridges have a sealed case with the primer inside the case. Striking the rim of the cartridge fires the bullet. Since there is no way for the primer blast to blow backward, there is no GSR to detect on the back of the shooter's hand. Figure 13.27 shows a handgun that does not produce GSR on the shooter's hand. It is a 22-caliber Ruger Mark I pistol.

FIGURE 13.27

The gap that the primer blast escapes through is shown in Figure 13.28. The 38 special on the right has the primer inserted, and the 38 special on the left shows the hole into which the primer is pressed.

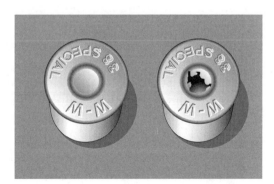

FIGURE 13.28

The sealed bottoms of 22-caliber cartridges are shown in Figure 13.29. There is no primer seam for gases to escape through.

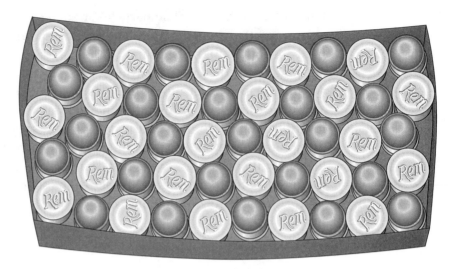

FIGURE 13.29

COLLECTION

Always unload a weapon before taking it to the crime lab. In picking up a weapon, never stick anything down the barrel; put on gloves and pick up the weapon on an area unlikely to produce useful fingerprints. In the case of a handgun, it is recommended that the trigger guard or checkered part of the grip be used to lift the gun. A revolver must have each bullet removed from the cylinder, and it is important to mark each cylinder chamber and bullet and note which cylinder and bullet were in line with the barrel. Each bullet should be packaged separately using a soft material as packing. For a semiautomatic handgun the magazine can be removed and bullets already in the magazine left in place. The slide must also be pulled back to remove any bullet in the chamber. It is important to record the position of the hammer and any safeties. If a weapon is discovered submerged, it is important not to take it out of the water and try to dry it. The weapon will certainly rust and cause a loss of fingerprint and barrel striation information. A submerged weapon should be sealed in a plastic container while still underwater. The plastic container, filled with the water and the gun, should then be delivered to the crime lab. Once there, the gun can be removed from the container and dried out under a nitrogen atmosphere which will prevent any rusting. How to pick up a revolver by the trigger guard is shown in Figure 13.30.

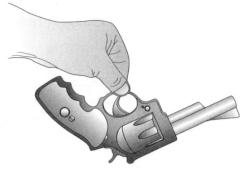

FIGURE 13.30

Figure 13.31 shows how to pick up a revolver by the grip.

FIGURE 13.31

To remove the bullets from a revolver, the cylinder should be opened and the bullets extracted (Figure 13.32).

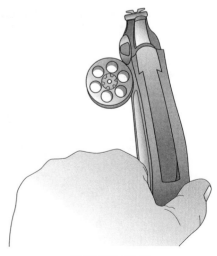

FIGURE 13.32

Some revolvers break open at the top so that the bullets can be removed (Figures 13.33 and 13.34).

FIGURE 13.33

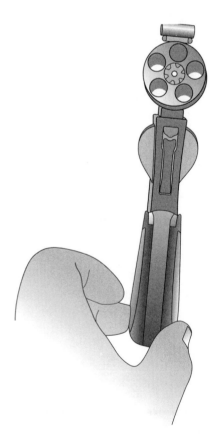

FIGURE 13.34

Figure 13.35 shows a semiautomatic 9-mm handgun. This weapon can be unloaded by releasing the magazine (the button on the right bottom of the trigger guard). Any ammunition still in the magazine can be left there. The slide must also be pulled back to empty any round in the chamber. Figure 13.36 shows the magazine removed, slide pulled back, and the bullet that was in the chamber next to the pistol.

FIGURE 13.35

FIGURE 13.36

In Figure 13.37 note the position of the hammer. This Taurus 9-mm model PT 99 AF has a half-cocked position that prevents the weapon from being fired by pulling the trigger.

FIGURE 13.37

Any bullets found at the crime scene should be removed in a way that does not compromise any of the striation marks on the sides of the bullets. If a bullet is embedded in a wall, the wall around the bullet should be removed and the section of wall with the bullet still embedded in it should sent to the crime lab. Once at the crime lab more sophisticated techniques can be used to dissolve the wall and remove the bullet without causing any damage. Never use a penknife to pry a bullet from an object. While this might be acceptable in movies, it may render a perfectly good bullet useless for comparison. If a bullet is lodged in a victim, the investigator can wait until a doctor removes it during surgery or autopsy.

REVIEW QUESTIONS

1. Black powder was discovered by the

   A. Black Panthers   B. English
   C. Swiss   D. Chinese

2. Early handguns lacked accuracy because of the absence of

   A. sights   B. rifling
   C. scopes   D. lead projectiles

3. The term *pistol* comes from the name of

   A. the inventor of the handgun
   B. a part of a plant
   C. a town in Tuscany, Italy
   D. a hand tool

4. A round lead ball weighing ½ lb just fits into the barrel of which gauge of shotgun?

   A. 12   B. 16
   C. 20   D. 410

5. Which gauge of shotgun has the largest-diameter barrel?

   A. 12   B. 16
   C. 20   D. 410

6. Which gauge is not really a gauge but a caliber?

   A. 12   B. 16
   C. 20   D. 410

7. Rifling is put in a gun barrel to make the bullet

   A. tumble   B. go faster
   C. penetrate steel   D. twist

8. Rifling in a gun barrel makes a bullet fly

    A. faster   B. straighter
    C. quieter   D. higher

9. The caliber of a rifle is determined by the distance from

    A. land to land   B. groove to groove
    C. breech to muzzle   D. base of bullet to nose

10. A revolver is a handgun that has the ammunition in a

    A. magazine   B. tube
    C. cylinder   D. breech

11. When the trigger of a semiautomatic pistol is pulled, the gun

    A. fires once   B. fires once and reloads
    C. keeps on firing   D. none of the above

12. Most police officers in the Unites States carry

    A. revolvers   B. single-shot handguns
    C. semiautomatic pistols   D. shotguns

13. Rifling is put into gun barrels by the twisting action of what type of cutter?

    A. broach   B. button
    C. mandrel   D. all of the above

14. Which type of cutter does not really cut the metal but uses compression?

    A. broach   B. button
    C. mandrel   D. all of the above

15. According to the Geneva Convention, Articles of War, the military cannot use expanding bullets that would cause unnecessary suffering. For this reason the U.S. military uses which type of bullet?

    A. FMJ   B. JHP
    C. SJHP   D. SP

16. A bullet recovered from a victim has a mass of 9.74 g. What is its mass in grains?

    A. 9.74   B. 100
    C. 150   D. 200

17. A bullet fragment that is 0.50 in long shows a rate of twist of about 14.5. What caliber is the bullet likely to be?

    A. 22   B. 357
    C. 40   D. 45

18. To match a bullet recovered from a victim with a suspect's weapon, the gun must be

A. put under a microscope
B. fitted to the questioned bullet
C. disassembled
D. test-fired into a water tank

19. A cartridge case can be matched to a gun by comparing which markings?

A. extractor
B. ejector
C. firing pin
D. all of the above

20. Which caliber of gun does not leave GSR on the shooter's hand?

A. 22
B. 38
C. 357
D. 45

21. A victim of a shotgun blast has a wound about 10 in in diameter. A reasonable estimate of the distance from the shotgun to the victim at the time of the shooting is

A. 10 ft
B. 10 yd
C. 6 yd
D. greater than 20 yd

22. The system that allows forensic scientists to enter digitally captured images of fired bullets is known as

A. IAFIS
B. CODIS
C. NIBIN
D. GSR

23. An exit wound is _____ than an entrance wound and has _____ margins.

A. smaller, inverted
B. smaller, everted
C. larger, inverted
D. larger, everted

24. A contact wound shows what on the skin?

A. a clean hole
B. a star pattern
C. nothing
D. small circular holes

25. One of the best methods for determining gunshot residue is

A. SEM/EDX
B. TLC
C. paraffin
D. GC/MS

Answers

1. D	10. C	18. D
2. B	11. B	19. D
3. C	12. C	20. A
4. A	13. D	21. B
5. A	14. B	22. C
6. D	15. A	23. D
7. D	16. C	24. B
8. B	17. A	25. A
9. A		

CHAPTER 14

GLASS

TERMS YOU SHOULD KNOW

borosilicate	fused silica	radial
concentric	jigsaw	refractive index
density	Kimax	safety glass
flat glass	laminated glass	soda lime
float glass	Pyrex	soft glass
fractures	quartz	tempered glass

CHEMICAL TYPES OF GLASS

There are three main chemical types of glass of interest to the forensic scientist: fused silica, soda lime (soft), and borosilicate. The main component of glass is the chemical silicon dioxide (SiO_2), which is more commonly referred to as sand. Even though sand is plentiful, glass used to be relatively rare and expensive because of the high temperatures (higher than 3000°F) required to turn sand into glass. Glass made from pure sand is known as **quartz** or **fused silica**. Fused silica is the strongest and most thermally stable form of glass known. If a piece of fused silica is heated in a flame until it glows red and then plunged into ice cold water, it will not crack. The windows for the space shuttle are made of fused silica.

Eventually someone discovered that adding other chemicals could lower the melting point of pure sand. A mixture of soda (Na_2O) and lime (CaO) lowered the melting point of the mixture to about 1300°F and produced the glass known as **soda lime** or **soft glass**. Soda lime glass is relatively cheap to make and is used in many applications such as windows, bottles, jars, and most glass items that do not have to be heated. Soda lime glass is not very stable thermally and tends to shatter when heated.

In **borosilicate** glass the lime is replaced with boron oxide (B_2O_3), so it contains soda, boron oxide, and sand. The resulting mixture melts at about 1650°F and produces a glass that is more thermally stable than soda lime glass but not as stable as fused silica glass. Borosilicate glass can be heated and will not crack (it will, however, crack if it is heated and then plunged into cold water). For this reason borosilicate glass is used for cooking and laboratory glassware. Borosilicate glasses are sold under the trade names **Pyrex** and **Kimax**.

GLASS PROCESSING—FLAT, TEMPERED, AND SAFETY

The three different types of chemical glass can be manufactured into final products using one of three different processes: flat, tempered, and safety. **Flat glass** is probably the most common glass and is used for windows. It is made from soda lime glass and is sometimes referred to as annealed glass. (After flat glass is made, it is heated and then slowly cooled by a process known as annealing, which removes any thermal stress in the glass and makes it stronger.) Flat glass can be made by rolling glass between metal drums to produce a glass known as sheet or plate glass. This glass picks up many distortions from the drums, and for this reason the process has been replaced with the float method. **Float glass** is produced by using a bath of molten tin to support the glass as it is being manufactured. This method produces distortion-free glass, which is then annealed.

In 1903 Edouard Benedictus, a French scientist, was working in his laboratory when he accidentally knocked over a glass flask and it fell to the ground. The flask broke, but the glass stayed in place because its surface was covered with a thin film of cellulose nitrate, a liquid plastic. The same week a newspaper in Paris ran an article about the increasing number of automobile accidents in the city. The main cause of injury and death was a result of drivers and passengers being cut by windshield glass. Edouard Benedictus realized that a thin-film of plastic could keep all the pieces of glass intact even if the windshield were broken. **Safety glass**, sometimes referred to as **laminated glass**, normally has three layers, two layers of soda lime glass with a thin film of plastic sandwiched between. A diagram of laminated glass is shown in Figure 14.1. The front windshield of all cars sold in the United States must be made of safety glass. The term *safety* is normally stamped right on the glass.

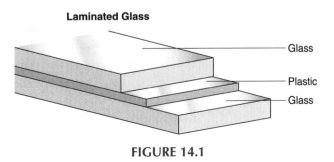

FIGURE 14.1

Another type of glass is **tempered glass**. Soda lime glass can be heated to about 1150°F, at which point it softens. Blowing jets of air against the surface of the glass then rapidly cools it. The surface of the glass solidifies before the inside, creating tension, and this makes the glass very strong. One can use the analogy of a balloon: The rubber of a balloon is very soft when there is no air in it. When the balloon is filled with air, the rubber surface becomes very hard because of the tension created by air pressure. The analogy can be taken even further: If the balloon is stuck with a pin, it will explode. If the surface of tempered glass is compromised, the glass will disintegrate into thousands of tiny fragments. Because this is actually considered a safety feature, the side and back windows of many cars are made of tempered glass. In an accident these windows disintegrate into many of tiny particles that are not likely to cut anyone. However, because windows help keep people from being ejected from vehicles, many groups are pushing the government to require that all automobile windows be made from laminated glass.

DENSITY AND REFRACTIVE INDEX

The density and refractive index (η) of glass vary according to the chemical type of the glass and the manufacturing process. The forensic scientist can determine the refractive index and density and tell what type of glass a fragment is made of. Within the same type of glass there are small variations in the density and refractive index that can help link a small glass fragment recovered from the sole of a suspect's shoe with the glass from a house window shattered in a burglary.

The **density** of glass fragments can be determined by the flotation method. A small shard of glass is put in a vial filled with bromoform. Since the density of bromoform is greater than that of glass, the shard floats. Next, either bromobenzene or ethanol is added drop by drop and the solution mixed with each addition. When the density of the mixture is the same as that of the glass, the shard neither sinks nor floats but is suspended about halfway between the top and bottom of the solution as if it is weightless. The mass and volume of the solution are then measured using a graduated cylinder and an electronic balance. Dividing the mass of the solution by the volume of the solution gives the density of the glass.

The **refractive index** of glass, as mentioned in Chapter 5, is a measure of how much it bends light. To determine the refractive index a glass shard is placed on a microscope slide and a drop of oil with a refractive index higher than that of the glass is added. The slide is then mounted in a special type of microscope that has a heated stage and a thermocouple to measure the temperature. As the temperature is increased, the refractive index of the oil decreases. When the refractive index of the oil and the glass are exactly the same, the lines of light pass straight through and the shard disappears. Automated microscopes interfaced with computers can perform the analysis and automatically determine the refractive index of the glass fragment.

TYPES OF FRACTURES

When a high-speed projectile passes through a glass window, it punctures the glass rather than causing the whole pane to shatter. The entrance side of the window shows a smaller, more regular hole, and the exit side of the window shows a larger, more irregular hole. In addition, two types of fracture patterns are produced. Small **concentric** circles form around the hole on the exit side. Radial fractures begin at the hole and radiate out like the spokes on a wheel, always stopping on preexisting fracture lines. Radial fractures can be used to determine the order in which multiple gunshots have been fired through a window.

Figure 14.2 is a sketch of a bullet passing through a window from left to right in which the entrance hole is shown to be smaller than the exit hole.

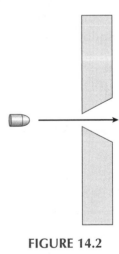

FIGURE 14.2

Figure 14.3 is a sketch of a window with the concentric and radial fractures labeled.

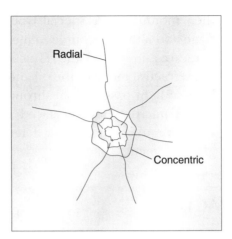

FIGURE 14.3

Radial fractures were used to help determine what really happened in a case that occurred several years ago. Two men, who were acquaintances, were drinking and watching a football game on television. They got into a heated argument, and one left saying he was going to get his gun and come back. When the police responded at the scene they found one man, with a gun, shot dead on the lawn outside the house. The other man was inside the house, also with a gun. He told the police that he saw, through his living room window, the other man waving a gun. He then went and got his own gun. He said the man outside fired his gun into his house and that he fired back in defense and the shot killed the man on the lawn. The police took the living room window to the crime lab to see if the physical evidence could corroborate the man's story. There were two holes in the window as shown in Figure 14.4.

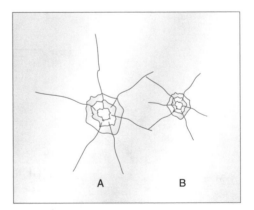

FIGURE 14.4

Bullet hole A had a larger hole on the outside of the window, and bullet hole B had a larger hole on the inside of the window. This meant that bullet hole A was from the shot fired by the man inside the house and bullet hole B was from the shot fired by the man standing on the lawn outside the house. Since the radial lines emanating from bullet hole B end on radial fractures from bullet hole A, bullet hole A was present first. This means that the man inside the house was the first to fire. The man outside was already fatally wounded when he fired a shot back into the house.

MATCHING GLASS SAMPLES

A forensic scientist is often asked if a glass fragment found at a crime scene can be matched to a glass fragment found on a suspect. If the glass fragment is very small, such as a tiny glass shard adhering to the suspect's clothing or shoes, the forensic scientist can determine the refractive index and density of the sample. This information can be used to determine the probability that the fragment of glass found on the suspect is from the same source of glass as that at the crime scene. This makes the glass sample class characteristic evidence.

However, sometimes the fragments of glass (this also applies to plastics, ceramics, and paint chips) are large enough that the randomly generated edges can be matched together like pieces of a **jig-saw** puzzle. This makes the glass evidence individual characteristic. An example of this type of match is shown in Figure 14.5. In this hypothetical case fragment A was found on the carpet of a burglarized house near a window that had been broken to gain access to the home. A suspect is arrested nearby, and a careful brushing of the suspect's clothing produces fragment B. The forensic scientist can use the matching edges of the two glass fragments to prove that the suspect was present at the crime scene.

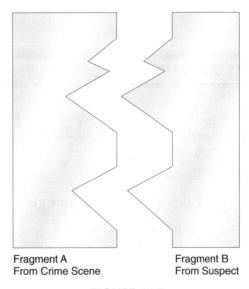

Fragment A
From Crime Scene

Fragment B
From Suspect

FIGURE 14.5

Sometimes a forensic scientist must reconstruct an entire window from the fragments left at the crime scene. This can be a daunting task if there are many pieces to fit together. Two techniques used to simplify the task involve ultraviolet light and polarized light. Ultraviolet light is absorbed by the side of the glass that was in contact with the liquid tin used in the flotation method of manufacturing flat glass. This allows the forensic scientist to arrange all the glass fragments from a window with the same side up. Polarized light is then used to make the stress lines in the glass visible. These lines can be used to help align the pieces of glass to reconstruct the window and can even be used to determine if a piece of glass found on a suspect matches the glass from the crime scene. Two pieces of flat glass held between two crossed polarizers are shown in Figure 14.6. Evidence like this can be used to connect a suspect to a crime scene even if there are no contact edges to match.

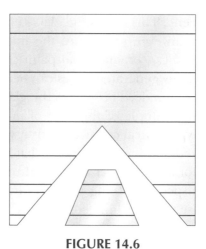

FIGURE 14.6

REVIEW QUESTIONS

1. The purest type of glass is called

   A. fused silica   B. soda lime
   C. borosilicate   D. ceramic

2. Cooking or laboratory glass is also called

   A. fused silica   B. soda lime
   C. borosilicate   D. ceramic

3. Soft glass is also called

   A. fused silica   B. soda lime
   C. borosilicate   D. ceramic

4. The strongest and most thermally stable form of glass is known as

   A. fused silica   B. soda lime
   C. borosilicate   D. ceramic

5. Float glass is produced using a bath of molten

   A. tin   B. mercury
   C. silver   D. lead

6. Safety glass is also known as _____ glass.

   A. soft   B. laminated
   C. tempered   D. flint

7. Soda lime glass, which is suddenly cooled from the outside, is called _____ glass.

   A. soft   B. laminated
   C. tempered   D. flint

8. The density of glass fragments is normally determined by the _____ method.

   A. paraffin   B. TLC
   C. hot stage microscope D. flotation

9. The refractive index of glass fragments is determined by the _____ method.

   A. paraffin   B. TLC
   C. hot stage microscope D. flotation

10. When a shard of glass is in a liquid of the same density, it

   A. floats
   B. sinks
   C. dissolves
   D. is suspended in the middle

11. When a shard of glass is in a liquid of the same refractive index, it

   A. disappears   B. dissolves
   C. looks darker   D. looks lighter

12. Fractures emanating outward from a hole are called _____ fractures.

   A. concentric   B. radial
   C. entrance   D. exit

13. Concentric fractures form on which side of glass?

    A. entrance   B. exit
    C. both   D. impossible to tell

14. Radial fractures always terminate on

    A. laminated glass   B. tempered glass
    C. existing fractures   D. all of the above

15. The exit side of a bullet hole in a glass window is _____ the entrance hole.

    A. smaller than   B. the same as
    C. larger than   D. impossible to locate

16. Refractive index and density serve as _____ evidence.

    A. individual characteristic   B. class characteristic
    C. fingerprint   D. hearsay

17. A jigsaw fit of larger glass fragments serves as _____ evidence.

    A. individual characteristic   B. class characteristic
    C. fingerprint   D. hearsay

18. Flat glass absorbs ultraviolet light on one side because of its contact with

    A. tin   B. mercury
    C. silver   D. lead

19. Stress striations in glass can be seen using _____ light.

    A. laser   B. ultraviolet
    C. infrared   D. polarized

20. Glass fragments can be found on a suspect's

    A. clothing   B. shoes
    C. hair   D. all of the above

Answers

1. A	8. D	15. C
2. C	9. C	16. B
3. B	10. D	17. A
4. A	11. A	18. A
5. A	12. B	19. D
6. B	13. B	20. D
7. C	14. C	

CHAPTER 15

HAIR

TERMS YOU SHOULD KNOW

anagen	cortex	keratinized
bulb	cuticle	medulla
Canada balsam	discontinuous	medullary index
catagen	follicle	spinous
continuous	follicular tag	telogen
coronal	imbricate	trace

THE HAIR FOLLICLE

Hair is composed mostly of protein produced from the hair **follicle**. The follicle is fed by tiny blood vessels and is shown in Figure 15.1.

Hair can be used for drug analysis because anything present in the bloodstream is also incorporated into the hair. The protein of the hair is **keratinized**, which makes it very strong. Hair is a very persistent form of physical evidence. Samples of hair from Napoleon are still around and have been tested for the presence of arsenic.

COMPONENTS OF HAIR—MEDULLA, CORTEX, AND CUTICLE

Human hair has three layers called the cuticle, cortex, and medulla. The **cuticle** is the outermost layer of the hair. It is made from keratinized proteins that are very strong and protect the inside of the hair. Cuticles look like shingles on the roof of a house.

The **cortex** is the middle portion of the hair extending from the cuticle to the medulla and containing the pigment granules.

The **medulla** is the central structure or core of the hair. In the case of human hair it may or may not be present. There are three common classifications of the medulla: fragmented or **trace**, interrupted or **discontinuous**, and **continuous**. Examples of these patterns are shown in Figure 15.2.

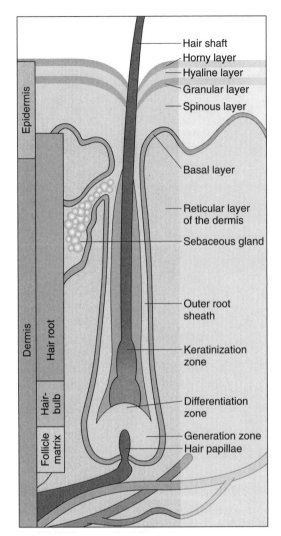

FIGURE 15.1

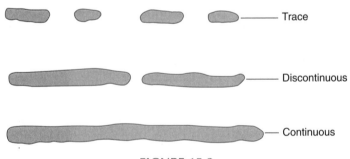

FIGURE 15.2

CUTICLE PATTERNS AND THE MEDULLARY INDEX

The cuticles of different species display different patterns. This allows the forensic investigator to determine to which species a hair belongs. Consider a jogger out West who is discovered dead. Was the attacker human or an animal? Forensic scientists can analyze the cuticle pattern of any hairs left at the crime scene and determine the answer. Humans have a very fine cuticle pattern, called **imbricate**, which is shown in Figure 15.3. The overlapping shingles of the cuticle always point toward the tip. In Figure 15.3 the root of the hair is on the left and the tip of the hair is on the right.

FIGURE 15.3

In Figure 15.4 a human hair is shown magnified 550 × by an SEM.

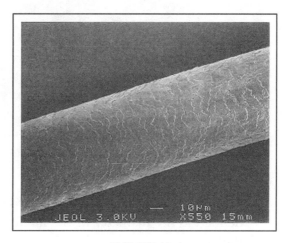

FIGURE 15.4

Animal hair often has much rougher cuticles, such as spinous or coronal. **Spinous** cuticle patterns are found on the hair of minks, seals, cats, and other animals and are not found on humans. The spinous pattern is shown in Figure 15.5.

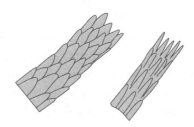

FIGURE 15.5

Coronal cuticle patterns are found on the hair of rodents and bats. The coronal pattern is shown in Figure 15.6. The hair from a bat is shown in Figure 15.7.

FIGURE 15.6

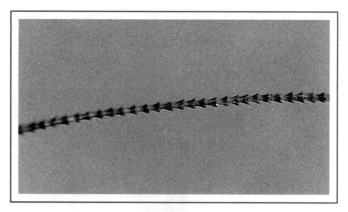

FIGURE 15.7

Another important feature of hair is the **medullary index**, which is defined as the diameter of the medulla divided by the diameter of the hair.

$$\text{Medullary index} = \frac{\text{diameter of medulla}}{\text{diameter of hair}}$$

In humans, the medullary index is always less than ⅓, and in animals it is greater than ½. The medulla traps air, which allows the hair to act as a better thermal insulator. It tends to be more important, and hence more prominent, in animals that need more protection from the cold.

To see the cuticle, a hair can be mounted directly on a glass slide (known as a dry mount) and viewed under a microscope using reflected light. To see the medulla, a drop of **Canada balsam** is put on the hair (known as a wet mount). Because it has about the same refractive index as the cuticle of the hair, the cuticle disappears and the forensic scientist can easily see and measure the medulla.

COMPARISON OF HAIR SAMPLES

Samples of hair from the crime scene can be compared to hair samples obtained from a suspect. Hairs from humans show a certain natural variability, and for this reason a representative sample of hair must be collected from the suspect. Head hairs tend to be uniform in diameter down the entire length of the shaft and have a circular cross section. Beard hairs have a triangular cross section. Pubic hairs have varying diameters and tend to be kinked. A pubic hair is shown in Figure 15.8.

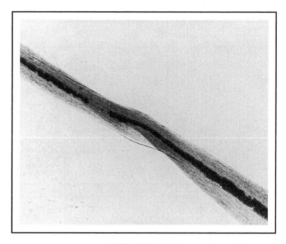

FIGURE 15.8

It is recommended that at least 25 head hairs or pubic hairs be randomly collected from a suspect. There should be a combination of hairs pulled and combed from various regions.

To compare hair samples, the forensic scientist uses a comparison microscope. The diameters of the hair, medulla (if present), and pigment granules are all compared. It is important to take into account that there may be a significant time interval between when the sample was found at the crime scene and when the hair was collected from the suspect. Forensic scientists use the rule of thumb that hair grows at a constant rate of about 1 cm per month. Hair coloring looks almost like a paint job on the surface of the hair. Natural hair color comes from the tiny pigment granules in the cortex of the hair. Hair that is bleached has had the color removed from these pigment granules. If hair found at the crime scene shows coloring 1 cm from the root and hair collected from a suspect 1 month later shows the same coloring 2 cm from the root, there is a good possibility that the two hair samples come from the same individual (assuming everything else matches up under the comparison microscope).

PHASES OF HAIR GROWTH

Microscopic examination of the root or bulb of a hair indicates what phase of growth the hair is in. Hair goes through three distinct phases of growth: anagen, catagen, and telogen. The **anagen** phase is the initial growth phase of the hair, and at this stage the hair is actively growing. A hair in the anagen phase is shown in Figure 15.9. Note the **bulb**.

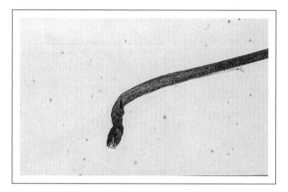

FIGURE 15.9

The **catagen** phase is a transition phase between the actively growing anagen phase and the dormant telogen phase. A hair in the catagen phase is shown in Figure 15.10. Note the **bulb**.

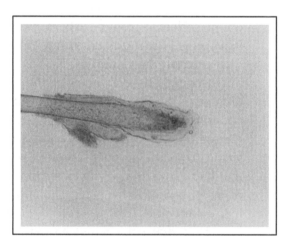

FIGURE 15.10

The **telogen** phase is the resting or dormant phase of hair growth. In the telogen phase the hair can fall out naturally. A hair in the telogen phase is shown in Figure 15.11. Note the **bulb**.

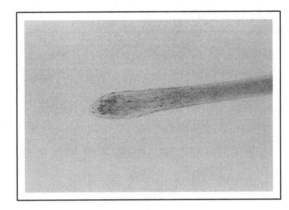

FIGURE 15.11

Figure 15.12 illustrates the idealized bulb shapes for the various stages of hair growth.

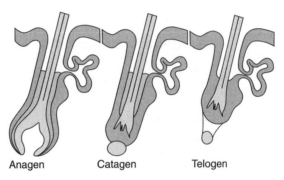

Anagen   Catagen   Telogen

FIGURE 15.12

FOLLICULAR TAGS

When a hair is forcibly removed, some of the tissue and blood vessels from the hair follicle and surrounding skin are sometimes removed with it. This adhering tissue is referred to as a **follicular tag**. While a hair itself is a poor source of DNA, the follicular tag can sometimes yield usable amounts of DNA. This can lead to the hair being an individual characteristic piece of evidence. Follicular tags are most common on the bulbs of hairs that have been forcibly removed. The absence of a follicular tag however, does not mean that the hair was not forcibly removed. Some hairs just come out clean, especially if they are in the telogen phase.

REVIEW QUESTIONS

1. Hair is mostly composed of

   A. protein   B. carbohydrate
   C. lipids   D. bone

2. The outer protein of hair is especially strong because it is

   A. thick   B. calcified
   C. keratinized   D. helical

3. Hair samples from Napoleon showed traces of

   A. French wine   B. arsenic
   C. dye   D. lead

4. The outer layer of the hair is called the

   A. cuticle   B. medulla
   C. cortex   D. root

5. The inside layer of the hair is called the

   A. cuticle   B. medulla
   C. cortex   D. root

6. The string of cells running down the center of the hair is called the

   A. cuticle   B. medulla
   C. cortex   D. root

7. The medullary index for humans is

   A. less than ⅓   B. equal to ⅓
   C. equal to ½   D. greater than ½

8. The medullary index for most animals is

   A. less than ⅓   B. equal to ⅓
   C. equal to ½   D. greater than ½

9. The cuticle pattern for humans is called

   A. coronal   B. spinous
   C. imbricate   D. none of the above

10. A common fluid used by forensic scientists to help see the medulla is

    A. acetone   B. clove oil
    C. bromobenzene   D. Canada balsam

11. Head hair tends to show what type of diameter along its shaft?

    A. uniform   B. kinked
    C. triangular   D. variable

12. Beard hair tends to show what type of diameter along its shaft?

    A. uniform   B. kinked
    C. triangular   D. variable

13. A least how many hairs should be removed from a suspect's head?

    A. 1   B. 12
    C. 25   D. 100

14. What is the average rate at which hair grows per month?

    A. 1 cm   B. 1 in
    C. 1/2 cm   D. 2 in

15. The growth phase of hair is called the _____ phase.

    A. anagen   B. catagen
    C. telogen   D. bulb

16. The phase between the actively growing phase and the dormant phase is called the _____ phase.

    A. anagen   B. catagen
    C. telogen   D. bulb

17. The resting or dormant stage of hair growth is called the _____ phase.

    A. anagen   B. catagen
    C. telogen   D. bulb

18. DNA can sometimes be extracted from the _____ adhering to the hair root.

    A. follicular tag   B. proteins
    C. lipids   D. pigments

19. Pigment cells are generally located in the _____ of the hair.

    A. cuticle   B. medulla
    C. cortex   D. root

20. Hair samples are best matched using a

    A. stereomicroscope   B. polarizing microscope
    C. SEM   D. comparison microscope

Answers

1. A	8. D	15. A
2. C	9. C	16. B
3. B	10. D	17. C
4. A	11. A	18. A
5. C	12. C	19. C
6. B	13. C	20. D
7. A	14. A	

CHAPTER 16

FINGERPRINTS

TERMS YOU SHOULD KNOW

12-point match	epidermis	Physical Developer
anthropometry	friction ridges	plastic fingerprints
bifurcation	Henry system	ridge characteristics
crossing	iodine fuming	ridge ending
crossover	island	short ridge
cyanoacrylate	latent fingerprints	silver nitrate
dermis	minutiae	spur
dusting powders	ninhydrin	Superglue fuming
enclosure	papillae	visible fingerprints

HISTORY OF PERSONAL IDENTIFICATION

In the eighth century the Chinese used thumbprints to seal important documents. There is no record of whether they were actually used for identification, and there was no systematic classification. Quntilian, a Roman lawyer, made use of a bloody handprint in a murder case in 1000 A.D. and the work of Francis Galton set the theoretical background for the use of fingerprints as a means of personal identification.

In 1879 Alphonse Bertillon published his first book on **anthropometry**, a personal identification method based on 11 body measurements. This was the first system of personal identification used by the police. In 1892 Francis Galton published the book *Fingerprints* and proposed the use of fingerprints as a means of personal identification. In his book, Galton explained the many different characteristics present in a fingerprint and how they can combine to form a unique print for each person. He did a statistical analysis of the possible combinations of the characteristics and showed that fingerprints are unique. He also demonstrated that fingerprints are permanent and don't change with a person's age like bone measurements. Police still favored the system of anthropometry, partly because it worked and partly because it was the system they were used to. All prison records were based on anthropometry.

In 1902 the New York Civil Service began the practice of fingerprinting everyone who took a civil service exam. In 1903 a man by the name of William West was convicted and sent to Leavenworth Penitentiary. When convicted, he received an extra severe sentence because he was a repeat offender. He protested the sentence, stating that he had never been convicted before. When William West arrived at prison, the officials made the 11 body measurements and found that they matched the anthropometry measurements of another prisoner already at Leavenworth and also named William West. The two men looked alike as well, which made it difficult for prison officials to tell them apart. This spelled the end of anthropometry. In 1903 the New York State prison system started fingerprinting all the inmates. And in 1904, because of the William West case, Leavenworth Penitentiary also switched to fingerprinting as its primary means of personal identification. In 1905 the U.S. Army began using fingerprints, and the U.S. Department of Justice set up the Bureau of Criminal Identification in Washington, DC, to centralize and standardize the use of fingerprinting in the United States. In 1907 the U.S. Navy began using fingerprints, and the Bureau of Criminal Identification was moved to Leavenworth Penitentiary. In 1918 Edmond Locard recommended that 12 points of comparison be required to prove the identity of an individual. In 1924 the U.S. Congress established the FBI as the central repository for all fingerprint information. In 2004 the FBI crime lab identification section began using the Integrated Automated Fingerprint Identification System (IAFIS) with more than 46 million records in its database. The more than 200 million fingerprint cards already collected are still kept on file.

THREE FUNDAMENTAL PRINCIPLES OF FINGERPRINTS

There are three guiding principles that make fingerprints especially useful for personal identification in forensic science. These are known as the three fundamental principles of fingerprints. The first principle is that fingerprints are unique. They are an image of the **friction ridges** present on the surfaces of the fingers, which give us better gripping ability especially on wet surfaces. This is similar to the function of treads on car tires. These raised ridges of skin are formed randomly when the fetus is inside the womb. They do not form unending parallel lines but have different characteristics called **minutiae**. There are various kinds of **ridge characteristics** or minutiae including the following (Figure 16.1).

Bifurcation: A single friction ridge that has split into two

Ridge ending: The point where a friction ridge ends

Short ridge: A single friction ridge that runs only a short distance

Dot (island): A friction ridge that is about as long as it is wide

Enclosure: A single ridge that splits in two and then comes back together to form a single ridge again

Spur: A bifurcation in which one of the ridges ends after a short distance

Crossing: Two ridges that cross over one another and form an X

Crossover: A short ridge that runs between two parallel ridges.

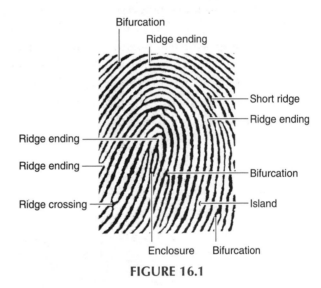

FIGURE 16.1

With the advent of computerized fingerprint scanning, the most important minutiae are bifurcations and ridge endings. In fact, many experts consider bifurcations and ridge endings the only true minutiae, with all the rest being combinations of the two.

There are many more possible combinations of these minutiae then there are people on the earth. This means that every fingerprint is unique. In more than 100 years of recording fingerprints, no two people have ever been found to have the same fingerprints. Even the fingerprints of identical twins (who have the same DNA) are different. In a court case, the forensic scientist often shows a point-by-point comparison of minutiae to establish the identity of the person who left the fingerprint. It is customary to show at least a **12-point match** (Figure 16.2), but the exact number depends on the print and on the expert's experience.

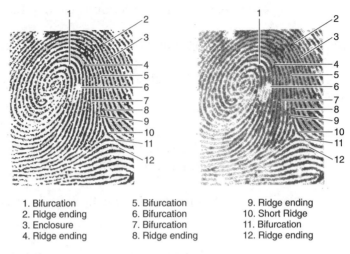

1. Bifurcation	5. Bifurcation	9. Ridge ending
2. Ridge ending	6. Bifurcation	10. Short Ridge
3. Enclosure	7. Bifurcation	11. Bifurcation
4. Ridge ending	8. Ridge ending	12. Ridge ending

FIGURE 16.2

The second fundamental principle of fingerprinting is that fingerprints do not change over a person's lifetime. The longest interval on record involved a man who was arrested in his late seventies and a fingerprint search showed that he had been arrested 60 years earlier. Simply removing the skin does not change a fingerprint pattern. The friction ridge pattern is determined in the womb by the dermal **papillae**, cells that form a layer between the **epidermis** and the **dermis** (Figure 16.3).

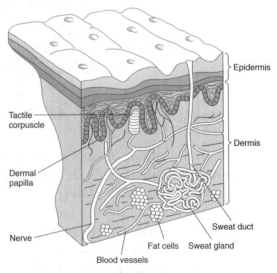

FIGURE 16.3

The papillae are about 2 mm beneath the surface of the skin and are a negative template of the friction ridges on the surface of the skin. A cut deep enough to cause a displacement of the papillae also causes a displacement, or a scar, on the surface of the skin. The scar does not change the fingerprint.

The notorious bank robber John Dillinger tried to remove his fingerprints by using a corrosive acid. He had the outer layer of the skin (the epidermis) removed by acid and had plastic surgery performed on his face to conceal his identity. He was shot and killed on July 22, 1934, during the famous "lady in red" incident outside the Biograph Theater (Figure 16.4).

FIGURE 16.4

The term *lady in red* derives from the incident in which the FBI was looking for Dillinger, and an informant, Ana Cumpanas, stepped forward and said she would be going to the theater with him in the near future. She wanted the cash reward offered for the capture of Dillinger and to be allowed to stay in the United States (she was scheduled for deportation back to Romania as an undesirable alien). She was told to wear a bright red dress so that the agents waiting outside the theater could easily spot both her and her date, John Dillinger. When she exited the theater, the agents attempted to arrest the man she was with, but he fled. The agents shot and killed the man, but there was some question whether he was truly John Dillinger. The fingerprints of the dead man were taken, and in spite of the presence of a tremendous amount of scar tissue, the FBI was able to match them to those of John Dillinger from fingerprint records taken earlier in his career.

The third fundamental principle of fingerprints is that they display patterns that allow them to be classified. This is not as important nowadays, but before the advent of computerized fingerprint searches all matches had to be done manually. It was impossible for an agent to manually compare a fingerprint card with 200 million cards kept on file at the FBI, and for this reason fingerprint cards were broken down into small groups or classifications. The primary FBI system (also known as the **Henry system**) was based on the presence of whorls on the fingers. There are three basic fingerprint patterns: loop, whorl, and arch. Each finger is assigned a numerical value, depending on which finger it is, if it has a whorl pattern (Table 16.1). If it has a loop or an arch it is assigned a zero. The numbers are added up in the numerator and in the denominator, and the resulting fraction is known as the Henry, or FBI primary, classification. Many people do not have any whorl patterns in their fingerprints and have a Henry classification of 1/1. About 25% of the population falls into this category.

16	+	8	+	4	+	2	+	1	+	1
Right index		Right ring		Left thumb		Left middle		Left pinky		
Right thumb		Right middle		Right pinky		Left index		Left ring		
16	+	8	+	4	+	2	+	1	+	1

TABLE 16.1

Finger	Whorl Value	Finger	Whorl Value
Right thumb	16	**Left thumb**	4
Right index	16	**Left index**	2
Right middle	8	**Left middle**	2
Right ring	8	**Left ring**	1
Right pinky	4	**Left pinky**	1

The author has the fingerprint patterns given in Table 16.2.

TABLE 16.2

Finger	Pattern	Value	Finger	Pattern	Value
Right thumb	Whorl	16	**Left thumb**	Loop	0
Right index	Loop	0	**Left index**	Loop	0
Right middle	Arch	0	**Left middle**	Loop	0
Right ring	Whorl	8	**Left ring**	Loop	0
Right pinky	Loop	0	**Left pinky**	Loop	0

This results in the following fraction.

$$\frac{0 + 8 + 0 + 0 + 0 + 1}{16 + 0 + 0 + 0 + 0 + 1} = \frac{9}{17}$$

Somewhere in the FBI headquarters there is a box in the 9/17 classification section with the author's fingerprint card (the card is the result of a pistol permit and not a criminal offense).

VISUALIZATION OF LATENT AND PLASTIC FINGERPRINTS

In general, three types of fingerprints can be found at the crime scene: visible, plastic, and latent. **Visible fingerprints** can be easily seen by the investigator and photographed without any preparation. Examples of visible fingerprints include those made by oil, grease, paint, or blood. **Plastic fingerprints** are made in soft material that takes an impression of the fingerprint. Plastic fingerprints can be present in pools of blood after they have hardened. **Latent fingerprints** are fingerprints that are invisible to the human eye. Latent fingerprints require treatment to make them visible. These procedures make the oils and salts left behind when an object is touched visible to the eye. The oils and salts are produced by the sweat glands that feed into the friction ridges of the epidermis (Figure 16.5).

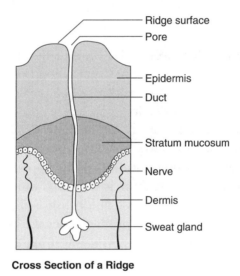

Cross Section of a Ridge

FIGURE 16.5

Latent fingerprints can be visualized by many methods. In fact, this is an area of intense research and new methods are being discovered all the time. These techniques can be separated into two groups, physical and chemical.

Physical methods include the use of lasers and dusting powders. Lasers work because there are chemicals in the skin secretions left behind by the finger touching the surface that undergo fluorescence. When these chemicals are exposed to a shorter wavelength (such as ultraviolet) and reemit the light in the visible range, the process is called fluorescence. The investigator normally wears goggles that block any ultraviolet and interfering light. The advantage of lasers is that large areas can be covered in a relatively short period of time. The disadvantage is that the method is not as sensitive as some others although treatment with certain chemicals helps increase the natural fluorescence of fingerprints.

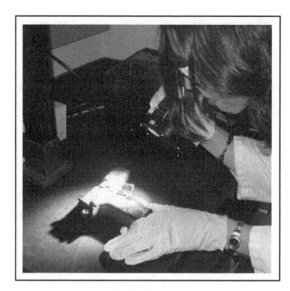

FIGURE 16.6

Dusting powders are used in one of the oldest and most trusted methods of latent fingerprint visualization (Figure 16.6). The oils left behind are slightly sticky, and very fine particles adhere to surfaces. If the particles, or dusting powders, contrast well with the background, latent fingerprints will become visible. Black dusting powders are well suited to white surfaces, and white powders are used on dark surfaces. Dusting powders can be applied using different techniques. The most common is a brush, which can be camel hair, feather duster, or fiberglass. The brush is dipped into the powder, and the powder is gently sprinkled over the print. Excess powder is very gently brushed off or blown away using a can of compressed air. A magnetic brush can be used with special magnetic dusting powder to remove the excess without ever coming in contact with the print. Many modern dusting powders are also fluorescent. In the case of fluorescent powder the lights can be turned off and an ultraviolet light turned on, and the fingerprint glows in the dark. The contrast between the surface and the powder is not important for fluorescent powders. Dusting works best on hard, nonporous surfaces.

Chemical methods of latent fingerprint identification include **Superglue fuming**, iodine sublimation, ninhydrin, and silver nitrate. Superglue is composed of the chemical cyanoacrylate ester. When **cyanoacrylate** fumes come in contact with the oils of a latent fingerprint, a chemical reaction occurs. The cyanoacrylate polymerizes into a hard, white substance that forms an exact image of the fingerprint. A fuming hood can be used to treat large objects, but a simpler procedure is to use a small fish tank with a cover. A metal cap is placed on a light bulb inside the tank. The object to be fumed is placed inside the tank, a few drops of Superglue are put in the cap, and the light bulb is turned on. In a few minutes the image of the fingerprint appears. Since the image is milky white, the contrast is not always good, but there are several fluorescent dyes that can be applied to a Superglue-fumed fingerprint to enhance the image. Additionally, a cyanoacrylate print can be dusted with powder and the print lifted (Figure 16.7).

FIGURE 16.7

Iodine is a solid at room temperature, but it undergoes sublimation (goes directly into the vapor phase) when heated. The iodine vapor coats the unsaturated oils of a latent fingerprint, producing a golden-brown image. The image will quickly fade unless it is sprayed with a dilute solution of starch. The starch reacts with the iodine, creating a dark blue image of the latent fingerprint. **Iodine fuming** can be done in a cabinet or tank, like Superglue fuming, but it also has been used in larger enclosed areas such as the inside of a car.

Ninhydrin is a chemical that can be sprayed from an aerosol can onto a latent fingerprint. The object is then put in a warming oven and left to develop for about 24 h. This method is very sensitive and easy to use (Figure 16.8).

FIGURE 16.8

Silver nitrate reacts with chloride in the salts of latent fingerprints. The product of the reaction is the white solid silver chloride. The silver chloride print is then exposed to intense light, which causes a photoreduction of the silver salt to silver metal. The silver metal forms a black image of the print. The salts from a fingerprint will outlast the oils (which are organic) if there is no water to wash the salts away. Silver nitrate has been used to develop latent fingerprints on documents more than 2000 years old. Most forensic investigators use a mixture of silver nitrate, ferric nitrate, ferrous ammonium sulfate, citric acid, and *N*-dodecylamine acetate called **physical developer**. The item to be visualized is first dipped in a maleic acid prewash and then put in physical developer.

RECORDING AND LIFTING OF FINGERPRINTS

Fingerprints should always be photographed as soon as they are visualized. A camera fitted with a fixed-length adapter is used to produce a one-to-one image. A fingerprint camera is shown in Figure 16.9.

FIGURE 16.9

If the fingerprint is on a piece of paper or a weapon, the entire carrier of fingerprint should be sent to the crime lab with the fingerprint still on it. If the fingerprint is on an immovable object, or one too large to send to the crime lab, the fingerprint should be lifted. This is accomplished using a clear plastic with adhesive on one side called lifting tape (Figure 16.10). In a pinch, clear masking or packing tape can also be used. The tape is placed over the visualized fingerprint and then removed and placed on a white or black background card (whichever provides the best contrast). Fingerprints on porous surfaces, such as paper, are best visualized by using a chemical technique such as iodine fuming, ninhydrin, or physical developer.

FIGURE 16.10

INTEGRATED AUTOMATED FINGERPRINT IDENTIFICATION SYSTEM

Fingerprints are very useful in confirming personal identification. When a person is arrested, they are always fingerprinted, and these prints can be sent to the FBI to check a defendant's identity. This must be positively established before the trial since the person might have previous convictions, which would affect the sentencing, or might be wanted for another, more serious crime. The police cannot always count on the criminal to tell them their true identity, so their fingerprints can be sent to the FBI, which keeps more than 47 million fingerprint records.

Before the advent of the Integrated Automated Fingerprint System (IAFIS), fingerprint cards had to be classified manually and visually checked against all the fingerprint cards in a group. A typical turnaround time was about 2 weeks. The biggest problem was that the classification system was based on ten fingerprints. This was fine for the identification of an arrested defendant, but a criminal was hardly ever cooperative enough to leave good fingerprints from all ten fingers at a crime scene. Single or partial prints recovered at the crime scene could be checked against those for only a small group of suspects. In the 1970s the FBI, the British Home Office, and the Japanese National Police Agency developed a computerized method of scanning fingerprint images into a computer and creating software to digitize the minutiae. The system was called the automated fingerprint identification system (AFIS). An explanation of how AFIS works is given in Figure 16.11 from the state of California fingerprint imaging system.

Fingerprint pattern classifications are used to subdivide large databases in traditional law enforcement AFIS applications.

Reference print

Candidate fingerprint minutiae file

Statistical correlation

FINGERPRINT MINUTIAE

Minutiae points are the X, Y coordinates and ridge direction vector associated with ridge endings or bifurcations that naturally occur in all fingerprints

FIGURE 16.11

Scanning was originally done using fingerprint cards, but now there are specialized scanners that can scan a person's fingers directly. The main drawback of the original AFIS was that several different systems were available from different manufacturers that were not compatible with each other. The FBI set a standard to make all the records compatible, and the new system was called IAFIS. The great thing about IAFIS is that the search is not based on a ten-finger system, so a partial fingerprint can be searched against all 47 million records. This has made fingerprints a much more important piece of physical evidence, which is why there is so much renewed interest in the development of latent prints. The FBI describes their latent print unit and IAFIS as follows.

The Latent Print Unit conducts all work pertaining to the examination of latent prints on evidence submitted to the FBI Laboratory. Latent prints are impressions produced by the ridged skin on human fingers, palms, and soles of the feet. Unit examiners analyze and compare latent prints to known prints of individuals in an effort to make identifications or exclusions. The uniqueness, permanence, and arrangement of the friction ridges allow Unit examiners to positively match two prints and to determine whether an area of a friction ridge impression originated from one source to the exclusion of all others. A variety of techniques, including use of chemicals, powders, lasers, alternate light sources, and other physical means, are employed in the detection and development of latent prints. In instances where a latent print has limited quality and quantity of detail, Unit personnel may perform microscopic examinations in order to effect conclusive comparisons.

In 1999 the FBI developed and implemented a new automated fingerprint system known as the Integrated Automated Fingerprint Identification System (IAFIS). Although IAFIS is primarily a ten-print system for searching an individual's fingerprints to determine whether a prior arrest record exists and then maintaining a criminal arrest record history for each individual, the system also offers significant latent print capabilities. Using IAFIS, a latent print specialist can digitally capture latent print and ten-print images and perform several functions with each. These include:

Enhancement to improve image quality;

Comparison of latent fingerprints against suspect ten-print records retrieved from the criminal fingerprint repository;

Searches of latent fingerprints against the ten-print fingerprint repository when no suspects have been developed;

Automatic searches of new arrest ten-print records against an unsolved latent fingerprint repository; and

Creation of special files of ten-print records in support of major criminal investigations.

Using the IAFIS fingerprint search capability against data from the FBI Criminal Justice Information Services (CJIS) Division, which maintains the world's largest repository of fingerprint records, the Unit has made identifications in cases for which no known suspects were named for comparison purposes and in cases in which latent prints on crime scene-related evidence were not identified with suspects named in the investigation.

Personnel from the Latent Print Unit also form the nucleus of the FBI Disaster Squad, which renders assistance in identifying victims at disaster scenes. This squad may be deployed upon official request from the ranking law enforcement official at the scene, the medical examiner or coroner in charge of victim identification, the ranking official of a public transportation carrier, the National Transportation Safety Board, the Federal Aviation Administration, or the U.S. Department of State in instances of foreign disasters involving U.S. citizens. Since 1940, the Disaster Squad has responded to over 200 disasters worldwide and has identified over half of the victims by fingerprints or footprints.

Unit personnel use special techniques in the examination of fingers and hands of unknown deceased individuals to obtain identifiable prints. Automated searches of identifiable prints can be conducted in the IAFIS database, which contains over 36 million individuals' known fingerprints. If classifiable prints are obtained from all ten fingers, manual searches can also be conducted in the CJIS civil fingerprint file.

The Unit also provides training in all aspects of latent print work to local, state, federal, and foreign law enforcement personnel. In addition, the Unit conducts research to evaluate new technologies, procedures, and equipment.

Occasionally, in matters initiated by entities outside the FBI, the Unit will serve as a final authority when the authenticity, value, and/or identification of friction ridge impressions is questioned or challenged.

IAFIS has made the search of the FBI's enormously large fingerprint database a rapid process. However, this process is not 100% accurate, and the identification of a match always requires a human expert. In January 2004, Jeremy Bryan Jones was arrested in Georgia for trespassing. He gave the police an alias, John Paul Chapman, because he was wanted for rape, sodomy, and jumping bond. An arrest warrant was out for him under his true name, Jeremy Bryan Jones. Jones was fingerprinted, using an IAFIS scan and the results were checked against the 47 million records in the IAFIS system. The system did not correctly match Jones prints, which were already in the database, and instead created a new file under the name Chapman. Jeremy Bryan Jones was arrested and freed a total of three times because of this computer glitch. It is believed that he was responsible for the murder of four women during that time.

IAFIS handles more than 50,000 fingerprint comparisons everyday, resulting in the arrest of thousands of criminals every month. It takes about 5 min for the IAFIS to search its database, and it has dramatically improved the arrest rate associated with fingerprints. While no human error was involved in the Jeremy Bryan Jones case, the FBI is conducting an internal review to determine what went wrong and how to improve the system.

REVIEW QUESTIONS

1. Initially, most police departments used which system of personal identification?

   A. anthropometry   B. fingerprinting
   C. photographs   D. DNA

2. The fingerprint system was adopted at Leavenworth after two people, both named _____, could not be distinguished by body measurements.

   A. Jesse James   B. William West
   C. Al Capone   D. John Dillinger

3. The first principle of fingerprints is that fingerprints

   A. are hard to forge   B. are unique
   C. do not change with age   D. display patterns

4. The second principle of fingerprints is that fingerprints

   A. are hard to forge   B. are unique
   C. do not change with age   D. display patterns

5. The third principle of fingerprints is that fingerprints

   A. are hard to forge   B. are unique
   C. do not change with age   D. display patterns

6. A single friction ridge that splits into two ridges is called a

   A. bifurcation   B. ridge ending
   C. enclosure   D. dot

7. A friction ridge that is about as long as it is wide is called a

   A. bifurcation   B. ridge ending
   C. enclosure   D. dot

8. It is customary to show how many points of comparison when comparing fingerprints in court?

   A. 2   B. 4
   C. 12   D. 24

9. The friction ridge pattern of a fingerprint is established by the

   A. dermis   B. dermal papillae
   C. sweat pores   D. sweat gland

10. A famous outlaw who tried to hide his fingerprints by dissolving his fingertip skin with acid was

    A. Al Capone   B. Richard Hauptmann
    C. William West   D. John Dillinger

11. The Henry system is based on which pattern?

    A. loops   B. whorls
    C. arches   D. none of the above

12. A person has a whorl on his right thumb, right middle finger, and left middle finger. This person has what primary FBI classification?

    A. 1/1   B. 3/25
    C. 17/25   D. 25/25

13. A fingerprint that can be easily seen is called a _____ print.

    A. visible   B. plastic
    C. latent   D. partial

14. A fingerprint embedded in a soft material is called a _____ print.

    A. visible   B. plastic
    C. latent   D. partial

15. A fingerprint that is invisible is called a _____ print.

    A. visible   B. plastic
    C. latent   D. partial

16. Cyanoacrylate esters are used to visualize latent prints in which method?

    A. physical developer   B. infrared photography
    C. Superglue   D. dusting powders

17. Physical developer contains which chemical?

    A. silver nitrate   B. cyanoacrylate
    C. carbon   D. iodine

18. At a crime scene a fingerprint on a coffee cup should be

    A. lifted
    B. broken off
    C. sent to the crime lab on the cup
    D. none of the above

19. The first thing to do after visualizing a fingerprint is to

    A. lift it   B. photograph it
    C. all of the above   D. none of the above

20. Which methods are particularly useful for visualizing prints on porous surfaces?

    A. iodine fuming
    C. physical developer
    B. ninhydrin
    D. all of the above

21. The computerized system used by the FBI to search a fingerprint database of more than 47 million records is known as

    A. NIBIN
    C. IAFIS
    B. CODIS
    D. ATF

22. The Henry system of fingerprint classification requires how many prints?

    A. one
    C. five
    B. two
    D. ten

23. Assuming good quality, the IAFIS requires how many prints for a match?

    A. one
    C. five
    B. two
    D. ten

24. The final identification match is always done by a

    A. computer
    C. forensic expert
    B. judge
    D. lawyer

25. IAFIS can search its 47 million record database in

    A. 24 h
    C. 5 min
    B. 1 h
    D. 1 day

Answers

1. A	10. D	18. C
2. B	11. B	19. B
3. B	12. B	20. D
4. C	13. A	21. C
5. D	14. B	22. D
6. A	15. C	23. A
7. D	16. C	24. C
8. C	17. A	25. C
9. B		

CHAPTER 17

IMPRESSIONS AND TOOL MARKS

TERMS YOU SHOULD KNOW

alginate	dental stone	polysulfide
aspect ratio	electrostatic dust	polyvinylsiloxane
base	lifter	Snow Print Wax
calcium sulfate	gypsum	striation marks
cast	Permlastic	tool marks
catalyst	plaster of Paris	

THEORY OF IMPRESSION MATCHING

Tool marks are made when a harder object comes in contact with a softer object, leaving marks on it. A tool such as a screwdriver is machined to certain dimensions, and this machining process leaves unique **striation marks** in the metal of the tool. One of the first things an investigator looks for at a suspect's home is the suspect's toolbox. Any tools used in the commission of a crime leave unique scratch marks behind. These striation marks can be used to match a tool to an object it came into contact with at the crime scene.

In the case of a burglary where a robber forced entry into a house by jimmying a window lock, the first thing an investigator looks for, once a suspect is in custody, is the suspect's tools. Any screwdrivers are sent to the crime lab along with the window lock. When a screwdriver is first made, the microscopic imperfections in the blade make it unique. As it is used, more imperfections are added and the blade becomes more unique. Once at the crime lab, a **cast** is made of the scratch marks left on the window lock from the forced entry. The questioned screwdriver blades are used to scrape a soft metal such as lead. The forensic scientist scrapes the blades across the lead using both sides of the blades and different angles. The cast and the lead brick with the scrapings are placed under a comparison microscope to see if the striation marks match.

In 1932 the infant son of Charles and Anne Lindbergh was kidnapped from his nursery. A handmade wooden ladder used to gain entrance to a second-floor window (Figure 17.1), a ransom note, some muddy footprints, and a chisel were the only clues left at the crime scene.

FIGURE 17.1

The ransom was paid, but the infant was never returned. His body was eventually found in the woods near the Lindbergh home. A suspect, Richard Hauptmann, was eventually arrested. One of the first things forensic investigator Arthur Koehler looked for was Richard Hauptmann's toolbox. In it he found the hand plane used to construct the homemade ladder. The imperfections in the plane's blade caused unique striation marks on any wood it was used on. Test pieces of wood planed with this tool displayed the same striation marks found on the wooden ladder left at the Lindbergh home. This proved that Richard Hauptmann's plane was used to make the ladder used in the kidnapping.

Impressions can sometimes be discovered in the most unusual places. A man was found dead in the early morning hours on the side of a road in Binghamton, NY—the responding police officers could tell just from the condition of the body that he had been the victim of a hit-and-run accident. There had been a rainstorm that night, so no tire tracks were visible. There was also an absence of any skid marks, indicating that the driver had not stopped for the pedestrian. In a search of the crime scene the police noticed a van parked on the side of the road, and on closer inspection saw that there was a man asleep behind the wheel. The police knocked on the car window and proceeded to question the driver. He explained that he was out driving in the early hours of the morning and was too tired to make it home. The rain was also a factor in his decision to pull over and rest. He said that he had almost fallen asleep and lost control of the van. It had fishtailed in the driving rain, and when he regained control of the vehicle, he decided to pull over and get some sleep. When the police looked at the other (passenger) side of the van, they were shocked to see the impression of the pedestrian in the side of the van. The driver did not even know that he had struck someone. A police sketch of the van is shown in Figure 17.2.

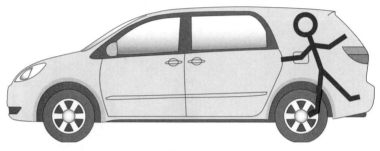

FIGURE 17.2

Another example of the forensic use of impressions is the following. The steering column (Figure 17.3) of a stolen vehicle had been broken open with some type of tool in order to reach the ignition and disable the steering wheel lock. A suspect located near the vehicle was found to have a screwdriver (Figure 17.4) in his backpack. The investigating officer submitted the steering column to the crime lab along with the screwdriver to see if it might have been used in the crime.

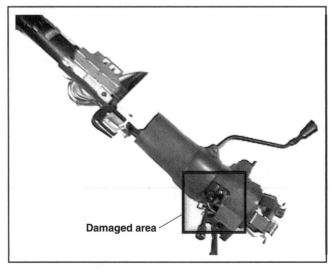

Damaged area

FIGURE 17.3

FIGURE 17.4

The steering column was examined, and an area of striated tool marks was found on a small internal part (Figure 17.5). A cast of the questioned tool mark was obtained using a dental rubber casting medium (Figure 17.6) so that the tool mark could be examined microscopically (it's tough to put a steering column under a microscope!).

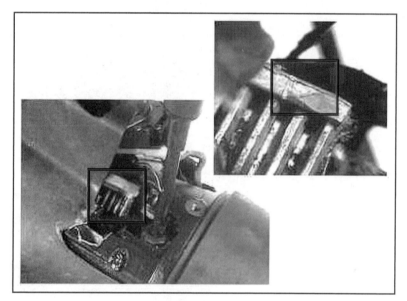

FIGURE 17.5

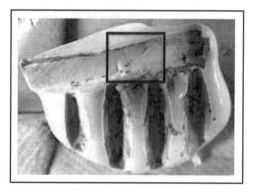

FIGURE 17.6

Standards were then made with the questioned screwdriver. The tip of the screwdriver was pulled across a sheet of soft lead at various angles and in different directions. Casts of the "test" tool marks were then made by the same method used for the questioned tool mark on the steering column (Figure 17.7). The cast of the tool mark standard was compared to the cast of the tool mark from the steering column using a comparison microscope. The results are seen in Figures 17.8 and 17.9.

FIGURE 17.7

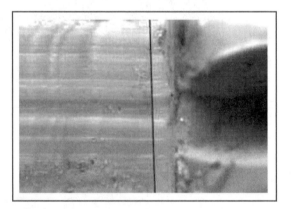

FIGURE 17.8

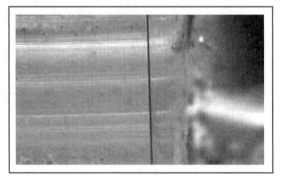

FIGURE 17.9

DENTAL STONE, PERMLASTIC, AND SILICONE-BASED IMPRESSION MATERIALS

There are three materials commonly used in forensic science to make casts of tool marks and other impressions: dental stone, Permlastic, and polyvinylsiloxane. **Dental stone** is a very fine grade of **calcium sulfate** (sometimes known as **alginate, gypsum,** or **plaster of Paris**) that was developed for dentists to take dental impressions. Dental stone is normally the material of choice when making a cast of bite marks, shoeprints, and tire prints. A container of dental stone is shown in Figure 17.10.

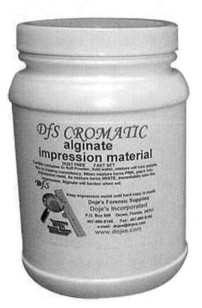

FIGURE 17.10

Dental stone is prepared by mixing about 2 parts alginate with 1 part water. The resulting paste is applied to the impression and allowed to set (for a few minutes to a few hours depending on size and temperature). Chromatic dental stone changes color, letting you know when to apply the paste and when it has set. In snow a waxy substance (called **Snow Print Wax**) is first sprayed over the impression, and then the cast is made. The process is shown in Figures 17.11 and 17.12.

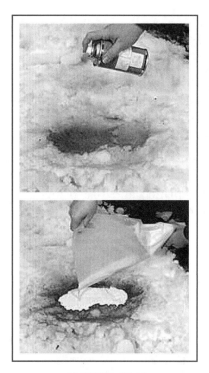

FIGURE 17.11

FIGURE 17.12

Permlastic (polysulfide) and **polyvinylsiloxane** are both used to take the impressions of smaller objects like bite marks or scratches left behind on a forced lock. Both products consist of two tubes (one **base** and one **catalyst**), which are connected so that equal amounts of each are dispensed. The two components are mixed, and the paste is applied to the impression. Both compounds polymerize in about 1/2 h to form an elastomeric (rubbery) solid which can then be pealed off the object. Both Permlastic and polyvinylsiloxane take extremely fine impressions. Tubes of Perlastic are shown in Figure 17.13, and tubes of polyvinylsiloxane are shown in Figure 17.14.

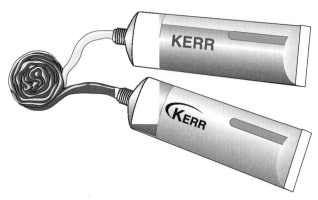

FIGURE 17.13

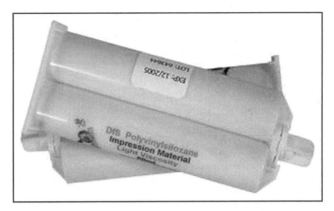

FIGURE 17.14

Footwear can also leave valuable impressions and prints behind at the crime scene. An **electrostatic dust lifter** can be used to charge a plastic film that has been placed over a footwear impression. The charged plastic lifts any dust particles from the impression, and they adhere to the film. These devices work best in a dry environment. Electrostatic dust lifters work well on paper, wood, carpet, linoleum, and concrete. Figure 17.15 shows a Pathfinder electrostatic dust print lifter.

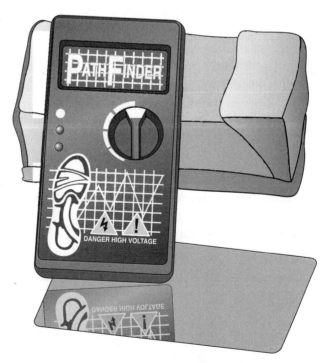

FIGURE 17.15

There are many Internet sites that provide data for matching footwear prints and tire track impressions to the manufacturer. A good place to start is the web site produced by Chesapeake Area Shoeprint and Tire Track (CAST) at *http://members.aol.com/varfee/mastssite/index.html*

Once the print or impression has been taken, the forensic scientist can develop a great deal of class characteristic evidence. Measurements of the length and width of footwear can be used to calculate the size of a shoe. The pattern produced by the sole of the shoe can be used to determine the manufacturer. A footwear print about 11.5 in long and about 4.3 in wide might indicate a size 8½D shoe. The tread patterns are often specific to different manufacturers. Many popular sneaker manufacturers actually put the name of the company (Addias, for example) in the tread design or the company symbol (Reebok often includes its two lines with a third intersecting logo). Once a suspect is apprehended, the forensic investigator is often asked if a positive match can be made between the suspect's footwear and the print left behind at the crime scene. All shoes of a certain type are the same when they come off the production line. However, once a person starts wearing a shoe, random and unique wear patterns begin to appear. Some people put more pressure on one side of the foot than on the other, and the tread picks up cuts, scraps, and foreign objects, which can make each footprint unique. The forensic scientist takes the suspect's footwear, inks it on a pad, and presses it against a piece of white paper much as in taking a person's fingerprint. The print is compared to any left at the crime scene, and a point-by-point match can be presented to the court just as in the case of a fingerprint.

An identical process can also be used for a tire track print or impression. The width of the tread impression gives the first number in the size of a tire. For example, the tire size 235/60R16 stands for a tire that has a 235-mm-wide tread with an **aspect ratio** (the ratio of the height of the sidewall of the tire to the width of the tread times 100) of 60. It is also a radial and fits on a 16-in-diameter wheel. Multiplying the decimal aspect ratio (the aspect ratio divided by 100) by the width of the tire gives the height of the sidewall of the tire. A tire impression left at a crime scene that was about 9.3 in wide and showed a repeating imperfection mark every 84.7 in of travel is consistent with this size tire. To prove this, the width can be converted from inches to millimeters by multiplying by 25.4 mm/in.

$$\text{Width (mm)} = \text{width (in)} \times 25.4 \text{ mm/in}$$
$$= 9.3 \text{ in} \times 25.4 \text{ mm/in} = 236 \text{ mm}$$

This value is consistent with a size 235 tire. The height of the sidewall can be calculated by multiplying the width of the tread by the aspect ratio times 100.

$$\text{Height of sidewall} = 9.3 \times 60/100 = 5.6 \text{ in}$$

The overall diameter (height) of the tire is the diameter of the wheel plus twice the height of the sidewall:

$$\text{Overall diameter} = \text{wheel diameter} + 2 \times \text{sidewall height}$$
$$= 16 \text{ in} + 2 \times 5.6 = 27.2 \text{ in}$$

The overall circumference of the tire is

$$\text{Overall circumference} = 3.14 \times \text{diameter}$$
$$= 3.14 \times 27.2 \text{ in} = 85.4 \text{ in}$$

Any imperfection in the tire tread would be expected to repeat every 85.4 in, which is consistent with what was found at the crime scene. Exact widths and diameters of tires vary depending on the manufacturer and on inflation, so the numbers are always approximate.

Tread patterns are often unique, and patented, for each manufacturer, so a brand of tire can often be determined from the tread pattern. As the vehicle is driven, the tires develop unique wear patterns. Some wear faster on the front tires, and some on the back. Wear can take place more on the inside of the tires, the middle, or the outside, and wear may show scalloping along the edges. There may be random cuts, nicks, or stones in the tread. These all leave unique impressions at the crime scene that can be used to positively associate the vehicle with the crime.

REVIEW QUESTIONS

1. A screwdriver used to force a lock leaves a

   A. residue   B. tool mark
   C. vapor   D. trade mark

2. Impression evidence left at the Lindbergh infant kidnapping included

   A. a ladder   B. footprints
   C. a chisel   D. all of the above

3. A suspect's tool is compared to the striation tool marks left on an object by

   A. fitting the tool to the object
   B. photographing both
   C. using the tool to scratch lead
   D. looking for residue

4. Which of the following items can leave valuable impression evidence?

   A. tools   B. teeth
   C. tires   D. all of the above

5. The forensic scientist _____ was able to match the hand plane in Richard Hauptmann's toolbox with the marks on the ladder left at the Lindbergh home.

   A. Edmond Locard   B. Arthur Koehler
   C. Paul Kirk   D. Calvin Goddard

6. The wood used to make the ladder used in the Lindbergh infant kidnapping was matched to Richard Hauptmann's

   A. attic   B. garage
   C. family room   D. basement

7. In Binghamton, NY, the impression of a _____ on the side of a van led to the driver's arrest.

   A. dog   B. utility pole
   C. man   D. stop sign

8. The random striation marks cause by a tool form what type of evidence?

   A. individual characteristic   B. class characteristic
   C. hearsay   D. testimonial

9. The impression material made from calcium sulfate is known as

   A. alginate   B. Permlastic
   C. polyvinylsiloxane   D. none of the above

10. The impression material made from polysulfide is known as

    A. alginate   B. Permlastic
    C. polyvinylsiloxane D. none of the above

11. Large casts, like those of tire tracks, are best made using

    A. alginate   B. Permlastic
    C. polyvinylsiloxane D. none of the above

12. Permlastic and polyvinylsiloxane are both two-component mixtures that require one part base and one part

    A. acid   B. monomer
    C. polymer   D. catalyst

13. Footprints left behind on a carpet at a crime scene can be recovered using a/an

    A. piece of tape
    C. electrostatic dust lifter
    B. ink pad
    D. wet paper

14. A tire track found at a crime scene measures 7.5 in in width. What is the tread width in millimeters?

    A. 160
    C. 210
    B. 190
    D. 230

15. A cut in the tread of a tire track repeats every 84.8 in. The overall diameter of the tire is how many inches?

    A. 22
    C. 27
    B. 24
    D. 30

16. A 185/60R14 tire has what sidewall height in inches?

    A. 2.4
    C. 4.4
    B. 3.4
    D. 5.4

17. A 185/60R14 tire has what overall circumference in inches?

    A. 71.6
    C. 77.2
    B. 65.4
    D. 84.8

18. To take an impression in snow the impression should first be sprayed with

    A. lacquer
    C. Pam
    B. hair spray
    D. Snow Print Wax

Answers

1. B	7. C	13. C
2. D	8. A	14. B
3. C	9. A	15. C
4. D	10. B	16. C
5. B	11. A	17. A
6. A	12. D	18. D

CHAPTER 18

PAINT

TERMS YOU SHOULD KNOW

acrylate	enamels	polyurethane
base coat	flash rust	primer
binders	lacquers	pyrolysis GC
clear coat	latex	solvent
control	pigments	thermoplastic
cross-linking	polymers	thermoset
electro coat primer		

PIGMENTS, BINDERS, AND SOLVENTS

Many types of surfaces are painted to give the surface color, to protect the surface, or both. When these surfaces become part of a crime scene, it is up to the forensic scientist to determine if the paint can be a valuable piece of evidence. This requires a basic understanding of what paint is.

Paint is a mixture of three components: solvent, pigment, and binder. The **solvent** is the liquid that dissolves the pigment and binder into a solution. When paint is applied to a surface, the solvent evaporates and leaves the pigment and binder behind. When a forensic scientist analyzes paint, only the pigment and binder are normally present. Spray paint in aerosol cans often uses a quickly evaporating alcohol as a solvent. House paints typically use water.

Pigments are chemicals that are added to paint to give it color. They can be organic or inorganic compounds and can be identified by spectroscopy. Different manufacturers use different pigments; thus the chemicals used to make Ford red are different from the chemicals used to make Ferrari red and can easily be identified by chemical analysis.

Binders are chemicals that hold the pigment to the surface that has been painted. They are chemicals that undergo polymerization (the process by which smaller binder molecules combine to form larger macromolecules like plastic) to form a protective coating like a plastic skin over the painted object. Paints are often named after the binder used. Binders include **latex, acrylate, polyurethane**, and oil.

Paints can also be **lacquers** and **enamels**. The **polymers** in lacquers lie on top of one another. Older GM cars used to be painted with acrylic lacquers. After a car was painted it was subjected to heat which caused the polymers to flow. Lacquers are said to be **thermoplastic** (they soften when heated). A sketch of the acrylate polymers in a lacquer are shown in Figure 18.1.

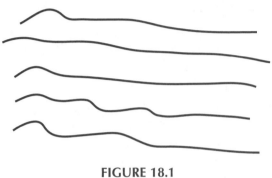

FIGURE 18.1

The polymers in enamel chemically attach to one another by a process called **cross-linking**. This can be the result of the paint being heated (**thermoset**) or a chemical reaction. Enamels are much more resistant to chemical attack, and all newer cars are painted with enamels. An old test for lacquers (called the GM test) was to drop a paint chip from a car into acetone (nail polish remover). If the paint chip dissolved, it was lacquer and probably from a GM car. A sketch of the acrylate polymers of an enamel cross-linking are shown in Figure 18.2.

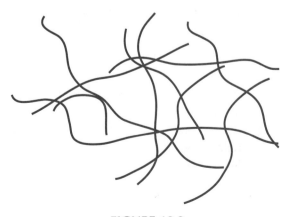

FIGURE 18.2

AUTOMOTIVE PAINT

Paint is often transferred in hit-and-run accidents and collisions. It is therefore important that the forensic scientist understand the automotive paint process.

Cars surfaces normally receive four layers of paint: electro coat primer, primer, base coat, and clear coat. The steel body of a car is very susceptible to **flash rust** (rapid rusting of a new metal surface). As soon as the body of the car is ready to be painted, the surface is thoroughly cleaned and run through a bath of **electro coat primer**. An electric current is passed through the metal car body, causing the primer to bond to the metal through an electrochemical process. The metal is now protected against corrosion, and the rest of the process can be completed when necessary.

The next coat is the **primer**. It is normally an epoxy-based compound that further protects the metal against corrosion and provides a good surface for the base coat. The color of the primer depends on the color of the base coat to be applied next.

The **base coat** is the layer of paint with the final color that will be seen. The base coat can be an acrylic or polyurethane enamel. To create certain effects the base coat can contain mica or aluminum flakes that give it an opalescent or metallic appearance.

The **clear coat** is a colorless binder without any pigment. It is applied over the base coat for two reasons. First, it protects the base coat against attack from ultraviolet light and from chemicals. Second, it also provides a glossier finish that adds depth to the color of the base coat. Most clear coats are polyurethane, although acrylic is still sometimes used.

PYROLYSIS GAS CHROMATOGRAPHY OF PAINT CHIPS

The method of choice used to identify fibers, **pyrolysis GC** (Chapter 11), is also used to identify the binder in automobile paint chips. A paint chip is inserted into the pyrolyzer, and the polymers of the binder are broken down into gases. The GC then analyzes these gases, and the results are displayed in the form of a pyrogram. Not only is the pyrogram used to determine the chemical class of the binder, but subtle differences in the polymer allow the forensic scientist to identify the automobile manufacturer. The pigment in the paint chip can be analyzed using a microspectrophotometer (Chapter 5). Automobile manufacturers often change paint formulations every few model years, which allows the forensic scientist to narrow down the field of suspect vehicles.

COLLECTION OF PAINT SAMPLES

A paint chip left behind at a crime scene can be of great value. It should be carefully packaged to prevent any damage to the edges. There is always a chance that it can be matched to a suspect's vehicle and that the random edges on the chip might match the damaged section of the car. The paint chip can be analyzed by pyrolysis GC and a microspectrophotometer to determine the manufacturer and possible makes and models of cars that have that particular paint formulation.

In the case of a suspect's vehicle, use a clean penknife or scalpel to scrape off small samples of paint. These samples can be about half the size of a postage stamp (about ¼ in by ¼ in) and must be scraped all the way down to the metal surface. This allows the matching of any layers visible in the paint. It is also important to always collect a **control**, that is, a paint sample taken from an area away from the damaged section of the car.

REVIEW QUESTIONS

1. Paint is a mixture of how many components?

   A. one   B. three
   C. five   D. six

2. The component of paint that gives it color is called

   A. pigment   B. binder
   C. solvent   D. plastic

3. The component of paint that dissolves the other components is called

   A. pigment   B. binder
   C. solvent   D. plastic

4. The component of paint that holds the pigment to a surface and provides protection is called

   A. pigment   B. binder
   C. solvent   D. plastic

5. A type of binder is

   A. latex   B. oil
   C. polyurethane   D. all of the above

6. An enamel paint is an example of

    A. thermoset   B. thermoplastic
    C. thermodynamic   D. thermostable

7. Lacquer paint is an example of

    A. thermoset   B. thermoplastic
    C. thermodynamic   D. thermostable

8. In the old GM test, acetone dissolved which type of paint?

    A. lacquer   B. enamel
    C. latex   D. polyurethane

9. Which type of paint has polymer molecules that are cross-linked?

    A. lacquer   B. enamel
    C. latex   D. polyurethane

10. How many layers of paint are on the average car?

    A. one   B. two
    C. three   D. four

11. The first coat of paint, which protects the metal from flash rust, is called the

    A. base coat   B. primer
    C. electro coat primer   D. clear coat

12. The coat of paint that protects the metal from corrosion and provides a good painting surface for the color coat is called the

    A. base coat   B. primer
    C. electro coat primer   D. clear coat

13. The coat of paint that contains the color is called the

    A. base coat   B. primer
    C. electro coat primer   D. clear coat

14. The coat of paint that contains binder but no pigment is called the

    A. base coat   B. primer
    C. electro coat primer   D. clear coat

15. The most common tool used to identify the binder of a paint chip is a

    A. visible spectrophotometer   B. polarizing microscope
    C. pyrolysis GC   D. SEM

16. A paint chip collected from a car should be about what size?

A. ¼ in × ¼ in
B. ½ in × ½ in
C. 1 in × 1 in
D. 2 in × 2 in

17. A paint chip collected from a car should be

A. round
B. scraped down to the bare metal
C. near the driver's side
D. washed before collection

18. A paint chip collected from a point away from any damage is called a/an

A. backup
B. surrogate
C. control
D. standard

19. If a paint chip is large, extra care should be taken in packaging it to prevent any damage to the edges. Then it can be used to make a

A. color comparison
B. pyrolysis chromatogram
C. layer comparison
D. jigsaw fit

Answers

1. B	8. A	14. D
2. A	9. B	15. C
3. C	10. D	16. A
4. B	11. C	17. B
5. D	12. B	18. C
6. A	13. A	19. D
7. B		

CHAPTER 19

QUESTIONED DOCUMENTS

TERMS YOU SHOULD KNOW

ALS	hologram	microprinting
anthrax	ink-jet printer	questioned
color shifting inks	intaglio	document
digital imaging	IR photography	security thread
electrum	laser printer	TLC
ESDA	linen	USSS
exemplar	Lydia lion	watermark

TYPES OF QUESTIONED DOCUMENTS

Any document whose source or authenticity is uncertain is referred to as a **questioned document**. These documents can include checks, letters, wills, contracts, records, tickets, and currency, and they can be analyzed for handwriting, ink, and paper. Documents can also be examined for information in the case of charred, shredded, obliterated, and indented writing.

The first currency was issued in about 600 B.C. in Lydia as a coin called the **Lydia lion** (Figure 19.1). It was made from a mixture of gold and silver called **electrum**. As soon as the first coins were made, the first counterfeits also appeared. Coins made from a cheap imitation mixture of copper and zinc started showing up. Since coins were minted by order of the king, it was considered treason to produce counterfeits. Counterfeiters were subject to the most severe forms of the death penalty such as being boiled in oil. In addition, all the property owned by the counterfeiter became the property of the crown.

FIGURE 19.1

In 1774 the British tried to stop the American war for independence by making U.S. currency worthless. They set up printing presses on their warships in New York harbor and hired printers to come aboard at night to print copies of the various currencies issued by the United States. The effort was successful enough to cause a huge devaluation of U.S. currency. General George Washington complained that it required a wheelbarrow full of money to buy a wheelbarrow full of food. The counterfeiting did not, however, affect the final outcome of the war.

In 1862 the U.S. Congress authorized the U.S. Treasury to print the first "greenbacks" or paper currency that we are familiar with today. In 1865 Congress established the **U.S. Secret Service (USSS)** to combat the counterfeiting of U.S. paper currency that was undermining public confidence in the new money. Initially, U.S. currency had three main security features that made it hard to copy. First, the currency is printed on a mixture of linen and paper, not just paper. Paper is derived from wood pulp, which yields very short, coarse fibers. **Linen** is derived from the much longer, stronger fibers of the flax plant. It is much more durable than paper and has a completely different feel. The linen is mixed with red and blue silk threads, which are very hard to copy and make it very easy to spot a counterfeit. The printing process itself is unique. It is called **intaglio** and involves the following as described by the U.S. Bureau of Engraving and Printing.

> The Bureau prints currency on high-speed, sheet-fed rotary presses which are capable of printing over 8,000 sheets per hour. Printing plates are covered with ink and then the surface of each plate is wiped clean which allows the ink to remain in the design and letter grooves of the plates. Each sheet is then forced, under extremely heavy pressure (estimated at 20 tons), into the finely recessed lines of the printing plate to pick up the ink. The printing impression is three dimensional in effect and requires the combined handiwork of highly skilled artists, steel engravers, and plate printers. The surface of the note feels slightly raised, while the reverse side feels slightly indented. This process is called intaglio printing.

The paper used to make U.S. currency comes from Crane & Company, Dalton, MA. Their web site can be accessed at http://www.crane.com/currency/. Crane & Company supply enough paper to the U.S. Bureau of Engraving and Printing to print about 9 billion notes each year. The U.S. Bureau of Engraving and Printing prints about 37 million notes per day, which are shipped to the 12 regional Federal Reserve banks.

In the past, it required a skilled engraver to scribe the lines in metal plates needed to counterfeit U.S. currency. In one famous case, handled by the USSS in 1876, Abraham Lincoln's body was almost stolen.

In the 1870s one the nation's largest counterfeiting rings was located in the city of Chicago. The counterfeiter's master engraver was a man by the name of Ben Boyd. When he was captured and imprisoned by the USSS, the whole Chicago operation ground to a halt. The gangsters were so dependent on Boyd's abilities that they came up with an outrageous idea. They decided to sneak into Oak Ridge Cemetery in Springfield, where Lincoln's coffin was kept on display, and steal the president's body and hold it for ransom. They planned to return the body only if the authorities freed Ben Boyd. Luckily, the would-be grave robbers had an informant in their group, and the authorities chased the robbers from the gravesite before the president's body was removed.

In 1990 less than 1% of all counterfeit U.S. currency was produced using a digital printer. Today, more than 40% of all counterfeit U.S. currency is produced using a digital printer. The use of **digital imaging** and color copiers has prompted the United States to add additional security items in U.S. currency. First, a security thread and microprinting were added in 1990. The security thread does not photocopy and fluoresces under ultraviolet (UV) light. The **microprinting** consists of very fine lines and small words that cause patterns that interfere with light transmission and therefore cannot be photocopied. The U.S. Bureau of Engraving and Printing has also added a watermark and color-shifting ink to keep one step ahead of would-be counterfeiters. With the advent of new copier technology the federal government is more concerned with 1 million people trying to counterfeit one note than with one person trying to counterfeit 1 million notes. Some explanations of the security features in U.S. currency from the U.S. Bureau of Engraving and Printing web site are as follows.

Evaluation Criteria

Effectiveness: Counterfeit deterrent effectiveness was tested by reprographic equipment manufacturers and government scientists. They also considered the ease of public and cash handler recognition.

Durability: Durability was tested rigorously. Tests included crumpling, folding, laundering, soiling, and soaking in a variety of solvents such as gasoline, acids, and laundry products.

Production costs: Research and production expenses will increase the cost of each note by about two cents. The Federal Reserve System has funded the development and introduction of the new currency through earnings the Federal Reserve receives primarily from interest on its holdings of United States government securities.

Appearance: The currency still has a familiar American look. The size of the notes, basic colors, historical figures and national symbols are not changing. New features were evaluated for their compatibility with the traditional design of United States currency.

The New Security Features

Watermark: The watermark is formed by varying paper density in a small area during the papermaking process. The image is visible as darker and lighter areas when held up to the light. Since the watermark does not copy on color copiers or scanners, it makes it harder to use lower denomination paper to print counterfeit notes in higher denominations and is a good way to authenticate the note. It depicts the same historical figure as the engraved portrait.

Color-shifting inks: These inks, used in the numeral on the lower right corner of the face of the note, change color when the note is viewed from different angles. The ink appears green when viewed directly and changes to black when the note is tilted.

Fine-line printing patterns: This type of line structure appears normal to the human eye but is difficult for current copying and scanning equipment to resolve properly. The lines are found behind the portrait on the front and around the historic building on the back.

Enlarged off-center portraits: The larger portrait can incorporate more detail, making it easier to recognize and more difficult to counterfeit. It also provides an easy way for the public to distinguish the new design from the old. The portrait is shifted off center to provide room for a watermark and unique "lanes" for the security thread in each denomination. The slight relocation also reduces wear on most of the portrait by removing it from the center, which is frequently folded. The increased image size can help people with visual impairments identify the note.

Low-vision feature: The Series 1996 $20 and $50 notes, and Series 1999 $5 and $10 notes have a large dark numeral on a light background on the lower right corner of the back. This numeral, which represents the denomination, helps people with low vision, senior citizens and others as well because it is easier to read. Also, a machine-readable feature has been incorporated for the blind. It will facilitate development of convenient scanning devices that could identify the denomination of the note.

Pre-Existing Security Features

Security thread: A security thread is a thin thread or ribbon running through a bank note substrate. All 1990 series and later notes, except the $1, include this feature. The note's denomination is printed on the thread. In addition, the threads of the new $5, $10, $20, and $50 notes have graphics in addition to the printed denomination. The denomination number appears in the star field of the flag printed on the thread. The thread in the new notes glows when held under a long-wave ultraviolet light. In the new $5 it glows blue, in the new $10 it glows orange, in the new $20 note it glows green, in the new $50 note it glows yellow, and in the new $100 note it glows red. Since it is visible in transmitted light, but not in reflected light, the thread is difficult to copy with a color copier which uses reflected light to generate an image. Using a unique thread position for each denomination guards against certain counterfeit techniques, such as bleaching ink off a lower denomination and using the paper to "reprint" the bill as a higher value note.

Microprinting: This print appears as a thin line to the naked eye, but the lettering easily can be read using a low-power magnifier. The resolution of most current copiers is not sufficient to copy such fine print. On the newly designed $5, microprinting can be found in the side borders and along the lower edge of the portrait's frame on the face of the note. On the new $10, microprinting appears in the numeral "10" in the lower left-hand corner and along the lower edge of the portrait's frame on the face of the note. On the Series 1996 $20 notes, microprinting appears in the lower left corner numeral and along the lower edge ornamentation of the oval framing the portrait. On the $50 notes, microprinting appears on the side borders and in Ulysses Grant's collar. On the $100 notes, microprinting appears in the lower left corner numeral and on Benjamin Franklin's coat. In 1990, 1993, and 1995 series notes, "The United States of America" is printed repeatedly in a line outside the portrait frame.

Nowadays the greatest percentage of counterfeit money is found abroad. There is about $480 billion in U.S. currency, and about two-thirds of it is overseas. United States currency is the de facto currency for many countries. About 80% of the counterfeit U.S. currency seized abroad comes from Colombia. In one process, the ink from a genuine $1 bill is removed by bleach and the paper is used to print a counterfeit $50 bill. The federal government plans a new design every 7 to 10 years to try to stay one step ahead of technology. Two possibilities include adding a **hologram** (Austria uses a picture of Mozart for a hologram) or even switching to clear plastic instead of paper. Figure 19.2 shows an Australian twenty dollar note made of plastic.

FIGURE 19.2

Documents sent to the lab require comparisons of handwriting, inks, checks, money, paper, and lottery tickets, to name a few. A document that has been charred (burned), erased, obliterated (written over), shredded, or indented can be brought to the questioned document section of the crime lab for analysis. There are many standardized techniques that document examiners use, including infrared (IR) photography, digital imaging, thin-layer chromatography, electrostatic imaging, microspectrophotometry, and alternate light sources (ALS).

The dyes used to make inks vary from manufacturer to manufacturer. Even though the blue ink from BIC, Parker, Paper Mate, Cross, and Pilot pens may all look the same to the unaided eye, they are all composed of different dyes. These different dyes give the ink from each manufacturer unique chemical and optical properties, which allow the document examiner to differentiate among various brands of pens.

IR photography makes use of the fact that the different organic chemicals that make up ink dyes absorb infrared light in different ways. Sometimes writing is covered to hide some piece of information. If the ink used in the obliteration is different from the ink used in the original writing, infrared photography can sometimes be used to "see" through the top layer of ink and reveal what is underneath. Figure 19.3 shows an example of this effect. The first image represents a sample of writing that has been obliterated, and the second is the same image as seen with infrared photography.

FIGURE 19.3

The use of infrared imaging can also show when a document has been altered. Figure 19.4 is from the FBI document examination section.

FIGURE 19.4

The writing on charred and indented paper can often be visualized using an alternate light source. An **ALS** produces a highly collimated beam of light that can create shadows that enable indented or charred writing to be clearly seen. Alternate light sources can be produced using fiber optics or lasers.

A digital scanner can be used to scan an obliterated document into a computer. Be sure to select the maximum resolution and color depth even if it is a black-and-white image. Next, use digital image editing software such as Adobe Photoshop or JASC Paint Shop Pro to increase the contrast of the image and sharpen fuzzy lines. A computer can enhance slight variations in the image that are not visible to the unaided human eye. A simulated charred image is shown in Figure 19.5.

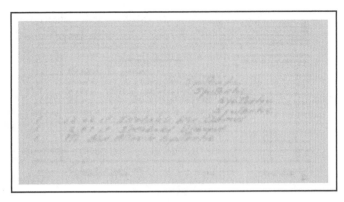

FIGURE 19.5

When the image was scanned by a digital color scanner and the contrast enhanced by software, the image in Figure 19.6 was obtained.

FIGURE 19.6

Thin-layer chromatography (TLC), (Chapter 4) can separate the dye components of inks. A dot of ink is put on a sheet of paper about 1 in from the bottom. The paper is placed in a glass tank filled with a mixture of water and methanol to a height of about 1/2 in. As capillary action draws the solvent up the paper, the ink dyes travel at different rates. The distance the dye travels divided by the distance the solvent travels is known as the retention factor. Each dye has its own characteristic retention factor, and this can be used to determine the identity of the dyes and the manufacturer of the ink.

Many forensic document examiners use a new device called an **electrostatic detection apparatus (ESDA)**, which works on the principle that charged surfaces attract small particles. The charge on the surface of paper varies because of any irregularities (such as indentations) that affect the paper's ability to attract toner particles. The manufacturer of the ESDA[2] gives the following description on its web site.

The New ESDA^2—Outstanding Technology with Improved Design

More sensitive than oblique lighting

Simple to operate

Produces permanent 1 to 1 transparencies

Responds only to indented writing—ignores visible script

Nondestructive—leaves documents uncontaminated

ESDA is the leading technology for detecting indented writing on questioned documents. ESDA works by creating an invisible electrostatic image of indented writing, which is then visualized by the application of charge sensitive toners. The sensitive imaging process reacts to sites of microscopic damage to fibers at the surface of a document, which have been created by abrasive interaction with overlying surfaces during the act of handwriting.

A New Image Development System

Traditionally, cascade developers have been used in the image development process but ESDA^2 is supplied with a new system—the Toner Pad—a technique that ensures a cleaner operation while maintaining excellent sensitivity. A soft, brushed-textile pad impregnated with toner is simply wiped across the surface of the imaging film to produce visible images of any indented writing. The new system is cleaner to use, removes the need to handle loose powder and eliminates the problems associated with under- or overtoned images. ESDA^2 retains the standard cascade developer, however, for those who prefer the traditional method of image development.

New A3 Vacuum Bed with Filter System

The larger, removable vacuum bed and wider imaging film enable documents up to 310 mm × 440 mm to be processed and ESDA^2 also features a powerful extraction fan and filter to remove any airborne toner particles.

Document Preparation

A new large capacity document humidifier is also provided; this increases the sensitivity of documents prior to the ESDA^2 electrostatic imaging process.

Making a Permanent Record

Images of indented writing can be made permanent by the simple process of laminating the developed images with the provided transparent self-adhesive plastic film.

ESDA²—the Complete System

ESDA² is designed for examining all types of documents up to A3 size and is supplied with one reel of imaging film, cascade developer, 50 toner pads, a pack of fixing film, and document humidifier.

Figure 19.7 shows the ESDA² along with a sample of indented writing and the same sample after treatment with ESDA².

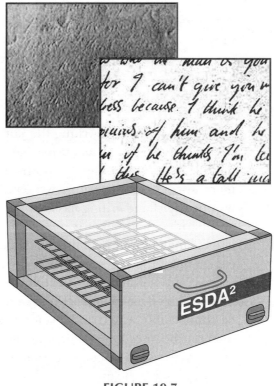

FIGURE 19.7

Microspectrophotometers (Chapter 5) can analyze the infrared and visible light absorbed by ink dyes. A microspectrophotometer has the advantage of being able to zoom in on a single line on a questioned $50 bill or on a single stroke of ink on a questioned check.

Sometimes a question arises as to when a document was written. Someone might claim to have love letters written by Napoleon. The U.S. Secret Service is the expert on questioned documents: Besides analyzing the paper, they can analyze the ink and date the formulation. If the letters were written using an ink formulation that wasn't available until 1960, then they could not have come from Napoleon. The USSS has the largest collection of inks in the world that can be used for comparison. Another technique that can be employed involves silver nitrate. Ink formulations contain chloride, which diffuses into the paper at a characteristic rate. When the paper is sprayed with silver nitrate, the chlorides react and form the white precipitate silver chloride. By measuring the distance the chloride has traveled from the ink, the date the document was written can be established.

HANDWRITING ANALYSIS

Forensic document examiners are often requested to analyze handwriting samples to see if they are from the same person or are forgeries. The examiner might be requested to determine if the handwriting from a ransom or stick-up note matches the handwriting of the suspect. Handwriting is a neuromuscular activity that is learned when we are about 7 years old. At first there is an attempt to make everyone's handwriting the same, and we are taught to reproduce a template of letters using paper with dotted lines across the middle. As we grow older, the dotted lines disappear and we become more worried about what we write rather than how we write. By our twenties our handwriting has become constant and we have our own peculiarities that makes it unique. Features such as the spacing of letters, angle, slant, pressure, shape, and so on, help a handwriting expert tell if the two samples were written by the same individual.

There are certain rules to follow when obtaining a handwriting sample (called an **exemplar**) from a suspect. First, the suspect should be comfortably seated and given a pen and paper as similar to that used for the questioned document as possible. Second, the contents of the questioned document should be dictated. The suspect must never be shown the questioned document. This forces the suspect to decide on spacing, indentation, punctuation, abbreviation, spelling, and a hundred of minute features that the handwriting expert can use for the comparison. If the writing sample is very small, like a signature, it is best to combine it with other writing and repeat the task several times.

A famous example of the use of handwriting analysis involved the letters containing **anthrax** mailed through the U.S. mail to Senator Tom Daschle (Figures 19.8 and 19.9).

FIGURE 19.8

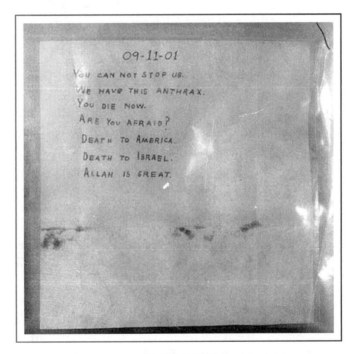

FIGURE 19.9

PRINTED DOCUMENT ANALYSIS

In the past, most printed material was produced by typewriters, and it was fairly easy to determine the brand of the machine by font and spacing. An individual typewriter could be identified by spacing irregularities and microscopic imperfections in the keys. While the typewriter has gone the way of the Dodo bird, the same principles are used today to help forensic examiners determine the source of a printed document.

First, the paper is examined. There are different kinds of paper varying in weight, strength, size, grade, watermark, treatment, and coating. Writing paper is often bleached with chlorine to make it white and then coated with clay particles to aid in the absorption of ink. Analysis of the paper often yields the type and brand. The next step is to analyze the ink used in the printing. In the case of an **ink-jet printer** different companies such as Lexmark, Canon, Hewlett Packard, and so on, use different chemical formulations for their ink cartridges. Analysis of the ink yields the manufacturer of the ink and the printer. Ink-jet printer heads themselves wear as they are dragged back and forth across the paper, which leads to microscopic imperfections in the printing. These can often be used to determine if a printed page came from a suspect's printer. The feed mechanism can also cause microscopic marks to be left behind on the paper.

In the case of a **laser printer** or a photocopier the ink is usually carbon particles that have been burned into the paper in the fusion stage. A laser printer or a photocopier works by applying a positive charge to a circular drum made of selenium or some compound of selenium. In the case of a LaserJet printer, the laser sweeps across the drum as it rotates. Where the laser strikes, the positive charge is lost and no ink is printed on that section of the paper. In the case of a photocopier, the light from the image is used to expose the selenium drum. The drum is rotated over negatively charged toner particles picked up by the sections of the drum that are still positively charged. A piece of paper is then positively charged and passes over the rotating drum. The toner particles are then transferred to the paper. The paper passes through a fusion stage where the carbon particles are burned permanently into the paper. The drum material is soft and begins to wear as soon as it is used. Microscopic striation marks are produced on the drum, and their images are transferred to the paper. This allows investigators to match a printed document with an individual printer. The toners on a laser printer or a photocopier also vary in particle size and composition. Some copiers even use a liquid toner. Analysis of the toner can help the forensic scientist determine the manufacturer of the laser printer or photocopier that produced the printed document.

Sometimes the background of a printed document can help in a forensic investigation. In the early days of the New York State lottery, which started in 1967, the tickets were preprinted with numbers by a firm in New Jersey. They were sold to the public, and a winning ticket number was drawn from those sold. If you had the winning ticket, you had 1 year to claim your prize. One year no one came forward to claim the prize, and then shortly before the one year was up, a man stepped forward with the winning lottery ticket. The next week a woman stepped forward with the winning lottery ticket. Both tickets had the winning number, and forensic examination of the paper and ink confirmed them to be genuine lottery tickets. In those days lottery players with the numbers before and after the winning number also won small consolation prizes. Since both these tickets had been turned in, the document examiners were able to compare the backgrounds (the tickets were printed on a rolling stock of paper with the emblem of the state of New York printed in the background). In the case of the woman's ticket the backgrounds matched perfectly with the backgrounds of the tickets printed directly before and after the winning ticket. The background of the man's ticket did not match. When confronted with the evidence, the man confessed. A relative of his worked for the company in New Jersey that printed the tickets. When no one stepped forward to claim the prize, he thought that the winning ticket must have been accidentally discarded or lost and came up with the idea of sneaking into the ticket-printing business and setting the machine to print the winning number on genuine paper using the genuine machine.

An example of a stamp that could be used to solve a crime because it matched the preceding stamp in a roll is shown in Figure 19.10 from the FBI web site.

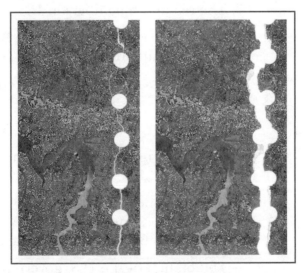

FIGURE 19.10

REVIEW QUESTIONS

1. A questioned document is a document with

   A. a lot of questions
   B. a connection to a crime
   C. a chain of custody
   D. an uncertain source or authenticity

2. The use of currency began in about

   A. 2000 B.C.   B. 1000 B.C.
   C. 600 B.C.   D. 100 B.C.

3. The first currency was the

   A. Lydia lion   B. Egyptian scarab
   C. sand dollar   D. Spanish doubloon

4. A mixture of gold and silver is called

   A. white gold   B. electrum
   C. fool's gold   D. brass

5. A mixture of copper and zinc is called

   A. white gold   B. electrum
   C. fool's gold   D. brass

6. U.S. dollars are made of

   A. paper   B. cotton
   C. paper and linen   D. silk

7. The red and blue fibers in U.S. currency are

   A. paper   B. cotton
   C. paper and linen   D. silk

8. The process by which U.S. currency is printed is called

   A. intaglio   B. engraving
   C. printing   D. photocopying

9. The paper used to make U.S. currency comes from

   A. the U.S. Mint
   B. the Danbury Mint
   C. Crane & Company, Dalton, MA
   D. the U.S. Bureau of Engraving and Printing

10. The branch of the U.S. government charged by Congress to combat counterfeiting is the

   A. FBI   B. USSS
   C. DEA   D. ATF

11. Today, more than _____ of all counterfeit U.S. currency is produced using a digital printer.

   A. 10%   B. 20%
   C. 40%   D. 80%

12. The U.S. Bureau of Engraving and Printing has added which feature to stay ahead of new copier technology?

    A. security thread   B. microprinting
    C. watermark   D. all of the above

13. Color-shifting inks appear green when viewed directly and change to _____ when the note is tilted.

    A. black   B. red
    C. gold   D. blue

14. In 1870 the USSS prevented would-be counterfeiters from stealing the body of _____ and holding it for ransom.

    A. George Washington   B. Abraham Lincoln
    C. Thomas Jefferson   D. Ulysses S. Grant

15. The U.S Bureau of Engraving and Printing prints about _____ notes each year.

    A. 37 million   B. 100 million
    C. 1 billion   D. 9 billion

16. The greatest percentage of counterfeit U.S. currency is found

    A. in New York City   B. in Hawaii
    C. abroad   D. in San Diego

17. About 80% of the counterfeit U.S. currency found abroad comes from

    A. Colombia   B. China
    C. Mexico   D. Korea

18. The U.S Bureau of Engraving and Printing plans on introducing a new design every _____ to stay one step ahead of counterfeiters.

    A. year   B. 2 years
    C. 5 years   D. 7 to 10 years

19. Differences in inks can be detected using

    A. TLC   B. infrared photography
    C. microspectrophotometry   D. all of the above

20. Indented writing can be visualized using

    A. an ink pad   B. electrostatic detection
    C. infrared photography   D. TLC

21. The USSS has the largest collection of _____ in the world

    A. documents   B. guns
    C. inks   D. trench coats

22. The length of time that ink has been on a document can be determined by the migration of _____ into the paper.

    A. chloride   B. dyes
    C. alcohol   D. water

23. A specimen of a person's handwriting is called a/an

    A. example   B. exemplar
    C. instrument   D. test

24. In the case of a laser printer the letters are formed by burning carbon particles into the paper in the _____ stage

    A. copier   B. toner
    C. drum   D. fusion

25. In laser printing, microscopic imperfections in the _____ are pressed into the toner and the paper, and can sometimes be used to help identify a printing source.

    A. copier   B. toner
    C. drum   D. fusion

Answers

1. D	10. B	18. D
2. C	11. C	19. D
3. A	12. D	20. B
4. B	13. A	21. C
5. D	14. B	22. A
6. C	15. D	23. B
7. D	16. C	24. D
8. A	17. A	25. C
9. C		

CHAPTER 20

COMPUTER CRIME

TERMS YOU SHOULD KNOW

BIOS	EXT2FS	OS
caches	FAT	SD card
CD-ROM	Linux	swap file
CMOS	MacOS X	Unix
Compact Flash cards	Microsoft Windows	USB flash drives
DVD	NTFS	

OPERATING SYSTEMS

Computer crime is of growing concern at all levels of police agencies. A computer can be the victim of a crime (hacked into and its contents deleted or stolen), in which case it is called a computer crime, or a computer can be used in conjunction with a crime (illegal transactions or images stored on a computer), in which case it is normally called a computer-related crime. Computers use a **basic input and output system (BIOS)** that is saved in complementary metal oxide semiconductor (CMOS) integrated circuits (chips) on the computer motherboard. BIOS handles the initial turning on of the computer and the reading of information from the hard, disk, compact disc read-only memory (CD-ROM), and digital video disk (DVD) drives. The BIOS then reads the **operating system (OS)** from the hard drive. It is the operating system that most people using a computer interact with. The majority of computers use the **Microsoft Windows** operating system. These include **Windows XP**, 2000, Me, 98SE, 95, 3.11, and others. The majority of new computers are shipped with Windows XP. Apple computers use their own operating system. The present version is called **MacOS X**. Most other computers use some version of **Unix** such as **Linux** or Sun. Different operating systems save data using different methods. It is important for the forensic scientist to understand the differences among the systems in order to be able to recover data or information. Older versions of Windows use a **file allocation table (FAT)** file system (FAT12, FAT16, or FAT32). Windows XP and 2000 use a newer, more secure **NT file system (NTFS)**. Linux uses **EXT2FS** and MacOS X.

ANALYSIS OF HARD DRIVES

Sometimes the forensic scientist is asked to recover data from a hard drive. The drive may be damaged, erased, or encrypted. Hard drives are made of multiple platters containing a material that can be easily magnetized. In the event of physical damage the platters can be removed and the data read. An old trick is to put a hard drive in a freezer. The data can often be read while the platters are cold. If the data has been erased, it is often still possible to recover all the files. When a file is deleted, the only thing that is erased is the reference to the file saved in a special location on the hard drive. This reference lists where on the hard drive all the pieces of the file are stored (all the pieces are not always saved together). There are various programs available for all the operating systems that can recover deleted files.

The case of Molly and Clayton Daniels, described in Chapter 21, is a good example of a computer-related crime. The couple tried to fake the death of Clayton Daniels to avoid jail time and collect insurance money. They dug up a body, placed it in Clayton Daniels' car, and set it on fire. The body was burned beyond recognition. The couple also obtained fake documents to establish a new identity for Clayton Daniels, including a birth certificate and a Texas driver license. When the police were able to prove the body in the burned car was not that of Clayton Daniels, one of the first things they seized as evidence was the couple's computer.

Windows has ways of storing information about every web site you visit. These include a history folder containing a copy of all the links to pages you have visited on the Internet. Two other folders contain temporary Internet files, cookies, and pages viewed. The cookies file is generated by a web site when you view it and stores information such as preferences at that site on your computer. This information is stored in a text file. The entire web page can also be stored on your computer in a temporary Internet file, which allows for rapid viewing of a web page. Other information, such as keystrokes and passwords, can be temporarily stored in areas known as **caches, swap files**, fragments, and slack space.

When the Daniels' computer was analyzed, the police discovered that Molly Daniels had surfed the web for information on how to burn a body, deceive arson investigators, and obtain a new identity, as well as a list of plastic surgeons.

There are programs that can completely erase all the data on a hard drive. When an investigator comes upon a computer that may have valuable information, it should never be shut down by clicking on the turn-off-computer icon. Many professionals have their computers set up so that a special sequence of keys must be depressed or the hard drive will be erased. The recommended procedure is to just pull the power cord out of the wall. The computer can then be taken to the crime lab.

Computer files can also be stored on other devices such as disks, CD-ROMs, DVDs, CompactFlash cards, secure digital (SD) cards, and **USB flash drives**. Flash drives are becoming very popular on college campuses. They are often attached to key rings and can be carried in one's pocket. A common 1-GB flash drive is shown in Figure 20.1. It can be inserted into the USB port of a computer, and data can be saved just as on a hard drive. Some USB flash drives have a biometric fingerprint identification system built right into the stick.

FIGURE 20.1

A storage device that is common in cameras and computers, and can be switched between the two, is a **CompactFlash card** or a **SD card**. It is about the size of a postage stamp. A CompactFlash card is shown in Figure 20.2. There are commercially available software programs that can recover files and images from these devices even if they have been deleted.

FIGURE 20.2

HACKING

Windows has swap file, system, and web browser caches that operate invisibly while a computer is being used. A forensic scientist can analyze these caches of information to see what the operator of the computer was doing.

REVIEW QUESTIONS

1. The system that handles the turning on of a computer is called the

   A. OS
   C. NTFS
   B. BIOS
   D. FAT

2. Windows XP uses the _____ file system.

   A. FAT16
   C. NTFS
   B. FAT32
   D. EXT2FS

3. When a file is erased, only the _____ in deleted.

   A. data
   C. hard drive
   B. file
   D. reference to the file

4. The majority of new home computers are shipped with the _____ OS.

   A. Windows 98
   C. Windows XP
   B. Windows 2000
   D. Apple Mac OS X

5. If a computer is to be seized for evidence, it should be turned off by

   A. clicking on Shutdown
   B. pressing Ctrl-Alt-Del
   C. pulling the power cord
   D. pressing the soft Shutdown key

6. Portable devices for storing data include

   A. UBS flash drives
   C. CD-ROMs and DVDs
   B. SD cards
   D. all of the above

7. Some USB flash drives are protected from unauthorized use by

   A. key locks
   C. iris scanners
   B. fingerprint readers
   D. combination locks

Answers

1. B   3. D   5. C   7. B
2. C   4. C   6. D

CHAPTER 21

DNA PROFILING

TERMS YOU SHOULD KNOW

adenine	elimination sample	PCR
Alec Jeffreys	forensic file	RFLP
chromosome	gene	STRs
CODIS	guanine	thermal cycler
cytosine	mitochondrial DNA	thymine
DNA	nuclear DNA	zygote
DNA amplifier	offender database	

INTRODUCTION TO DNA

We all start as a single cell called a **zygote**. This cell, formed by the union of a sperm and an egg, contains all the information needed to make blood cells, muscle tissue, insulin, hair color, and so on. These millions of bits of information are stored in the **deoxyribonucleic acid (DNA)** located in the nucleus of the cell (Figure 21.1). A bit of inherited information, such as the color of your eyes, is contained in a specific section of the DNA called the **gene**. DNA is an extremely long polymer made from the four nucleotides **adenine** (A), **guanine** (G), **cytosine** (C), and **thymine** (T). It is the sequence of A, T, G, and C that codes for the information in each gene much like the letters of the alphabet code for a word when they are put in the correct sequence. The DNA molecule is wrapped in a compact structure called a **chromosome**.

Human cells have 23 pairs of chromosomes in the nucleus of each cell. Even though we start out as a single cell, we have about 60 trillion cells when we are born. Each of the 60 trillion cells that make up the human body has the same DNA as the original zygote. In addition, everyone's DNA is unique (except that of identical twins because they were formed from the same cell).

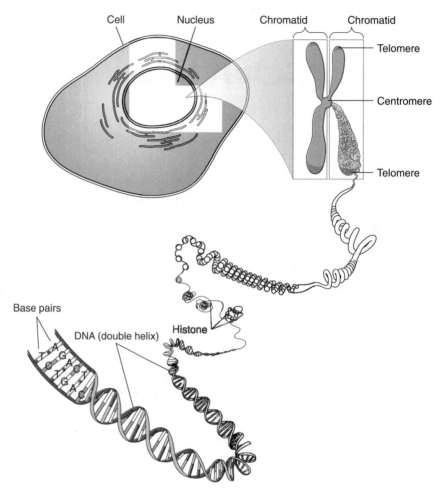

FIGURE 21.1

In 1983 and 1986 two young girls (Lynda Mann and Dawn Ashworth) were raped and murdered in the town of Narborough, England. The modus operandi was very similar in both cases, which led the police to believe that the same person had committed both crimes. A 17-year hospital employee confessed to the 1986 murder but not to the 1983 murder. The police were sure the two were connected, so for the first time they had samples of DNA from semen recovered from both victims analyzed. The samples were sent to **Alec Jeffreys** and his colleagues at Leicester University, who had developed a new procedure for DNA "fingerprinting." The results of the analysis indicated that the same person had committed both crimes. However, the police were shocked to find that the DNA left at the crime scene did not match that of the person who had confessed to the crime. After spending 3½ months in prison he was released.

The police then carried out a massive screening of DNA collected from the town's 1400 residents. Colin Pitchfork was caught trying to persuade someone to give him a DNA sample, and his DNA was found to be a perfect match for the DNA sample recovered from the two victims. He was arrested and convicted for the rape and murder of the two young girls, marking the first time that DNA fingerprinting was used to solve a crime.

FORENSIC VALUE OF DNA EVIDENCE

The DNA in every cell of your body is the same. This means that the DNA in your blood cells is the same as the DNA in your saliva, semen, skin, and hair. DNA evidence is similar to fingerprint evidence. The DNA sample collected from a crime scene must be compared to the DNA sample obtained from the suspect. A point-by-point comparison is made, and if any of the features of the DNA from the suspect do not match the crime scene DNA, it must be from another individual. The following are rich sources of DNA: saliva, blood, and semen. DNA can sometimes be obtained from sweat, skin, and hair, and it is up to the forensic investigators to collect the proper specimens.

DNA evidence can be used to both convict the guilty and exonerate the innocent. In the case of the New York Central Park jogger, DNA evidence played a vital role in releasing five men falsely convicted of the crime.

In the evening of April 19, 1989, a 28-year-old investment banker was jogging in New York's Central Park at about 9:00 P.M. She was found near death at about 2:00 A.M. the next morning at the north end of the park. She had been brutally attacked, raped, and left for dead with a fractured skull and a blood loss of 75%. The woman was in a coma for 12 days but eventually recovered. She suffered a complete loss of memory regarding the incident.

The police already had a group of 14- to 15-year-old teenaged boys who had been arrested for various incidents they had committed in Central Park that evening. They explained to the police that they had been "wilding," which included a series of random attacks. The police found two head hairs and one pubic hair on the T-shirt of one of the suspects. An expert witness testified that these hairs were similar to those of the victim. Four of the teenagers confessed to the crime and implicated a fifth. All five were convicted of the brutal crime and sentenced to jail.

In January 2002, Matias Reyes, already in jail for rape, murder, and robbery, confessed to the Central Park jogger crime. DNA samples were obtained from Matias Reyes, and they matched the DNA from semen recovered from the victim's body and socks, proving he was the one who had committed the crime. A further investigation of the hair samples found on the teenagers showed that they did not come from the victim. On December 19, 2002, a New York State Supreme Court Judge, Charles Tejeda, vacated the convictions against all five teenagers after they had served from 5 to 13 years for a crime they never committed.

TECHNIQUES OF DNA ANALYSIS

There are two main techniques used for the analysis of DNA, restriction fragment length polymorphism (RFLP), and polymerase chain reaction (PCR). The choice of which method to use can depend on the amount of DNA evidence that can be recovered from the crime scene. **RFLP** requires a relatively large amount of DNA. In the case of blood this represents a stain about the size of a quarter. **PCR** is more sensitive and for blood requires only the volume equivalent to the head of a pin. Since PCR is so sensitive, it is very important to take measures to prevent any contamination of the DNA sample. DNA has even been found by the FBI on the back of an envelope where the criminal had licked the adhesive to seal it.

PCR is so sensitive because the first step is DNA amplification. The two strands of DNA can be separated by heating a solution of the DNA to a temperature of about 90°C. At this temperature the DNA unwinds (Figure 21.2).

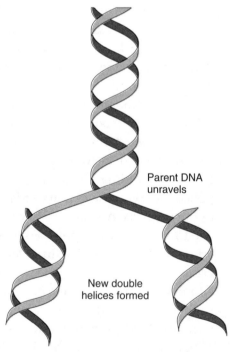

Parent DNA
unravels

New double
helices formed

FIGURE 21.2

The solution then cools down, and an enzyme called polymerase makes two new DNA strands, which are exact duplicates of the original. About 4 min are required for the complete process (cycle) to occur, which takes place in a **thermal cycler** or **DNA amplifier**. An Applied Biosystems DNA amplifier is shown in Figure 21.3.

FIGURE 21.3

If the cycle can be repeated every 4 min, the instrument can perform about 30 cycles in about 2 h. The amount of DNA is doubled with each cycle, which means that after 2 h it has been amplified 2^{30} or 1 billion times. This is what makes PCR so sensitive. It works best with short sequences of DNA such as **short tandem repeats (STRs)** with a length of about four base pairs.

MITOCHONDRIAL DNA

Up until now, the discussion about DNA has focused on the DNA found inside the nucleus of the cell (**nuclear DNA**). There is, however, another type of DNA present in the cell outside the nucleus. It is contained in small structures called mitochondria, which are responsible for producing chemical energy for the cell. This DNA is called **mitochondrial DNA**. Mitochondrial DNA is much smaller than nuclear DNA, but it is much more persistent. Bones that are thousands of years old have had their mitochondrial DNA successfully extracted. However, the potential forensic use of mitochondrial DNA for personal identification has two drawbacks. First, unlike nuclear DNA, the mitochondrial DNA in your cells is an exact copy of the mitochondrial DNA in your mother's cells. Identical copies of mitochondrial DNA are passed down from a mother to all her offspring. This means that brothers and sisters all have the same mitochondrial DNA and that all the children of sisters also have the same mitochondrial DNA. This makes for a poor personal identification system but has proved useful in the fields of forensic anthropology and genealogy. In this work, the mitochondrial DNA must be tested against a known DNA sample. The DNA of living descendents who can be traced back through maternal lines to the person of interest can be used as comparison standards.

Two famous cases in which mitochondrial DNA was used involved Jesse James and the last czar of Russia, Alexander. There was always some controversy surrounding the death of Jesse James in 1882. Did he really die or had someone else been buried in his grave. Mitochondrial DNA was extracted from teeth from the body buried in Jesse James' grave and was matched, which proved that the body truly was that of Jesse James. In this case, the comparison mitochondrial DNA sample came from a grandchild of Jesse's sister.

The deaths of Czar Nicholas and Czarina Alexandra have always been shrouded in mystery. The bodies were shot, bayoneted, thrown down a mineshaft, set on fire, and then doused with acid. In 1991 bones were discovered in a pit near where they reportedly had been kept. Mitochondrial DNA was extracted from the bones and found to match that of Britain's Prince Philip, who was related to Alexandra through his mother. The tests confirmed the bones as belonging to Nicolas and Alexandra and three of their daughters.

A recent case illustrating the usefulness of mitochondrial DNA involved Clayton Daniels, who pleaded guilty to sexual assault charges in 2004. He was allowed to remain out of jail but was required to meet with his probation officer as part of his sentence. After he failed to show up for a scheduled meeting, he was given a 30-day jail sentence. Just a few days before he was to start serving his sentence, in June 2004, the police discovered his Chevrolet at the bottom of a cliff. A body was in the driver's seat, but there had been an extensive fire and the body had been burned beyond recognition. His co-workers raised $1000 for his funeral, and his wife, Molly Daniels, collected his $110,000 life insurance.

Soon after the funeral Molly Daniels introduced neighbors to her "new" boyfriend, Jake Gregg. Jake looked a lot like Clayton, and the police became very suspicious. The fire had been so intense that the investigators had had samples analyzed and found traces of charcoal lighter fluid that had been used to start the blaze. There were no skid marks at the scene of the accident. Since the body had been burned beyond recognition, the police had samples from it analyzed for mitochondrial DNA. They also took samples from Clayton Daniels' mother and found that the DNA did not match. A search warrant was obtained, and an analysis of Molly's computer showed that she had researched how to burn a body and how to obtain a new identity for Clayton, as well as a list of plastic surgeons. Molly confessed to the crime and explained that the body in the car was that of Charlotte Davis, an 81-year-old woman who had died and was buried in a cemetery a few miles away. The couple had dug up the body and used it to try to fake the death of Clayton Daniels.

COLLECTION AND PRESERVATION OF DNA EVIDENCE

It is very important to take steps to prevent any possible contamination of the crime scene. No eating, drinking, or smoking should be allowed. Avoid touching anything unless you are wearing examination gloves. In fact, you should wear two layers of gloves and change the outer layer each time you touch a new piece of physical evidence. Don't even use the phone at the crime scene; your breath could contaminate valuable DNA evidence. Anyone with a cold or cough should be excluded from the area. All evidence that might carry DNA should be air-dried and placed in a nonairtight paper bag.

The main sources of DNA evidence found at crime scenes include sweat, saliva, blood, semen, hair, and skin. Since many of these are invisible to the naked eye, the investigator must look for carriers of DNA evidence, including bloodstains, knives, drinking glasses, clothes, cigarettes, phones, and so on.

It is very important that the investigator collect elimination and reference samples. **Elimination** and **reference samples** are taken from anyone, besides the suspect, whose DNA may be at the crime scene. In the case of a burglary, the DNA from anyone who had lawful access to the crime scene should be collected, and it is always a good idea to collect DNA samples from police officers and investigators in case any of their DNA has contaminated the crime scene. In the case of a sexual assault, reference and elimination samples should be collected from the victim and from any consensual partners from the previous 4 days.

USE OF DNA IN IDENTIFICATION

The use of DNA as a means of personal identification requires that each individual be different. The sections of DNA that code for proteins, such as insulin, are the same for everyone. In fact, almost all of one's DNA codes for something important. However, there are regions within the DNA that contain repeating sequences of the nucleotides A, T, G, and C. These regions are referred to as tandem repeats and seem to be randomly dispersed in the general population, making them unique. Forensic science is mostly interested in the short tandem repeats STRs of four nucleotides since these work best with PCR. One STR of interest is called TH01. It is the name given to the DNA sequence AATG. A certain individual might have a STR containing four of these:

AATG AATG AATG AATG
TTAC TTAC ATAC TTAC

Everyone has two of each type of STR, one from their father and one from their mother. This tends to create two bands for each STR analyzed by electrophoresis (if the person is homozygous for that STR, there will only be one band).

DNA has quickly become the preferred method of forensic investigation. The U.S. military now routinely collects a drop of blood from each recruit for a DNA profile. In the case of massive trauma or a disaster, a sample of DNA may be all that's available to identify a person.

COMBINED DNA INDEX SYSTEM

The **Combined DNA Index System (CODIS)** is a database of DNA types from every state. It is maintained by the FBI, and police agencies are allowed to search it for any matches with DNA profiles. A DNA profile is the result of PCR analysis of 13 different DNA locations. The probability of all 13 locations matching at random is about 1 in 600 trillion. This makes a CODIS match as good as, if not more positive than, a fingerprint match. Sometimes DNA matching is referred to as DNA fingerprinting since the match is as reliable as a fingerprint match. The database stores DNA profiles in two groups. The first is the convicted **offender database**. People convicted of certain crimes have a blood sample taken, and the DNA profile from that sample is entered into the CODIS offender database. The type of crime that requires entry into the CODIS system varies from state to state. All states require people who commit felony sex offenses to be entered, some states require everyone convicted of felonies to be entered, and one state enters anyone who is arrested. The other database is referred to as the **forensic file**. It contains DNA profiles obtained from crime scenes. A match with a profile in the forensic file is called a forensic hit (a match in the offender file is called an offender hit). A forensic hit indicates that the perpetrator of the crime you are investigating has committed another crime somewhere else.

The FBI publishes the following brochure describing its CODIS system.

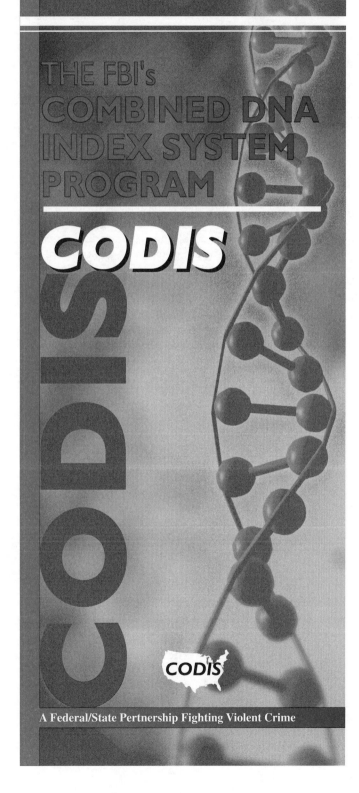

U.S. Department of Justice
Federal Bureau of Investigation

THE FBI's
COMBINED DNA
INDEX SYSTEM
PROGRAM

CODIS

CODIS

A Federal/State Pertnership Fighting Violent Crime

MISSION

The FBI Laboratory's **CO**mbined **D**NA **I**ndex **S**ystem (CODIS) blends forensic science and computer technology into an effective tool for solving violent crimes. CODIS enables federal, state, and local crime labs to exchange and compare DNA profiles electronically, thereby linking crimes to each other and to convicted offenders.

BACKGROUND and STATUS

CODIS began as a pilot project in 1990 serving 14 state and local laboratories. The DNA Identification Act of 1994 (Public Law 103 322) formalized the FBI's authority to establish a national DNA index for law enforcement purposes. In October 1998, the FBI's National DNA Index System (NDIS) became operational. CODIS is implemented as a distributed database with three hierarchical levels (or tiers) – local, state, and national. NDIS is the highest level in the CODIS hierarchy, and enables the laboratories participating in the CODIS Program to exchange and compare DNA profiles on a national level. All DNA profiles originate at the local level (LDIS), then flow to the state (SDIS) and national levels. SDIS allows laboratories within states to exchange DNA profiles. The tiered approach allows state and local agencies to operate their databases according to their specific legislative or legal requirements.

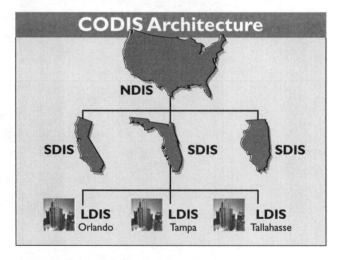

The FBI provides CODIS software, together with installation, training, and user support, free of charge to any state and local law enforcement labs performing DNA analysis. Today, CODIS is installed in more than 100 laboratories. NDIS already contains more than 210,000 profiles from 24 states and the FBI. In addition, all 50 states have passed legislation authorizing the collection of biological samples from convicted offenders for DNA databasing.

INDEXES

CODIS generates investigative leads in crimes where biological evidence is recovered from the crime scene using two indexes: the forensic and offender indexes.

The **Forensic Index** contains DNA profiles from crime scene evidence.

The **Offender Index** contains DNA profiles of individuals convicted of sex offenses (and other violent crimes) with many states now expanding legislation to include other felonies.

Matches made among profiles in the Forensic Index can link crime scenes together; possibly identifying serial offenders. Based on a match, police in multiple jurisdictions can coordinate their respective investigations, and share the leads they developed independently. Matches made between the Forensic and Offender Indexes provide investigators with the identity of the perpetrator(s). After CODIS identifies a potential match, qualified DNA analysts in the laboratories responsible for the matching profiles contact each other to validate or refute the match.

DNA DATABASE LEGISLATION

On a parallel course with the acceptance of DNA evidence in the United States, states have enacted DNA database legislation requiring the collection of blood samples from convicted offenders and storage and analysis of such samples in State DNA databases. In 1991 the FBI Laboratory issued Legislative Guidelines with recommended provisions to be included in State laws, such as definition, access and disclosure, compatibility, expungement, and penalties for unauthorized disclosure.

The complete coverage of State DNA database laws occurred in 1998 with all 50 states having enacted legislation. This legislation requires persons convicted of felony sex offenses (and other crimes, depending on each state's statute) to provide biological samples for DNA analysis. These samples are analyzed and entered into the CODIS database. The FBI hopes that eventually, all 50 states will include all felony offenses.

MEASURING SUCCESS

Ultimately, the success of the CODIS program will be measured by the crimes it helps solve. CODIS's primary metric, the "Investigation Aided" is defined as a case that CODIS assisted through a hit (a match produced by CODIS that would not otherwise have been developed). As of December 1999, CODIS has produced over 600 hits assisting in more than 1,100 investigations.

QUALITY ASSURANCE

The FBI takes an active role in assuring the quality of the results in the database. For example, the DNA Identification Act of 1994 established a DNA Advisory Board (DAB) to develop, revise, and recommend standards for quality assurance. The DAB fulfilled its mission by recommending two quality assurance documents to the Director of the FBI, resulting in the issuance of the *Standards for Forensic DNA Testing Labs and Standards for Convicted Offender Labs*.

THE FUTURE

There has been a sharp increase in the demand for CODIS services due to two factors – (1) advances in the technologies supporting human genome research and (2) increased awareness of the crime reduction potential of forensic DNA by executive and legislative bodies at the State, Local, and National levels, as well as by the general public. In fact, many law enforcement officials consider forensic DNA analysis the most significant advance in forensic science since fingerprints. As a result, states are rapidly expanding the scope and size of their CODIS databases.

Over the past five years about one-half of the States have expanded the scope of their original DNA database legislation (e.g., six states are including all felons in their database, in the past year about five States have expanded the scope of their legislation, and one State now covers all arrested persons). There is currently a backlog of over 500,000 convicted offender samples to be analyzed simply because a majority of states' analyses efforts are unable to keep pace with the collection of these samples. Plus, many labs are doing retests using the new STR technology. The FBI Laboratory is committed to building an infrastructure throughout the U.S. to support the CODIS program and will continue to work with State and local forensic laboratories to achieve the full potential of this investigative tool.

CODIS SUCCESS STORIES

FLORIDA & IOWA;

February 2000: In 1995, an unidentified woman's body was found on an off-ramp along an interstate in Des Moines, IA. After identifying the victim, police began looking at truck drivers as suspects, due to the location of the body. The Iowa Department of Public Safety sent biological evidence left at the crime scene to the FBI Laboratory for DNA analysis. The FBI Lab analyzed the evidence, and developed a DNA profile of the perpetrator. The profile was uploaded to CODIS, where NDIS matched it to the Florida offender. At the time of the hit, the offender was incarcerated in a Florida prison for a sexual assault conviction in early 1999. After identifying the offender, police discovered that he possessed a commercial trucking license.

MISSOURI;

January 2000: In December 1997, the St. Louis Police Dept. had their first cold Forensic Hit using RFLP technology. The hit involved two 1996 cases where young girls were abducted from bus stops and raped. The cases occurred at opposite ends of the city, and police were unable to identify a suspect. In 1999, the St. Louis Police Dept. decided to re-run one of the cases using STR technology, hoping to develop new leads in the case. In January 2000, CODIS matched the reanalyzed 1996 case hit to a 1999 rape case. Dominic Moore, a suspect identified by police in the 1999 case, had confessed to the 1999 rape along with two other 1999 rapes. After the January 2000 CODIS hit, police were able to identify Moore as the perpetrator of the two 1996 rapes.

VIRGINIA;

March 1999: In October 1987, the Prince George County Police Department in Virginia responded to a phone call from a woman who said that she had been raped and stabbed. Police officers arrived at the woman's home shortly after the call was received, but the woman had already bled to death from multiple stab wounds. The Virginia Division of Forensic Science in Richmond developed a DNA profile from the evidence left at the crime scene. Twelve years later, CODIS matched the crime scene profile to the DNA profile of a convicted rapist who had been incarcerated in a Virginia prison since 1989.

REVIEW QUESTIONS

1. DNA stands for

   A. deoxyribonucleic acid   B. ribonucleic acid
   C. DNA numbering analysis   D. do not ask

2. A single cell containing the DNA from both the mother and the father is called a/an

   A. bacteria   B. sperm
   C. egg   D. zygote

3. A piece of inherited information, such as blood type, is called a

   A. zygote   B. sperm
   C. gene   D. egg

4. The four nucleotides that code for the information on DNA are

   A. A, B, C, D   B. A, G, T, C
   C. A, G, U, C   D. W, X, Y, Z

5. Human cells have _____ pairs of chromosomes.

   A. 12   B. 20
   C. 23   D. 60

6. DNA is packed into the nucleus of the cell on structures called

   A. golgi   B. mitochondria
   C. chloroplasts   D. chromosomes

7. The scientist who developed DNA fingerprinting and analyzed the first DNA samples used to solve a crime was

   A. James Watson   B. Francis Crick
   C. Alec Jeffreys   D. Linus Pauling

8. In the first DNA fingerprinting case in Narborough, England, the DNA recovered from the victims _____ the DNA from the 17-year hospital employee who confessed to the crime.

   A. matched   B. didn't match
   C. was too degraded to match D. closely matched

9. A good source of DNA is

   A. saliva   B. semen
   C. blood   D. all of the above

10. The most sensitive method of DNA analysis is

    A. PCR   B. RFLP
    C. EMIT   D. RIA

11. DNA unwinds at a temperature of about

    A. 50°C   B. 70°C
    C. 80°C   D. 90°C

12. The structure of DNA is called a/an

    A. alpha-helix   B. double helix
    C. pleated sheet   D. spiral

13. After 30 cycles of a DNA amplifier, the original DNA has been multiplied _____ times.

    A. 1 million   B. 100 million
    C. 1 billion   D. 100 billion

14. A form of DNA that is the same in all siblings and comes directly from the mother is called _____ DNA.

    A. nuclear   B. ribosomal
    C. transfer   D. mitochondrial

15. A sample of DNA taken from an investigator is referred to as a/an _____ sample.

    A. elimination   B. blind
    C. duplicate   D. surrogate

16. An example of the use of mitochondrial DNA to identify remains based on living relatives involved

    A. Jimmy Hoffa   B. Jesse James
    C. John Dillinger   D. Napoleon Bonaparte

17. Mitochondrial DNA is _____ nuclear DNA.

    A. less persistent than   B. more persistent than
    C. as persistent as   D. none of the above

18. Modern DNA fingerprinting focuses on DNA sequences of four nucleotides called

    A. RFLPs   B. PCRs
    C. STRs   D. ALSs

19. The computerized system used by the FBI to search its DNA database is called

    A. IAFIS   B. NIBIN
    C. DBASE   D. CODIS

20. The FBI DNA database stores the DNA profiles in _____ group(s).

    A. one   B. two
    C. three   D. four

21. CODIS is based on the matching of how many DNA locations?

    A. 10   B. 12
    C. 13   D. 23

22. A CODIS match with DNA from a crime scene is called a/an _____ hit.

    A. forensic   B. offender
    C. false   D. positive

23. The CODIS database presently contains about _____ profiles.

    A. 10,000   B. 210,000
    C. 1 million   D. 47 million

24. There are presently about _____ laboratories that create DNA profiles for the CODIS database.

    A. 10   B. 50
    C. 100   D. 500

Answers

1. A	9. D	17. B
2. D	10. A	18. C
3. C	11. D	19. D
4. B	12. B	20. B
5. C	13. C	21. C
6. D	14. D	22. A
7. C	15. A	23. B
8. B	16. B	24. C

PART IV

THE FUTURE OF FORENSIC SCIENCE

CHAPTER 22

FUTURE TRENDS IN FORENSIC SCIENCES

Author's note. This chapter offers predictions of future events based on current trends. It represents the author's opinion as to what the future holds based on the current state of criminalistics and the sciences behind it.

EVIDENCE RESPONSE TEAMS

The growing sensitivity of analytical instrumentation requires greater training and equipment in the area of physical evidence collection. At this time only larger cities have specialized evidence collection units that can drive to the crime scene in a well-equipped van and thoroughly search a crime scene. Evidence collection technicians (probably graduates of a future 2-year AAS degree program) will wear protective clothing to prevent any contamination of the evidence. They will carry lasers, ultraviolet lights, and special goggles to help visualize latent fingerprints and seminal stains. They will be able to select portable instruments from the van as necessary, depending on the crime scene. These will include trace evidence vacuums, combustion sniffers, infrared imaging systems, handheld GC/MS, X-ray fluorescence systems, and Raman spectral instruments.

TERRORISM

The threat of terrorism is a prominent concern for any forensic scientist. Criminologists will need to be trained to detect and handle weapons of mass destruction. The forensic scientist of the future will require training in the fields of bioterrorism and ionizing radiation and will need to be protectively clothed to handle such situations. Entering crime scenes where these types of weapons have been used will require specialized clothing, breathing systems, inoculations, and radiation, chemical, and biological monitors.

HAZARDOUS MATERIALS RESPONSE UNITS

The proliferation of clandestine laboratories for making drugs, explosives, and biological weapons means that criminal investigators will be exposed to more and more hazardous materials. The production of 1 lb of methamphetamine produces 6 lb of toxic waste. Future forensic scientists will need to protect themselves from the exposure to toxic compounds at the crime scene and will have to learn how to properly collect, package, and dispose of toxic substances according to state and federal guidelines.

THE NEW FBI CRIME LAB

In April 2003, the FBI opened its new 500,000-ft^2 laboratory building in Quantico, VA. The new building has some of the most advanced forensic research equipment in the world, and is headquarters to more than 650 examiners and technicians. The new lab cost about $130 million to build and provides free analysis of any type of physical evidence for international, federal, state, and local police agencies. The new building has three five-story towers and was designed from the start to handle physical evidence. Clean rooms are kept separate from offices and have completely filtered air. Two-thirds of each floor is lab space and is sealed off from other areas. Each lab even has an elevator dedicated just to the transportation of evidence.

NEW ANALYTICAL INSTRUMENTS IN THE FUTURE

The mass spectrometer is quickly becoming the premier detector in the analytical laboratory. Most organic analysis is done using GC/MS. The advent of higher-resolution mass spectrometers with greater sensitivity has led researchers to an instrument that can analyze elements as well as organic compounds. This instrument is called an inductively coupled argon plasma mass spectrometer. The main drawback of GC/MS is that higher-molecular-weight compounds cannot be vaporized. In the future, liquid chromatography will probably supplant gas chromatography as the method of choice for introducing organic compounds, even explosives, into the mass spectrometer. The analytical laboratory of the future will probably have a centralized mass spectrometer detector with a GC, LC, ICAP, and laser desorption unit to introduce organic and inorganic samples into the mass spectrometer.

The advent of DNA analysis has led to a great many positive identifications because of the individual characteristic nature of DNA evidence. Presently, the analysis of DNA evidence is highly technical and requires time. It is hoped that in the future a portable device will be able to take samples and quickly produce results. A portable device could be taken to the crime scene and used to analyze any trace evidence that could yield the identity of the criminal. The portable DNA analyzer could be a wireless device that could be tied into the CODIS system and instantaneously identify any individuals who were at the crime scene.

CONTROL OF CRIME LABS BY THE COURTS

A controversial suggestion made by some forensic scientists has been to move the control of crime labs from state police and place them under the control of the courts or the state governments. This is intended to give both prosecutor and defense equal access to the expertise and capabilities of the crime lab. There are sometimes ethical concerns arising from the fact that both the budget and the control of the crime lab are under the authority of the police. Sometimes the cost of the lab is justified by the conviction rate. There is a concern that the results of the analysis help support the conviction of the suspect.

BIOMETRICS

The science of electronically measuring some physical attribute of a person as a means of personal identification is called biometrics. The following can be used in biometrics: voice recognition, fingerprint recognition, retinal recognition, DNA recognition, iris recognition, face recognition, and hand recognition. Some computers are already available with biometric fingerprint scanners that are much more secure than passwords. The applications of biometrics are endless. Some items in which biometrics has already been incorporated include doors, safes, cell phones, computers, disks, time locks, identification cards, and credit cards.

GLOSSARY OF FORENSIC TERMS

Actus rea – guilty by act.

Addiction – physical or psychological dependence caused by a drug.

AFIS – Automated Fingerprint Identification System.

Algor mortis – The cooling of a body after death because of loss of heat to the surroundings.

Allege – To make an accusation without any proof.

Allele – One of the different forms of each of the genes contributed by parents to offspring that determines a trait such as blood type.

Anthropology – The study of skeletal remains to determine age, sex, race, and identification.

Anthropometry – A system of personal identification invented by Alphonse Bertillon based on 11 body measurements and on photographs.

Autopsy – A surgical procedure involving the dissection of a body to determine the previous health of the individual and the cause of death.

BAC – The blood alcohol content (or blood alcohol concentration) of a person based on the grams of alcohol per 100 mL of blood.

Ballistics – The study of ammunition, firearms, and the trajectory of projectiles fired from them.

Barbiturate – A depressant synthesized from the chemical barbituric acid.

Biological evidence – Evidence from living systems such as blood, sweat, saliva, and semen. In general, biological evidence must be packaged in a nonairtight container and refrigerated at 4°C.

Biology – The science that studies living systems. In forensics biologists often help in the identification of plants and vegetation and in the analysis of body fluids and DNA.

Blood spatter – The pattern formed by blood as it strikes a surface. Blood spatter analysis can often reveal how an injury occurred.

Body temperature – The temperature of a body taken rectally or by insertion in the liver. The temperature can be used to estimate the time of death.

Bullet – Ammunition that is fired from a weapon. Bullets are often made of a metal such as lead.

Cannabis – *Cannabis sativa* is the formal Latin name for the marijuana plant.

Chain of custody – A document tracing the persons responsible for evidence from the time it is collected at the crime scene to the time it is turned over to the court.

Chromatography – The separation of a complex mixture into pure compounds.

Clandestine – Secret, covert, underground, or illegal.

Club drug – One of the common classes of drugs popular at nightclubs and raves, such as MDMA, GHB, ketamine, methamphetamine, and Rohypnol.

Cocaine – A stimulant extracted from the coca leaf of South America.

CODIS – The Combined DNA Index System maintained by the Federal Bureau of Investigation. This database allows the DNA from a crime scene to be coded and searched against the DNA from convicted offenders and other crime scenes.

Comparison microscope – A microscope that combines the field of view of two microscopes to allow the comparison of bullets, hairs, fibers, and other physical evidence.

Confirmatory – A method that determines the identity of a compound with a high degree of certainty.

Coroner – A person charged with investigating any death that was deemed suspicious. Originally appointed by the king, the word means "from the crown." These individuals are now appointed or elected.

Corroborate – To provide supporting evidence or confirmation of the truth of something.

Cortex – The inside part of the hair containing the color pigments and the medulla.

Criminal profiling – A psychological representation of a suspect based on the crime, crime scene, victim, physical evidence, testimony, and behavior.

Criminalistics – The application of scientific methods to solving crimes.

Cuticle – The outside part of the hair, which is made of very strong, keratinized proteins.

Date rape drug – Rohypnol and GHB are drugs that are sometimes used in drug-facilitated sexual crimes. The drug can render the victim unable to resist and unable to remember what happened.

Deposition – An official statement in writing given by a witness under oath.

Diener – A person who assists the pathologist during an autopsy.

DNA – The basic unit of genetic information contained in the nucleus of each cell. Each person's DNA is unique and can be used to determine the source of a biological sample.

Double helix – The structure of DNA, which can be represented as a twisted ladder.

Drug (illegal) – A substance taken to produce a change in feeling, perception, or behavior. Most illegal drugs are taken to create a euphoric effect.

Electrophoresis – A technique that uses a voltage applied to a gel plate to separate various biological substances.

Entomology – The study of the birth, death, and life cycles of insects.

Euphoria – A deep sense of well-being, a really good feeling.

Everted – Turned outward. An exit wound has everted edges.

Evidence – Anything that can be used to determine the facts of a criminal case, including testimonial and physical evidence.

Exigent evidence – Evidence that is in danger of immediate loss or destruction.

Expert witness – A person with specialized knowledge who helps the jury to understand the evidence presented in a trial.

External examination – A study of the outside of the body, which the pathologist performs first.

Fingerprint – A unique system of lines left behind when the friction ridges of the finger come in contact with a surface. The patterns and ridge characteristics can be used to uniquely identify an individual.

Fluorescence – The process by which a substance can absorb a shorter wavelength and reemit the light as a longer wavelength. In forensic science UV light is often used, and fluorescent samples reemit visible light, which allows investigators to locate substances such as seminal fluid.

Forensic science – The application of science to law.

Gas chromatography (GC) – The separation of a complex mixture into pure compounds by heating the sample and causing it to change into the gaseous state. The gases are then forced through a column where the separation occurs. Specialized detectors are used to determine when each compound exits the column.

Grand jury – A body of between 16 and 23 people impaneled by a superior court to look at evidence and decide whether it is sufficient to send a case to trial.

Gunshot residue (GSR) – The remnants of burned and unburned smokeless powder on the victim or the remnants of burned primer powder on the shooter.

Habeas corpus – To have or produce the body.

Hair – Protein structures produced by hair follicles in the skin, which can be used for comparison and sometimes identification.

Hallucinogen – A chemical substance that produces an alteration in a person's perception or thought processes.

Hashish – The resin formed from the flowering top of the female *Cannabis* plant. It can be smoked or chewed.

Homicide – The intentional, deliberate taking of a human life.

IAFIS – Integrated Automated Fingerprint System

Jurisprudence – The study of law.

Latent – Invisible to the unaided eye.

Livor mortis – The settling of blood to the lowest point in the body after death.

Locard's principle – A statement by Edmond Locard, considered to be the "father of modern forensic science," which can best be summarized as "Every contact leaves a trace." This is considered to be the founding principle of forensic science.

Manslaughter – The accidental or nonintentional taking of another person's life.

Marijuana – The common name for the *Cannabis sativa* plant which contains the hallucinogen delta-9-tetrahydrocannabinol (THC).

Mass – The amount of matter present in a sample.

Mass spectrometry (MS) – A confirmatory method that normally uses the output of a gas chromatograph to provide a gaseous sample of a pure compound. The molecules of the compound are then fragmented and charged. These fragments are then separated and counted according to their mass.

Medical examiner – A physician who is authorized by the state to investigate suspicious deaths. The medical examiner is expected to determine the cause and manner of death and whether a homicide or threat to public safety exists.

Mens rea – Guilty in mind, meaning that the person has conscious intent to commit a crime.

Mitochondria – Small units found in the cells of the body that produce the energy needed by the cell.

Mitochondrial DNA – A small circular sequence of DNA that is passed unchanged from mother to offspring. All siblings have the exact mitochondrial DNA in their cells, and it can often be extracted from skeletal remains long after nuclear DNA has completely disintegrated.

Murder – The intentional taking of another person's life without any legal justification. First-degree murder involves planned or premeditated murder or murder that occurs in the commission of a felony crime; second-degree murder involves the intent to murder without the element of premeditation.

Narcotic – A chemical that is derived from opium or has opiumlike properties. Sometimes this term is incorrectly applied to all abused drugs.

Odontology – The study of teeth. In forensics, an odontologist is normally a dentist with specialized training in identifying people from teeth and bite marks.

Opium – The dried resin of the capsule of the unripe poppy plant *Papaver somniferum*. The main active ingredient in the resin is morphine.

Pathologist – A physician who has had specialized training in determining the cause and manner of death by performing an autopsy.

Physical Evidence Recovery Kit (PERK) – A kit used by hospital staff to collect physical evidence from a rape victim.

Polygraph – An instrument that records electrical signals from the heart, breathing, and conductivity of the skin. The results of these measurements are used to form an opinion about the honesty or dishonesty of an individual. A polygraph is sometimes erroneously referred to as a lie detector.

Polymerase chain reaction (PCR) – A method of amplifying the amount of DNA in a sample by thermal cycling. The double helix of the DNA in a sample is separated by heating to about 95°C and then cooled. The process is repeated 20 to 30 times, and the process creates millions of new copies that are exact replicas of the original DNA.

Psychosis – A mental impairment that causes the affected individual to lose touch with reality.

Questioned documents – Documents from an uncertain source, including alterations, forgeries, and counterfeits.

Restriction fragment length polymorphism (RFLP) – The first method employed by forensic laboratories to match DNA from crime scene samples to individual suspects. While very accurate, the method required a large amount of DNA and used segments that were too large to be amplified by PCR. The technique was also labor-intensive and slow. STR has replaced RFPL.

Rigor mortis – The stiffening of the muscles of the body after death as a result of chemical changes. The contractions begin about 2 h after death.

Rule of sixes – A rule-of-thumb estimate of the distance between the muzzle of a shotgun and the victim. At a distance of 6 ft or less the wound appears as a single round hole. At a distance of up to 6 yd the wound appears as a central hole with many small pellet holes around it. At a distance greater than 6 yd the wound appears as a series of small pellet holes.

Scanning electron microscope (SEM) – A microscope that uses electrons instead of light to magnify objects up to 1 million times. It is often used to detect the cystolithic hairs on marijuana or to show gunshot residue on a shooter's hand.

Short tandem repeat (STR) – The most common technique used to match DNA samples from a crime scene and DNA from a suspect. The FBI CODIS system is based on short tandem repeats. Most commonly, STRs are sequences of four nucleotides (A, G, C, and T) that repeat many times in an individual's nuclear DNA.

Toolmarks – Impressions left behind when a harder material comes in contact with a softer material. The striation marks left behind can be used to link a tool to an object from the crime scene it may have come in contact with.

Toxicology – The study of drugs and poisons in the body.

Trace evidence – Evidence from a crime scene that cannot be discerned by the unaided eye. Trace evidence is often referred to as an invisible clue and requires a microscope or other sensitive instrument for analysis.

Ultraviolet light (UV) – Light of a shorter wavelength than visible light. Ultraviolet light is often separated into three regions – UV-A, UV-B, and UV-C. Many chemicals of forensic interest fluoresce in the presence of ultraviolet light.

STREET TERMS OF DRUGS AND DRUG TRADE

Street Terms of Drugs and the Drug Trade from the Executive Office of the President, Office of National Drug Control Policy, February 2004

007s – Methylenedioxymethamphetamine (MDMA)

100s – Lysergic acid diethylamide (LSD)

151 – Crack cocaine

2-for-1 sale – A marketing scheme designed to promote and increase crack sales

24-7 – Crack cocaine

25s – Lysergic acid diethylamide (LSD)

2CB – Nexus

3750 – Marijuana and crack rolled in a joint

40 – OxyContin pill

40-bar – OxyContin pill

420 – Marijuana use

45-minute pychosis – Dimethyltryptamine

69s – Methylenedioxymethamphetamine (MDMA)

714s – Methaqualone

80 – OxyContin pill

A – LSD; amphetamine

A-bomb – Marijuana cigarette with heroin or opium

A-boot – Under the influence of drugs

Abandominiums – Abandoned row houses where drugs are used

Abe – $5 worth of drugs

Abe's cabe – $5 bill

Abolic – Veterinary steroids

AC/DC – Codeine cough syrup

Acapulco gold – Marijuana from southwestern Mexico; marijuana

Acapulco red – Marijuana

Ace – Marijuana cigarette; PCP

Acid – LSD

Acid cube – Sugar cube containing LSD

Acid freak – Heavy user of LSD

Acid head – User of LSD

Acido (Spanish) – Hallucinogens; LSD

Ad – PCP; drug addict

Adam – Methylenedioxymethamphetamine (MDMA)

Aeon flux – Lysergic acid diethylamide (LSD)

Afgani indica – Marijuana

African – Marijuana

African black – Marijuana

African bush – Marijuana

African woodbine – Marijuana cigarette

Agonies – Withdrawal symptoms

Ah-pen-yen – Opium

Aimes – Amyl nitrite

Aimies – Amphetamine; amyl nitrite

AIP – Heroin from Afghanistan, Iran, or Pakistan

Air blast – Inhalants

Airhead – Marijuana user

Airplane – Marijuana

Al Capone – Heroin

Alice B. Toklas – Marijuana brownie

All lit up – Under the influence of drugs

All-star – User of multiple drugs

All-American drug – Cocaine

Alpha-ET – Alpha-ethyltryptamine

Ames – Amyl nitrite

Amidone – Methadone

Amoeba – PCP

Amp – Amphetamine; marijuana dipped in formaldehyde or embalming fluid, sometimes laced with PCP and smoked

Amp head – LSD user

Amp joint – Marijuana cigarette laced with some form of narcotic

Amped – High on amphetamines

Amped-out – Fatigue after using amphetamine

Amping – Accelerated heartbeat

AMT – Dimethyltryptamine

Amys – Amyl nitrite

Anadrol – Oral steroids

Anatrofin – Injectable steroids

Anavar – Oral steroids

Angel – PCP

Angel dust – PCP

Angel hair – PCP

Angel mist – PCP

Angel poke – PCP

Angie – Cocaine

Angola – Marijuana

Animal – LSD

Animal trank – PCP

Animal tranq – PCP

Animal tranquilizer – PCP

Antifreeze – Heroin

Apache – Fentanyl

Apple jacks – Crack cocaine

Are you anywhere? – Do you use marijuana?

Aries – Heroin

Arnolds – Steroids

Aroma of men – Isobutyl nitrite

Around the turn – Having gone through withdrawal period

Artillery – Equipment for injecting drugs

Ashes – Marijuana

Aspirin – Powder cocaine

Assassin of youth – Marijuana

Astro turf – Marijuana

Atom bomb – Marijuana mixed with heroin

Atshitshi – Marijuana

Aunt – Powder cocaine

Aunt Hazel – Heroin

Aunt Mary – Marijuana

Aunt Nora – Cocaine

Auntie – Opium

Auntie Emma – Opium

Aurora borealis – PCP

Author – Doctor who writes illegal prescriptions

B – Amount of marijuana needed to fill a matchbox

B-40 – Cigar laced with marijuana and dipped in malt liquor

B-bombs – Amphetamines; methylenedioxymethamphetamine (MDMA)

B.J.'s – Crack cocaine

Babe – Drug used for detoxification

Baby – Marijuana

Baby bhang – Marijuana

Baby habit – Occasional use of drugs

Baby T – Crack cocaine

Babysit – Guide someone through their first drug experience

Babysitter – Marijuana

Back breakers – LSD and strychnine

Back dex – Amphetamine

Back door – Residue left in a pipe

Back jack – Injecting opium; to inject a drug

Back to back – Smoking crack after injecting heroin or heroin used after smoking crack

Backtrack – Allow blood to flow back into a needle during injection

Backup – To prepare a vein for injection

Backwards – Depressants

Bad – Crack cocaine

Bad bundle – Inferior-quality heroin; damaged heroin

Bad go – Bad reaction to a drug

Bad seed – Marijuana; heroin; peyote

Bad rock – Crack cocaine

Bag – Container for drugs; a package of drugs, usually marijuana or heroin; a person's favorite drug

Bag bride – Crack-smoking prostitute

Bag man – Person who transports money; person who supplies narcotics or other drugs; a pusher

Bagging – Using inhalants

Baker – Person who smokes marijuana

Bale – Marijuana

Ball – Crack cocaine; Mexican black tar heroin

Balling – Vaginally implanting cocaine

Balloon – Heroin supplier; a penny balloon that contains narcotics

Ballot – Heroin

Bam – Amphetamine; depressants

Bamba – Marijuana

Bambalacha – Marijuana

Bambita – Desoxyn or an amphetamine derivative

Bambs – Depressants

Bammies – A poor quality of marijuana

Bammy – Marijuana

Banana split – Combination of 2C-B (Nexus) with other illicit substances, particularly LSD (lysergic acid diethylamide)

Banano – Marijuana or tobacco cigarettes laced with cocaine

Bang – Inhalants; to inject a drug

Banging – Under the influence of drugs

Bank bandit pills – Depressants

Bar – Marijuana

Barb – Depressants

Barbies – Depressants

Barbs – Cocaine

Barr – Codeine cough syrup

Barrels – LSD

Bart Simpson – Heroin

Basa – Crack cocaine

Base – Cocaine; crack

Base crazies – Searching on hands and knees for cocaine or crack

Base head – Person who bases

Baseball – Crack cocaine

Based out – To have lost control over basing

Bash – Marijuana

Basing – Crack cocaine

Basuco (Spanish) – Cocaine; coca paste residue sprinkled on a regular or marijuana cigarette

Bathtub crank – Poor-quality methamphetamine; methamphetamine produced in bathtubs

Bathtub speed – Methcathinone

Batman – Cocaine; heroin

Batmans – Methylenedioxymethamphetamine (MDMA)

Batt – IV needle; hypodermic needle

Batted out – Apprehended by the law

Battery acid – LSD

Batu – Smokable methamphetamine

Bazooka – Cocaine; crack; crack and tobacco combined in a joint; coca paste and marijuana

Bazulco – Cocaine

BC bud – Marijuana from British Columbia; synonymous with any high-grade marijuana from Canada

BDMPEA – Nexus

Beam – Cocaine

Beam me up Scottie – Crack dipped in PCP

Beam me up Scotty – PCP and crack

Beamer – Crack smoker

Beamers – Crack cocaine

Bean – A capsule containing drugs; MDMA (methylenedioxymethamphetamine)

Beannies – Methamphetamine

Beans – Crack cocaine; mescaline; amphetamine; depressants

Beast – Heroin; LSD

Beat – Crack cocaine

Beat artist – Person selling bogus drugs

Beat vials – Vials containing sham crack to cheat buyers

Beautiful boulders – Crack cocaine

Beavis and Butthead – LSD

Bebe – Crack cocaine

Bed bugs – Fellow addicts

Beedies – Cigarettes from India (resembling marijuana joints/vehicle for other drugs)

Beemers – Crack cocaine

Behind the scale – To weigh and sell cocaine

Beiging – Chemicals altering cocaine to make it appear to be of a higher purity; chemically altering cocaine to make it look brown

Belladonna – PCP

Belt – Effects of drugs

Belted – Under the influence of a drug

Belushi – Combination of cocaine and heroin

Belyando spruce – Marijuana

Bender – Drug party

Bennie – Amphetamine

Bens – Amphetamine; methylene-dioxymethamphetamine (MDMA)

Benz – Amphetamine

Benzedrine – Amphetamine; methyl-enedioxymethamphetamine (MDMA)

Benzidrine – Amphetamine

Bermuda triangles – Methylene-dioxymethamphetamine (MDMA)

Bernice – Cocaine

Bernie – Cocaine

Bernie's flakes – Cocaine

Bernie's gold dust – Cocaine

Bhang – Marijuana (Indian term)

Bibs – MDMA (methylene-dioxymethamphetamine)

Big 8 – 1/8 kilogram crack

Big bag – Heroin

Big bloke – Cocaine

Big C – Cocaine

Big D – LSD

Big doodig – Heroin

Big flake – Cocaine

Big H – Heroin

Big Harry – Heroin

Big man – Drug supplier

Big O – Opium

Big rush – Cocaine

Biker's coffee – Methamphetamine and coffee

Bill Blass – Crack cocaine

Billie hoke – Cocaine

Bin laden – Heroin (after September 11)

Bindle – Small packet of drug powder; heroin

Bing – Enough drug for one injection

Bingers – Crack addicts

Bingo – To inject a drug

Bings – Crack cocaine

Biphetamine – Amphetamine; methyl-enedioxymethamphetamine (MDMA)

Bipping – Snorting heroin and cocaine, either separately or together

Birdhead – LSD

Birdie powder – Cocaine; heroin

Biscuit – 50 rocks of crack

Bite one's lips – To smoke marijuana

Biz – Bag or portion of drugs

Bjs – Crack cocaine

Black – Marijuana; opium; metham-phetamine

Black acid – LSD; LSD and PCP

Black and white – Amphetamine

Black Bart – Marijuana

Black beauties – Amphetamine; depres-sants

Black beauty – Methamphetamine

Blackbirds – Amphetamine

Black bombers – Amphetamine

Black Cadillacs – Amphetamine

Black dust – PCP

Black eagle – Heroin

Black ganga – Marijuana resin

Black gold – High-potency marijuana

Black gungi – Marijuana from India

Black gunion – Marijuana

Black hash – Opium mixed with hashish

Black hole – The depressant high asso-ciated with ketamine

Black mo/black moat – Highly potent marijuana

Black mollies – Amphetamine

Black mote – Marijuana mixed with honey

Black pearl – Heroin

Black pill – Opium pill

Black rock – Crack cocaine

Black Russian – Opium mixed with hashish

Black star – LSD

Black stuff – Heroin; opium

Black sunshine – LSD

Black tabs – LSD

Black tar – Heroin

Black whack – PCP

Blacks – Amphetamine

Blade – Crystal methamphetamine

Blanca (Spanish) – Cocaine

Blanco (Spanish) – Heroin; cocaine

Blank – Container of nonnarcotic powder sold as heroin

Blanket – Marijuana cigarette

Blanks – Low-quality drugs

Blast – Cocaine; smoke crack; marijuana; smoke marijuana or crack

Blast a joint – To smoke marijuana

Blast a roach – To smoke marijuana

Blast a stick – To smoke marijuana

Blasted – Under the influence of drugs

Blaxing – Smoking marijuana

Blazing – Smoking marijuana

Blizzard – A white cloud in a pipe used to smoke cocaine

Block – Marijuana

Blockbusters – Depressants

Blonde – Marijuana

Blotter – Crack cocaine; LSD

Blotter acid – LSD; PCP

Blotter cube – LSD

Blow – Cocaine; to inhale cocaine; to smoke marijuana

Blow a fix/blow a shot – injection misses the vein and is wasted in the skin

Blow a stick – To smoke marijuana

Blow blue – To inhale cocaine

Blow coke – To inhale cocaine

Blow one's roof – To smoke marijuana

Blow smoke – To inhale cocaine

Blow the vein – To inject a drug

Blow up – Crack cut with lidocaine to increase size, weight, and street value

Blow your mind – Get high on hallucinogens

Blowcaine – Crack diluted with procaine

Blowing smoke – Marijuana

Blowout – Crack

Blows – Heroin

Blue – Crack cocaine; depressants; OxyContin

Blue acid – LSD

Blue angels – Depressants

Blue bag – Heroin

Blue barrels – LSD

Bluebirds – Depressants

Blue boy – Amphetamine

Blue bullets – Depressants

Blue caps – Mescaline

Blue chairs – LSD

Blue cheers – LSD

Blue clouds – Amytal (amobarbital sodium) capsules

Blue de hue – Marijuana from Vietnam

Blue devil – Depressants

Blue devils – Methamphetamine

Blue dolls – Depressants

Blue heaven – LSD

Blue heavens – Depressants

Blue kisses – Methylenedioxymethamphetamine (MDMA)

Blue lips – Methylenedioxymethamphetamine (MDMA)

Blue madman – PCP

Blue meth – Methamphetamine

Blue microdot – LSD

Blue mist – LSD

Blue mollies – Amphetamine

Blue moons – LSD

Blue Nile – Methylenedioxymethamphetamine (MDMA)

Blue nitro vitality – GBL-containing product

Blue sage – Marijuana

Blue sky blond – High-potency marijuna from Colombia

Blue star – Heroin

Blue tips – Depressants

Blue vials – LSD

Blunt – Marijuana inside a cigar; cocaine and marijuana inside a cigar

Bo – Marijuana

Bo-bo – Marijuana

Boat – PCP

Bobo – Crack cocaine

Bobo bush – Marijuana

Body-packer – Individual who ingests wrapped packets of crack or cocaine to transport

Body stuffer – Individual who ingests crack vials to avoid prosecution

Bogart a joint – Salivate on a marijuana cigarette; refuse to share

Bohd – Marijuana; PCP

Bolasterone – Injectable steroids

Bolivian marching powder – Cocaine

Bollo – Crack cocaine

Bolo – Crack cocaine

Bolt – Amphetamine; isobutyl nitrite

Bomb – Crack; heroin; large marijuana cigarette; high-potency heroin

Bomb squad – Name of crack-selling crew

Bomber – Marijuana cigarette

Bombido – Heroin; injectable amphetamine; depressants

Bombita (Spanish) – Heroin; amphetamine; depressants

Bombs away – Heroin

Bone – Marijuana; $50 piece of crack; high-purity heroin

Bonecrusher – Crack cocaine

Bones – Crack cocaine

Bong – Pipe used to smoke marijuana

Bonita (Spanish) – Heroin

Boo – Marijuana; methamphetamine

Boo boo bama – Marijuana

Book – 100-dosage units of LSD

Boom – Marijuana

Boomers – Psilocybin/psilocin; LSD

Boost – Crack cocaine; to steal; to inject a drug

Boost and shoot – Steal to support a habit

Booster – To inhale cocaine

Boot – To inject a drug

Boot the gong – To smoke marijuana

Booted – Under the influence of drugs

Bopper – Crack cocaine

Boppers – Amyl nitrite

Botray – Crack cocaine

Bottles – Crack vials; amphetamine

Boubou – Crack cocaine

Boulder – Crack cocaine; $20 worth of crack

Boulya – Crack cocaine

Bouncing powder – cocaine

Box labs – Small, mobile, clandestine labs used to produce methamphetamine

Boxed – In jail

Boy – Cocaine; heroin

Bozo – Heroin

Brain damage – Heroin

Brain pills – Amphetamines

Brain ticklers – Amphetamine

Brea (Spanish) – Heroin

Break night – Staying up all night on a cocaine binge until daybreak

Breakdown – $40 of Crack cocaine that can be broken down into $20 packages

Brewery – Place where drugs are made

Brick – Crack cocaine; cocaine; marijuana; 1 kilogram of marijuana

Brick gum – Heroin

Bridge or bring up – Ready a vein for injection

Britton – Peyote

Broccoli – Marijuana

Broja – Heroin

Broker – Go between in a drug deal; heavy drug user

Bromo – Nexus

Brown – Marijuana; heroin; methamphetamine

Brown bombers – LSD

Brown crystal – Heroin

Brown dots – LSD

Brown rhine – Heroin

Brown sugar – Heroin

Brown tape – Heroin

Brownies – Amphetamine

Browns – Amphetamine

Bubble gum – Cocaine; Crack cocaine; marijuana from Tennessee

Buck – Shoot someone in the head

Bud – Marijuana

Buda – Marijuana; a high-grade marijuana joint filled with crack

Buddha – Potent marijuana spiked with opium

Buffer – A woman who performs oral sex in exchange for crack; crack smoker

Bugged – Irritated; to be covered with sores and abscesses from repeated use of unsterile needles

Bull – Narcotics agent or police officer

Bulldog – Heroin

Bullet – Isobutyl nitrite; inhalants

Bullet bolt – Inhalants

Bullia capital – Crack; fake crack

Bullion – Crack cocaine

Bullyon – Marijuana

Bumblebees – Amphetamine

Bummer trip – Unsettling and threatening experience from PCP intoxication

Bump – Crack; fake crack; cocaine; boost a high; hit of ketamine ($20)

Bumper – Crack cocaine

Bumping up – Methylenedioxymethamphetamine (MDMA) combined with powder cocaine

Bundle – Heroin

Bunk – Fake cocaine; crack cocaine

Burese – Cocaine

Burn one – To smoke marijuana

Burn the main line – To inject a drug

Burn transaction – Selling a substance as a certain drug

Burned – Purchase fake drugs

Burned out – Collapse of veins from repeated injections; permanent impairment from drug abuse

Burnese – Cocaine

Burnie – Marijuana

Burnout – Heavy abuser of drugs

Bush – Marijuana; cocaine; PCP

Businessman's LSD – Dimethyltryptamine

Businessman's special – Dimethyltryptamine

Businessman's trip – Dimethyltryptamine

Busted – Arrested

Busters – Depressants

Busy bee – PCP

Butler – Crack cocaine

Butt naked – PCP

Butter – Marijuana; crack

Butter flower – Marijuana

Buttons – Mescaline

Butu – Heroin

Buzz – Under the influence of drugs

Buzz bomb – Nitrous oxide

C – Cocaine

C and M – Cocaine and morphine

C joint – Place where cocaine is sold

C-dust – Cocaine

C-game – Cocaine

C.S. – Marijuana

Caballo (Spanish) – Heroin

Cabbage head – An individual who will use or experiment with any kind of drug

Cabello (Spanish) – Cocaine

Caca – Heroin

Cactus – Mescaline

Cactus buttons – Mescaline

Cactus head – Mescaline

Cad/Cadillac – 1 ounce

Cadillac – Cocaine; PCP

Cadillac express – Methcathinone

Cafeteria use – Use of various drugs simultaneously, particularly sedatives or hypnotics

Cafeteria-style use – Using a combination of different club drugs

Caine – Cocaine; crack cocaine

Cakes – Round disks of crack

Calbo (Spanish) – Heroin

California cornflakes – Cocaine

California sunshine – LSD

Cam trip – High-potency marijuana

Cambodian red/Cam red – Marijuana from Cambodia

Came – Cocaine

Can – Marijuana; 1 ounce

Canade – Heroin/marijuana combination

Canadian black – Marijuana

Canamo – Marijuana

Canappa – Marijuana

Cancelled stick – Marijuana cigarette

Candy – Cocaine; crack cocaine; amphetamine; depressants

Candy blunt – Blunts dipped in cough syrup

Candy C – Cocaine

Candy flipping on a string – Combining or sequencing LSD with MDMA; mixing LSD, MDMA, and cocaine

Candy raver – Young people who attend raves; rave attendees who wear candy jewelry

Candy sugar – Powder cocaine

Candy-flipping – LSD mixed with Ecstasy

Candyman – Drug supplier

Cannabinol – PCP

Cannabis tea – Marijuana

Cap – Crack cocaine; LSD; a capsule of a drug

Cap up – Transfer bulk-form drugs to capsules

Capital H – Heroin

Caps – Heroin; psilocybin/psilocin; crack; Gamma-hydroxybutyrate (GHB)

Capsula (Spanish) – Crack cocaine

Carburetor – Crack stem attachment

Care bears – Methylenedioxymethamphetamine (MDMA)

Carga (Spanish) – Heroin

Carmabis – Marijuana

Carne (Spanish) – Heroin

Carnie – Cocaine

Carpet patrol – Crack smokers searching the floor for crack

Carrie – Cocaine

Carrie Nation – Cocaine

Carry – To be in posession of drugs

Cartucho (Spanish) – Package of marijuana cigarettes

Cartwheels – Amphetamine

Casper – Crack cocaine

Casper the Ghost – Crack cocaine

Cat – Methcathinone

Cat in the Hat – Methylenedioxymethamphetamine (MDMA)

Cat Valium – Ketamine

Catnip – Marijuana cigarette

Caviar – Combination of cocaine and marijuana; crack cocaine

Cavite all-star – Marijuana

CDs – Crack cocaine

Cecil – Cocaine

Cest – Marijuana

Chalk – Crack cocaine; amphetamine; methamphetamine

Chalked up – Under the influence of cocaine

Chalking – Chemically altering the color of cocaine so it looks white

Champagne – Combination of cocaine and marijuana

Chandoo/chandu – Opium

Channel – Vein into which a drug is injected

Channel swimmer – One who injects heroin

Chapopote (Spanish) – Heroin

Charas – Marijuana from India

Charge – Marijuana

Charged up – Under the influence of drugs

Charity – Methylenedioxymethamphetamine (MDMA)

Charley – Heroin

Charlie – Cocaine

Chase – To smoke cocaine; to smoke marijuana

Chaser – Compulsive crack user

Chasing the dragon – Crack mixed with heroin

Chasing the tiger – To smoke heroin

Chatarra (Spanish) – Heroin

Cheap basing – Crack

Check – Personal supply of drugs

Cheeba – Marijuana

Cheeo – Marijuana

Cheese – Heroin

Chemical – Crack cocaine

Chemo – Marijuana

Cherry meth – Gamma-hydroxybutyrate (GHB)

Chewies – Crack cocaine

Chiba – Heroin

Chiba chiba – High-potency marijuana from Colombia

Chicago black – Marijuana (term from Chicago)

Chicago green – Marijuana

Chicken feed – Methamphetamine

Chicken powder – Amphetamine

Chicken scratch – Searching on hands and knees for crack or cocaine

Chicle (Spanish) – Heroin

Chief – LSD; mescaline

Chiefing – To smoke marijuana

Chieva – Heroin

Chillum – An object used to smoke opium, hashish, and marijuana

China cat – High-potency heroin

China girl – Fentanyl

Chinatown – Fentanyl

China white – Heroin; fentanyl; synthetic heroin

Chinese molasses – Opium

Chinese red – Heroin

Chinese tobacco – Opium

Chip – Heroin

Chipper – Occasional user; occasional heroin user; occasional Hispanic user

Chipping – Using drugs occasionally

Chippy – Cocaine

Chips – tobacco or marijuana cigarettes laced with PCP

Chira – Marijuana

Chiva/chieva (Spanish) – Heroin

Choco-fan – Heroin

Chocolate – Marijuana; opium; amphetamine

Chocolate chip cookies – MDMA combined with heroin or methadone

Chocolate chips – LSD

Chocolate Ecstasy – Crack made brown by adding chocolate milk during production

Chocolate rock – Crack smoked together with heroin

Chocolate Thai – Marijuana

Choe – Cocaine

Cholly – Cocaine

Chorals – Depressants

Christina – Amphetamine

Christmas bud – Marijuana

Christmas rolls – Depressants

Christmas tree – Marijuana; amphetamine; methamphetamine; depressant

Christmas tree meth – Green methamphetamine produced using Drano crystals

Chronic – Marijuana; marijuana mixed with crack

Chrystal methadrine – Methylenedioxymethamphetamine (MDMA)

Chucks – Hunger following withdrawal from heroin

Chunky – Marijuana

Churus – Marijuana

Cid – LSD

Cigarette paper – Packet of heroin

Cigarrode cristal – PCP

Cinnamon – Methamphetamine

Circles – Rohypnol

Citrol – High-potency marijuana from Nepal

CJ – PCP

Clam bake – Sitting inside a car or other small, enclosed space and smoking marijuana

Clarity – Methylenedioxymethamphetamine (MDMA)

Clear – Methamphetamine

Clear up – Stop drug use

Clicker – Crack mixed with PCP; marijuana dipped in formaldehyde and smoked

Clickums – A marijuana cigarette laced with PCP

Cliff-hanger – PCP

Climax – Crack; heroin; isobutyl nitrite; inhalants

Climb – Marijuana cigarette

Clips – Rows of vials heat-sealed together

Clocker – Entry-level crack dealers who sell drugs 24 h a day

Clocking paper – Profits from selling drugs

Closet baser – User of crack who prefers anonymity

Cloud – Crack cocaine

Cloud nine – Crack cocaine; methylenedioxymethamphetamine (MDMA)

Cluck – Crack smoker

Cluckers – Middlemen who facilitate the connection between buyers and sellers

Copilot – Amphetamine

Coasting – Under the influence of drugs

Coasts to coasts – Amphetamine

Coca – Cocaine

Cocaine blues – Depression after extended cocaine use

Cochornis – Marijuana

Cocktail – Cigarette laced with cocaine or crack; partially smoked marijuana cigarette inserted in regular cigarette; to smoke cocaine in a cigarette

Coco rocks – Dark-brown crack made by adding chocolate pudding during production

Coco snow – Benzocaine used as cutting agent for crack

Cocoa puff – To smoke cocaine and marijuana

Cocofan (Spanish) – Brown tar heroin

Coconut – Cocaine

Cod – Large amount of money

Coffee – LSD

Coke – Cocaine; crack cocaine

Coke bar – A bar where cocaine is openly used

Cola – Cocaine

Colas – Marijuana

Cold turkey – Sudden withdrawal from drugs

Coli – Marijuana

Coliflor tostao (Spanish) – Marijuana

Colombian – Marijuana

Colorado cocktail – Marijuana

Columbo – PCP

Columbus black – Marijuana

Combol – Cocaine

Come home – End an LSD "trip"

Come up – A person who sells drugs for money; to take a small amount of money and increase it to a large amount

Comeback – Benzocaine and mannitol used to adulterate cocaine for conversion to crack

Comic book – Lysergic acid diethylamide (LSD)

Conductor – LSD

Connect – Purchase drugs; supplier of illegal drugs

Contact lens – LSD

Cook – Drug manufacturer; mix heroin with water; heating heroin to prepare it for injection

Cook down – Process in which users liquify heroin in order to inhale it

Cooker – To inject a drug; person who manufactures methamphetamine

Cookies – Crack cocaine

Cooking up – To process powdered cocaine into crack

Cooler – Cigarette laced with a drug

Coolie – Cigarette laced with cocaine

Cop – Obtain drugs

Copping zones – Specific areas where buyers can purchase drugs

Coral – Depressant

Coriander seeds – Cash

Cork the air – To inhale cocaine

Corrine – Cocaine

Corrinne – Cocaine

Cosa (Spanish) – Marijuana

Cotics – Heroin

Coties – Codeine

Cotton – Currency; OxyContin

Cotton brothers – Cocaine, heroin, and morphine

Cotton fever – Critically high temperature associated with accidentally injecting cotton fibers into the bloodstream

Courage pills – Heroin; depressants

Course note – Bill larger than $2

Cozmo's – PCP

CR – Methamphetamine

Crack – Cocaine

Crack attack – Craving for crack

Crack back – Marijuana and crack

Crack cooler – Crack soaked in wine cooler

Crack gallery – Place where crack is bought and sold

Crack house – Place where crack is used

Crack kits – Glass pipe and copper mesh

Crack spot – Area where people can purchase crack; place where crack is sold but not used

Cracker jack – Crack smoker

Crackers – LSD; Talwin and Ritalin combination is injected and produces an effect similar to the effect of heroin mixed with cocaine

Crank – Crack cocaine; heroin; amphetamine; methamphetamine; methcathinone

Cranking up – To inject a drug

Crankster – Someone who uses or manufactures methamphetamine

Crap – Low-quality heroin

Crash – Sleep off effects of drugs

Crazy coke – PCP

Crazy Eddie – PCP

Crazy weed – Marijuana

Credit card – Crack stem

Crib – Crack cocaine

Crimmie – Cigarette laced with crack

Crink – Methamphetamine

Cripple – Marijuana cigarette

Cris – Methamphetamine

Crisscross – Amphetamine

Crisscrossing – The practice of setting up a line of cocaine next to a line of heroin; the user places a straw in each nostril and snorts about half of each line; then the straws are crossed and the remaining lines are snorted

Cristal (Spanish) – Methylene-dioxymethamphetamine (MDMA)

Cristina (Spanish) – Methamphetamine

Cristy – Smokable methamphetamine

Croak – Crack mixed with methamphetamine; methamphetamine

Crop – Low-quality heroin

Cross tops – Amphetamine

Crossles – Methamphetamine

Crossroads – Amphetamine

Crown crap – Heroin

Crumbs – Tiny pieces of crack

Crunch and Munch – Crack cocaine

Crush and rush – Method of methamphetamine production in which starch is not filtered out of the ephedrine or pseudoephedrine tablets.

Cruz (Spanish) – Opium from Veracruz, Mexico

Crying weed – Marijuana

Cryppie – Marijuana

Crypto – Methamphetamine

Cryptonie – Marijuana

Crystal – Cocaine; amphetamine; methamphetamine; PCP

Crystal glass – Crystal shards of methamphetamine

Crystal joint – PCP

Crystal meth – Methamphetamine

Crystal methadrine – Amphetamine

Crystal T – PCP

Crystal tea – LSD

Cube – LSD; 1 ounce

Cubes – Marijuana tablets; crack cocaine

Culican – High-potency marijuana from Mexico

Cupcakes – LSD

Cura (Spanish) – Heroin

Cushion – Vein into which a drug is injected

Cut – Adulterate drugs

Cut deck – Heroin mixed with powdered milk

Cycline – PCP

Cyclones – PCP

D – LSD; PCP

Dabble – Use drugs occasionally

Dagga – Marijuana from South Africa

Dama blanca (Spanish) – Cocaine

Dance fever – Fentanyl

Dank – Marijuana; the practice of lacing cigarettes with formaldehyde

Dawamesk – Marijuana

Dead on arrival – Heroin

Dead president – Heroin

Dead road – Methylenedioxymethamphetamine (MDMA)

Debs – Amphetamine; methylenedioxymethamphetamine (MDMA)

Deca-duabolin – Injectable steroids

Decadence – Methylenedioxymethamphetamine (MDMA)

Deck – 1 to 15 grams of heroin, also known as a bag; packet of drugs

Deeda – LSD

Delatestryl – Injectable steroids

Demo – Crack stem; sample-size quantity of crack

Demolish – Crack

Dep-testosterone – Injectable steroids

Desocsins – Methamphetamine

Desogtion – Methamphetamine

DET – Dimethyltryptamine

Detroit pink – PCP

Deuce – Heroin; $2 worth of drugs

Devil drug – Crack cocaine

Devil's dandruff – Crack cocaine; powder cocaine

Devil's dick – Crack pipe

Devil's dust – PCP

Devilsmoke – Crack cocaine

Dew – Marijuana

Dews – $10 worth of drugs

Dex – Amphetamine; methylenedioxymethamphetamine (MDMA)

Dexedrine – Amphetamine; methylenedioxymethamphetamine (MDMA)

Dexies – Amphetamine

Diablito (Spanish) – Combination of crack cocaine and marijuana in a joint

Diambista – Marijuana

Diamond folds – Folded paper used to package drugs

Diamonds – Amphetamines; methylenedioxymethamphetamine (MDMA)

Dianabol – Veterinary steroids; veterinary and oral

Dice – Crack cocaine

Diesel – Heroin

Diet pills – Amphetamine

Dihydrolone – Injectable steroids

Dimba – Marijuana from West Africa

Dime – Crack cocaine; $10 worth of crack

Dime bag – $10 worth of drugs

Dime special – Crack cocaine

Dime's worth – Amount of heroin needed to cause death

Ding – Marijuana

Dinkie dow – Marijuana

Dinosaurs – Populations of heroin users in their forties and fifties

Dip – Crack cocaine

Dipper – PCP

Dipping out – Crack runners taking a portion of crack from vials

Dirt – Heroin

Dirt grass – Inferior-quality marijuana

Dirties – Marijuana cigarettes with powdered cocaine added to them

Dirty basing – Crack cocaine

Dirty joints – Combination of crack cocaine and marijuana

Disco biscuit – Depressants; methylenedioxymethamphetamine (MDMA)

Disco biscuits – Depressants; methylenedioxymethamphetamine (MDMA)

Disco pellets – Stimulant

Discorama – Inhalants

Disease – Drug of choice

Ditch – Marijuana

Ditch weed – Inferior-quality marijuana

Djamba – Marijuana

DMT – Dimethyltryptamine; PCP

Do a joint – Marijuana

Do a line – To inhale cocaine

Do it Jack – PCP

DOA – Crack; heroin; PCP

Doctor – Methylenedioxymethamphetamine (MDMA)

Doctor shopping – The practice of going from doctor to doctor to obtain prescriptions for pharmaceuticals

Dog – Good friend

Dog food – Heroin

Dogie – Heroin

Dollar – $100 worth of drugs

Dolls – Amphetamines; depressant; methylenedioxymethamphetamine (MDMA)

Domes – LSD

Domestic – Locally grown marijuana

Domex – PCP and MDMA

Dominican knot – The torn and knotted corner of a baggie containing drugs

Dominoes – Amphetamine

Don Jem – Marijuana

Don Juan – Marijuana

Dona Juana (Spanish) – Marijuana

Dona Juanita (Spanish) – Marijuana

Donk – Marijuana/PCP combination

Doob – Marijuana

Doobee – Marijuana

Doobie/dubbe/duby – Marijuana

Doogie/doojee/dugie – Heroin

Dooley – Heroin

Doosey – Heroin

Dope – Marijuana; heroin; any other drug

Dope fiend – A person who is drug-dependent; crack addict

Dope smoke – To smoke marijuana

Dopium – Opium

Doradilla – Marijuana

Dors and 4's – Combination of Doriden and Tylenol 4

Doses – LSD

Dosure – Lysergic acid diethylamide

Dots – LSD

Doub – $20 rock of crack

Double-breasted dealing – Dealing cocaine and heroin together

Double bubble – Cocaine

Double-cross – Amphetamine

Double dome – LSD

Double rock – Crack diluted in procaine

Double trouble – Depressants

Double-up – When a crack dealer delivers an extra rock as a marketing ploy to attract customers

Double-ups – A $20 rock that can be broken into two $20 rocks

Double yoke – Crack cocaine

Dove – $35 piece of crack

Dover's deck – Opium

Dover's powder – Opium

Down – Codeine cough syrup

Downer – Depressants

Downie – Depressants

Dr. Feelgood – Heroin

Draf – Marijuana; Ecstasy, with cocaine

Draf weed – Marijuana

Drag weed – Marijuana

Dragon rock – Mixture of heroin and crack

Draw up – To inject a drug

Dream – Cocaine

Dream gun – Opium

Dream stick – Opium

Dreamer – Morphine

Dreams – Opium

Dreck – Heroin

Drink – PCP

Drivers – Amphetamine; methylenedioxymethamphetamine (MDMA)

Drop – To swallow drugs

Dropper – To inject a drug

Dropping – Wrapping methamphetamine in bread and then consuming it

Drowsy high – Depressants

Dry high – Marijuana

Dry up – To inject drugs

Dub – When a crack dealer delivers an extra rock as a marketing ploy to attract customers

Dube – Marijuana

Duby – Marijuana

Duct – Cocaine

Due – Residue of oils trapped in a pipe after smoking base

Duji – Heroin

Dujra – Heroin

Dujre – Heroin

Dummy dust – PCP

Dump – To vomit after taking drugs

Durabolin – Injectable steroids

Durong – Marijuana

Duros (Spanish) – Marijuana

Dust – Marijuana mixed with various chemicals; cocaine; heroin; PCP

Dust blunt – Marijuana/PCP combination

Dust joint – PCP

Dust of angels – PCP

Dusted parsley – PCP

Dusting – Adding PCP, heroin, or another drug to marijuana

Dymethzine – Injectable steroids

Dynamite – Cocaine mixed with heroin

Dyno – Heroin

Dyno-pure – Heroin

E – Ecstasy (Methylenedioxymethamphetamine; MDMA)

E-bombs – MDMA (methylenedioxymethamphetamine)

E-puddle – Sleeping due to MDMA use/exhaustion

E-tard – Person under the influence of MDMA (methylenedioxymethamphetamine)

Earth – Marijuana cigarette

Easing powder – Opium

Eastside player – Crack cocaine

Easy lay – Gamma-hydroxybutyrate (GHB)

Easy score – Obtaining drugs without difficulties

Eating – Taking a drug orally

Ecstasy – Methylenedioxymethamphetamine (MDMA)

Egg – Crack cocaine

Eggs – Heroin in rock form

Egyptians – Methylenedioxymethamphetamine (MDMA)

Eight ball – 1/8 ounce of drugs

Eightball – Crack mixed with heroin

Eighth – Heroin

El diablito (Spanish) – Cocaine, marijuana, heroin, and PCP

El diablo (Spanish) – Cocaine, marijuana, and heroin

El gallo ("rooster") – Marijuana

El perico ("parrot") – Cocaine

Elbows – One pound of methamphetamine

Electric Kool-Aid – LSD

Electric Kool-aid – Crack cocaine

Elephant – Marijuana; PCP

Elephant flipping – Use of PCP and MDMA

Elephant trank – PCP

Elephant tranquilizer – PCP

Elephants – Methylenedioxymethamphetamine (MDMA)

Elvis – LSD

Embalming fluid – PCP

Emergency gun – Instrument used to inject other than a syringe

Emsel – Morphine

Endo – Marijuana

Energizer – PCP

Enoltestovis – Injectable steroids

Ephedrone – Methcathinone

Equipose – Veterinary steroids

Erth – PCP

Esnortiar (Spanish) – Cocaine

Esra – Marijuana

Essence – Methylenedioxymethamphetamine (MDMA)

Estuffa – Heroin

ET – Alpha-ethyltryptamine

Eve – Methylenedioxymethamphetamine (MDMA)

Everclear – Cocaine; gamma-hydroxybutyrate (GHB)

Exiticity – Methylenedioxymethamphetamine (MDMA)

Explorer's club – Group of LSD users

Eye opener – Crack; amphetamine

Eye openers – Amphetamine

Factory – Place where drugs are packaged, diluted, or manufactured

Fake STP – PCP

Fall – Arrested

Fallbrook redhair – Marijuana, (term from Fallbrook, CA)

Famous dimes – Crack cocaine

Fantasia – Dimethyltryptamine

Fantasy – Gamma-hydroxybutyrate (GHB)

Fast – Methamphetamine

Fast white lady – Powder cocaine

Fastin – Amphetamine; methylene-dioxymethamphetamine (MDMA)

Fat bags – Crack cocaine

Fatty – Marijuana cigarette

Feed bag – Container for marijuana

Feeling – Marijuana

Feenin – Behavior associated with a person craving cocaine or other addictive substances when they are unavailable

Felix the cat – LSD

Ferry dust – Heroin

Fi-do-nie – Opium

Fields – LSD

Fiend – Someone who smokes marijuana alone

Fifteen cents – $15 worth of drugs

Fifty-one – Crack; crack sprinkled on tobacco

Finajet/finaject – Veterinary steroids

Fine stuff – Marijuana

Finger – Marijuana cigarette

Finger lid – Marijuana

Fingers – The cutoff fingers of surgical gloves used to package drugs

Fir – Marijuana

Fire – Crack and methamphetamine; to inject a drug

Fire it up – To smoke marijuana

Firewater – GBL-containing product

Firewood – Marijuana

First line – Morphine

Fish scales – Crack cocaine

Five C note – $500 bill

Five cent bag – $5 worth of drugs

Five dollar bag – $50 worth of drugs

Five-way – Combines snorting of heroin, cocaine, methamphetamine, ground-up flunitrazepam pills, and drinking alcohol

Fives – Amphetamine

Fix – To inject a drug

Fizzies – Methadone

Flag – Appearance of blood in the vein

Flake – Cocaine

Flakes – PCP

Flame cooking – Smoking cocaine base by putting the pipe over a stove flame

Flamethrowers – Cigarette laced with cocaine and heroin; heroin, cocaine, and tobacco

Flash – LSD; the rush of cocaine injection

Flat blues – LSD

Flat chunks – Crack cut with benzocaine

Flatliners – 4-Methylthioamphetamine

Flave – Powder cocaine

Flea powder – Low-purity heroin

Flex – Fake crack (rock cocaine)

Flipping – Methylenedioxymethamphetamine (MDMA)

Florida snow – Cocaine

Flower – Marijuana

Flower flipping – Ecstasy (MDMA) mixed with mushrooms

Flower tops – Marijuana

Fly Mexican Airlines – To smoke marijuana

Flying – Under the influence of drugs

Foil – Heroin

Following that cloud – Searching for drugs

Foo foo – Cocaine

Foo foo stuff – Heroin; cocaine

Foo-foo dust – Cocaine

Foolish powder – Cocaine; heroin

Footballs – Amphetamine

Forget me drug – Rohypnol

Forget pill – Rohypnol

Forget-me pill – Rohypnol

Forwards – Amphetamine

Four-leaf clover – Methylene-dioxymethamphetamine (MDMA)

Fraho/frajo – Marijuana

Freebase – To smoke cocaine; crack cocaine

Freebasing – Smoking crack cocaine

Freeze – Cocaine; renege on a drug deal

French blue – Amphetamine

French fries – Crack cocaine

Fresh – PCP

Friend – Fentanyl

Fries – Crack cocaine

Frios **(Spanish)** – Marijuana laced with PCP

Frisco special – Cocaine, heroin, and LSD

Frisco speedball – Cocaine, heroin, and a dash of LSD

Friskie powder – Cocaine

Frontloading – The process of transferring a drug solution from one syringe to another

Fry – Marijuana cigarettes dipped in embalming fluid, sometimes also laced with PCP; crack cocaine

Fry daddy – Crack and marijuana; cigarette laced with crack; marijuana joint laced with crack

Fry sticks – Marijuana cigarettes dipped in embalming fluid, sometimes also laced with PCP

Fu – Marijuana

Fuel – Marijuana mixed with insecticides; PCP

Fuete – Hypodermic needle

Fuma D'Angola (Portugese) – marijuana

Furra – Heroin

G – $1000 or 1 gram of drugs; term for an unfamiliar male; gamma-hydroxybutyrate (GHB)

G-riffic – Gamma-hydroxybutyrate (GHB)

G-rock – One gram of rock cocaine

G-shot – Small dose of drugs used to hold off withdrawal symptoms until a full dose can be taken

G.B. – Depressants

Gaffel – Fake cocaine

Gaffus – Hypodermic needle

Gage/gauge – Marijuana

Gagers – Methcathinone

Gaggers – Methcathinone

Gaggler – Amphetamine; Methylenedioxymethamphetamine (MDMA)

Galloping horse – Heroin

Gallup – Heroin

Gamma oh – Gamma-hydroxybutyrate (GHB)

Gamot – Heroin

Gange – Marijuana

Gangster – Marijuana; person who uses or manufactures methamphetamine

Gangster pills – Depressants

Ganja – Marijuana (term from Jamaica)

Gank – Fake crack

Ganoobies – State of being stoned and laughing uncontrollably

Garbage – Inferior-quality marijuana; low-quality heroin

Garbage heads – Users who buy crack from street dealers instead of cooking it themselves

Garbage rock – Crack cocaine

Gash – Marijuana

Gasper – Marijuana cigarette

Gasper stick – Marijuana cigarette

Gato (Spanish) – Heroin

Gauge butt – Marijuana

GBH – Gamma-hydroxybutyrate (GHB)

GBL – Gamma-butyrolactone; used in making gamma-hydroxybutyrate (GHB)

Gee – Opium

Geek – Crack mixed with marijuana

Geek joints – Cigarettes or cigars filled with tobacco and crack; a marijuana cigarette laced with crack or powdered cocaine

Geeker – Crack users

Geep – Methamphetamine

Geeter – Methamphetamine

Geeze – To inhale cocaine

Geezer – To inject a drug

Geezin a bit of dee gee – To inject a drug

George – Heroin

George smack – Heroin

Georgia home boy – Gamma-hydroxybutyrate (GHB)

Get a gage up – To smoke marijuana

Get a gift – Obtain drugs

Get down – To inject a drug

Get high – To smoke marijuana

Get lifted – Under the influence of drugs

Get off – To inject a drug; get high

Get-off houses – Private places where heroin users can purchase and use heroin for a fee

Get the wind – To smoke marijuana

Get through – Obtain drugs

Getgo – Methamphetamine

Getting roached – Using Rohypnol

Getting snotty – Using heroin

Ghana – Marijuana

GHB – Gamma-hydroxybutyrate

Ghost – LSD

Ghostbusting – Smoking cocaine; searching for white particles in the belief that they are crack

Gick monster – Crack smoker

Gift-of-the-sun – Cocaine

Gift-of-the-sun-god – Cocaine

Giggle smoke – Marijuana

Giggle weed – Marijuana

Gimmick – Drug injection equipment

Gimmie – Crack and marijuana; marijuana joint laced with crack

Gin – Cocaine

Girl – Cocaine; crack cocaine; heroin

Girlfriend – Cocaine

Giro house – Nonbank financial institutions for businesses frequently used by drug traffickers to launder drug proceeds

Give wings – Inject someone or teach someone to inject heroin

Glacines – Heroin

Glad stuff – Cocaine

Glading – Using an inhalant

Glass – Heroin; amphetamine; hypodermic needle; methamphetamine

Glass gun – Hypodermic needle

Glo – Crack cocaine

Gluey – One who sniffs or inhales glue

Go – Amphetamines; methylene-dioxymethamphetamine (MDMA)

Go into a sewer – To inject a drug; inject in the vein

Go loco – To smoke marijuana

Go on a sleigh ride – To inhale cocaine

Go-fast – Methcathinone; crank; methamphetamine

Goat – Heroin

Goblet of jam – Marijuana

God's drug – Morphine

God's flesh – LSD; psilocybin/psilocin

God's medicine – Opium

Gold – Marijuana; crack cocaine; heroin

Gold dust – Cocaine

Gold star – Marijuana

Golden – Marijuana

Golden dragon – LSD

Golden eagle – 4-Methylthioamphetamine

Golden girl – Heroin

Golden leaf – Very high-quality marijuana

Golf ball – Crack cocaine

Golf balls – Depressants

Golpe – Heroin

Goma (Spanish) – Black tar heroin; opium

Gondola – Opium

Gone, shot to the curb – Lost everything to crack

Gong – Marijuana; opium

Gonj – Marijuana

Goob – Methcathinone

Good – PCP; heroin

Good and plenty – Heroin

Good butt – Marijuana cigarette

Good giggles – Marijuana

Good go – Proper amount of drugs for the money paid

Good H – Heroin

Good horse – Heroin

Good lick – Good drugs

Good stuff – High-potency drug, especially marijuana

Goodfellas – Fentanyl

Goody-goody – Marijuana

Goof butt – Marijuana cigarette

Goofball – Cocaine mixed with heroin; depressants

Goofers – Depressants

Goofy's – LSD

Goon – PCP

Goon dust – PCP

Goop – Gamma-hydroxybutyrate (GHB)

Gopher – Person paid to pick up drugs

Gorge – Marijuana

Goric – Opium

Gorilla biscuits – PCP

Gorilla pills – Depressants

Gorilla tab – PCP

Got it going on – Fast sale of drugs

Graduate – Completely stop using drugs; progress to stronger drugs

Gram – Hashish

Granulated orange – Methamphetamine

Grape parfait – LSD

Grass – Marijuana

Grass brownies – Marijuana

Grasshopper – Marijuana

Grata – Marijuana

Gravel – Crack cocaine

Gravy – Heroin; to inject a drug

Grease – Currency

Great bear – Fentanyl

Great hormones at bedtime – Gamma-hydroxybutyrate (GHB)

Great tobacco – Opium

Greek – Combination of marijuana and powder cocaine

Green – Inferior-quality marijuana; ketamine; PCP

Green buds – Marijuana

Green double domes – LSD

Green dragons – Depressants

Green frog – Depressants

Green goddess – Marijuana

Green goods – Paper currency

Green leaves – PCP

Green single dome – LSD

Green tea – PCP

Green triangles – Methylene-dioxymethamphetamine (MDMA)

Green wedge – LSD

Greenies – Amphetamines; methylene-dioxymethamphetamine (MDMA)

Greens – Marijuana

Greens/green stuff – Paper currency

Greeter – Marijuana

Gremmies – Combination of cocaine and marijuana

Greta – Marijuana

Grey shields – LSD

Griefo – Marijuana

Griefs – Marijuana

Grievous bodily harm – Gamma-hydroxybutyrate (GHB)

Grifa (Spanish) – Marijuana

Griff – Marijuana

Griffa – Marijuana

Griffo – Marijuana

Grit – Crack cocaine

Groceries – Crack cocaine

Ground control – The guide or caretaker during a hallucinogenic experience

Grow(s) – Marijuana-growing operations (indoor and outdoor)

Gum – Opium; methylene-dioxymethamphetamine (MDMA)

Guma – Opium

Gun – To inject a drug; needle; hypodermic needle

Gunga – Marijuana

Gungeon – Marijuana

Gungun – Marijuana

Gunja – Marijuana

Gutter – Vein into which a drug is injected

Gutter junkie – Addict who relies on others to obtain drugs

GWM – Methylenedioxymethamphetamine (MDMA)

Gym candy – Steroids

Gyve – Marijuana cigarette

H – Heroin

H and C – Heroin and cocaine

H-bomb – Ecstasy (MDMA) mixed with heroin

H caps – Heroin

Hache – Heroin

Hail – Crack cocaine

Haircut – Marijuana

Hairy – Heroin

Half – ½ ounce

Half a football field – 50 rocks of crack

Half elbows – ½ pound of methamphetamine

Half-G – $500

Half-load – 15 bags (decks) of heroin

Half-moon – Peyote

Half-piece – ½ ounce of heroin or cocaine

Half-track – Crack cocaine

Half-a-C – $50 bill

Hamburger Helper – Crack cocaine

Hammerheading – MDMA (methylenedioxymethamphetamine) used in combination with Viagra

Hand-to-hand – Direct delivery and payment

Hand-to-hand man – Transient dealers who carry small amounts of crack

Hanhich – Marijuana

Hanyak – Smokable methamphetamine

Happy cigarette – Marijuana cigarette

Happy drug – Methylenedioxymethamphetamine (MDMA)

Happy dust – Cocaine

Happy pill – Methylenedioxymethamphetamine (MDMA)

Happy powder – Cocaine

Happy stick – Marijuana and PCP combination

Happy sticks – PCP

Happy trails – Cocaine

Hard ball – Crack cocaine

Hard candy – Heroin

Hard line – Crack cocaine

Hard rock – Crack cocaine

Hard stuff – Heroin; opium

Hardware – Isobutyl nitrite; inhalants

Harry – Heroin

Harsh – Marijuana

Has – Marijuana

Hats – LSD

Have a dust – Cocaine

Haven dust – Cocaine

Hawaiian – Very high-potency marijuana

Hawaiian black – Marijuana

Hawaiian homegrown hay – Marijuana

Hawaiian sunshine – LSD

Hawk – LSD

Hay – Marijuana

Hay butt – Marijuana cigarette

Hayron – Heroin

Haze – LSD

Hazel – Heroin

HCP – PCP

He man – Fentanyl

Head drugs – Amphetamine

Headlight – LSD

Head shop – Store specializing in the sale of drug paraphernalia

Heart-on – Inhalants

Hearts – Amphetamine

Heat – The police or narcotics officers

Heaven – Cocaine; heroin

Heaven and Hell – PCP

Heaven dust – Cocaine; heroin

Heavenly blue – LSD

Heeled – Having plenty of money

Helen – Heroin

Hell – Crack cocaine

Hell dust – Heroin

Henpecking – Searching on hands and knees for crack

Henry – Heroin

Henry VIII – Cocaine

Her – Cocaine

Hera – Heroin

Herb – Marijuana

Herb and Al – Marijuana and alcohol

Herba – Marijuana

Herbal bliss – Methylenedioxymethamphetamine (MDMA)

Herms – PCP

Hero – Heroin

Hero of the underworld – Heroin

Heroina (Spanish) – Heroin

Herone – Heroin

Hessle – Heroin

Hiagra in a bottle – Inhalants

Highball – Inhalants

Highbeams – The wide eyes of a person on crack

Hikori – Peyote

Hikuli – Peyote

Hillbilly heroin – OxyContin

Him – Heroin

Hinkley – PCP

Hippie crack – Inhalants

Hippieflip – Use of mushrooms and MDMA (methylenedioxymethamphetamine)

Hironpon – Smokable methamphetamine

Hit – To smoke marijuana; marijuana cigarette; crack cocaine

Hit house – House where users go to shoot up and leave the owner drugs as payment

Hit the hay – To smoke marijuana

Hit the main line – To inject a drug

Hit the needle – To inject a drug

Hit the pit – To inject a drug

Hitch up the reindeers – To inhale cocaine

Hitter – Little pipe designed for only one hit

Hitters – People who inject others who have hard-to-find veins in exchange for drugs

Hitting up – To inject a drug

Hocus – Marijuana; opium

Hog – PCP

Holding – Possessing drugs

Holiday meth – Green methamphetamine produced using Drano crystals

Holy terror – Heroin

Hombre (Spanish) – Heroin

Hombrecitos (Spanish) – Psilocybin

Homegrown – Marijuana

Homicide – Heroin cut with scopolamine or strychnine

Honey – Currency

Honey blunts – Marijuana cigars sealed with honey

Honey oil – Ketamine; inhalants

Honeymoon – Early stages of drug use before addiction or dependency develops

Hong-yen – Heroin in pill form

Hooch – Marijuana

Hooked – Addicted

Hooter – Cocaine; marijuana

Hop/hops – Opium

Hopped up – Under the influence of drugs

Horn – To inhale cocaine; crack pipe; to inhale a drug

Horning – To inhale cocaine; heroin

Horse – Heroin

Horse heads – Amphetamine

Horse tracks – PCP

Horse tranquilizer – PCP

Horsebite – Heroin

Hospital heroin – Diluadid

Hot dope – Heroin

Hot heroin – Heroin poisoned to give to a police informant

Hot ice – Smokable methamphetamine

Hot load/hot shot – Lethal injection of a narcotic

Hot-rolling – Liquefying methamphetamine in an eye dropper and then inhaling it

Hot stick – Marijuana cigarette

Hotcakes – Crack cocaine

House fee – Money paid to enter a crack house

House piece – Crack given to the owner of a crack house or apartment where crack users congregate

How do you like me now? – Crack cocaine

Hows – Morphine

HRN – Heroin

Hubba – Crack cocaine

Hubba pigeon – Crack users looking for rocks on the floor after a police raid

Hubba, I am back – Crack cocaine

Hubbas – Crack

Hubbas (northern California) – Crack; I am back

Huff – Inhalants

Huffer – Inhalant abuser

Huffing – To sniff an inhalant

Hug drug – Methylenedioxymethamphetamine (MDMA)

Hugs and kisses – Combination of
methamphetamine and methylenedioxymethamphetamine (MDMA)

Hulling – Using others to get drugs

Hunter – Cocaine

Hustle – Attempt to obtain drug customers

Hyatari – Peyote

Hydro – Amphetamine; high-quality
methamphetamine; marijuana; methylenedioxymethamphetamine
(MDMA); marijuana grown in water
(hydroponic)

Hype – Heroin addict; an addict; methylenedioxymethamphetamine
(MDMA)

Hype stick – Hypodermic needle

I am back – Crack

Iboga – Amphetamine; methylenedioxymethamphetamine (MDMA)

Ice – Cocaine; Crack cocaine; smokable
methamphetamine; methamphetamine; methylenedioxymethamphetamine (MDMA); phencyclidine (PCP)

Ice cream habit – Occasional use of
drugs

Ice cube – Crack cocaine

Icing – Cocaine

Idiot pills – Depressants

Igloo – Methylenedioxymethamphetamine (MDMA)

Ill – PCP

Illies – Marijuana dipped in PCP

Illing – Marijuana dipped in PCP

Illy – Marijuana cigarettes soaked in
embalming fluid and dried

Illy momo – PCP

In – Connected with drug suppliers

Inbetweens – Amphetamine; depressants

Inca message – Cocaine

Indian boy – Marijuana

Indian hay – Marijuana from India

Indian hemp – Marijuana

Indica – Species of *Cannabis* found in
hot climates; grows to 3.5 to 4 feet

Indo – Marijuana term from northern
California

Indonesian bud – Marijuana; opium

Instaga – Marijuana

Instagu – Marijuana

Instant zen – LSD

Interplanetary mission – Travel from
one crackhouse to another to search
for crack

Isda – Heroin

Issues – Crack cocaine

J – Marijuana cigarette

Jab/job – To inject a drug

Jack – Steal someone else's drugs

Jack up – To inject a drug

Jackpot – Fentanyl

Jag – Keep a high going

Jam – Cocaine; amphetamine

Jam cecil – Amphetamine

Jamaican gold – Marijuana

Jamaican red hair – Marijuana

Jane – Marijuana

Jay – Marijuana cigarette

Jay smoke – Marijuana

Jee gee – Heroin

Jefferson airplane – Used match cut in
half to hold a partially smoked marijuana cigarette

Jejo – Cocaine

Jellies – Depressants; MDMA in gel
caps

Jelly – Cocaine

Jelly baby – Amphetamine

Jelly bean – Amphetamine; depressants

Jelly beans – Crack cocaine

Jerry Garcias – Methylenedioxymethamphetamine (MDMA)

Jerry Springer – Heroin

Jet – Ketamine

Jet fuel – PCP; methamphetamine

Jib – Gamma-hydroxybutyrate (GHB)

Jim Jones – Marijuana laced with
cocaine and PCP

Jive – Marijuana; heroin; drugs

Jive doo jee – Heroin

Jive stick – Marijuana

Joharito – Heroin

Johnson – Crack cocaine

Joint – Marijuana cigarette

Jojee – Heroin

Jolly bean – Amphetamine

Jolly green – Marijuana

Jolly pop – Casual user of heroin

Jolt – Strong reaction to drugs; to inject a drug

Jones – Heroin

Jonesing – Need for drugs

Joy – Heroin

Joy flakes – Heroin

Joy juice – Depressants

Joy plant – Opium

Joy pop – To inject a drug

Joy popping – Occasional use of drugs

Joy powder – Cocaine; heroin

Joy smoke – Marijuana

Joy stick – Marijuana cigarette; marijuana and PCP combination

Ju-ju – Marijuana cigarette

Juan Valdez (Spanish) – Marijuana

Juanita (Spanish) – Marijuana

Juggle – Sell drugs to another addict to support a habit

Juggler – Teen-aged street dealer

Jugs – Amphetamine

Juice – PCP; steroids

Juice joint – Marijuana cigarette sprinkled with crack

Juja – Marijuana

Jum – Sealed plastic bag containing crack

Jumbos – Large vials of crack sold on the streets; marijuana mixed with crack

Junco – Heroin

Junk – Cocaine; heroin

Junkie – Addict

Junkie kits – Glass pipe and copper mesh

K – PCP

K-blast – PCP

K-hole – Periods of ketamine-induced confusion; the depressant high associated with ketamine

Kabak – Marijuana; Turkish marijuana

Kabayo – Heroin

Kabuki – Crack pipe made from a plastic rum bottle and a rubber spark plug cover

Kaff – Very potent marijuana from Morocco, Lebanon, and other Arab/Middle Eastern countries

Kaksonjae – Smokable methamphetamine

Kalakit – Marijuana

Kali – Marijuana

Kangaroo – Crack

Kansas grass – Marijuana

Kaps – PCP

Karachi – Heroin, phenobarbital, and methaqualone

Karo – Codeine cough syrup

Kate bush – Marijuana

Kawaii electric – Marijuana

Kaya – Marijuana

KB – Marijuana

Kee – Marijuana

Kentucky blue – Marijuana

Kester plant – Drugs hidden in the rectum

Ket – Ketamine

Key – Marijuana

KGB (killer green bud) – Marijuana

Khat – Amphetamine; methcathinone; methylenedioxymethamphetamine (MDMA)

Khayf – Very potent marijuana from Morocco, Lebanon, and other Arab/Middle Eastern countries

Ki – Marijuana

Kibbles and Bits – Small crumbs of crack

Kick – Inhalants; getting off a drug habit

Kick stick – Marijuana cigarette

Kicker – OxyContin

Kiddie dope – Prescription drugs

Kief – Very potent marijuana from Morocco, Lebanon, and other Arab/Middle Eastern countries

Kiff – Marijuana cigarette; very potent marijuana from Morocco, Lebanon, and other Arab/Middle Eastern countries

Killer – Marijuana; PCP

Killer green bud – Marijuana

Killer joints – PCP

Killer weed – Marijuana

Killer weed (1980s) – Marijuana and PCP

Kilo – 2.2 pounds

Kilter – Marijuana

Kind – Marijuana

Kind bud – High-quality marijuana

King – Cocaine

King bud – Marijuana

King ivory – Fentanyl

King Kong pills – Depressants

King's habit – Cocaine

Kissing – The exchange of plastic-wrapped rocks (crack) by kissing or through mouth-to-mouth transfer

Kit – Equipment used to inject drugs

Kit kat – Ketamine

Kitty flipping – Use of ketamine and MDMA

KJ – PCP

Kleenex – Methylenedioxymethamphetamine (MDMA)

Klingons – Crack addicts

Kokomo – Crack cocaine

Kona gold – Marijuana

Kools – PCP

Krippy – Marijuana

Kryptonite – Crack cocaine; marijuana

Krystal – PCP

Krystal joint – PCP

Kumba – Marijuana

KW – PCP

L – LSD

L.A. – Long-acting amphetamine

L.A. glass – Smokable methamphetamine

L.A. ice – Smokable methamphetamine

L.L. – Marijuana

La buena (Spanish) – Heroin

La chiva ("goat") – Heroin

La rocha – Rohypnol

Lace – Cocaine and marijuana

Lactone – GBL

Lady – Cocaine

Lady caine – Cocaine

Lady snow – Cocaine

Lakbay diva – Marijuana

Lamborghini – Crack pipe made from a plastic rum bottle and a rubber spark-plug cover

Las mujercitas (Spanish) – Psilocybin

Lason sa daga – LSD

Late night – Cocaine

Laugh and scratch – To inject a drug

Laughing gas – Nitrous oxide

Laughing grass – Marijuana

Laughing weed – Marijuana

Lay back – Depressants

Layout – Equipment for taking drugs

LBJ – Heroin; LSD; PCP

Leaf – Cocaine; marijuana

Leak – Marijuana/PCP combination

Leaky bolla – PCP

Leaky leak – PCP

Lean – Codeine cough syrup

Leapers – Amphetamine

Leaping – Under the influence of drugs

Legal speed – Over-the-counter asthma drug; trade name—MiniThin

Lemon 714 – PCP

Lemon drop – Methamphetamine with a dull-yellow tint

Lemonade – Heroin; poor-quality drugs

Leno (Spanish) – Marijuana

Lenos – PCP

Lens – LSD

Lethal weapon – PCP

Letter biscuits – MDMA (methylenedioxymethamphetamine)

Lettuce – Money

LG (lime green) – Marijuana

Lib (Librium) – Depressants

Lid – 1 ounce of marijuana

Lid poppers – Amphetamine

Lid proppers – Amphetamine

Light stuff – Marijuana

Lightning – Amphetamine

Lima – Marijuana

Lime acid – LSD

Line – Cocaine

Liprimo – Marijuana and crack rolled in a joint

Lipton tea – Poor-quality drugs

Liquid E – Gamma-hydroxybutyrate (GHB)

Liquid Ecstasy – Gamma-hydroxybutyrate (GHB)

Liquid G – Gamma-hydroxybutyrate (GHB)

Liquid lady – Cocaine dissolved in water and ingested as a nasal spray

Liquid X – Gamma-hydroxybutyrate (GHB)

Lit up – Under the influence of drugs

Little bomb – Heroin; amphetamine; depressants

Little ones – PCP

Little smoke – Marijuana; LSD; psilocybin/psilocin

Live ones – PCP

Llesca – Marijuana

Load – 25 bags of heroin

Load of laundry – Methamphetamine

Loaded – High

Loaf – Marijuana

Lobo – Marijuana

Locker room – Isobutyl nitrite; inhalants

Loco (Spanish) – Marijuana

Loco weed (Spanish) – Marijuana

Locoweed – Marijuana

Log – Marijuana cigarette; PCP

Logor – LSD

Loony Toons – LSD

Loose shank – Marijuana

Loused – Covered by sores and abscesses from repeated use of unsterile needles

Love – Crack cocaine

Love affair – cocaine

Love boat – Marijuana dipped in formaldehyde; PCP; blunts mixed with marijuana and heroin; blunts mixed with marijuana and PCP

Love drug – Depressants; methylenedioxymethamphetamine (MDMA)

Love flipping – Use of mescaline and MDMA

Love leaf – Marijuana/PCP combination

Love pearls – Alpha-ethyltryptamine

Love pill – Methylenedioxymethamphetamine (MDMA)

Love pills – Alpha-ethyltryptamine

Love trip – Mescaline and methylenedioxymethamphetamine (MDMA)

Love weed – Marijuana

Loveboat – PCP; combination of PCP and marijuana

Lovelies – Marijuana laced with PCP

Lovely – PCP

Lover's speed – Methylenedioxymethamphetamine (MDMA)

Lovers' special – Methylenedioxymethamphetamine (MDMA)

LSD – Lysergic acid diethylamide

Lubage – Marijuana

Lucy in the sky with diamonds – LSD

Ludes – Depressants; methaqualone

Luding out – Depressants

Luds – Depressants

Lunch money drug – Rohypnol

M – Marijuana; morphine

M&M – Depressant

M.J. – Marijuana

M.O. – Marijuana

M.S. – Morphine

M.U. – Marijuana

Ma'a – Crack cocaine (Samoan)

Macaroni – Marijuana

Macaroni and cheese – $5 pack of marijuana and a dime bag of cocaine

Machinery – Marijuana

Macon – Marijuana

Maconha – Marijuana

Mad dog – PCP

Madman – PCP

Mafu (Spanish) – Marijuana

Magic – PCP

Magic dust – PCP

Magic mushroom – Psilocybin/psilocin

Magic smoke – Marijuana

Mainline – To inject a drug

Mainliner – Person who injects into the vein

Make up – Need to find more drugs

Mama coca – Cocaine

Manhattan silver – Marijuana

Manteca (Spanish) – Heroin

MAO – Amphetamines; methylenedioxymethamphetamine (MDMA)

Marathons – Amphetamine

Marching dust – Cocaine

Marching powder – Cocaine

Mari – Marijuana cigarette

Maria pastora – *Salvia divinorum*

Marimba (Spanish) – Marijuana

Marshmallow reds – Depressants

Mary – Marijuana

Mary and Johnny – Marijuana

Mary Ann – Marijuana

Mary Jane – Marijuana

Mary Jonas – Marijuana

Mary Warner – Marijuana

Mary Weaver – Marijuana

Maserati – Crack pipe made from a plastic rum bottle and a rubber spark-plug cover

Matchbox – ¼ ounce of marijuana or 6 marijuana cigarettes

Matsakow – Heroin

Maui wauie – Marijuana from Hawaii

Maui-wowie – Marijuana; methamphetamine

Max – Gamma-hydroxybutyrate dissolved in water and mixed with amphetamines

Maxibolin – Oral steroids

Mayo – Cocaine; heroin

MDM – Methylenedioxymethamphetamine (MDMA)

MDMA – Methylenedioxymethamphetamine

Mean green – PCP

Medusa – Inhalants

Meg – Marijuana

Megg – Marijuana cigarette

Meggie – Marijuana

Mellow yellow – LSD

Mercedes – Methylenedioxymethamphetamine (MDMA)

Merchandise – Drugs

Merck – Cocaine

Merk – Cocaine

Mesc – Mescaline

Mescal – Mescaline

Mese – Mescaline

Messorole – Marijuana

Meth – Methamphetamine

Meth head – Methamphetamine regular user

Meth monster – One who has a violent reaction to methamphetamine

Meth speedball – Methamphetamine combined with heroin

Methatriol – Injectable steroids

Methedrine – Amphetamines; methylenedioxymethamphetamine (MDMA)

Methlies Quik – Methamphetamine

Methyltestosterone – Oral steroids

Mexican brown – Marijuana; heroin

Mexican crack – Methamphetamine with the appearance of crack; methamphetamine

Mexican green – Marijuana

Mexican horse – Heroin

Mexican locoweed – Marijuana

Mexican mud – Heroin

Mexican mushrooms – Psilocybin/psilocin

Mexican red – Marijuana

Mexican reds – Depressants

Mexican speedballs – Crack and methamphetamine

Mexican Valium – Rohypnol

Mezc – Mescaline

MFT – Nexus

Mickey Finn – Depressants

Mickey's – Depressant; LSD

Microdot – LSD

Midnight oil – Opium

Mighty Joe Young – Depressants

Mighty mezz – Marijuana cigarette

Mighty Quinn – LSD

Mighty white – A form of crack cocaine that is hard, white, and pure

Mind detergent – LSD

Mini beans – Amphetamine; methylenedioxymethamphetamine (MDMA)

Minibennie – Amphetamine

Mint leaf – PCP

Mint weed – PCP

Mira (Spanish) – Opium

Miss – To inject a drug

Miss Emma – Morphine

Missile basing – Crack liquid and PCP

Mission – Trip out of the crackhouse to obtain crack

Mist – PCP; crack smoke in the bottom of a glass pipe

Mister blue – Morphine

Mitsubishi – Methylenedioxymethamphetamine (MDMA)

Mix – A term used to refer to cocaine or a drug environment

Mixed jive – Crack cocaine

Mo – Marijuana

Modams – Marijuana

Mohasky – Marijuana

Mohasty – Marijuana

Mojo – Cocaine; heroin

Money talks – Heroin

Monkey – Cigarette made from cocaine paste and tobacco; drug dependency; heroin

Monkey dust – PCP

Monkey tranquilizer – PCP

Monoamine oxidase – Amphetamine; methylenedioxymethamphetamine (MDMA)

Monos (Spanish) – Cigarette made from cocaine paste and tobacco

Monster – Cocaine

Monte – Marijuana from South America

Mooca/moocah – Marijuana

Moon – Mescaline

Moon gas – Inhalants

Moonrock – Crack mixed with heroin

Moonstone – When a dealer shaves a slice of methylenedioxymethamphetamine (MDMA) into a bag of heroin

Mooster – Marijuana

Moota/mutah – Marijuana

Mooters – Marijuana cigarette

Mootie – Marijuana

Mootos – Marijuana

Mor a grifa – Marijuana

More – PCP

Morf – Morphine

Morning shot – Amphetamine; methylenedioxymethamphetamine (MDMA)

Morning wake-up – First blast of crack from the pipe

Morotgara – Heroin

Morpho – Morophine

Mortal combat – High-potency heroin

Mosquitos – Cocaine

Mota/moto (Spanish) – Marijuana

Mother – Marijuana

Mother's little helper – Depressants

Motorcycle crack – Methamphetamine

Mouth worker – One who takes drugs orally

Movie star drug – Cocaine

Mow the grass – To smoke marijuana

Mu – Marijuana

Mud – Heroin; opium

Muggie – Marijuana

Muggle – Marijuana

Muggles – Marijuana

Mujer (Spanish) – Cocaine

Mule – Carrier of drugs

Murder 8 – Fentanyl

Murder one – Heroin and cocaine

Murotugora – Heroin

Mushrooms – Psilocybin/psilocin

Musk – Psilocybin/psilocin

Muta – Marijuana

Mutha – Marijuana

Muzzle – Heroin

Nail – Marijuana cigarette

Nailed – Arrested

Nanoo – Heroin

Nazimeth – Methamphetamine

Nebbies – Depressants

Nemmies – Depressants

New acid – PCP

New addition – Crack cocaine

New Jack swing – Heroin and morphine

New magic – PCP

Nexus – 2-(4-Bromo-2,5-diethoxyphenyl)-
ethylamine; also just known as 2CB

Nexus flipping – Use of Nexus (2-CB)
and MDMA

Nice and easy – Heroin

Nickel bag – $5 worth of drugs; heroin

Nickel deck – Heroin

Nickel note – $5 bill

Nickelonians – Crack addicts

Niebla (Spanish) – PCP

Nieve (Spanish) – Cocaine

Nigra – Marijuana

Nimbies – Depressants

Nineteen – Amphetamine; methylenedioxymethamphetamine (MDMA)

Nix – Stranger among the group

No worries – Depressant

Nod – Effects of heroin

Nods – Codeine cough syrup

Noise – Heroin

Nontoucher – Crack user who doesn't
want affection during or after smoking crack

Northern lights – Marijuana from
Canada

Nose – Cocaine; heroin

Nose candy – Cocaine

Nose drops – Liquified heroin

Nose powder – Cocaine

Nose stuff – Cocaine

NOX – Use of nitrous oxide and MDMA

Nubs – Peyote

Nugget – Amphetamine

Nuggets – Crack cocaine

Number – Marijuana cigarette

Number 3 – Cocaine; heroin

Number 4 – Heroin

Number 8 – Heroin

Nurse – Heroin

O – Opium

O.J. – Marijuana

O.P. – Opium

O.P.P. – PCP

O.Z. – One ounce of a drug substance

Octane – PCP laced with gasoline

Ogoy – Heroin

Oil – Heroin; PCP

Old garbage – Heroin

Old Navy – Heroin

Old Steve – Heroin

On a mission – Searching for crack
and/or being high on crack

On a trip – Under the influence of
drugs

On ice – In jail

On the ball – When a dealer shaves a
slice of methylenedioxymethamphetamine (MDMA) into a bag of heroin

On the bricks – Walking the streets

On the nod – Under the influence of
narcotics or depressant

One and one – To inhale cocaine

One and ones – Talwin and Ritalin
combination is injected and produces
an effect similar to the effect of
heroin mixed with cocaine.

One bomb – 100 rocks of Crack
cocaine

One-on-one house – Where cocaine
and heroin can be purchased

One-plus-one sales – Selling cocaine
and heroin together

One tissue box – 1 ounce of crack

One way – LSD; heroin

One-fifty-one – Crack; crack sprinkled
on tobacco

One-stop shop – Place where more
than one drug is sold

Onion – 1 ounce of crack cocaine

Oolies – Marijuana cigarettes laced
with crack

Ope – Opium

Optical illusions – LSD

Orange bandits – Methylenedioxymethamphetamine (MDMA)

Orange barrels – LSD

Orange crystal – PCP

Orange cubes – LSD

Orange haze – LSD

Orange line – Heroin

Orange micro – LSD

Orange wedges – LSD

Oranges – Amphetamine

Organic Quaalude – Gamma-hydroxy-butyrate (GHB)

Os – OxyContin

Outer limits – Crack and LSD

Owsley – LSD

Owsley's acid – LSD

Ox – OxyContin

Oxicotten – A semisynthetic opiate

Oxy – OxyContin

Oxy 80's – A semisynthetic opiate

Oxycet – A semisynthetic opiate

Oxycotton – OxyContin

Oyster stew – Cocaine

Oz – Inhalants

Ozone – Marijuana, PCP, and crack cigarette; marijuana cigarette; PCP

OZs – Methamphetamine

P – Peyote; PCP

P-dogs – Combination of cocaine and marijuana

P-dope – 20% to 30% pure heroin

P-funk – Crack mixed with PCP; heroin

P.R. – Panama red

Pack – Marijuana; heroin

Pack a bowl – Marijuana

Pack of rocks – Marijuana cigarette

Pakaloco – Marijuana ("crazy tobacco")

Pakalolo – Marijuana

Pakistani black – Marijuana

Panama cut – Marijuana

Panama gold – Marijuana

Panama red – Marijuana

Panatella – Large marijuana cigarette

Pancakes and syrup – Combination of glutethimide and codeine cough syrup

Pane – LSD

Pangonadalot – Heroin

Panic – Drugs not available

Paper – A dose unit of heroin; 1/10 gram or less of the drug ice or methamphetamine

Paper acid – LSD

Paper bag – Container for drugs

Paper blunts – Marijuana within a paper casing rather than a tobacco leaf casing

Paper boy – Heroin peddler

Papers – Folded paper used to package drugs

Parabolin – Oral steroids; veterinary steroid

Parachute – Crack and PCP smoked; heroin; smokable crack and heroin mixture

Parachute down – Use of MDMA after heroin

Paradise – Cocaine

Paradise white – Cocaine

Pariba – Powder cocaine

Parlay – Crack cocaine

Parsley – Marijuana; PCP

Party pack – Combination of 2C-B (Nexus) with other illicit drugs, particularly MDMA (methylenedioxymethamphetamine; Ecstasy)

Paste – Crack cocaine

Pasto (Spanish) – Marijuana

Pat – Marijuana

Patico (Spanish) – Crack cocaine

Paz (Spanish) – PCP

PCPA – PCP

Peace – PCP; LSD

Peace pill – PCP

Peace tablets – LSD

Peace weed – PCP

Peaches – Amphetamine

Peanut – Depressants

Peanut butter – Methamphetamine; PCP mixed with peanut butter

Pearl – Cocaine

Pearls – Amyl nitrite

Pearly gates – LSD

Pebbles – Crack cocaine

Peddler – Drug supplier

Pee Wee – Crack cocaine; $5 worth of crack

Peep – PCP

Peeper(s) – MDMA user(s)

Peg – Heroin

Pellets – LSD

Pen yan – Opium

Pep pills – Amphetamine

Pepsi habit – Occasional use of drugs

Percia – Cocaine

Percio – Cocaine

Perfect high – Heroin

Perico (Spanish) – Cocaine

Perlas (Spanish) – Street dealer (heroin)

Perp – Fake crack made of candle wax and baking soda

Peruvian – Cocaine

Peruvian flake – Cocaine

Peruvian lady – Cocaine

Peter – Depressants

Peter Pan – PCP

Peth – Depressant

Peyote – Mescaline

Pharming – Consuming a mixture of prescription substances

Phennies – Depressants

Phenos – Depressants

Philly blunts – Marijuana

Pianoing – Using the fingers to find lost crack

Picking – Searching on hands and knees for cocaine or crack

Piece – Cocaine; crack cocaine; 1 ounce

Piedra (Spanish) – Crack cocaine

Pig killer – PCP

Piggybacking – Simultaneous injection of two drugs; sequential use of more than one methylenedioxymethamphetamine (MDMA) tablet

Pikachu – Pills containing PCP and Ecstasy

Piles – Crack cocaine

Pill houses – Residences where pills are illicitly sold

Pill ladies – Female senior citizens who sell OxyContin

Pills – OxyContin

Pimp – Cocaine

Pimp your pipe – Lending or renting crack pipe or stem

Pin – Marijuana

Pin gon – Opium

Pin yen – Opium

Ping-in-wing – To inject a drug

Pingus – Rohypnol

Pink – Methamphetamine

Pink blotters – LSD

Pink elephants – Methamphetamine

Pink hearts – Amphetamine; methamphetamine

Pink ladies – Depressants

Pink panther – LSD

Pink panthers – Methylenedioxymethamphetamine (MDMA)

Pink robots – LSD

Pink wedges – LSD

Pink witches – LSD

Pipe – Crack pipe; marijuana pipe; vein into which a drug is injected; mix drugs with other substances

Pipero (Spanish) – Crack user

Pit – PCP

Pits – PCP

Pixies – Amphetamine

Plant – Hiding place for drugs

Playboy bunnies – Methylenedioxymethamphetamine (MDMA)

Playboys – Methylenedioxymethamphetamine (MDMA)

Pluto – Heroin

Pocket rocket – Marijuana; marijuana cigarette

Pod – Marijuana

Point – A needle

Poison – Heroin; fentanyl

Poke – Marijuana; to smoke marijuana

Pollutants – Amphetamines; methylenedioxymethamphetamine (MDMA)

Polo – Mixture of heroin and motion sickness drug

Polvo (Spanish) – Heroin; PCP

Polvo blanco (Spanish) – Cocaine

Polvo de angel (Spanish) – PCP

Polvo de estrellas (Spanish) – PCP

Pony – Crack cocaine

Pony packs – Folded paper used to package drugs

Poor man's coke – Methamphetamine

Poor man's heroin – Talwin and Ritalin combination is injected and produces an effect similar to the effect of heroin mixed with cocaine

Poor man's pot – Inhalants

Pop – To inhale cocaine

Poppers – Isobutyl nitrite; amyl nitrite; methamphetamine

Poppy – Heroin

Pot – Marijuana

Potato – LSD

Potato chips – Crack cut with benzocaine

Potlikker – Marijuana

Potten bush – Marijuana

Powder – Cocaine HCL; heroin; amphetamine

Powder diamonds – Cocaine

Power puller – Rubber piece attached to crack stem

Pox – Opium

Predator – Heroin

Prescription – Marijuana cigarette

Press – Cocaine; crack cocaine

Pretendica – Marijuana

Pretendo – Marijuana

Primbolin – Injectable and oral steroids

Prime time – Crack cocaine

Primo – Crack; marijuana mixed with cocaine; crack and heroin; heroin, cocaine and tobacco

Primo square – A marijuana joint laced with crack

Primobolan – Injectable and oral steroid

Primos – Cigarette laced with cocaine and heroin

Product – Crack cocaine

Proviron – Oral steroids

Pseudocaine – Phenylpropanolamine, an adulterant for cutting crack

Puff the dragon – To smoke marijuana

Puffer – Crack smoker

Puffy – PCP

Pulborn – Heroin

Pullers – Crack users who pull at parts of their bodies excessively

Pumpers – Steroids

Pumping – Selling crack

Pure – Heroin

Pure love – LSD

Purple – Ketamine

Purple barrels – LSD

Purple caps – Crack cocaine

Purple flats – LSD

Purple gel tabs – Lysergic acid diethylamide (LSD)

Purple haze – LSD; Crack cocaine; marijuana

Purple hearts – LSD; amphetamine; depressants

Purple ozoline – LSD

Purple rain – PCP

Push – Sell drugs

Push shorts – To cheat; sell short amounts

Pusher – Metal hanger or umbrella rod used to scrape residue out of crack stems; one who sells drugs

Q – Depressants

Qat – Methcathinone

Quads – Depressants

Quarter – ¼ ounce or $25 worth of drugs

Quarter bag – $25 worth of drugs

Quarter moon – Hashish

Quarter piece – ¼ ounce

Quartz – Smokable methamphetamine

Quas – Depressants

Queen Ann's lace – Marijuana

Quicksilver – Isobutyl nitrite; inhalants

Quill – Cocaine; heroin; methamphetamine

Quinolone – Injectable steriods

R-2 – Rohypnol

Racehorse Charlie – Cocaine; heroin

Ragweed – Inferior-quality marijuana; heroin

Railroad weed – Marijuana

Rainbow – LSD

Rainbows – Depressants

Rainy day woman – Marijuana

Rambo – Heroin

Rane – Cocaine; heroin

Rangood – Marijuana grown wild

Rap – Criminally charged; to talk with someone

Raspberry – Female who trades sex for crack or money to buy crack

Rasta weed – Marijuana

Rave – All-night dance parties frequently designed to enhance a hallucinogenic experience through music and lights

Rave energy – Methylenedioxymethamphetamine (MDMA)

Raw – Crack cocaine; high-purity heroin

Raw fusion – Heroin

Raw hide – Heroin

Razed – Under the influence of drugs

Ready rock – Cocaine; Crack cocaine; heroin

Real tops – Crack cocaine

Recompress – Change the shape of cocaine flakes to resemble "rock"

Recycle – LSD

Red – Under the influence of drugs; methamphetamine

Red and blue – Depressants

Red bud – Marijuana

Red bullets – Depressants

Red caps – Crack cocaine

Red chicken – Heroin

Red Cross – Marijuana

Red Devil – Depressants; PCP; heroin

Red devils – Methylenedioxymethamphetamine (MDMA)

Red dirt – Marijuana

Red eagle – Heroin

Red lips – LSD

Red phosphorus – Smokable speed

Red rock – Heroin

Red rock opium – Heroin, barbital, strychnine, and caffeine

Red rum – Heroin, barbital, strychnine, and caffeine

Red stuff – Heroin, barbital, strychnine, and caffeine

Redneck cocaine – Methamphetamine

Reds – Depressants

Reefer – Marijuana

Reefers – Marijuana cigarette

Regular P – Crack cocaine

Reindeer dust – Heroin

RenewTrient – GBL-containing product

Res – Potent residue left as a result of smoking crack which is scraped and smoked

Rest in peace – Crack cocaine

Revivarant – GBL-containing product

Revivarant-G – GBL-containing product

Reynolds – Rohypnol

Rhine – Heroin

Rhythm – Amphetamine

Rib – Rohypnol; methylenedioxymethamphetamine (MDMA)

Rider – 5 kilograms of heroin sometimes provided at no cost per 100 kilograms of cocaine imported from Colombia

Riding the wave – Under the influence of drugs

Rig – Equipment used to inject drugs

Righteous bush – Marijuana

Ringer – Good hit of crack; hear bells

Rip – Marijuana

Rippers – Amphetamine

Ritual spirit – Methylenedioxymethamphetamine (MDMA)

Ritz and Ts – A combination of Ritalin and Talwin injected

Roach – Butt of marijuana cigarette

Roach clip – Holds partially smoked marijuana cigarette

Roach-2 – Rohypnol

Roacha – Marijuana

Roaches – Rohypnol

Roachies – Rohypnol

Road dope – Amphetamine

Roapies – Rohypnol

Roasting – Smoking marijuana

Robin's egg – Stimulant

Robutal – Rohypnol

Roca (Spanish) – Crack cocaine; methylenedioxymethamphetamine (MDMA)

Rochas dos – Rohypnol

Roche – Rohypnol

Rock – Methamphetamine

Rock attack – Crack cocaine

Rock house – Place where crack is sold and smoked

Rock star – Female who trades sex for crack or money to buy crack; a person who uses rock cocaine

Rock(s) – Cocaine; crack cocaine

Rocket caps – Dome-shaped caps on crack vials

Rocket fuel – PCP

Rockets – Marijuana cigarette

Rockette – Female who uses crack

Rocks of hell – Crack cocaine

Rocky III – Crack

Roid rage – Aggressive behavior caused by excessive steroid use

Roller – To inject a drug

Rollers – Police

Rolling – Methylenedioxymethamphetamine (MDMA)

Rolls Royce – Methylenedioxymethamphetamine (MDMA)

Rompums – Marijuana with horse tranquilizers

Roofies – Rohypnol

Rooster – Crack cocaine

Root – Marijuana

Rope – Marijuana; rohypnol

Rophies – Rohypnol

Rophy – Rohypnol

Ropies – Rohypnol

Roples – Rohypnol

Rosa (Spanish) – Amphetamine

Rose Marie – Marijuana

Roses – Amphetamine

Rough stuff – Marijuana

Row-shay – Rohypnol

Rox – Crack cocaine

Roxanne – Cocaine; crack

Royal blues – LSD

Roz – Crack cocaine

Rubia (Spanish) – Marijuana

Ruderalis – Species of *Cannabis*, found in Russia, grows 1 to 2.5 feet

Ruffies – Rohypnol

Ruffles – Rohypnol

Rugs – Marijuana

Runners – People who sell drugs for others

Running – Methylenedioxymethamphetamine (MDMA)

Rush – Cocaine; isobutyl nitrite; inhalants

Rush hour – Heroin

Rush snappers – Isobutyl nitrite

Russian sickles – LSD

Sack – Heroin

Sacrament – LSD

Sacred mushroom – Psilocybin

Salad – Marijuana

Salt – Heroin

Salt and pepper – Marijuana

Salty water – Gamma-hydroxybutyrate (GHB)

Sam – Federal narcotics agent

Sancocho (Spanish) – To steal

Sandoz – LSD

Sandwich – Two layers of cocaine with a layer of heroin in the middle

Sandwich bag – $40 bag of marijuana

Santa Marta (Spanish) – Marijuana

Sasfras – Marijuana

Satan's secret – Inhalants

Satch – Papers, letter, cards, clothing, etc., saturated with drug solution; used to smuggle drugs into prisons or hospitals

Satch cotton – Fabric used to filter a solution of narcotics before injection

Sativa – Species of *Cannabis* found in cool, damp climate; grows up to 18 feet

Scaffle – PCP

Scag – Heroin

Scat – Heroin

Scate – Heroin

Schmeck – Cocaine

Schmiz – Methamphetamine

Schoolboy – Cocaine; codeine

Schoolcraft – Crack cocaine

Schwagg – Marijuana

Scissors – Marijuana

Scooby snacks – Methylenedioxymethamphetamine (MDMA)

Scoop – Gamma-hydroxybutyrate (GHB)

Scootie – Methamphetamine

Score – Purchase drugs

Scorpion – Cocaine

Scott – Heroin

Scottie – Cocaine

Scotty – Cocaine; crack; the high from crack

Scrabble – Crack cocaine

Scramble – Crack cocaine; low-purity, adulterated heroin

Scrape and snort – To share crack by scraping off small pieces to snort

Scratch – Money

Scrub – Marijuana

Scruples – Crack cocaine

Scuffle – PCP

Seccy – Depressants

Second to none – Heroin

Seconds – Second inhalation of crack from a pipe

Seeds – Marijuana

Seggy – Depressants

Sen – Marijuana

Seni – Peyote

Serial speedballing – Sequencing cocaine, cough syrup, and heroin over a 1- to 2-day period

Sernyl – PCP

Serpico 21 – Cocaine

Server – Crack dealer

Sess – Marijuana

Set – Place where drugs are sold; Talwin and Ritalin combination is injected and produces an effect similar to the effect of heroin mixed with cocaine

Seven-Up – Crack cocaine

Sevenup – Cocaine; crack

Sewer – Vein into which a drug is injected

Sextasy – Ecstasy used with Viagra

Sezz – Marijuana

Shit – Heroin

Shabu – Ice; Crack cocaine; methamphetamine; methylenedioxymethamphetamine (MDMA)

Shake – Marijuana; powder cocaine

Shaker/baker/water – Materials needed to freebase cocaine: shaker bottle, baking soda, water

Sharps – Hypodermic needles

She – Cocaine

Shebanging – Mixing cocaine with water and squirting it up the nose

Sheet rocking – Crack and LSD

Sheets – PCP

Sherm – Psychedelic mushrooms

Sherm sticks – PCP

Sherman stick – Crack cocaine combined with marijuana in a blunt

Shermans – PCP

Sherms – Crack cocaine; PCP; cigars dipped in or laced with PCP

Shmeck/schmeek – Heroin

Shoot – Heroin

Shoot the breeze – Nitrous oxide

Shoot/shoot up – To inject a drug

Shooting gallery – Place where drugs are used

Shoppers – Individuals who buy drugs for others, sometimes keeping some of the drug for themselves

Shot – To inject a drug; an amount of cocaine; 10 shot or 20 shot

Shot down – Under the influence of drugs

Shot to the curb – Person who has lost it all to crack

Shotgun – Inhaling marijuana smoke forced into one's mouth by another's exhaling

Shrile – Powder cocaine

Shrooms – Psilocybin/psilocin

Siddi – Marijuana

Sightball – Crack cocaine

Silk – Heroin

Silly putty – Psilocybin/psilocin

Simple Simon – Psilocybin/psilocin

Sinse (Spanish) – Marijuana

Sinsemilla – Potent variety of marijuana

Sixty-two – 2½ ounces of poor-quality crack

Skag – Heroin

Skee – Opium

Skeegers/skeezers – Crack-smoking prostitutes

Sketch – Methamphetamine

Sketching – Coming down from a speed-induced high

Skid – Heroin

Skied – Under the influence of drugs

Skin popping – Injecting drugs under the skin; to inject drugs on any part of the body without hitting a vein

Skittling – Abuse of cold tablets containing dextromethorphan (a cough suppressant)

Skuffle – PCP

Skunk – Marijuana; heroin

Skunkweed – Marijuana

Slab – A large piece of Crack cocaine the size of a stick of chewing gum

Slam – To inject a drug

Slammin'/slamming – Amphetamine; methylenedioxymethamphetamine (MDMA)

Slanging – Selling drugs

Sleep – Gamma-hydroxybutyrate (GHB)

Sleep-500 – Gamma-hydroxybutyrate (GHB)

Sleeper – Heroin; depressants

Sleet – Crack cocaine

Sleigh ride – Cocaine

Slick superspeed – Methcathinone

Slime – Heroin

Smack – Heroin

Smears – LSD

Smoke – Marijuana; crack cocaine; heroin and crack

Smoke a bowl – Marijuana

Smoke Canada – Marijuana

Smoke houses – Crack houses

Smoke-out – Under the influence of drugs

Smoking – PCP

Smoking gun – Heroin and cocaine

Smurf – Cigar dipped in embalming fluid

Smurfs – Methylenedioxymethamphetamine (MDMA)

Snackies – Methylenedioxymethamphetamine (MDMA) adulterated with mescaline

Snap – Amphetamine

Snappers – Isobutyl nitrite

Sniff – To inhale cocaine; methcathinone; inhalants

Sniffer bag – $5 bag of heroin intended for inhalation

Snop – Marijuana

Snort – To inhale cocaine; powder cocaine; use an inhalant

Snorting – Using inhalant

Snorts – PCP

Snot – Residue produced from smoking amphetamine

Snotballs – Rubber cement rolled into balls, burned, and the fumes inhaled

Snotty – Heroin

Snow – Cocaine; heroin; amphetamine

Snowbird – Cocaine user; cocaine

Snow coke – Crack

Snow pallets – Amphetamine

Snow seals – Cocaine and amphetamine

Snow white – Cocaine

Snowball – Cocaine and heroin

Snowcones – Cocaine

Snowmen – LSD

Soap – Gamma-hydroxybutyrate (GHB); Crack cocaine; methamphetamine

Soap dope – Methamphetamine with a pinkish tint

Society high – Cocaine

Soda – Injectable cocaine

Soft – Powder cocaine

Softballs – Depressants

Soles – Hashish

Soma – PCP

Somali tea – Methcathinone; khat

Somatomax – Gamma-hydroxybutyrate (GHB)

Sopers – Depressants

Soup – Crack cocaine

South Parks – Lysergic acid diethylamide

Space – Crack cocaine

Space base – Crack dipped in PCP; hollowed-out cigar refilled with PCP and crack

Space cadet – Crack dipped in PCP

Space dust – Crack dipped in PCP

Space ship – Glass pipe used to smoke crack

Spaceball – PCP used with crack

Spackle – Methamphetamine

Spark it up – To smoke marijuana

Sparkle – Methamphetamine that has a somewhat shiny appearance

Sparkle plenty – Amphetamine

Sparklers – Amphetamine

Special K – Ketamine

Special la coke – Ketamine

Speckled birds – Methamphetamine

Spectrum – Nexus

Speed – Crack cocaine; amphetamine; methamphetamine

Speed for lovers – Methylene-dioxymethamphetamine (MDMA)

Speed freak – Habitual user of methamphetamine

Speedball – Cocaine mixed with heroin; crack and heroin smoked together; methylphenidate (Ritalin) mixed with heroin; amphetamine

Speedballing – To shoot up or smoke a mixture of cocaine and heroin; Ecstasy mixed with ketamine; the simultaneous use of a stimulant with a depressant

Speedballs-nose-style – The practice of snorting cocaine

Speedboat – Marijuana, PCP, and crack combined and smoked

Speedies – Methylenedioxymetham-phetamine (MDMA) adulterated with amphetamine

Spider – Heroin

Spider blue – Heroin

Spike – Heroin cut with scopolamine or strychnine; to inject a drug; needle; hypodermic needle

Spivias – Amphetamine; methylene-dioxymethamphetamine (MDMA)

Splash – Amphetamine

Spliff – Large marijuana cigarette

Splim – Marijuana

Split – Adulterated drugs; to leave; half and half

Splitting – Rolling marijuana and cocaine into a single joint

Splivins – Amphetamine

Spoon – 1/16 ounce of heroin; paraphernalia used to prepare heroin for injection

Spoosh – Methamphetamine

Spores – PCP

Sporos – Methaqualone

Sporting – To inhale cocaine

Spray – Inhalants

Sprung – Person just starting to use drugs

Square mackerel – Marijuana (term from Florida)

Square time Bob – Crack cocaine

Squirrel – Combination of PCP and marijuana, sprinkled with cocaine and smoked; marijuana, PCP, and crack combined and smoked; LSD

Stack – Marijuana

Stackers – Steroids

Stacking – Taking steroids without a prescription; use of three or more methylenedioxymethamphetamine (MDMA) tablets in combination

Stacks – Methylenedioxymethamphet-amine (MDMA) adulterated with heroin or crack

Star – Cocaine; amphetamine; meth-cathinone

Star dust – PCP

Star-spangled powder – Cocaine

Stardust – Cocaine; PCP

Stars – Methylenedioxymethamphet-amine (MDMA)

Stash – Place to hide drugs

Stash areas – Drug storage and distribution areas

Stat – Methcathinone

Steerer – Person who directs customers to spots for buying crack; worker who directs buyers to where drugs are sold

Stem – Cylinder used to smoke crack

Stems – Marijuana

Step on – Dilute drugs

Stick – Marijuana; PCP

Stink weed – Marijuana

Stoned – Under the influence of drugs

Stones – Crack cocaine

Stoney weed – Marijuana

Stoppers – Depressants

Stove top – Crystal methamphetamine; methamphetamine

STP – PCP

Straw – Marijuana cigarette

Strawberries – Depressants

Strawberry – LSD; female who trades sex for crack or money to buy crack

Strawberry fields – LSD

Strawberry shortcake – Amphetamine; methylenedioxymethamphetamine (MDMA)

Strung out – Heavily addicted to drugs

Studio fuel – Cocaine

Stuff – Heroin

Stumbler – Depressants

Sugar – Cocaine; crack cocaine; heroin; LSD

Sugar block – Crack cocaine

Sugar boogers – Powder cocaine

Sugar cubes – LSD

Sugar lumps – LSD

Sugar weed – Marijuana

Sunshine – LSD

Super – PCP

Super acid – Ketamine

Super C – Ketamine

Super grass – PCP; marijuana with PCP; marijuana

Super ice – Smokable methamphetamine

Super joint – PCP

Super kools – PCP

Super pot – Marijuana

Super weed – PCP

Super X – Combination of methamphetamine and methylenedioxymethamphetamine (MDMA)

Superlab – Clandestine laboratories capable of producing 10 pounds of methamphetamine in 24 hours

Superman – LSD

Supermans – Methylenedioxymethamphetamine (MDMA)

Surfer – PCP

Sustanon 250 – Injectable steroids

Swag – Marijuana

Swallower – An individual used as a drug courier

Swans – Methylenedioxymethamphetamine (MDMA)

Sweet dreams – Heroin

Sweet Jesus – Heroin

Sweet Lucy – Marijuana

Sweet stuff – Cocaine; heroin

Sweeties – Amphetamine; methylenedioxymethamphetamine (MDMA)

Sweets – Amphetamine

Swell up – Crack cocaine

Swishers – Cigars in which tobacco is replaced with marijuana

Synthetic cocaine – PCP

Synthetic THT – PCP

T – Cocaine; marijuana

T-buzz – PCP

T.N.T. – Heroin; fentanyl

Tabs – LSD; methylenedioxymethamphetamine (MDMA)

TAC – PCP

Tachas – Methylenedioxymethamphetamine (MDMA)

Tail lights – LSD

Taima – Marijuana

Taking a cruise – PCP

Takkouri – Marijuana

Talco (Spanish) – Cocaine

Tango and Cash – Fentanyl

Tar – Crack and heroin smoked together; heroin; opium

Tardust – Cocaine

Taste – Heroin; small sample of drugs

Taxing – Price paid to enter a crack house; charging more per vial depending on race of customer or if not a regular customer

Tea – Marijuana; PCP

Tea party – To smoke marijuana

Teardrops – Dose units of crack packaged in the cutoff corners of plastic bags

Tecata (Spanish) – Heroin

Tecatos – Hispanic heroin addict

Teenager – Cocaine

Teeth – Cocaine; crack cocaine

Ten pack – 1000 dose units of LSD

Tens – Amphetamine; methylene-dioxymethamphetamine (MDMA)

Tension – Crack cocaine

Tex-Mex – Marijuana

Texas pot – Marijuana

Texas shoe shine – Inhalants

Texas tea – Marijuana

Thai sticks – Bundles of marijuana soaked in hashish oil; marijuana buds found on short sections of bamboo

Thanie – Heroin

THC – Tetrahydrocannabinol

The beast – Heroin

The C – Amphetamine; methcathinone

The devil – Crack cocaine

The ghost – LSD

The hawk – LSD

The witch – Heroin

Therobolin – Injectable steroids

Thing – Cocaine; crack cocaine; heroin; main drug interest at the moment

Thirst monster – Crack smoker

Thirst monsters – Heavy crack smokers

Thirteen – Marijuana

Thirty-eight – Crack sprinkled on marijuana

Thoroughbred – Drug dealer who sells pure narcotics

Thrust – Isobutyl nitrite; inhalants

Thrusters – Amphetamine

Thumb – Marijuana

Thunder – Heroin

Tic – PCP in powder form; methamphetamine

Tic tac – PCP

Tick tick – Methamphetamine

Ticket – LSD

Tie – To inject a drug

Tigre (Spanish) – Heroin

Tigre blanco (Spanish) – Heroin

Tigre del norte (Spanish) – Heroin

Timothy Leary – Lysergic acid diethylamide (LSD)

Tin – Container for marijuana

Tina – Methamphetamine; crystal methamphetamine; methamphetamine used with Viagra

Tio – Cocaine-laced marijuana cigarette

Tish – PCP

Tissue – Crack cocaine

Titch – PCP

Tits – Black tar heroin

TNT – Fentanyl

Toke – To inhale cocaine; to smoke marijuana; marijuana

Toke up – To smoke marijuana

Toliet water – Inhalants

Tolly – Toluene, chemical contained in many inhalants

Tom and Jerries – Methylene-dioxymethamphetamine (MDMA)

Toncho – Octane booster which is inhaled

Tongs – Heroin

Tooles – Depressants

Tools – Equipment used for injecting drugs

Toonies – Nexus

Toot – Cocaine; to inhale cocaine

Tooties – Depressants

Tootsie Roll – Heroin

Top drool – Heroin

Top gun – Crack cocaine

Topi – Mescaline

Topo (Spanish) – Crack

Tops – Peyote

Torch – Marijuana

Torch cooking – Smoking cocaine base by using a propane or butane torch as a source of flame

Torch up – To smoke marijuana

Tornado – Crack cocaine

Torpedo – Marijuana and crack

Toss up – Crack cocaine; female who trades sex for crack or money to buy crack

Toss-ups – Crack cocaine

Totally spent – Hangover feeling that is an adverse effect of methylenedioxymethamphetamine (MDMA)

Toucher – User of crack who wants affection before, during, or after smoking crack

Tout – Person who introduces buyers to sellers

Touter – Person who stands on the street and advertises a drug

Toxy – Opium

Toys – Opium

TR-6s – Amphetamine

Track – To inject a drug

Tracks – Row of needle marks on a person

Tragic magic – Crack dipped in PCP

Trails – Cocaine; LSD-induced perception that moving objects leave multiple images or trails behind them

Train – Heroin

Trank – PCP

Tranq – Depressants

Trap – Hiding place for drugs

Trapped vehicles – Vehicles with secret compartments used to conceal drugs

Trash – Methamphetamine

Trauma – Marijuana

Travel agent – LSD supplier

Tray – $3 bag of marijuana

Trays – Bunches of vials

Trey – Small rock of crack cocaine

Trip – LSD; alpha-ethyltryptamine

Triple A – Marijuana from British Columbia

Triple crowns – Methylenedioxymethamphetamine (MDMA)

Triple folds – Folded paper used to package drugs

Triple Rolexes – Methylenedioxymethamphetamine (MDMA)

Triple stacks – Methylenedioxymethamphetamine (MDMA)

Troll – Use of LSD and MDMA

Troop – Crack cocaine

Trophobolene – Injectable steroid

Truck drivers – Amphetamine

Trupence bag – Marijuana

Ts and Rits – Talwin and Ritalin combination is injected and produces an effect similar to the effect of heroin mixed with cocaine

Ts and Rs – Talwin and Ritalin combination is injected and produces an effect similar to the effect of heroin mixed with cocaine

Tuie – Depressants

Turbo – Marijuana and crack

Turf – Place where drugs are sold

Turkey – Cocaine; amphetamine

Turnabout – Amphetamine

Turned on – Introduced to drugs; under the influence

Tustin – Marijuana

Tutti-frutti (Portuguese) – Flavored cocaine

Tutus – Methylenedioxymethamphetamine (MDMA)

Tweak mission – A person on a mission to find crack

Tweaker – Crack user looking for drugs on the floor after a police raid

Tweaking – Drug-induced paranoia; peaking on speed; desperately searching for crack

Tweaks – Crack cocaine

Tweek – Methamphetaminelike substance

Tweeker – Methcathinone

Tweety Birds – Methylenedioxymethamphetamine (MDMA)

Twenties – $20 vials or bags of crack

Twenty – $20 rock of crack

Twenty rock – Crack cocaine

Twenty-five – LSD

Twin towers – Heroin (after September 11)

Twinkie – Crack cocaine

Twist – Marijuana cigarette

Twisters – Crack and methamphetamine

Twists – Small plastic bags of heroin secured with a twist tie

Twistum – Marijuana cigarette

Two for Nine – Two $5 vials or bags of crack for $9

United States P – Amphetamine; methylenedioxymethamphetamine (MDMA)

Ultimate – Crack cocaine

Ultimate xphoria – Methylenedioxymethamphetamine (MDMA)

Uncle – Federal agents

Uncle Milty – Depressants

Unkie – Morphine

Unotque – Marijuana

Up against the stem – Addicted to smoking marijuana

Uppers – Amphetamine

Uppies – Amphetamine

Ups and downs – Depressants

Uptown – Powder cocaine

Utopiates – Hallucinogens

Uzi – Crack; crack pipe

V – The depressant Valium

Vega – A cigar wrapping refilled with marijuana

Venus – Nexus

Vidrio (Spanish) – Heroin

Viper – Marijuana smoker

Viper's weed – Marijuana

Vita-G – Gamma-hydroxybutyrate (GHB)

Vitamin K – Ketamine

Vitamin R – Ritalin (methylphenidate)

Vodka acid – LSD

Wac – PCP on marijuana

Wack – PCP

Wacky weed – Marijuana

Wafers – Methylenedioxymethamphetamine (MDMA)

Wake and bake – Marijuana

Wake ups – Amphetamine

Wash – Methamphetamine

Wasted – Under the influence of drugs; murdered

Water – Blunts; methamphetamine; PCP; a mixture of marijuana and other substances within a cigar; gamma-hydroxybutyrate (GHB)

Water-water – Marijuana cigarettes dipped in embalming fluid, sometimes also laced with PCP

Watercolors – Lysergic acid diethylamide (LSD)

Wave – Crack cocaine

Wedding bells – LSD

Wedge – LSD

Weed – Marijuana; PCP

Weed tea – Marijuana

Weight trainers – Steroids

Weightless – High on crack

West Coast – Methylphenidate (Ritalin)

West Coast turnarounds – Amphetamine; methylenedioxymethamphetamine (MDMA)

Wet – Blunts mixed with marijuana and PCP; methamphetamine; marijuana cigarettes soaked in PCP (embalming fluid) and dried

Whack – Crack cocaine; heroin and PCP; Crack/PCP mixture or marijuana laced with insecticides

Whackatabacky – Marijuana

Wheat – Marijuana

Wheels – Methylenedioxymethamphetamine (MDMA)

When-shee – Opium

Whiffledust – Amphetamine; methylenedioxymethamphetamine (MDMA)

Whippets – Nitrous oxide

White – Heroin; amphetamine

White ball – Crack cocaine

White boy – Heroin; powder cocaine

White cloud – Smoke that collects in bottom of crack pipe; crack smoke

White cross – Amphetamine; methamphetamine

White diamonds – Methylenedioxymethamphetamine (MDMA)

White dove – Methylenedioxymethamphetamine (MDMA)

White dragon – Powder cocaine; heroin

White dust – LSD

White ghost – Crack cocaine

White girl – Cocaine; heroin

White horizon – PCP

White horse – Cocaine; heroin

White junk – Heroin

White lady – Cocaine; heroin

White lightning – LSD

White mosquito – Cocaine

White nurse – Heroin

White Owsley's – LSD

White powder – Cocaine; PCP

White Russian – Marijuana

White stuff – Heroin

White sugar – Crack cocaine

White tornado – Crack cocaine

White-haired lady – Marijuana

Whiteout – Inhalants; isobutyl nitrite

Whites – Amphetamine; folded paper used to package drugs

Whiz bang – Cocaine; heroin and cocaine

Wicked – A potent brand of heroin

Wicky stick – PCP, marijuana, and crack

Wigging – Odd behavior resulting from the use of mind-altering drugs

Wigits – Methylenedioxymethamphetamine (MDMA)

Wild cat – Methcathinone mixed with cocaine

Window glass – LSD

Window pane – LSD; crack cocaine

Wings – Cocaine; heroin

Winstrol – Oral steroids

Winstrol V – Veterinary steroids

Witch – Cocaine; heroin

Witch hazel – Heroin

Wobble weed – PCP

Wolf – PCP

Wolfies – Rohypnol

Wollie – Rocks of crack rolled into a marijuana cigarette or in a cigar

Wonder star – Methcathinone

Woo blunts – Marijuana; marijuana combined with cocaine

Woola blunt – Marijuana and heroin combination

Woolah – Hollowed-out cigar refilled with marijuana and crack

Woolas – Cigarettes laced with cocaine; crack sprinkled on marijuana cigarette

Woolie – Marijuana and heroin combination

Woolies – Marijuana and crack or PCP

Wooly blunts – Marijuana and crack or PCP

Wooties – Crack smoked in marijuana joints

Work – Methamphetamine

Working – Selling crack

Working bags – Bags containing several small rocks of crack cocaine

Working fifty – Crack rock weighing 1/2 gram or more

Working half – Crack rock weighing 1/2 gram or more

Working man's cocaine – Methamphetamine

Works – Equipment for injecting drugs

Worm – PCP

Wrecking crew – Crack cocaine

WTC – Heroin (after September 11)

X – Marijuana; amphetamine; methylenedioxymethamphetamine (MDMA)

X-ing – Methylenedioxymethamphetamine (MDMA)

X-pills – Methylenedioxymethamphetamine (MDMA)

XTC – Methylenedioxymethamphetamine (MDMA)

Ya ba – A pure and powerful form of methamphetamine from Thailand; "crazy drug"

Yahoo/yeaho – Crack cocaine

Yale – Crack cocaine

Yam – Crack cocaine

Yao – Powder cocaine

Yayoo – Crack cocaine

Yeah-O – Crack cocaine

Yeh – Marijuana

Yellow – LSD; depressants

Yellow bam – Methamphetamine

Yellow bullets – Depressants

Yellow dimples – LSD

Yellow fever – PCP

Yellow jackets – Depressants; methamphetamine

Yellow powder – Methamphetamine

Yellow submarine – Marijuana

Yellow sunshine – LSD

Yen pop – Marijuana

Yen shee suey – Opium wine

Yen sleep – Restless, drowsy state after LSD use

Yeo – Crack

Yeola – Marijuana and crack

Yerba (Spanish) – Marijuana

Yerba mala (Spanish) – PCP and marijuana

Yerhia – Marijuana

Yesca – Marijuana

Yesco – Marijuana

Yeyo (Spanish) – Cocaine

Yimyom – Crack cocaine

Ying yang – LSD

Z – 1 ounce of heroin

Zacatecas purple – Marijuana from Mexico

Zambi – Marijuana

Zay – A mixture of marijuana and other substances within a cigar; blunts

Ze – Opium

Zen – LSD

Zero – Opium

Zigzag man – Marijuana; LSD; marijuana rolling papers

Zip – Cocaine

Zol – Marijuana cigarette

Zombie – PCP; heavy user of drugs

Zombie weed – PCP

Zonked – Extremely high on drugs

Zooie – Holds butt of marijuana cigarette

Zoom – Marijuana laced with PCP; PCP

Zoomer – Individual who sells fake crack and then flees

Zoquete (Spanish) – Heroin

Zulu – Bogus crack

ACKNOWLEDGMENTS

This book has not been prepared in consultation with, nor is it endorsed by, any state or federal government agency.

Page 7: Quotation is from Edmond Locard, *Technical Police Laboratory* (Lyon, France, 1929).

Page 10: Quotation is from Janice Long, *Chemical & Engineering News*, Vol. 79, No. 4 (2002), p. 38.

Page 72: Photos are courtesy of Athena Research & Consulting LLC. © 2005 by Athena Research & Consulting LLC. All rights reserved.

Page 82: Quotation is from R. C. Murray and J. C. F. Tedrow, *Forensic Geology* (Englewood Cliffs, NJ: Prentice Hall, 1991).

Pages 99–100: Evidence Submissions Form is courtesy of the Georgia Bureau of Investigation.

Pages 114–116: Excerpt from Article VII: Opinions and Expert Testimony is courtesy of the Department of Justice, United States Government.

Pages 140–142: Excerpt from Michigan vs. Tyler is courtesy of the State of Michigan. The case can be accessed through Findlaw, which links to cases in the public domain.

Pages 142–143: Excerpt from Michigan vs. Tyler is courtesy of the Supreme Court, United States Government. This case can be accessed through Findlaw.

Page 149: Poster is courtesy of the Federal Bureau of Investigation (FBI), United States Goverment.

Page 151: Quotation is from the Thermo Electron Corporation web site (www.thermo.com). © copyright 2005 Thermo Electron Corporation. All rights reserved.

Page 167: National Drug Threat Assessment matrix is courtesy of the Department of Justice, United States Government.

Pages 177–178: Table of New York State alcohol- and drug-related penalties is courtesy of New York State.

Page 181: Tables on male and female body are from W. Miller and R. Munoz, *How to Control Your Drinking* (Albuquerque, University of New Mexico Press, 1982), pp. 8–11.

Pages 183–184: Quotation is courtesy of The National Highway Traffic Safety Administration (NHTSA), United States Government.

Page 187: Quotation is from Draeger Safety Diagnostics, Inc. web site (www.draeger.com). © copyright 2005 Draeger Safety Diagnostics, Inc. All rights reserved. Courtesy of Draeger Safety Diagnostics, Inc.

Pages 198, 200, 202–205: Photos are courtesy of the FirearmsID.com web site (firearmsid.com). © copyright 2005 FirearmsID.com. All rights reserved.

Page 202: Photo is courtesy of the FBI, United States Government.

Pages 206, 208: Photos are courtesy of the Forensic Medicine for Medical Students web site (www.forensicmed.co.uk). © copyright 2005 Forensics for Medical Students. All rights reserved.

Pages 229–232: Photos are courtesy of the FBI, United States Government.

Page 241: Photo is courtesy of the FBI, United States Government.

Page 244: Photo is courtesy of the FBI, United States Government.

Pages 249–250: Excerpt from the Latent Print Unit is courtesy of the FBI, United States Government.

Pages 256–258: Photos are courtesy of the FirearmsID.com web site (firearmsid.com). © copyright 2005 FirearmsID.com. All rights reserved.

Page 273: Quotation is from the Bureau of Engraving and Printing, United States Government.

Pages 274–276: Excerpt is from the Bureau of Engraving and Printing, United States Government.

Pages 280–281: Quotation is from the Foster and Freeman Ltd. web site (www.fosterfreeman.co.uk). © copyright 2005 Foster and Freeman Ltd. All rights reserved.

Page 283: Photos are courtesy of the FBI, United States Government.

Pages 301–305: Excerpt from CODIS is courtesy of the FBI, United States Government.

Pages 320–360: List in Appendix A is courtesy of the Executive Office of the President, Office of National Drug Control Policy, United States Government.

INDEX